Green Computing for Sustainable Development

Green computing is a revolutionary technique that addresses environmental sustainability. It uses an eco-friendly approach to the design, manufacture, and use of computing resources. This is achieved by cutting down on electronic waste, using renewable energy sources, and consuming less energy. Recyclable materials with minimal environmental impact, software engineering techniques that are optimized, and energy-efficient hardware are examples of many approaches. Advanced technologies such as low-power processors, smart grids, and virtualized computing environments contribute to energy efficiency and waste reduction. Furthermore, integrating green computing with renewable energy sources amplifies its positive impact on the environment. The adoption of green computing practices promotes a circular economy, encourages resource conservation, and supports climate action.

Green Computing for Sustainable Development features chapters that explore issues that are concerned with furthering sustainability and green computing. Highlights include the following:

- Neuro-symbolic green computing combining neural networks' learning abilities with symbolic AI's logical reasoning while promoting environmentally friendly practices
- Energy-efficient data management, resource provisioning, and the importance of monitoring carbon footprints
- The intersection of green computing and wildlife conservation, highlighting how energy-efficient technologies can revolutionize conservation efforts
- The integration of geospatial information systems (GIS) and remote sensing (RS) as innovative solutions for sustainable development
- The role of information and communication technology (ICT) in promoting health and well-being
- The importance of green computing due to growing environmental concerns related to information technology
- The integration of AI in sustainable farming practices
- The synergy between green computing practices and economic growth in achieving sustainable development

- The integration of green computing with e-waste management to tackle environmental challenges in the IT sector
- How the "green Internet of Things" (IoT) is transforming smart city development by integrating ecological awareness and sustainability into urban planning

This book covers the wide range of principles essential for achieving long-term sustainability. It is a step toward fostering a balanced relationship between technological advancement and environmental stewardship.

Green Computing for Sustainable Development

Edited by
Thipendra P. Singh, Niharika Singh,
Amar Ramdane-Cherif, Ravi Tomar,
and Richa Choudhary

CRC Press
Taylor & Francis Group
Boca Raton London New York

CRC Press is an imprint of the
Taylor & Francis Group, an **Informa** business
AN AUERBACH BOOK

Designed cover image: Web Large Image (Public)

First edition published 2025
2385 NW Executive Center Drive, Suite 320, Boca Raton FL 33431

and by CRC Press
4 Park Square, Milton Park, Abingdon, Oxon, OX14 4RN

CRC Press is an imprint of Taylor & Francis Group, LLC

ISBN: 9781032737720 (hbk)
ISBN: 9781032748696 (pbk)
ISBN: 9781003471356 (ebk)

DOI: 10.1201/9781003471356

Typeset in Times
by KnowledgeWorks Global Ltd.

Contents

Preface

Green computing is a revolutionary technique that addresses environmental sustainability. It uses an eco-friendly approach to design, manufacture, and use computing resources. This is achieved by cutting down on electronic waste, using renewable energy sources, and consuming less energy. Recyclable materials with minimal environmental impact, software engineering techniques that are optimized, and energy-efficient hardware are examples of many approaches. This improves living quality and harmonizes IT operations with sustainable aims.

Sustainable development benefits from green computing through significant reductions in carbon footprints and resource depletion. Advanced technologies such as low-power processors, smart grids, and virtualized computing environments contribute to energy efficiency and waste reduction. Furthermore, integrating green computing with renewable energy sources amplifies its positive impact on the environment. The adoption of green computing practices promotes a circular economy, encourages resource conservation, and supports climate action. Embracing these principles is essential for achieving long-term sustainability and fostering a balanced relationship between technological advancement and environmental stewardship.

This edited volume contains well-curated 13 chapters on various above paradigms to address green computing for sustainable development.

First chapter discusses neuro-symbolic green computing which merges neuro-symbolic AI with green computing to create intelligent, sustainable, and energy-efficient systems. This approach combines neural networks' learning abilities with symbolic AI's logical reasoning while promoting environmentally friendly practices. The chapter covers key components like neuro-vector-symbolic architectures and hybrid reasoning networks, highlighting benefits such as enhanced energy efficiency and reduced carbon footprints. It aligns with the UN Sustainable Development Goals, supporting clean energy and sustainable practices. Future prospects include integrating AI with renewable energy, developing energy-efficient hardware, and advancing real-time environmental monitoring.

The chapter on software approach to green computing explores sustainable practices in green computing through software-centric approaches. It reviews the literature on energy-efficient software development, focusing on code optimization, modularization, and dynamic resource management. The role of green software growth procedures and open-source initiatives for collaborative innovation is analyzed. It also covers energy-efficient data management, resource provisioning, and the importance of monitoring carbon footprints. Emerging technologies like AI, IoT, and blockchain are examined for their potential in green computing. The chapter concludes with a framework for green software development, addressing regulatory compliance and promoting power-efficient IT practices.

Chapter 3 explores the intersection of green computing and wildlife conservation, highlighting how energy-efficient technologies can revolutionize conservation efforts. It examines the use of green computing in monitoring wildlife habitats, enhancing conservation through data analytics, and raising environmental awareness.

By showcasing synergies between IT and conservation, the chapter aims to inspire collaboration on sustainable solutions. Practical examples and case studies offer a roadmap for leveraging green computing to advance wildlife conservation practices.

Chapter on the role of remote sensing and GIS in sustainable computing practices addresses environmental concerns arising from rapid advancements in computing, including resource demands, e-waste, energy consumption, and global warming. It highlights green computing as a vital solution for sustainable practices. The integration of geospatial information systems (GIS) and remote sensing (RS), with their real-time satellite imagery capabilities, offers innovative solutions for sustainable development. The chapter emphasizes the transformative role of GIS and RS in sustainable computing and explores their synergy with computing technologies to address environmental challenges and promote a sustainable future.

The next chapter examines the role of information and communication technology (ICT) in promoting health and well-being. It covers various ICT applications, including access to health information, telemedicine, health monitoring with wearables, electronic health records, mobile health apps, e-pharmacy, and healthcare management systems. The integration of ICT in healthcare has expanded access, enhanced efficiency, and improved service quality, addressing how technology contributes to a healthier and smarter world.

Chapter 6 emphasizes the importance of green computing due to growing environmental concerns related to information technology. It explores the transition from traditional IT practices to ecologically responsible ones, focusing on energy-efficient hardware, low-power CPU design, and sustainable IT infrastructure. The chapter highlights the use of renewable energy sources like solar and wind to reduce greenhouse gas emissions, aligning IT with broader sustainability goals. It also addresses ethical lifecycle management, promoting longer product lifecycles, recycling, and sustainable design to minimize e-waste. Virtualization and cloud computing are discussed for their role in maximizing resource usage and reducing energy consumption. The chapter stresses the need for industry standards and regulatory frameworks to ensure environmentally responsible practices. Overall, it presents green computing as a critical step toward a sustainable and eco-conscious digital infrastructure, impacting social, economic, and environmental realms.

The role of artificial intelligence (AI) in sustainable agriculture is explored in Chapter 7. This aims to meet society's needs without compromising future natural resources. Sustainable farming balances social equity, economic profitability, and environmental health. Technological advancements in machinery, seeds, fertilizers, and farming methods have enhanced profitability. However, while AI aids complex decision-making, it requires substantial computational infrastructure, consuming significant resources and generating heat. The chapter emphasizes the need for a balanced approach to integrating AI into sustainable farming practices.

Chapter 8 explores the connection between information and communication technology (ICT) and education using bibliometric analysis. It provides a theoretical foundation for ICT's relevance in green computing, highlighting its need, importance, current trends, and challenges in education. Through science mapping and performance analysis, the chapter identifies research trends, prolific countries, authors, highly cited articles, and key keywords in the "ICT in education" domain. It also examines the current research status and future trends using bibliographic coupling and co-word analysis.

Chapter on integration of green computing and economic growth explores the synergy between green computing practices and economic growth in achieving sustainable development. It reviews the literature on the benefits of green computing, including cost savings, efficiency gains, job creation, and market demand shifts. The chapter also examines the importance of government policies, international collaboration, and funding in meeting Sustainable Development Goals (SDGs). Emphasizing the need for an expert workforce, it highlights future trends and proposes a multi-criteria optimization model that considers economic indicators, green computing adoption, and environmental impact for future research.

Chapters 10 and 11 explore the impact of information and communication technology (ICT) on teaching self-safety laws to children and women. The extensive use of mobile applications has become handy in this endeavor. Chapter 11 highlights UNICEF's Right Runner app, designed to educate kids and teens about their rights in an engaging way. This chapter discusses how women can benefit from smartphone apps for personal safety and protection. It also examines the role of mobile apps in bridging the gap between effective learning and motivational appeal, offering a valuable self-protective resource for users.

E-waste management is one of the major areas in sustainable development. The chapter on this topic examines the integration of green computing with e-waste management to tackle environmental challenges in the IT sector. It emphasizes how sustainable computing practices—such as reducing energy consumption and promoting responsible recycling—can minimize the environmental impact of IT operations. Simultaneously, effective e-waste management focuses on proper disposal, recycling, and policy frameworks to address the environmental and health risks of electronic waste. The chapter advocates for education, community engagement, and technological innovation to foster sustainable practices and achieve a circular economy in IT consumption and e-waste management.

The last chapter explores how the "green Internet of Things" (IoT) is transforming smart city development by integrating ecological awareness and sustainability into urban planning. It highlights how green IoT can address environmental challenges through efficient energy management, waste reduction, and carbon footprint minimization. IoT-enabled sensors and smart grids enhance real-time data analysis, optimizing resource use and protection. Applications include advanced traffic management, intelligent waste systems, and energy and water management, all contributing to sustainable urban environments. The chapter underscores green IoT's potential to reshape smart cities, creating efficient, eco-friendly urban spaces and promoting sustainable development.

Overall, this edited volume presents a very timely intervention into a very important topic toward sustainability. We expect it to be interesting to the readers.

Editors

Thipendra P. Singh is a professor of Artificial Intelligence and working as pro vice chancellor at Chandigarh University, Uttar Pradesh, India. A doctorate in Computer Science from Jamia Millia Islamia University, New Delhi. Dr. Singh is also a fellow of IEI and a senior member of IEEE. He has been editor/author of more than 20 books on various allied topics of Computer Science and contributed more than 100 research papers in various international journals and conferences.

Niharika Singh is backed by a decade of robust experience in technical consultancy, mentoring, and training. Currently, she is working as a data engineer in MPAC, Canada. Holding a Ph.D. in Deep Learning (Computer Science Engineering) from UPES, Dehradun, India, she has significantly contributed to both academia and industry.

Amar Ramdane-Cherif is a full professor at the University of Versailles, Paris-Saclay, France, where he works in the systems engineering laboratory. He has already written 7 book chapters, 50 international journal papers, and about 200 international conference articles. His research interests include ambient intelligence, semantic representation of knowledge, modeling of the ambient environment, and multimodal interaction between person/machine and machine/environment.

Ravi Tomar is a senior architect at Persistent Systems, India. His research interests include wireless sensor networks, image processing, data mining and warehousing, computer networks, big data technologies, and VANET. He has authored 130+ papers in different research areas, filled four Indian patent, edited 6 books, and authored 4 books.

Richa Choudhary holds a doctoral degree in the field of game theory and machine learning. Currently she is working as assistant professor in the Department of Computer Science Engineering-AIML, Panipat Institute of Engineering & Technology, Panipat, India.

Acknowledgments

Editing a book is harder than we thought. This requires a tremendous level of coordination among different stakeholders: contributing authors, editors, and publishers. This becomes even tougher when all these stay a distance apart and in different time zones.

To begin with, the editors want to thank all those who were directly or indirectly involved in the project.

Next, the editors feel thankful to their families, colleagues, and well-wishers who helped them in crucial times in achieving this milestone.

Editors also want to put on record their appreciation for their respective organizations, **University of Petroleum and Energy Studies, Bennett University, Chandigarh University, University of Paris-Saclay, and Persistent Systems**, and their respective management for providing them with such a wonderful opportunity to grow them academically.

Though the entire period of editing the book was filled with many ups and downs, the time with colleagues at the office was worth of price. Many times at low feelings, people around them kept them going which is appreciable on their part and editors want to heartfully thank them all.

Above and over, editors feel thankful to the almighty for showering all His blessings upon them to complete this project.

1 Neuro-Symbolic Green Computing and Its Integration with UN Sustainability Goals

Bikram Pratim Bhuyan and Amar Ramdane-Cherif

1.1 INTRODUCTION

Neuro-symbolic green computing represents a pioneering approach to artificial intelligence (AI), merging the strengths of neuro-symbolic AI with the principles of green computing. This interdisciplinary methodology aims to develop intelligent systems that are both highly efficient and environmentally sustainable. By combining the pattern recognition capabilities of neural networks with the logical reasoning strengths of symbolic AI and embedding these within a framework of sustainable computing practices, neuro-symbolic green computing addresses the growing need for powerful AI systems that also minimize environmental impact.

A practical example of neuro-symbolic green computing can be seen in smart city energy management. Imagine a city that employs neuro-symbolic AI to optimize its energy consumption and improve resilience against climate-related events. The system integrates neural networks and symbolic AI to analyze data from various sensors distributed throughout the city. These sensors monitor real-time data on energy consumption, weather conditions, and renewable energy generation from solar panels and wind turbines.

Neural networks process this unstructured data to predict energy demand and renewable energy supply. Symbolic AI components then apply logical rules to manage the energy grid efficiently. For instance, during periods of high renewable energy generation, the system prioritizes the use of solar and wind power, reducing reliance on non-renewable sources. Additionally, the system can forecast weather events, such as storms, and adjust energy storage and distribution strategies accordingly to ensure stability and minimize disruptions.

Furthermore, the data centers supporting this smart city initiative implement green computing practices. They operate on renewable energy sources and make use of energy-efficient hardware and cooling systems. This integrated approach not only enhances the city's energy efficiency but also significantly reduces its carbon footprint.

This chapter introduces the concept of neuro-symbolic green computing, a hybrid approach that integrates the advanced capabilities of neuro-symbolic AI

DOI: 10.1201/9781003471356-1

with the principles of green computing to create intelligent, sustainable, and efficient computational systems. The structure of the chapter is organized into several sections. The chapter includes an overview of neuro-symbolic computing in Section 1.2, discussing its key components, benefits, and challenges, followed by an exploration of green computing principles and their importance in Section 1.3. It further details the integration of neuro-symbolic AI with green computing in Section 1.4 to optimize energy use and reduce carbon footprints, illustrating the latest techniques such as neuro-vector-symbolic architectures (NVSA), hybrid reasoning networks, bootstrapping language-image pre-training (BLIP) fine-tuning, and differentiable programming. The chapter also aligns neuro-symbolic green computing with UN Sustainable Development Goals (SDG) (UN SDGs) in Section 1.5, particularly SDGs 7, 9, 11, 12, and 13, highlighting its potential to promote clean energy, sustainable industrial practices, resilient infrastructure, responsible consumption, and climate action. Finally, it discusses the future of neuro-symbolic green computing in Section 1.6, emphasizing the enhanced integration of AI and renewable energy, development of energy-efficient hardware, scalable AI systems, real-time environmental monitoring, AI-driven policy support, and continuous learning and adaptation. Section 1.7 acts as the conclusion of the chapter.

1.2 NEURO-SYMBOLIC COMPUTING: AN OVERVIEW

Neuro-symbolic computing (Bhuyan, Ramdane-Cherif, Tomar, & Singh, 2024) represents a paradigm shift in AI, aiming to combine the strengths of neural networks and symbolic AI to create more powerful, interpretable, and versatile systems. This method combines the structured reasoning of symbolic systems with neural networks' ability to learn. It makes it possible to solve challenging problems that require both data-driven continuous learning and logical discrete reasoning.

1.2.1 Key Components of Neuro-Symbolic Computing

Neural Networks form the foundational learning component of neuro-symbolic systems. These are computing models inspired by the human brain's architecture, consisting of interconnected nodes (neurons) arranged in layers. Neural networks are particularly adept at processing unstructured data, such as images, speech, and text, to perform tasks like classification, regression, and generation (the latest focus is on large language models). Neural networks (as multi-layer perceptrons) are very useful because they can learn from data. This is done through a process called training, in which the network changes its weights based on error-minimization methods like backpropagation and gradient descent. However, new types of neural networks, like Kolmogorov-Arnold Networks (Liu et al., 2024), are being developed as promising alternatives to multi-layer perceptrons. This ability to learn complex patterns and representations makes neural networks indispensable in applications ranging from image recognition to natural language processing.

On the other hand, symbolic AI contributes to the reasoning and interpretability aspects of neuro-symbolic systems. Symbolic AI operates through the manipulation of symbols and the application of logical rules, which allows it to represent knowledge and perform explicit reasoning tasks. This approach excels in domains requiring transparent, logical thought processes, such as theorem proving, knowledge representation, and solving puzzles. Symbolic AI's inherent explainability, where its reasoning process can be traced and understood, is crucial for applications that demand transparency and accountability, such as healthcare diagnostics and financial decision-making. Techniques within symbolic AI include rule-based systems, logic programming, ontologies, and knowledge graphs.

The real power of neuro-symbolic computing comes from the ways that neural networks and symbolic AI are combined (Garcez & Lamb, 2023). Hybrid architectures are a primary method of integration where neural networks are used to process raw data and extract features, which are then fed into symbolic reasoning modules. This division of labor allows each component to leverage its strengths—neural networks for perception and feature extraction and symbolic AI for reasoning and decision-making. Another key integration method is knowledge distillation (Gou, Yu, Maybank, & Tao, 2021), where knowledge learned by a neural network is transferred to a symbolic system. This process involves simplifying the complex, data-driven knowledge of neural networks into more interpretable, rule-based knowledge suitable for symbolic AI. Also, unified frameworks like neural theorem provers (Wang & Deng, 2020) and Logic Tensor Networks (Badreddine, Garcez, Serafini, & Spranger, 2022) combine learning and reasoning into one system, letting neural and symbolic parts interact in a dynamic way.

1.2.2 Benefits of Neuro-Symbolic Computing

Neuro-symbolic computing offers a notable benefit in its capacity to integrate data-driven learning with logical reasoning. Neural networks are highly proficient at identifying patterns from large quantities of organized, semi-structured, or unstructured data, including pictures, text, audio, and flat databases. Nevertheless, individuals of this kind often have difficulties when confronted with activities that need abstract reasoning, rule-based logic, or the management of structured knowledge. Symbolic AI, on the other hand, is particularly effective in these domains, allowing computers to carry out tasks such as theorem proving, planning, and knowledge-based reasoning.

However, symbolic AI by itself lacks the predictive capabilities of neural AI, since it encodes information in a discrete manner. By combining these two methodologies, neuro-symbolic systems are capable of addressing a wider array of tasks, acquiring knowledge from unprocessed input, and employing organized reasoning to resolve intricate issues. This dual functionality is especially advantageous in fields that need both perceptual and cognitive skills, such as autonomous driving, where the system must analyze visual information and make rational judgments based on rules and context.

Interpretability is a crucial consideration in the field of AI, particularly in situations when it is necessary for choices to be clear and comprehensible to human beings. Neural network models, although very effective, often function as "black boxes," making it challenging to determine how certain inputs result in particular outputs (Bhuyan, Tomar, & Fore, 2023). The absence of transparency can pose challenges in sectors such as healthcare, banking, and law, where comprehending the process of decision-making is crucial. Neuro-symbolic computing tackles this problem by integrating symbolic thinking, which is inherently comprehensible. Symbolic components employ logical norms and organized information, facilitating the comprehension of the reasoning process and offering unambiguous justifications for judgments. The capacity to comprehend AI systems promotes confidence and guarantees adherence to ethical and regulatory guidelines.

Neuro-symbolic systems are typically more **robust** and generalize better than purely neural or symbolic approaches. Neural networks can be sensitive to noisy or incomplete data, leading to brittle performance in real-world scenarios. Symbolic AI, while robust in reasoning, can struggle with the variability and ambiguity present in unstructured data. The integration of these approaches mitigates their individual weaknesses. Neuro-symbolic systems can leverage the robustness of symbolic reasoning to handle uncertainties and the adaptability of neural networks to process diverse data types. This combination enhances the system's ability to generalize from training data to new, unseen situations, making it more reliable and versatile in practical applications. Another benefit of neuro-symbolic computing is its potential for **scalability and efficiency**. Neural networks can process large amounts of data in parallel, making them suitable for handling big data applications. However, they can be computationally intensive and require significant resources for training and inference. Symbolic AI, while more computationally efficient for reasoning tasks, can struggle with scalability due to its reliance on predefined rules and structured data. Neuro-symbolic systems can optimize resource usage by leveraging the strengths of both approaches. For instance, neural networks can perform initial data processing and feature extraction, reducing the complexity of the input for the symbolic reasoning component. This division of labor allows for more efficient use of computational resources and facilitates scaling to larger, more complex problems.

Neuro-symbolic computing significantly enhances **problem-solving capabilities** by allowing systems to tackle tasks that require both learning and reasoning. This is particularly advantageous in fields such as scientific research, where complex hypotheses need to be tested against large datasets and logical consistency. In cybersecurity, for instance, neuro-symbolic systems can detect patterns of malicious activity (a task suited for neural networks) while simultaneously applying logical rules to identify potential threats and devise countermeasures. This combined approach allows for more comprehensive and effective problem-solving strategies.

Finally, neuro-symbolic systems offer greater **flexibility and adaptability** compared to purely neural or symbolic systems. They can be tailored to specific applications by adjusting the balance between neural learning and symbolic reasoning components. For example, in natural language processing, a neuro-symbolic system can use neural networks for understanding and generating text, while symbolic AI can handle tasks like parsing grammatical structures and applying linguistic rules (Wu, Li, Sun, & Lu, 2024). This adaptability makes neuro-symbolic computing suitable for a wide range of applications, from autonomous systems and robotics to finance and healthcare.

1.2.3 Challenges in Neuro-Symbolic Computing

While neuro-symbolic computing offers a promising hybrid approach that integrates the strengths of neural networks and symbolic AI, several challenges must be addressed to realize its potential fully. These challenges span from technical integration difficulties to scalability and standardization issues, which can impact the effectiveness and adoption of neuro-symbolic systems.

One of the foremost challenges in neuro-symbolic computing is the **complexity** involved in integrating neural networks and symbolic AI. These two approaches are fundamentally different: neural networks are data-driven and excel in learning as data is represented in a continuous space, while symbolic AI relies on predefined rules and logical structures in a discrete space to perform reasoning tasks. Combining these paradigms requires sophisticated integration techniques that can harmonize their disparate nature. Hybrid architectures need to be designed carefully to ensure that neural components can effectively communicate with symbolic modules, which often involves developing novel algorithms and frameworks that can bridge the gap between data-driven learning and rule-based reasoning. This integration complexity can slow down the development process and require significant computational resources.

The **lack of standardized frameworks and benchmarks** in neuro-symbolic computing poses a significant challenge. Without common standards, it is difficult to compare the performance and effectiveness of different neuro-symbolic approaches. This lack of benchmarks also hinders the ability to measure progress and identify best practices within the field. Establishing standardized protocols, evaluation metrics, and benchmarks is essential for fostering collaboration, guiding research efforts, and accelerating the development of robust neuro-symbolic systems. Standardization can also facilitate the transfer of successful methods and technologies across different application domains.

While one of the benefits of neuro-symbolic computing is enhanced interpretability, achieving this in practice can be challenging. The integration of neural networks and symbolic reasoning needs to be designed in a way that preserves the interpretability of the symbolic component while leveraging the learning capabilities of the neural component. This often requires innovative approaches to ensure that the reasoning process remains transparent and understandable, even as the system learns from data. Maintaining this balance is crucial, especially in applications where transparency and accountability are paramount.

Neuro-symbolic systems can be **resource-intensive**, both in terms of computational power and data requirements. Training large neural networks demands significant energy and computational resources, which can be environmentally and economically costly. Integrating symbolic AI adds another layer of complexity that can further increase resource consumption. This challenge is particularly pertinent in the context of green computing, which aims to minimize the environmental impact of computing technologies. Addressing the resource intensity of neuro-symbolic systems is crucial for making them more sustainable and aligning them with the goals of green computing. These challenges highlight the multifaceted nature of neuro-symbolic computing and underscore the need for continued research and innovation to overcome these hurdles. Addressing these issues not only enhances the capabilities of neuro-symbolic systems but also ensures their alignment with broader technological and environmental goals, including those of green computing. As we transition from the challenges in neuro-symbolic computing to the concept of green computing, it becomes clear that the sustainability and efficiency of computational systems are paramount. Green computing, or environmentally sustainable computing, focuses on designing, manufacturing, using, and disposing of computers, servers, and associated subsystems efficiently and effectively with minimal impact on the environment. It aims to reduce the carbon footprint of information technology (IT) systems and promote energy efficiency, contributing to broader sustainability goals. In the following section, we will explore the principles and practices of green computing, its importance, and its integration with advanced technologies like neuro-symbolic computing.

1.3 GREEN COMPUTING: AN OVERVIEW

Green computing (Saha, 2014), also known as environmentally sustainable computing, encompasses the design, manufacture, use, and disposal of IT systems in a way that minimizes environmental impact. This approach seeks to reduce the carbon footprint of IT operations, enhance energy efficiency, and promote sustainability throughout the lifecycle of computing devices. As the demand for computational power grows, green computing becomes increasingly critical in addressing the environmental challenges associated with the widespread use of technology.

1.3.1 Key Principles of Green Computing

Energy efficiency is at the core of green computing. It involves optimizing the energy consumption of computing devices, data centers, and IT infrastructure. Techniques such as dynamic power management, virtualization, and efficient cooling systems are employed to reduce energy usage. Energy-efficient hardware, including low-power processors and solid-state drives (SSDs), also play a significant role. By minimizing energy consumption, green computing not only lowers operational costs but also reduces greenhouse gas emissions.

The manufacturing process of computing devices has a significant environmental impact due to the extraction of raw materials, energy-intensive production, and the use of hazardous substances. Green computing promotes **sustainable manufacturing practices** by encouraging the use of eco-friendly materials, reducing waste, and improving the efficiency of production processes. Manufacturers are increasingly adopting practices such as recycling and reusing materials, reducing the use of toxic chemicals, and implementing environmentally friendly packaging solutions.

Optimizing the use of resources, including hardware, software, and network infrastructure, is another key aspect of green computing. This includes efficient utilization of computing resources through techniques like load balancing, resource pooling, and server consolidation. Cloud computing and virtualization are powerful tools in this regard, as they enable the sharing of resources among multiple users, reducing the need for excess hardware and minimizing idle capacity.

Electronic waste (e-waste) poses a significant environmental challenge due to the rapid obsolescence of electronic devices. Green computing addresses this issue by promoting **proper e-waste management practices**, including recycling, refurbishing, and responsible disposal of electronic products. Recycling programs aim to recover valuable materials from discarded devices, while refurbishing extends the lifespan of electronic products. Proper disposal methods ensure that hazardous substances do not contaminate the environment.

Incorporating **renewable energy sources**, such as solar, wind, and hydroelectric power, into IT operations is a crucial aspect of green computing. Data centers, which are significant consumers of energy, are increasingly powered by renewable energy to reduce their carbon footprint. This transition not only supports environmental sustainability but also contributes to energy security and cost savings in the long term.

1.3.2 Importance of Green Computing

The importance of green computing cannot be overstated, given the escalating environmental challenges and the increasing demand for computational power. The IT industry is responsible for a substantial portion of global energy consumption and carbon emissions. By adopting green computing practices, organizations can significantly reduce their environmental impact and contribute to global sustainability efforts.

Green computing helps mitigate the adverse environmental effects associated with the production, use, and disposal of computing devices. By reducing energy consumption and minimizing waste, green computing contributes to lower greenhouse gas emissions, reduced resource depletion, and decreased pollution.

Adopting green computing practices can lead to significant cost savings for organizations. Energy-efficient technologies and optimized resource usage reduce operational costs, while sustainable manufacturing and e-waste management practices can lower material costs and waste disposal expenses. Additionally, compliance with environmental regulations can prevent costly fines and enhance corporate reputation.

Green computing aligns with corporate social responsibility (CSR) initiatives (Chou, Chen, & Lin, 2023), demonstrating a commitment to environmental stewardship and sustainable development. Organizations that prioritize green computing practices can enhance their brand image, attract environmentally conscious customers and employees, and contribute positively to society.

The integration of green computing with advanced technologies, such as neuro-symbolic computing, holds great promise for creating more sustainable and efficient computational systems. Neuro-symbolic computing, which combines neural networks' learning capabilities with symbolic AI's logical reasoning, can benefit from green computing practices to enhance its sustainability.

Neuro-symbolic systems can be designed to be energy-efficient by optimizing the training and inference processes of neural networks and leveraging the computational efficiency of symbolic reasoning. Techniques such as model pruning, quantization, and hardware accelerators can be employed to reduce energy consumption without compromising performance.

Data centers supporting neuro-symbolic computing can implement green computing practices, such as using renewable energy sources, optimizing cooling systems, and improving server utilization. This reduces the environmental impact of running large-scale AI models and supports the sustainable growth of computational power.

The development of neuro-symbolic systems can incorporate sustainable practices, such as using recycled materials for hardware components, adopting energy-efficient software development practices, and ensuring proper e-waste management. This holistic approach ensures that AI advancements are aligned with environmental sustainability goals.

1.4 NEURO-SYMBOLIC GREEN COMPUTING

We introduce neuro-symbolic green computing as an interdisciplinary approach that combines the strengths of neuro-symbolic AI with the principles of green computing to create sustainable, efficient, and intelligent computational systems. **This field aims to leverage the pattern recognition and learning capabilities of neural networks with the logical reasoning and interpretability of symbolic AI while adhering to environmentally sustainable practices throughout the lifecycle of computing resources.**

Neuro-symbolic AI, as a hybrid approach, integrates neural networks with symbolic AI, allowing for the creation of AI systems that are both powerful and interpretable, capable of learning from data and applying logical rules to make decisions and solve problems. Green computing focuses on reducing the environmental impact of computing technologies by enhancing energy efficiency, promoting the use of renewable energy sources, and implementing sustainable manufacturing and disposal practices. It encompasses the design, use, and disposal of computing resources in a way that minimizes their ecological footprint.

Neuro-symbolic green computing, therefore, seeks to develop AI systems that not only achieve high performance and accuracy but also do so in an energy-efficient and environmentally friendly manner. This involves optimizing the computational processes of neuro-symbolic systems to reduce energy consumption, utilizing sustainable practices in the manufacturing and disposal of hardware, and integrating renewable energy sources to power data centers and other IT infrastructure.

1.4.1 Benefits of Neuro-Symbolic Green Computing

Neuro-symbolic green computing merges the strengths of neuro-symbolic AI with environmentally sustainable practices, offering a range of benefits that enhance both computational efficiency and ecological sustainability. This integration aims to address the growing demand for powerful AI systems while mitigating their environmental impact.

1. *Enhanced energy efficiency*: Neuro-symbolic green computing significantly enhances energy efficiency by optimizing the computational processes of AI systems. Traditional deep learning models require substantial

computational power and energy, leading to high operational costs and environmental impact. By integrating symbolic reasoning, which is computationally less intensive, with neural networks, these hybrid systems can achieve similar or superior performance with reduced energy consumption. Techniques such as model pruning, quantization (Tian, Luan, & Zheng, 2023), and hardware accelerators help reduce the energy requirements of AI systems, making them more sustainable.

2. *Reduced carbon footprint in data centers*: Data centers, which house the infrastructure for AI, are major energy consumers. Implementing neuro-symbolic AI within these centers can lead to more efficient use of computational resources. Symbolic AI can handle logical reasoning tasks, reducing the load on energy-intensive neural networks. Additionally, green computing practices like optimizing cooling systems, utilizing renewable energy sources, and enhancing server utilization can further decrease the environmental impact of data centers. This integration helps in reducing the overall carbon footprint of data-intensive AI operations.
3. *Prolonged hardware lifespan*: Neuro-symbolic green computing contributes to extending the lifespan of hardware. By optimizing computational tasks and reducing the need for continuous high-power processing, these systems decrease wear and tear on hardware components. This aligns with green computing goals of minimizing electronic waste and promoting the reuse and recycling of IT equipment. Sustainable hardware management not only reduces environmental impact but also lowers costs associated with frequent hardware replacements.
4. *Advanced problem-solving with lower environmental impact*: Neuro-symbolic systems enhance problem-solving capabilities while maintaining a lower environmental impact. For example, in healthcare, neuro-symbolic AI can efficiently analyze complex medical datasets to provide accurate diagnostics and treatment plans, reducing the computational power required compared to traditional deep learning approaches. Similarly, in environmental monitoring, these systems can process large-scale data efficiently, aiding in climate modeling and resource management with reduced energy consumption. This dual capability ensures effective problem-solving across various domains without compromising environmental sustainability.
5. *Scalability and adaptability*: Neuro-symbolic green computing offers scalability and adaptability, making it suitable for a wide range of applications. Scalable neuro-symbolic systems can dynamically adjust to different levels of computational demand, optimizing energy use accordingly. This flexibility ensures that AI applications can grow and adapt to new challenges without a proportional increase in energy consumption and environmental impact. By combining efficient learning and reasoning capabilities with sustainable practices, these systems can support diverse and evolving technological needs sustainably.
6. *Alignment with CSR goals*: Adopting neuro-symbolic green computing practices aligns with CSR initiatives. Organizations that prioritize sustainable AI practices can enhance their brand image, attract environmentally

conscious customers and employees, and contribute positively to society. By demonstrating a commitment to reducing environmental impact and promoting sustainability, companies can fulfill their CSR goals while leveraging advanced AI capabilities.

1.4.2 Latest Techniques in Neuro-Symbolic Green Computing

Neuro-symbolic green computing can advance rapidly, integrating cutting-edge techniques from both neuro-symbolic AI and green computing to create more efficient, sustainable, and intelligent systems. Here are some of the latest techniques and advancements to uplift this field.

1.4.2.1 Neuro-Vector-Symbolic Architectures

NVSA (Hersche, Zeqiri, Benini, Sebastian, & Rahimi, 2023) represent a significant advancement in the integration of neural networks and symbolic AI, combining the strengths of both to enhance performance, interpretability, and energy efficiency. This hybrid approach is particularly relevant to the goals of neuro-symbolic green computing, which seeks to develop intelligent systems that are both powerful and environmentally sustainable.

One of the primary contributions of NVSA to neuro-symbolic green computing is enhanced energy efficiency. By distributing computational tasks between neural networks and symbolic reasoning modules, NVSA reduces the overall computational load and energy consumption. Neural networks handle initial data processing and feature extraction, while symbolic components manage tasks requiring logical inference and decision-making. This division of labor ensures that each component operates within its optimal energy range, significantly reducing the need for extensive computation and frequent retraining.

NVSA frameworks are designed to be highly scalable and adaptable, capable of handling varying levels of computational demand. Techniques such as model pruning, which involves reducing the size of neural networks without sacrificing performance, further enhance scalability and energy efficiency. This scalability ensures that as the complexity of tasks increases, the system can efficiently allocate resources without a proportional increase in energy consumption.

Moreover, NVSA is particularly well-suited for implementation on energy-efficient hardware platforms. Advances in AI-specific accelerators and low-power processors can be effectively utilized within NVSA frameworks to maximize performance while minimizing energy use. These hardware solutions are crucial for deploying NVSA in real-world applications where power efficiency is a significant concern.

By optimizing computational processes and leveraging sustainable hardware, NVSA contributes to a lower carbon footprint for AI operations. Data centers, which are major energy consumers, benefit from the reduced load and optimized performance of NVSA systems. Incorporating renewable energy sources to power these data centers further enhances the environmental benefits, aligning with green computing goals.

The efficient operation of NVSA also reduces wear and tear on hardware components, extending their lifespan and reducing the frequency of replacements.

This contributes to a decrease in electronic waste (e-waste), which is a significant environmental concern. Sustainable management of hardware resources aligns with the principles of green computing, promoting the reuse and recycling of IT equipment.

In real-world applications, NVSA has demonstrated significant benefits. In healthcare, NVSA can process patient data efficiently and apply logical rules to interpret results, reducing the need for resource-intensive computations and enabling more sustainable healthcare solutions. In environmental monitoring, NVSA can analyze large datasets from environmental sensors, combining neural data processing with symbolic reasoning to make accurate predictions and decisions regarding climate change and resource management. In smart city applications, NVSA can optimize resource allocation, traffic management, and energy consumption by integrating real-time data analysis with logical decision-making frameworks.

1.4.2.2 Hybrid Reasoning Networks

Hybrid reasoning networks (Yu et al., 2021) represent a sophisticated approach within neuro-symbolic AI, integrating the statistical learning capabilities of neural networks with the logical reasoning strengths of symbolic AI. This integration aims to create systems that are not only highly efficient but also environmentally sustainable, aligning with the principles of neuro-symbolic green computing.

Hybrid reasoning networks utilize a comprehensive neuro-symbolic system to achieve robust, interpretable, and scalable reasoning capabilities. By combining neural networks' ability to handle unstructured data with symbolic AI's precision in logical reasoning, these networks address complex cognitive tasks more effectively than traditional AI models. The seamless interaction between neural and symbolic components allows for advanced problem-solving capabilities, making these networks particularly suitable for applications requiring both data-driven learning and structured reasoning. One of the key contributions of hybrid reasoning networks to neuro-symbolic green computing is their enhanced energy efficiency. By leveraging the strengths of both neural and symbolic components, these networks optimize computational tasks, reducing overall energy consumption. Neural networks handle initial data processing and feature extraction, while symbolic AI manages logical reasoning and decision-making tasks.

This division of labor ensures that each component operates at its most energy-efficient state, significantly lowering the computational load and associated energy costs.

Hybrid reasoning networks are also designed to be highly scalable and adaptable, capable of managing varying levels of computational demand. This scalability is crucial for maintaining energy efficiency as the complexity and scale of tasks increase. Techniques such as model compression and efficient resource allocation further enhance the scalability and adaptability of these networks, ensuring they can handle large-scale applications without a corresponding rise in energy consumption.

In addition to energy efficiency and scalability, hybrid reasoning networks contribute to green computing through their compatibility with energy-efficient hardware. These networks can be implemented on specialized AI accelerators and low-power processors, maximizing performance while minimizing energy use.

This compatibility with advanced hardware solutions is essential for deploying hybrid reasoning networks in real-world environments where energy efficiency is a priority.

The integration of renewable energy sources into the operational framework of hybrid reasoning networks further aligns with green computing principles. Data centers that deploy these networks can utilize solar, wind, and other renewable energy sources to power their operations, reducing the overall carbon footprint. This approach not only enhances sustainability but also supports the economic viability of large-scale AI deployments.

Hybrid reasoning networks also play a significant role in extending hardware lifespan and reducing electronic waste. By optimizing computational efficiency and reducing the need for continuous high-power processing, these networks decrease wear and tear on hardware components. This reduction in hardware strain leads to fewer replacements and upgrades, minimizing electronic waste and promoting sustainable IT practices.

In practical applications, hybrid reasoning networks demonstrate substantial benefits across various domains. In healthcare, these networks can process and analyze complex medical data, combining neural network-based data processing with symbolic reasoning to provide accurate diagnostics and treatment recommendations efficiently. In environmental monitoring, hybrid reasoning networks can analyze large datasets from sensors, using neural networks for data processing and symbolic AI for making logical inferences about environmental conditions and trends. In smart city initiatives, these networks optimize resource allocation, traffic management, and energy consumption by integrating real-time data analysis with structured reasoning frameworks, enhancing urban sustainability.

1.4.2.3 BLIP Fine-Tuning and Symbolic Rule Learning

BLIP (Li, Li, Savarese, & Hoi, 2023; Li, Li, Xiong, & Hoi, 2022) fine-tuning represents a sophisticated approach in neuro-symbolic AI, enhancing the integration between visual and textual data. BLIP leverages transformer models to handle image and text inputs, optimizing them for unified vision-language tasks. The pre-training process involves two stages. Initially, BLIP employs three losses: image-text contrastive (ITC) loss (Song et al., 2022) to align the visual and text transformers' feature spaces, image-text matching (ITM) loss (Li, Guo, Feng, Hwang, & Du, 2023) for binary classification of image-text pairs, and language modeling (LM) loss (Jozefowicz, Vinyals, Schuster, Shazeer, & Wu, 2016) for generating textual descriptions conditioned on images. This multi-objective optimization ensures the model is well-prepared to handle tasks like image captioning, visual question answering, and visual reasoning.

The second stage of BLIP pre-training refines the integration of visual information into the language model, enhancing the model's ability to generate accurate and contextually relevant text based on visual inputs. This comprehensive training framework allows BLIP to manage noisy data effectively by generating synthetic captions and filtering out inaccurate ones, significantly improving performance on downstream tasks.

Symbolic rule learning in BLIP enhances interpretability and logical reasoning capabilities by learning explicit rules from data. An example of this is the "pix2rule" framework (Cingillioglu & Russo, 2021), which processes images into objects, learns relationships between them, and extracts symbolic rules using a disjunctive normal form (DNF) layer. This hybrid architecture allows the system to handle complex tasks efficiently, even in the presence of noisy inputs.

BLIP fine-tuning and symbolic rule learning both contribute significantly to energy efficiency. BLIP's multi-stage pre-training reduces the need for extensive retraining, thus lowering computational power requirements. Similarly, symbolic rule learning's ability to extract and apply logical rules efficiently minimizes the computational load during inference, leading to reduced energy consumption.

These techniques are designed for high scalability and adaptability, which are crucial for maintaining energy efficiency as task complexity increases. BLIP's ability to handle large-scale vision-language tasks and symbolic rule learning's structured approach ensures that AI systems can manage varying computational demands without a corresponding rise in energy usage.

BLIP fine-tuning and symbolic rule learning are compatible with advanced AI accelerators and low-power processors, maximizing performance while minimizing energy use. This compatibility is essential for deploying neuro-symbolic systems in real-world environments where energy efficiency is a priority.

By optimizing computational efficiency and utilizing energy-efficient hardware, these techniques contribute to a lower carbon footprint for AI operations. Deploying such systems in data centers powered by renewable energy sources further enhances environmental benefits, aligning with green computing goals.

Efficient operation of these techniques reduces the strain on hardware components, extending their lifespan and reducing the frequency of replacements. This contributes to fewer issues related to electronic waste (e-waste), promoting sustainable IT practices.

1.4.2.4 Differentiable Programming

Differentiable programming (Liao, Liu, Wang, & Xiang, 2019) is a paradigm that allows complex computer programs, including those with control flows and data structures, to be differentiated end-to-end using automatic differentiation. This capability enables gradient-based optimization of program parameters, making it a powerful tool for enhancing the performance of machine learning models. The core idea is to make every part of a program differentiable, thus facilitating the integration of neural networks and symbolic reasoning within a single framework.

Differentiable programming builds upon various areas of computer science and applied mathematics, including automatic differentiation, graphical models, optimization, and statistics (Abadi & Plotkin, 2019). This programming paradigm not only supports the differentiation of programs but also introduces probability distributions over their execution, which allows for the quantification of uncertainty in program outputs. This approach is particularly useful in neuro-symbolic systems where the interplay between neural and symbolic components needs to be optimized continuously. Differentiable programming significantly enhances energy efficiency by streamlining the optimization process of neuro-symbolic systems. By enabling gradient-based optimization, it reduces the need for extensive and iterative training processes typical in traditional machine learning models.

This reduction in computational overhead translates directly to lower energy consumption, making AI systems more sustainable. The paradigm supports scalability and adaptability, which are crucial for managing the increasing complexity of neuro-symbolic systems. Differentiable programming allows for seamless scaling of models by efficiently optimizing various components within the system. This adaptability ensures that as the demand for computational resources grows, energy efficiency remains optimized, supporting sustainable growth in AI applications.

Differentiable programming is inherently compatible with modern AI hardware accelerators, such as GPUs and TPUs, which are designed for high efficiency in parallel processing tasks. This compatibility ensures that neuro-symbolic systems can leverage advanced hardware to maximize performance while minimizing energy consumption. The synergy between differentiable programming and energy-efficient hardware is crucial for developing sustainable AI systems that can operate effectively in real-world environments.

By optimizing computational processes and leveraging efficient hardware, differentiable programming contributes to a lower carbon footprint for AI operations. This is particularly important in large-scale deployments where energy consumption can be significant. The reduced computational load and enhanced efficiency help minimize the environmental impact of neuro-symbolic systems, aligning with the goals of green computing.

Efficient operation of neuro-symbolic systems using differentiable programming reduces the strain on hardware components, thereby extending their lifespan. This reduction in wear and tear leads to fewer replacements and upgrades, minimizing electronic waste (e-waste). Sustainable hardware management is a key aspect of green computing, promoting the reuse and recycling of IT equipment.

1.4.2.5 Energy-Efficient Hardware and Accelerators

Energy-efficient hardware and accelerators are crucial components in the quest for sustainable and powerful AI systems. These technologies are designed to maximize computational performance while minimizing energy consumption, making them ideal for neuro-symbolic green computing. The latest advancements in this field include GPUs, TPUs, and specialized AI accelerators that offer significant energy savings and performance boosts (Karunaratne, 2023).

Graphics processing units (GPUs) and tensor processing units (TPUs) have become the backbone of energy-efficient AI computing. GPUs, such as NVIDIA's H100 Tensor Core GPUs, are designed for parallel processing, making them highly efficient for training large AI models (Choquette, 2022). These GPUs provide substantial energy savings by accelerating workloads that would otherwise consume significant CPU resources. For example, NVIDIA's H100 GPUs have been shown to reduce energy consumption by up to 4× while delivering a 3× reduction in system costs.

Specialized AI accelerators, like IBM's Digital AI Cores, are tailored for specific AI tasks, enhancing energy efficiency (Gershon et al., 2024). These accelerators integrate computation and memory to overcome the von Neumann bottleneck, significantly improving performance and energy efficiency. IBM's efforts in developing analog AI cores further highlight the potential for substantial energy savings and enhanced performance by combining compute and memory functions in a single device.

Parallel computing techniques, enabled by energy-efficient hardware, are transforming industries that rely on computationally intensive tasks. In sectors like aerospace, automotive, and environmental modeling, parallel computing with GPUs has drastically reduced the time and energy required for simulations. For instance, computational fluid dynamics (CFD) simulations that previously consumed vast amounts of energy are now accelerated by GPUs, achieving up to 30× speedups and 4× energy savings (Tu, Yeoh, Liu, & Tao, 2023).

Energy-efficient hardware directly contributes to the sustainability of neuro-symbolic computing by reducing the energy required for training and inference of AI models. This is particularly important as the complexity and scale of neuro-symbolic systems increase. By leveraging GPUs, TPUs, and specialized AI accelerators, neuro-symbolic systems can achieve high performance with significantly lower energy consumption.

The scalability of energy-efficient hardware ensures that neuro-symbolic systems can handle increasing computational demands without a proportional rise in energy consumption. This adaptability is crucial for maintaining sustainable AI operations as data volumes and processing requirements grow.

Utilizing energy-efficient hardware reduces the carbon footprint of AI operations. Data centers and computational facilities powered by such hardware can significantly cut their energy usage, aligning with global sustainability goals. The reduction in energy consumption also translates to lower greenhouse gas emissions, making AI applications more environmentally friendly.

Efficient hardware usage extends the lifespan of computing components, reducing the frequency of replacements and upgrades. This contributes to a decrease in electronic waste (e-waste), promoting sustainable IT practices and reducing the environmental impact of discarded electronic devices.

1.4.2.6 Renewable Energy Integration

Renewable energy integration into data centers is a critical step toward achieving sustainability goals, particularly given the rising energy demands of neuro-symbolic AI-driven workloads. By incorporating renewable energy sources like solar, wind, and hydroelectric power, data centers can significantly reduce their carbon footprint and contribute to global decarbonization efforts. This approach not only supports environmental sustainability but also enhances the economic viability of large-scale AI operations.

Integrating renewable energy sources into data centers directly reduces the reliance on fossil fuels, thereby cutting greenhouse gas emissions. AI data centers, which consume vast amounts of energy, can significantly lower their carbon footprint by utilizing clean energy. For example, several data centers have adopted solar and wind power to meet their energy needs, thereby aligning their operations with broader environmental goals (Uddin & Rahman, 2012).

Renewable energy integration can be optimized using AI-driven energy management systems. These systems predict energy supply from renewable sources and adjust data center operations accordingly. For instance, during peak solar or wind generation periods, data centers can ramp up operations while scaling down during low generation periods. This dynamic adjustment helps in maintaining a balance between energy supply and demand, ensuring efficient use of available renewable energy.

AI data centers can serve as flexible loads on the power grid, adjusting their energy consumption based on grid conditions. This flexibility helps stabilize the grid by reducing demand during peak hours and increasing consumption when the renewable energy supply is high. Implementing such demand response strategies ensures that data centers operate sustainably without overburdening the grid, contributing to overall grid stability.

Governments and local authorities are increasingly providing incentives for renewable energy adoption in data centers. These incentives include subsidies, tax benefits, and support for infrastructure development. Such measures encourage data center operators to invest in renewable energy projects, further promoting the integration of sustainable energy sources into their operations.

Advancements in energy-efficient hardware and AI accelerators further complement renewable energy integration. For instance, the use of GPUs and specialized AI accelerators that consume less power can enhance the overall energy efficiency of data centers. Combining these technologies with renewable energy sources ensures that AI systems can operate at high-performance levels while minimizing environmental impact.

1.4.2.7 Federated Learning and Edge Computing

Federated learning (FL) (Li, Fan, Tse, & Lin, 2020) is a decentralized machine learning approach that enables the training of models across multiple devices or edge nodes without the need to transfer raw data to a central server. This method is particularly beneficial for preserving data privacy and security, as only model updates are shared rather than the data itself. In the context of neuro-symbolic computing, FL allows for the collective improvement of AI models by leveraging the diverse data generated at the edge, enhancing model robustness and performance.

Edge computing refers to the deployment of computational resources at the periphery of the network, closer to where data is generated. This setup reduces latency and bandwidth usage, as data processing occurs locally rather than in centralized data centers. Edge computing supports real-time data processing and decision-making, which is crucial for applications like autonomous vehicles, smart cities, and industrial automation (Yang et al., 2023).

FL and edge computing collectively improve energy efficiency by minimizing the need for data transfer to central servers. This reduction in data movement decreases the overall energy consumption of AI systems. Additionally, processing data locally at the edge reduces the load on central data centers, leading to significant energy savings. The distributed nature of these technologies ensures that computational tasks are balanced across multiple devices, optimizing resource usage and further reducing energy expenditure.

The integration of FL with edge computing enhances the scalability of AI systems. Edge devices, equipped with sufficient computational power, can train models locally and share updates, allowing the system to scale efficiently without overwhelming any single node. This adaptability is crucial for handling the increasing data volumes and processing requirements in neuro-symbolic systems, ensuring that they can grow sustainably.

By keeping data on local devices and only sharing model updates, FL ensures that sensitive information remains secure. This privacy-preserving approach is essential for applications in healthcare, finance, and other sectors where data confidentiality is paramount. Enhanced security measures and robust encryption protocols further protect the data during the transmission of model updates.

FL and edge computing contribute to a lower carbon footprint by reducing the reliance on large, centralized data centers, which are significant energy consumers. The localized processing of data means less energy is used to transmit data over long distances, and the distributed nature of the computation helps utilize renewable energy sources more effectively. This alignment with green computing principles ensures that AI advancements are sustainable and environmentally friendly.

The ability to process data in real-time at the edge is a significant advantage for applications that require immediate decision-making. For instance, in autonomous vehicles and industrial automation, edge computing ensures that critical decisions are made swiftly, enhancing operational efficiency and safety. The combination of FL and edge computing supports these real-time applications by enabling fast and efficient data processing close to the source.

1.5 NEURO-SYMBOLIC GREEN COMPUTING AND ITS INTEGRATION WITH UN SUSTAINABILITY GOALS

Integrating neuro-symbolic AI techniques with green computing principles aligns with the UN SDGs (Carlsen & Bruggemann, 2022), particularly those focused on climate action, affordable and clean energy, industry innovation, and sustainable cities.

1.5.1 SDG 7: Affordable and Clean Energy

Objective: To ensure access to affordable, reliable, sustainable, and modern energy for all.

Neuro-symbolic green computing enhances energy efficiency by optimizing the computational processes involved in AI, contributing significantly to SDG 7. This goal focuses on increasing the global share of renewable energy, improving energy efficiency, and ensuring universal access to modern energy services.

Neuro-symbolic green computing leverages the strengths of both neural networks and symbolic AI to optimize computational tasks. Traditional AI models, particularly deep learning networks, require substantial energy during training and inference. By integrating symbolic reasoning, which is less computationally intensive, these hybrid systems achieve similar or superior performance with reduced energy consumption. NVIDIA's H100 Tensor Core GPUs are specifically designed to accelerate AI workloads efficiently. These GPUs can reduce energy consumption by up to 4× while lowering system costs by 3×. This optimization supports the goal of increasing the share of renewable energy in the global energy mix by making AI operations more energy efficient and reducing their reliance on fossil fuels.

FL and edge computing further contribute to energy efficiency by reducing the need for data transfer to centralized servers. In FL, model training occurs locally on edge devices, and only model updates are shared, reducing the energy and bandwidth required for data transmission. Edge computing processes data locally, reducing latency and the energy required for data transfer. This distributed approach ensures efficient use of energy, supporting the increased use of renewable sources. In a smart grid scenario, edge devices equipped with FL capabilities can optimize energy distribution and usage. For instance, a network of solar panels and wind turbines can use edge computing to analyze energy production in real time, adjusting the energy distribution to where it is needed most. This system not only enhances energy efficiency but also supports the integration of renewable energy sources into the grid.

AI-driven energy management systems can predict energy supply from renewable sources like solar and wind and dynamically adjust data center operations. During peak renewable energy generation periods, data centers can increase processing activities while scaling down during periods of low generation. This dynamic adjustment helps maintain a balance between energy supply and demand, ensuring efficient use of available renewable energy. Google's data centers use AI to manage cooling systems, significantly reducing energy consumption. By leveraging AI for predictive maintenance and dynamic energy management, these data centers optimize their operations to utilize renewable energy efficiently, contributing to SDG 7 by reducing their carbon footprint and operational costs.

The development and deployment of energy-efficient hardware, such as GPUs, TPUs, and specialized AI accelerators, are crucial for neuro-symbolic green computing. These technologies are designed to maximize computational performance while minimizing energy consumption, ensuring that AI systems can operate efficiently even as the complexity and scale of tasks increase. IBM's Digital AI Cores integrate computation and memory, overcoming traditional bottlenecks and significantly improving energy efficiency. These accelerators are particularly effective for edge computing applications, where energy efficiency and real-time processing are critical.

Enhanced energy efficiency in AI operations directly reduces the carbon footprint. By lowering energy consumption, neuro-symbolic green computing reduces greenhouse gas emissions, aligning with global sustainability goals. The integration of renewable energy sources into AI infrastructure further amplifies these environmental benefits, making AI systems more sustainable and less reliant on fossil fuels. Amazon Web Services (AWS) has committed to powering its global infrastructure with 100% renewable energy by 2025. By leveraging energy-efficient AI technologies, AWS data centers can optimize their energy use, reduce operational costs, and significantly cut their carbon emissions (Ma, 2023).

1.5.2 SDG 9: Industry, Innovation, and Infrastructure

Objective: To build resilient infrastructure, promote inclusive and sustainable industrialization, and foster innovation.

Neuro-symbolic green computing aligns with SDG 9 by driving sustainable industrial innovation, enhancing infrastructure resilience, and fostering technological advancements. By optimizing energy efficiency and leveraging advanced AI technologies, this approach contributes to economic development while minimizing environmental impact.

Neuro-symbolic green computing enhances the resilience of infrastructure by integrating AI-driven predictive maintenance and optimization strategies. These systems can analyze large datasets from sensors embedded in infrastructure, predicting failures before they occur and optimizing maintenance schedules. This not only prolongs the lifespan of infrastructure but also reduces downtime and repair costs. Smart grids utilize neuro-symbolic AI to manage energy distribution efficiently. By analyzing real-time data from various sources, these systems can predict energy demand and adjust supply accordingly, minimizing energy wastage and improving grid reliability. This ensures a stable and resilient energy infrastructure that supports economic development and human well-being.

Neuro-symbolic green computing supports sustainable industrialization by optimizing manufacturing processes and enhancing resource efficiency. AI systems can monitor and control industrial operations in real time, reducing waste and improving productivity. By integrating symbolic reasoning, these systems provide interpretable insights that help industries make informed decisions about sustainability practices. In manufacturing, AI-driven predictive maintenance systems can monitor equipment performance and predict potential failures, allowing for timely interventions that prevent costly downtimes and reduce resource wastage. Companies like Siemens are leveraging AI to optimize their production lines, resulting in significant energy savings and improved operational efficiency.

The integration of advanced AI technologies with green computing principles fosters innovation across various sectors. Neuro-symbolic AI enhances the capabilities of traditional AI systems by providing more accurate and interpretable results, driving innovation in fields such as healthcare, transportation, and environmental management. In healthcare, neuro-symbolic AI systems can analyze complex medical data to provide precise diagnostics and personalized treatment plans. These systems leverage both the pattern recognition capabilities of neural networks and the logical reasoning of symbolic AI to deliver insights that are both accurate and understandable, facilitating better patient outcomes and advancing medical research.

By optimizing energy use and integrating renewable energy sources, neuro-symbolic green computing significantly reduces the environmental impact of industrial activities. AI-driven energy management systems can predict renewable energy availability and adjust industrial operations to maximize the use of clean energy, thereby reducing greenhouse gas emissions. Google's data centers use AI to optimize their cooling systems, significantly reducing energy consumption. By leveraging renewable energy sources and advanced AI technologies, these data centers operate more efficiently and with a lower carbon footprint, contributing to global climate action efforts.

1.5.3 SDG 11: Sustainable Cities and Communities

Objective: To make cities and human settlements inclusive, safe, resilient, and sustainable.

Neuro-symbolic green computing contributes significantly to achieving SDG 11 by leveraging advanced AI technologies to enhance urban resilience, optimize resource management, and foster sustainable urban development. This integration aligns with the goals of SDG 11, which focuses on improving urban planning, providing access to essential services, reducing environmental impact, and promoting sustainable transportation.

Neuro-symbolic green computing enhances urban resilience through predictive maintenance and optimization strategies powered by AI. These systems can analyze large datasets from sensors embedded in urban infrastructure, predicting failures before they occur and optimizing maintenance schedules. This proactive approach reduces downtime, prevents costly repairs, and extends the lifespan of critical infrastructure. In flood-prone areas, neuro-symbolic AI can predict flooding events by analyzing weather data and sensor inputs from rivers and drainage systems. This predictive capability allows cities to take preemptive actions, such as activating flood defenses and evacuating at-risk populations, thereby minimizing the impact of natural disasters.

Neuro-symbolic AI plays a crucial role in optimizing the management of urban resources, including energy, water, and waste. By integrating IoT and AI technologies, cities can monitor and control resource usage in real time, ensuring efficient distribution and reducing waste. In smart cities, AI-driven energy management systems can optimize the use of renewable energy sources by predicting energy supply from solar and wind power and adjusting consumption patterns accordingly. This not only improves energy efficiency but also supports the integration of renewable energy into the urban grid, contributing to reduced carbon emissions.

Sustainable urban mobility is a key component of SDG 11, and neuro-symbolic AI contributes by enhancing public transportation systems and promoting eco-friendly transportation options. AI can optimize traffic flow, reduce congestion, and encourage the use of public transport, cycling, and walking. Cities like Barcelona and Amsterdam have implemented AI-based traffic management systems that analyze real-time traffic data to optimize signal timings and reduce congestion. These systems also promote the use of public transport and cycling by providing real-time updates on transport schedules and bike-sharing availability, thereby reducing the reliance on private cars and lowering urban emissions.

Neuro-symbolic AI enhances the quality of life in urban areas by supporting the development of smart urban services. These services include smart lighting, waste management, and water distribution systems that adapt to real-time demands and optimize resource use. In cities like Singapore, smart lighting systems use AI to adjust street lighting based on pedestrian and vehicle activity, reducing energy consumption while ensuring safety. Similarly, AI-powered waste management systems optimize collection routes and schedules, reducing operational costs and environmental impact. Neuro-symbolic AI can also support urban inclusivity and safety by analyzing social data to identify areas needing improvement and by enabling more equitable access to city services. AI can help design and implement policies that address urban poverty and inequality, ensuring that all residents benefit from sustainable urban development. In New York City, AI is used to analyze demographic and social data to identify underserved communities and allocate resources more effectively. This ensures that urban development projects are inclusive and benefit all residents, particularly those in vulnerable situations.

1.5.4 SDG 12: Responsible Consumption and Production

Objective: To ensure sustainable consumption and production patterns.

Neuro-symbolic green computing plays a crucial role in advancing SDG 12 by optimizing resource use, reducing waste, and promoting sustainable production and consumption practices. This approach leverages the strengths of both neural networks and symbolic AI to enhance efficiency and sustainability across various industries.

Neuro-symbolic AI systems can significantly optimize the use of resources in production processes. By integrating AI-driven insights, industries can monitor and control resource consumption in real time, ensuring efficient use of materials and energy. These systems can identify inefficiencies and suggest improvements, leading to more sustainable production practices. In the manufacturing sector, AI can monitor equipment performance and predict maintenance needs, reducing downtime and resource wastage. Companies like Siemens have implemented AI solutions to optimize production lines, resulting in substantial energy savings and reduced material waste. This aligns with SDG 12's goal of achieving sustainable management and efficient use of natural resources.

Neuro-symbolic green computing also contributes to waste reduction through advanced waste management systems. AI can optimize the collection, sorting, and recycling processes, ensuring that materials are reused and recycled efficiently. This approach supports the circular economy model, where resources are continuously cycled back into the production process, minimizing waste generation. In waste management, AI systems can optimize the routing of collection trucks and improve the sorting of recyclables. For instance, smart waste bins equipped with sensors can notify collection services when they are full, optimizing collection routes and reducing fuel consumption. This leads to more efficient waste management practices and supports the goal of reducing global waste.

AI-driven systems can also encourage sustainable consumption by providing consumers with detailed information about the environmental impact of their purchases. By integrating AI with consumer applications, individuals can make informed decisions that favor sustainable products and services. Retail platforms can use AI to analyze and label products based on their environmental footprint, helping consumers choose eco-friendly options. Companies like Amazon have introduced features that highlight sustainable products, promoting responsible consumption patterns among their customers.

Industries can leverage neuro-symbolic AI to integrate sustainability into their operations. By adopting AI-driven sustainability reporting and compliance systems, companies can track their environmental impact and ensure adherence to regulatory standards. This transparency encourages businesses to adopt greener practices and reduce their ecological footprint. The automotive industry is increasingly adopting AI to optimize the production of electric vehicles (EVs) and manage the lifecycle of batteries. AI systems can track the environmental impact of EV production and suggest improvements, such as sourcing materials from sustainable suppliers or optimizing the recycling process for used batteries.

Neuro-symbolic green computing supports the transition from a linear to a circular economy by optimizing resource flows and ensuring materials are reused effectively. AI can help design products that are easier to recycle, extend the lifecycle of products through predictive maintenance, and manage end-of-life disposal sustainably. In the fashion industry, AI can optimize the design and production of garments to minimize waste and enhance recyclability. By analyzing material properties and manufacturing processes, AI can suggest designs that use fewer resources and are easier to recycle at the end of their lifecycle, supporting sustainable fashion practices.

1.5.5 SDG 13: Climate Action

Objective: To take urgent action to combat climate change and its impacts.

Neuro-symbolic green computing significantly contributes to SDG 13 by optimizing energy use, enhancing predictive capabilities, and supporting the integration of renewable energy sources. This approach leverages advanced AI technologies to mitigate climate change, improve resilience to climate-related hazards, and reduce greenhouse gas emissions.

Neuro-symbolic AI systems enhance energy efficiency by optimizing computational processes. These systems combine the data processing capabilities of neural networks with the logical reasoning strengths of symbolic AI, resulting in reduced energy consumption during AI model training and inference phases. This efficiency is crucial for lowering the carbon footprint of AI operations and aligns with climate action goals.

Neuro-symbolic AI enhances predictive capabilities, which are essential for climate change mitigation and adaptation. These systems can analyze large datasets from various sources, providing accurate predictions and early warnings for climate-related hazards such as floods, storms, and heat waves. This capability supports better planning and response strategies, reducing the impact of natural disasters.

The integration of renewable energy sources into AI infrastructure is crucial for sustainable climate action. Neuro-symbolic AI can optimize the use of renewable energy by predicting supply from sources like solar and wind and dynamically adjusting energy consumption patterns. This ensures efficient utilization of clean energy, reducing reliance on fossil fuels.

By improving energy efficiency and supporting the use of renewable energy, neuro-symbolic green computing directly contributes to reducing the carbon footprint of AI operations. Lower energy consumption translates to fewer greenhouse gas emissions, aligning with the goals of the Paris Agreement and SDG 13.2 (Dzebo, Iacobuţă, & Beaussart, 2023), which calls for integrating climate change measures into national policies and strategies.

1.6 FUTURE OF NEURO-SYMBOLIC GREEN COMPUTING

Neuro-symbolic green computing is set to play a transformative role in the future of AI, merging the robust learning capabilities of neural networks with the logical reasoning strengths of symbolic AI. This hybrid approach not only enhances the performance and interpretability of AI systems but also aligns with sustainability goals, making AI technologies more environmentally friendly. Here are some key directions and advancements expected in the future of neuro-symbolic green computing:

1. *Enhanced integration of AI and renewable energy*: Future developments in neuro-symbolic AI are likely to see deeper integration with renewable energy sources. AI systems will increasingly optimize their operations based on the availability of renewable energy, ensuring that they consume power most efficiently when it is derived from clean sources like solar and wind. This will involve advanced predictive models that can forecast energy supply fluctuations and adjust AI workloads accordingly to maximize the use of renewable energy.
2. *Advanced hardware and accelerators*: The development of specialized AI accelerators that are energy-efficient will continue to be a focus. These accelerators, such as GPUs and TPUs specifically designed for AI tasks, will become more prevalent, reducing the energy footprint of AI computations. Innovations in this area will include hardware that integrates more closely with neuro-symbolic AI frameworks, enabling even greater efficiencies by minimizing data movement and optimizing computational workflows.
3. *Scalable and resilient AI systems*: Neuro-symbolic AI systems will be designed to scale efficiently across various domains, from small edge devices to large data centers. This scalability will be coupled with enhanced resilience, ensuring that AI systems can maintain high performance and reliability even under varying environmental conditions and energy availability. Techniques like FL will be crucial, allowing AI models to be trained across distributed networks without the need for centralized data collection, thereby reducing energy consumption and enhancing data privacy.
4. *Real-time environmental monitoring and management*: Future neuro-symbolic AI systems will play a critical role in environmental monitoring and management. These systems will be capable of real-time data analysis and decision-making, providing insights into environmental changes and enabling timely responses to natural disasters and climate-related events. By integrating vast amounts of data from various sensors and sources, neuro-symbolic AI can offer accurate predictions and actionable intelligence for climate action initiatives.

5. *AI-driven policy and decision support*: Neuro-symbolic AI will also help policymakers and businesses make informed decisions that align with sustainability goals. These AI systems will provide transparent, interpretable insights into the potential impacts of different policies and actions, helping to ensure that decisions are both effective and environmentally responsible. By simulating various scenarios, neuro-symbolic AI can help identify the most sustainable paths forward.
6. *Continuous learning and adaptation*: Future neuro-symbolic AI systems will feature continuous learning capabilities, allowing them to adapt to new data and changing conditions dynamically. This adaptability will be crucial for maintaining efficiency and effectiveness in the face of evolving environmental challenges and energy landscapes. Such systems will be able to update their models and strategies in real time, ensuring optimal performance and sustainability at all times.

1.7 CONCLUSION

In conclusion, neuro-symbolic green computing merges the advanced learning capabilities of neural networks with the logical reasoning of symbolic AI within a framework of sustainable computing practices. This approach addresses the increasing demand for powerful AI systems while minimizing environmental impact. By optimizing energy efficiency and integrating renewable energy sources, neuro-symbolic green computing significantly reduces the carbon footprint of AI operations. It also enhances resource efficiency, supports sustainable industrial practices, and promotes resilient infrastructure and urban systems, aligning with key UN SDGs. The future of this interdisciplinary field promises advancements in scalable AI systems, real-time environmental monitoring, AI-driven policy support, and continuous learning, ensuring AI technologies contribute positively to global sustainability efforts.

ACKNOWLEDGMENT

This work is supported by the "ADI 2022" project funded by IDEX Paris-Saclay, ANR-11-IDEX-0003-02.

REFERENCES

Abadi, M., & Plotkin, G. D. (2019). A simple differentiable programming language. *Proceedings of the ACM on Programming Languages*, *4* (POPL), 1–28.

Badreddine, S., Garcez, A. d., Serafini, L., & Spranger, M. (2022). Logic tensor networks. *Artificial Intelligence*, *303*, 103649.

Bhuyan, B. P., Ramdane-Cherif, A., Tomar, R., & Singh, T. (2024). Neuro-symbolic artificial intelligence: A survey. *Neural Computing and Applications*, *36* (21), 12809–12844.

Bhuyan, B. P., Tomar, R., & Fore, V. (2023). Knowledge representation to expound deep learning black box. In *Future connected technologies* (pp. 113–128). CRC Press.

Carlsen, L., & Bruggemann, R. (2022). The 17 united nations' sustainable development goals: A status by 2020. *International Journal of Sustainable Development & World Ecology*, *29* (3), 219–229.

Choquette, J. (2022). NVIDIA hopper GPU: Scaling performance. In *2022 IEEE hot chips 34 symposium (HCS)* (pp. 1–46).

Chou, D. C., Chen, H.-G., & Lin, B. (2023). Green it and corporate social responsibility for sustainability. *Journal of Computer Information Systems, 63* (2), 322–333.

Cingillioglu, N., & Russo, A. (2021). pix2rule: End-to-end neuro-symbolic rule learning. *arXiv preprint arXiv:2106.07487.*

Dzebo, A., Iacobuţă, G. I., & Beaussart, R. (2023). *Paris agreement and the sustainable development goals: Evolving connections.* JSTOR.

Garcez, A., & Lamb, L. C. (2023). Neurosymbolic AI: The 3rd wave. *Artificial Intelligence Review, 56* (11), 12387–12406.

Gershon, T., Seelam, S., Belgodere, B., Bonilla, M., Hoang, L., & Barnett, D., … others (2024). The infrastructure powering IBM's gen AI model development. *arXiv preprint arXiv:2407.05467.*

Gou, J., Yu, B., Maybank, S. J., & Tao, D. (2021). Knowledge distillation: A survey. *International Journal of Computer Vision, 129* (6), 1789–1819.

Hersche, M., Zeqiri, M., Benini, L., Sebastian, A., & Rahimi, A. (2023). A neuro-vector-symbolic architecture for solving raven's progressive matrices. *Nature Machine Intelligence, 5* (4), 363–375.

Jozefowicz, R., Vinyals, O., Schuster, M., Shazeer, N., & Wu, Y. (2016). Exploring the limits of language modeling. *arXiv preprint arXiv:1602.02410.*

Karunaratne, G. (2023). *In-memory vector symbolic architectures* (Unpublished doctoral dissertation). ETH Zurich.

Li, J., Li, D., Savarese, S., & Hoi, S. (2023). Blip-2: Bootstrapping language-image pre-training with frozen image encoders and large language models. In *International conference on machine learning* (pp. 19730–19742).

Li, J., Li, D., Xiong, C., & Hoi, S. (2022). Blip: Bootstrapping language-image pre-training for unified vision-language understanding and generation. In *International conference on machine learning* (pp. 12888–12900).

Li, L., Fan, Y., Tse, M., & Lin, K.-Y. (2020). A review of applications in federated learning. *Computers & Industrial Engineering, 149*, 106854.

Li, Z., Guo, C., Feng, Z., Hwang, J.-N., & Du, Z. (2023). Integrating language guidance into image-text matching for correcting false negatives. *IEEE Transactions on Multimedia, 26*, 103–116.

Liao, H.-J., Liu, J.-G., Wang, L., & Xiang, T. (2019). Differentiable programming tensor networks. *Physical Review X, 9* (3), 031041.

Liu, Z., Wang, Y., Vaidya, S., Ruehle, F., Halverson, J., Soljačić, M., …, & Tegmark, M. (2024). KAN: Kolmogorov-Arnold networks. *arXiv preprint arXiv:2404.19756.*

Ma, N. (2023). AWS solutions for new energy wind solar farm management. In *Third EAGE digitalization conference and exhibition* (Vol. 2023, pp. 1–5).

Saha, B. (2014). Green computing. *International Journal of Computer Trends and Technology (IJCTT), 14* (2), 46–50.

Song, S., Wan, J., Yang, Z., Tang, J., Cheng, W., Bai, X., & Yao, C. (2022). Vision-language pre-training for boosting scene text detectors. In *Proceedings of the IEEE/CVF conference on computer vision and pattern recognition* (pp. 15681–15691).

Tian, Y., Luan, T. H., & Zheng, X. (2023). An empirical study on model pruning and quantization. In *International conference on broadband communications, networks and systems* (pp. 111–125).

Tu, J., Yeoh, G. H., Liu, C., & Tao, Y. (2023). *Computational fluid dynamics: A practical approach.* Elsevier.

Uddin, M., & Rahman, A. A. (2012). Energy efficiency and low carbon enabler green it framework for data centers considering green metrics. *Renewable and Sustainable Energy Reviews, 16* (6), 4078–4094.

Wang, M., & Deng, J. (2020). Learning to prove theorems by learning to generate theorems. *Advances in Neural Information Processing Systems*, *33*, 18146–18157.

Wu, X., Li, Y.-L., Sun, J., & Lu, C. (2024). Symbol-LLM: Leverage language models for symbolic system in visual human activity reasoning. *Advances in Neural Information Processing Systems*, *36*.

Yang, X., Wang, Z., Hu, X. S., Kim, C. H., Yu, S., Pajic, M., & Li, H. H. (2023). Neurosymbolic computing: Advancements and challenges in hardware-software co-design. *IEEE Transactions on Circuits and Systems II: Express Briefs*, *71* (3), 1683–1689.

Yu, W., Liang, J., Ji, L., Li, L., Fang, Y., Xiao, N., & Duan, N. (2021). Hybrid reasoning network for video-based commonsense captioning. In *Proceedings of the 29th ACM international conference on multimedia* (pp. 5213–5221).

2 Software Approach for Green Computing

Daniel Dauda Wisdom, Kingsley T. Igulu, Ugwunna Charles Okechukwu, Isaac Oniovosah Ayetuoma, Omilodi Babatola Moses, and Eti Friday Irikefe

2.1 INTRODUCTION

Green computing, known as green information technology (IT), is the strategic, designing, manufacturing, as well as disposing of computing devices, systems, and software in an ecologically accountable manner. Green computing involves a holistic method of minimizing the ecological impact of IT such that energy efficiency and resource utilization are reduced [1].

In the emerging digital era, the propagation of IT infrastructure, data centers, as well as electronic devices has increased energy consumption and carbon emissions of IT devices. Based on key estimates, the IT division accounts for a considerable number of global electricity energy consumption, causing greenhouse gas (GHG) emissions as well as ecological environmental ruin. Green computing raises an important concern with an imperative strategy to mitigate the ecological impact of IT operations, fostering meaningful development with sustainable Green IT in the digital era [2].

The advantages of green computing are that green IT has the possible ability to solve the (ecological) environmental concerns same time improve the economic and social benefits of green IT. By through approving sustainable practices throughout the IT lifecycle, establishments can minimize energy consumption, similarly reducing electronic waste, while lowering their carbon footprint. Additionally, green computing initiatives could result in efficiency by enhancing energy efficiency, resource optimization, and lifecycle management of IT devices [3].

In green computing, software method occupies a central position with an important approach for achieving environmental sustainability. Distinct from hardware approaches that focus primarily on energy consumption at the hardware level, the software method influences state-of-the-art algorithms, design principles, and advanced methodologies to reduce energy usage and make the most of resource efficiency in software applications [3]. Figure 2.1 depicts green computing.

The software method for green computing includes improving software design, development, deployment, as well as maintenance practices to reduce energy consumption and environmental impact. This involves writing energy-efficient code, designing energy-aware architectures, and implementing dynamic resource management techniques while embracing environmental software development strategies [4]. Thus, establishments can produce software methods that not only meet

DOI: 10.1201/9781003471356-2

FIGURE 2.1 Green computing.

functional requirements but also obey the environmental best practices. Whether via the use of well-organized algorithms, the adoption of virtualization skills, or the implementation of energy-aware programming methods, the software method empowers developers and IT professionals to make meaningful contributions toward ecological development [4].

2.1.1 Chapter Organization

The rest of the chapter is organized as follows: Section 2.2 discusses the related literature while Section 2.3 talks about embracing sustainability. Optimizing code efficiency for energy conservation is the topic of Section 2.4 while various energy-aware design principles have been elucidated in Section 2.5 of the chapter. A framework for software approach for green computing is presented in Section 2.6 and the chapter concludes with Section 2.7.

2.2 RELATED LITERATURE

A study on the overview of green computing presented in [1] focuses on the field's present trends, obstacles, and potential paths forward to investigate recent developments and determine the difficulties encountered in the field of green computing. To address advances and trends in green computing in the future, based on observations and previously published research, the study provides a descriptive review or overview of the subject. The study sheds light on the situation of green computing today, the difficulties encountered, and possible advancements in the future. Comprehensive data analysis or empirical research findings, particular case studies or instances that highlight the tendencies and difficulties, have been mentioned.

To achieve environmental sustainability, a thorough examination of the literature on green computing solutions in data centers has been proposed in [3], with a focus on resource management, energy usage, and storage systems. Understanding the main obstacles and new developments in data center green computing will help to advance this field's practical applications and future study. Examining the body of research on green computing solutions in data centers, the methodology entails completing a study of the literature. It probably entails analyzing and synthesizing pertinent research, and figuring out recurring themes, with important conclusions. The study highlights how sophisticated algorithms and techniques are required to manage virtual machine (VM) layouts, optimize network topologies, and distribute resources dynamically.

A study examining the trade-off between environmental sustainability and software quality criteria has been published in [4], with a special focus on making software greener. The goals were to examine the trade-offs associated with producing greener software, investigate database software's energy consumption, and comprehend how software quality criteria relate to environmental sustainability. The methodology combined empirical and case study methodologies with quantitative research methods. This required using various software frameworks in controlled experiments and empirical assessments. Initial findings showed considerable potential for energy savings in database software. To guarantee precision and dependability in measurement and conclusion, the study additionally concentrated on the validity of the research design and experimentation. Building a dynamic goal model to support sustainability needs is part of the next effort.

To overcome the dearth of creative methodologies and teaching materials in computer science education, the study [5] promotes the incorporation of green software principles. In light of the quick improvements in technology, it highlights the advantages of including green software themes for the environment, society, and students. The significance of teaching students how to use green software, the identification of pedagogical difficulties, the provision of solutions, and the promotion of curriculum integration are among the main goals. Methodologically, surveys of academics and teachers were carried out, and the results showed that there are few resources and courses available for teaching green software in higher education. Current approaches to pedagogical problems are examined, with an emphasis on software developers' deficiency in methods, expertise, and resources for creating ecologically friendly software. The study highlights the necessity for researchers and industry to work together.

The study paper [6] focuses on green computing and new difficulties in the IT business. The author suggests taking a closer look at green computing techniques and their increasing significance. The goal of the paper is to increase public knowledge of green computing initiatives and the difficulties in implementing them. The methodology consists of a survey of the body of literature along with a quick analysis of the problems and conditions of green computing practices today. Green computing is a more general term with an emphasis on methods and techniques. Nevertheless, the report does not present novel research findings or a thorough review of certain green computing techniques. The research study emphasizes how important it is to conduct more green computing research, especially in academic settings. They stress the significance of looking into efficient and effective ways to handle e-waste.

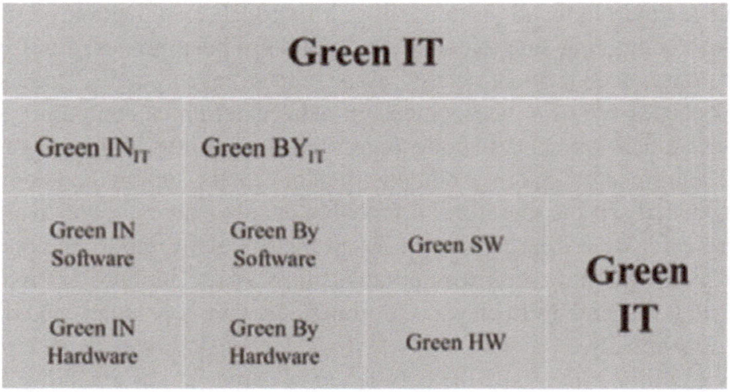

FIGURE 2.2 Green in software by hardware and IT.

To achieve large energy savings, the authors in [7] proposed replacing traditional desktop computers with laptops in workplace situations. Comparing desktop and laptop energy consumption for common workloads is one of the research study's goals. It examines how much less energy is used by thin clients and software-based power management systems in comparison to laptops. It also examines the viability and implications of a laptop-based business while considering variables other than energy usage (cost, user requirements). The research methodology employed in the study gathered power usage information for up to 15 months from more than 100 computers (laptops and desktops) and compared the energy consumption trends of desktops and laptops by data analysis and evaluated current thin client options by calculating their power consumption. The findings demonstrated that laptops used a lot less energy than desktop computers.

Green cloud broker as reported in [8] is a system that distributes cloud resources according to cost, environment, and energy efficiency. Figure 2.2 depicts green in software by hardware and IT.

The research study aims to create a cloud resource allocation system that takes the environment's impact and cost into account and cuts down on cloud data centers' energy utilization and GHG emissions. It attempts to make the choice of cloud service provider for users automatic, based on green metrics. It developed a mechanism using functions to allocate resources considering user preferences for both cost and green composite metrics.

2.3 EMBRACING SUSTAINABILITY

Computing is currently the change in paradigm toward sustainability. Green computing is a requirement among various other initiatives to reduce carbon emissions and ecological footprints. Green computing, however, mainly aims beyond mere operation efficiency through technological advances toward environment protection. Among all these strategies, benefits in all computing contexts to enable potential improvements in energy efficiency and resource optimization, with minimal environmental impact, point to the software approach as one of the most promising [9].

This is much more subtle compared to the hardware-oriented solutions that mostly bring solutions to the rise in energy consumption and electronic waste overflow. It translates to subsumption into new algorithms, streamlining code structures, and the adoption of principles of sustainable design. This approach is key in terms of balancing computational needs with environmental sustainability through efficient resource allocation, intelligent management of workloads, and adoption of energy-efficient programming methodologies. Cloud computing also places another layer on these efforts by allowing dynamic scaling and resource pooling to maximize energy efficiency and reduce idle capacity [7].

2.4 OPTIMIZING CODE EFFICIENCY FOR ENERGY CONSERVATION

In the approach of green computing through software, two of the basic strategies are code efficiency and optimization, not just to save energy but also to reduce environmental impact. This section emphasizes the techniques intended to develop energy-efficient code and deliberates on the ways it can help in reducing energy consumption within software applications [8].

2.4.1 Reducing Unwanted Computations

The most efficient way of enhancing code efficiency is to reduce unwanted superfluous calculations.

This involves identifying and removing repetitive operations, loops, or calculations that do not add value to the functionality required of the software. With attention to detail in code reviews and performance profiling, developers can spot places in programs where efficiency can be improved to refactor code into more effective execution paths [8]. Other mechanisms useful for avoiding unnecessary computation include memorization, caching, and lazy evaluation. Memorization basically consists of caching the results of expensive function calls and, when the same inputs are seen again, avoiding the precomputation, to recover and return the precomputed result. Similarly, caching often-accessed data or intermediate results can speed up succeeding computation, and, in the end, save energy by keeping CPU usage and memory access to a minimum. Besides, optimization of algorithms for time complexity can save lots of energy by reducing computational resources used in running code. It can be done by selecting algorithms with lower time complexities and avoiding the selection of inefficient data structures/algorithms that consume lots of resources. Hence, this allows developers to achieve high enhancement in code efficiency and saving energy [8].

2.4.2 Impact of Efficient Coding Practices on Energy Consumption

Efficient coding practices in most areas of software applications help to reduce energy consumption. Considering the execution of a code, this would lower power usage with less CPU cycle, memory access, and disk-operation requirements; hence, it would lower operational costs for computing infrastructure, which is a direct result of energy-efficient algorithms and optimizations.

Also, energy-efficient code leverages the performance and responsiveness of software applications. Improvement in user experience and productivity by curtailing processing overhead and latency leads to the satisfaction of conserving energy through optimum code.

Therefore, in highly distributed computing environments or cloud-based systems, energy-efficient code might realize huge energy savings. Thus, by lessening the computational load to servers and data centers, and energy-efficient software applications mean minimal overall power consumption and carbon emissions—adding up to positive sustainability goals in organizations and for the environment.

Optimizing the code efficiency to conserve power is one of the pivotal approaches in green computing techniques that not only reduce power consumption but also minimize the environmental impact. A developer can then move a step ahead in achieving energy conservation with higher efficiency and sustainability by incorporating various mechanisms that reduce extra or useless computations, optimize algorithms, and enhance the performance of the code [10, 11].

2.5 ENERGY-AWARE DESIGN PRINCIPLES

Designing software architectures in an energy-aware manner is one of the prime evaluations for ensuring minimum energy consumption and increasing sustainability. In this regard, the current section deals with the way in which the design patterns are contributing to the enhancement of efficiency in software development.

2.5.1 Modularization and Component Reuse

Modularization is a software design strategy that involves dividing software systems into smaller components, with every component handling specific functionalities or tasks. The approach enhances flexibility, maintainability, scalability, and energy efficiency, through isolating functionality within modular units, developers can optimize the efficiency of power usage by activating only necessary components where necessary [12, 13].

2.5.2 Role of Design Patterns in Energy-Efficient Software Development

Design patterns are very important in software development as they represent a reusable solution for common design problems. These patterns are traditionally concentrated on enhancing the quality, maintainability, and scalability of the software, and their use in energy-efficient practices of the software.

For example, the Observer pattern and the State pattern enable event-driven architectures. These types of architectures allow a device to optimally respond to a change in system state or the occurrence of an outside event without using power when these are queried in a continuous manner. It saves power by not wasting nonessential computational costs.

Furthermore, the Singleton and Flyweight patterns allow the optimization of resources by only creating one instance of the specified objects or resources and reusing them as and when required. This approach is useful for minimizing the memory used and the overhead on the CPU, resulting in better power savings with good performance.

2.5.3 Dynamic Resource Management and Virtualization

Dynamic resource management and virtualization are critical aspects of a green computing strategy that might be taken within a cloud. Dynamic resource allocation allows facilities for the reallocation of resources at run time for scheduling CPU, memory, and storage resources based on best-fit policies in view of the variability in workload. Virtualization is technology-agnostic and makes use of two main entities: hypervisors and containers, to achieve hardware abstraction or isolation and create multiple virtual instances that subdivide the main infrastructure.

Dynamic resource management and virtualization technologies in the setting of cloud computing act as a key factor in optimizing energy efficiency, providing only the needed resources for the specific instance according to workload needs.

Different scaling of computational resources, which occurs dynamically in response to demand, can provide the efficient use of computational resources by cloud providers; thereby, it reduces the extra loss of energy due to unwanted idle capacity or overprovisioning [14].

Developments in Human Society Advertisement Feature Degree of Pooling and Aggregation Obtaining the network capacity necessary to run the high-volume workloads generated by end-users depends on the ability to allocate critical resources. The hypervisor and managers of public cloud vendor servers pool VMs, all of which regardless run as seen by the end needs. Close to bounded good virtualization, this provides source aggregation through the transformation of corporal hardware into virtual occurrences or VM managers even out the workloads.

2.5.4 Benefits of Resource Pooling and Workload Balancing in Reducing Energy Waste

The pooling of resources can be defined as aggregate computing resources from various physical servers into a joint pool that is available to be allocated dynamically to virtual instances when and where needed. By means of resource pooling, providers of cloud services can be facilitated to improve the utilization of resources and keep them efficient, which are essential for not wasting energy unnecessarily, related to unused or idle capacity.

Workload consolidation is the act of combining several workloads into the smallest number of physical servers or computing nodes possible. This not only optimizes resources but also wipes out redundancy and underutilization, thus imbuing much more efficiency with little operational cost.

It has many advantages in resource pooling and workload consolidation in meeting the objective of minimizing energy waste within cloud computing setups. The first of these approaches enables cloud providers to achieve economies of scale, as they use minimal resources across many tenants or numerous applications—therefore, less final amount of energy consumption per workload.

On the other hand, it reduces the general data center energy efficiency by the number of physical servers that have been disposed of in running some workload. This eventually lessens the sum of physical servers that are kept on needlessly, subsequently lowering the operational overhead and allowing vast sums of energy to be saved, eventually having a positive outcome in environmental conservation [15].

2.5.5 Green Software Development Methodologies

Green software development methodologies mark a shift toward sustainable practices within the software development lifecycle. The Agile approach stresses iterative development, collaboration, and adaptability in response to change, breaking down software development into units, with an incremental iteration. Moreover, Agile enables teams to deliver functional software more frequently and adjust to evolving requirements. The iterative aspect promotes sustainability allowing teams to focus on features that provide the most value while reducing waste as well as unnecessary development efforts [16].

DevOps focuses mainly on improving collaboration and integration between development and operations teams to automate processes, streamline workflows, and expedite software delivery. Via breaking down barriers and encouraging cross-functional teamwork, DevOps shortens cycle times, enhances efficiency, and elevates the quality of software deployments. This approach of continuous integration and delivery (CI/CD) approach minimizes environmental impact just in time [16].

Lean principles advocate for improving value with minimal waste via the software development lifecycle. Through the elimination of non-value-added activities, minimum batch sizes, and optimized workflows, Lean software development weakens lead times and enhances efficiency, maximizing the quality of software products.

Sustainable software development framework (SSDF) integrates sustainability principles into the software development process, highlighting the consideration of environmental, social, and economic factors across software product lifecycles. SSDF incorporates sustainability metrics, guidelines, and best practices to empower developers to make informed decisions that mitigate environmental impact with optimized development [17].

2.5.6 How These Methodologies Promote Sustainability

Agile methodologies support iterative development cycles, allowing teams to deliver incremental improvements and promptly respond to feedback. Via concentrating on delivering value through small, iterative increments, Agile mitigates the risk of over-engineering and diminishes the environmental impact of software development by swiftly dodging unnecessary features and functionalities.

Agile and DevOps emphasize very effective feedback loops, through which teams may retrieve not only stakeholder and user feedback but also outputs from automated testing. Such a feedback-driven approach helps a team to identify and fix problems at the earliest possible opportunity, rework is reduced, and overall quality is enhanced for software products. By putting in place such feedback loops, development can reduce waste and maximize the efficiency of resources, besides reducing the ecological footprint that software development causes.

Agile, DevOps, and Lean foster a culture of incremental improvement by having teams reflect on their processes to identify areas that could benefit from incremental changes. In this way, the continuous improvement enabled by these practices allows teams to find and reduce inefficiencies, identify and trim down waste, and enhance the long-term sustainability of software development. As such, Agile, DevOps, and other Green Software Development practices emphasize sustainability involving iterative development, feedback loops, and continuous improvement.

2.5.7 Open-Source Initiatives and Collaborative Innovations

Open-source software acts like the fuel that allows collaborative innovations and thus sustainability in the high-tech industry by offering its services for free to one and all [18].

2.5.7.1 How Open-Source Software Enables Collaborative Innovation and Sustenance

Open-source software can be made accessible and transparent through free access of its source code to allow inspection, modification, or sharing for respective use. Avoiding this way could foster collaboration among developers, researchers, or organizations for collective innovation, development, or customization of software solutions for key needs and challenges [13].

Open-source initiatives rely on the community's engagement with people from all parts of the world, developers, and contributors who describe the problems, share experiences, and advance the technology. This fosters a culture of innovation, creativity, and inclusiveness whereby contributions from all types of expertise and collective resources can be called into play to address very complex problems, including those related to sustainability and environmental concerns.

Open-source software embraces this iterative development model for continuous improvement and innovation. Open-source projects develop through an iterative sequence of growth, feedback, and refinement that is very dynamic in nature. As a result, new features, improvements, and optimizations are developed quickly to address emerging needs and challenges. In an iterative way, it makes agile, adaptable, and resilient, thereby ensuring projects continue to be responsive to changing technological and environmental landscapes [19, 20].

Open-source initiatives facilitate extensive knowledge sharing and capacity building by providing platforms for learning, collaboration, and skill development. Through a transparent exchange of code, documentation, and best practices, open-source communities empower individuals and organizations to acquire new skills, deepen their understanding of technology, and contribute effectively to collaborative innovation efforts.

2.5.7.2 Case Studies of Successful Open-Source Projects Focused on Green Computing

1. ***Open energy dashboard (OED):*** OED is a collaboration-based, open-source, project-level monitoring and data analysis system for building and facility energy consumption. By providing means of aggregating and real-time displaying facility energy usage information, OED implements an energy problem solution approach aiming at resource harnessing and carbon emission reduction opportunities identification [21].
2. ***Open compute project (OCP):*** This is an open-source initiative targeted at the development of energy-efficient hardware solutions for data centers and cloud computing environments. Through collaboration on open hardware designs, specifications, and best practices, OCP enables organizations to reduce energy consumption, increase efficiency, and minimize the environmental impact of data center operations. This naturally creates a sense of openness in the project and stimulates innovation, competition, and knowledge exchange in a way that keeps energy efficiency and sustainability at the very cutting edge across the industry.
3. ***Open Green Web (OGW):*** The OGW is a repository of sustainable practices and tools to help when creating websites and applications. Offering resources, guidelines, and toolkits, this repository helps with energy-efficient development and supports developers in optimizing performance, resource usage, and carbon emission reduction. This project will foster collaboration, and sharing of knowledge, and further enable web developers, designers, and environmental advocates to contribute to making a greener and more sustainable environment for the web [22, 23].

2.5.8 Energy-Efficient Data Management and Processing

Effective management and processing of data are essential for improving efficiency and power consumption in computing environments. This section investigates strategies to optimize the storage, retrieval, and processing of data, aiming to minimize energy usage. Methods employed involve data compression, deduplication, and distributed computing, respectively [1, 9].

2.5.8.1 Exploring Strategies for Optimizing Data Management and Processing

Implementing data compression techniques minimizes the storage space required for data, thereby decreasing energy consumption associated with storage and transmission. Via compressing the data before storage or transfer, establishments can lessen dataset sizes, resulting in lower storage costs and reduced energy use. Common compression algorithms like ZIP, GZIP, and LZ4 effectively reduce file sizes while maintaining data integrity systematically [24].

Deduplication identifies and eliminates duplicate data copies within storage systems. This process decreases storage needs, lowers power consumption, and enhances storage efficiency by eliminating redundant data. Deduplication can operate at different levels, such as file level, block level, or byte level, depending on the granularity needed for duplicate detection.

Distributed computing frameworks, such as Apache Hadoop and Apache Spark, distribute data processing tasks across multiple nodes or servers to enable parallel execution and enhance performance, by leveraging idle computing resources more effectively through workload distribution, organizations can reduce energy consumption and improve system efficiency.

Efficient data lifecycle management involves optimizing storage and processing resources throughout the data's lifecycle, from creation to disposal. By implementing policies for data retention, archiving, and deletion, organizations can reduce stored data volumes, resulting in lower storage costs with lessened energy consumption [25].

2.5.8.2 Techniques for Energy-Efficient Data Management

Data compression techniques reduce the size of data files, thereby lowering storage requirements and decreasing energy consumption. In compressing data before storage or transmission, organizations can optimize storage resources and minimize energy usage associated with data storage and transmission [26].

Deduplication eliminates redundant copies of data within storage systems, effectively reducing storage needs and energy consumption. By means of identifying and removing duplicate data, organizations can enhance storage efficiency and lessen energy usage related to storing and managing redundant data.

Distributed computing frameworks distribute data processing tasks across multiple nodes or servers, enabling parallel execution and improved performance. By leveraging distributed computing frameworks, organizations can utilize computing resources more efficiently, leading to reduced energy consumption with enhanced system effectiveness.

Efficient data lifecycle management encompasses managing data from creation to disposal, optimizing storage and processing resources throughout the data's lifecycle. By implementing data retention policies as well as leveraging automated data lifecycle management tools, organizations can minimize energy usage associated with data storage and processing. This results in lesser energy consumption and reduced environmental effects [27].

2.5.9 Energy-Aware Resource Provisioning in Data Centers

Energy-efficient resource provisioning in data centers is essential for minimizing energy wastage and optimizing operational costs amid the rapid expansion of digital services and escalating demand for computational resources. Data centers have emerged as major energy consumers, prompting the development of various techniques and strategies aimed at enhancing resource provisioning efficiency while prioritizing workload demands and energy conservation [28].

One approach involves dynamically allocating resources according to the current workload demands. Constant monitoring of resource utilization and workload patterns enables data center operators to scale resources up or down as required.

This dynamic allocation makes sure resources are provisioned whenever they are in use, thus wasting low power during times of low demand.

Virtualization technology makes it possible to consolidate several VMs onto fewer physical servers. This consolidation ensures the reduction of the total energy used through the exploitation of server utilization. The intelligent resource management systems optimize VM placement and migration to minimize energy use while meeting the performance strategy [29].

Using predictive analytics—based on historical data and machine-learning algorithms—long-term workload demand can be predicted. With such foresight, data center operators are able to adjust resource provisioning to tie in with foreseen demand, thus avoiding under- and overprovisioning scenarios that can potentially lead to energy inadequacies [30].

Competence-oriented scheduling algorithms with respect to energy aspects not only schedule tasks to be run but also may renounce executing any task whenever best possible, thereby achieving minimum power consumption. Such algorithms consider workload characteristics, server efficiencies, and cooling inferences to maximally utilize resources at minimal energy use.

Whereas renewable resources in the form of solar or wind may be introduced to boost the efficiency of energy in the data center, for the reduction of GHGs and verified carbon standards, the Solar Radiation Modification (SRMs) should dynamically alter the provisioning of resources in tandem with the sources' availability, thus ensuring that workloads run under renewable energy sources as much as possible [21].

It allows effective cooling systems and resource management based on temperature requirements, which, in turn, keeps the desired high service levels intact without excessive energy consumption.

The success of realizing energy efficiency in data centers is rooted in intelligent resource management systems that make up resource deployment and utilization to reduce energy wastage. Such systems can utilize real-time monitoring, predictive analytics, and sophisticated algorithms to optimize resource provisioning, workload scheduling, and energy consumption [21].

2.5.10 Green Software Procurement and Vendor Management

Green software approach and vendor management are the two greatest contributors to the success of a sustainability scheme in an organization, since they contribute most significantly to overall environmental and ecological impacts associated with the usage and development of software [3]

2.5.10.1 Selection of Green Software Vendors and Products

Look for vendors that have a clear environmental policy and commitment to sustainability. These policies must contain targets for the reduction of carbon emissions, promotion of renewable energy sources, limiting generated waste, and developing and incorporating environmentally friendly operations [4]. Prefigure software products incorporating energy-efficient algorithms, better resource usage, and lower power consumption when in operation. Prioritize those vendors committing themselves to performance enhancement through the life cycle of their software package.

Conduct an end-to-end assessment of the software's impact on the environment from up-scaling to the point of deployment to its end-of-life disposal strategies. In this regard, service vendors are concerned with sustainability in the growth of software by using eco-friendly materials to reduce packaging wastes and offering alternatives for recycling or reusing the software at the end of its life.

Evaluate the carbon footprint of using the software, including what's in their servers' energy consumption, data transmission, and user behavior. Prefer vendors who provide transparent commentary about the carbon emission associated with their software and offer tools or features through which users can reduce their environmental impact [5].

2.5.10.2 Relevance of Environmental Impact Considerations

Software use is directly responsible for carbon emissions from energy use related to software, datacenter operation, and hardware production. Organizations can reduce the carbon footprint and environmental impact they produce by choosing the right eco-friendly software vendors and products.

Environmental sustainability is increasingly addressed by establishments as a part of their corporate social responsibility. Establishments can show responsibility for the sustainable development of society by applying factoring in the environmental impact into their decisions on software procurement and adapting their practice to the existing opportunities of society.

Eco-friendly software solutions are aimed at making the software energy-friendly and optimizing resources that would then translate into cost savings on the establishment. Cost savings are done through energy efficiency and resource optimization. Utility bills go down, and operational cost comes down as well, so organizations could benefit.

Environmental considerations are important for regulatory compliance and risk management. By adopting a proactive approach to discussing environmental impact in software acquisition, organizations have been able to mitigate risks related to regulatory non-compliance, reputational damage, and environmental liabilities [6].

Embracing green software procurement allows room for innovation in such resolutions. By supporting eco-friendly vendors and products, establishments might foster innovative development of technology that is the best possible in terms of environmental sustainability to have an upcoming society that is also more conscious toward eco-friendliness.

2.5.11 Carbon Footprint Monitoring and Reporting

It is important to manage and report on carbon footprinting as part of software applications and IT infrastructure. This section enlists the importance of measuring and monitoring carbon footprints and discusses a rough gauge of tools and frameworks for assessment [7].

2.5.11.1 Importance of Measuring and Monitoring Carbon Footprint

It is critical in measuring and monitoring the carbon emissions of the software applications and IT infrastructure in relation to the environmental impact. Calculating the carbon emissions provides pinpointed areas in the administrations' software and IT infrastructures that contribute most to environmental impact, thus enabling achievements in the best efforts of performance optimization with sustainable practices.

Carbon footprint management enables governments or organizations to set achievable objectives and targets for reducing environmental footprint [8]. Moreover, authorities and interested parties ask institutions to disclose their environmental practice, including carbon emissions. Carbon footprint management allows organizations to meet better transparency and better regulation rules and standards. Optimizing energy use, and improved resource efficiency with minimal waste, is one way organizations could reduce their operational costs relating to power consumption and environmental influence.

2.5.11.2 Tools and Frameworks for Carbon Footprint Assessment and Reporting

There are various carbon accounting tools and software platforms designed to assist organizations in gauging, pursuing, and reporting carbon emissions. These tools naturally offer functionalities for data collection, analysis, and reporting, allowing establishments to quantify their carbon footprint across different activities and areas [10].

Energy monitoring systems allow organizations to monitor real-time energy consumption across their IT infrastructure, including servers, data centers, and networking equipment. It allows for carbon footprint calculations with precision, as the energy monitoring data can be integrated with factors of carbon emission for reporting purposes.

LCA frameworks identify the net environmental impacts resulting from products and services across the life cycle, from mining raw materials to disposal. Governments can use the methodologies and tools of an LCA to establish the carbon footprint of software applications and IT infrastructures, and such methodologies include factors like hardware manufacturing, software development, and operational energy use [11].

Carbon footprint calculators are easy and simple tools that, at best, provide a rough estimate of carbon emissions attributed to an activity, in this case, software practice, website hosting, or cloud computing. Less advanced in scope than the tools for full-scale carbon accounting, these calculators will still give organizations a fast and easy way to begin the process of carbon footprint assessment and reporting.

Facilities can refer to existing industry standards and guides for measuring and reporting carbon footprints, such as the Greenhouse Gas Protocol, ISO 14064, or the Carbon Disclosure Project. These schemes embrace standard approaches and reporting formats, which support uniformity and comparability across organizations and industries.

2.5.12 Energy-Efficient Computing Technologies

The need to increase computational power and reduce the environmental impact of IT infrastructure puts a requirement for energy-efficient computing technologies.

Some of these emerging technologies, especially artificial intelligence (AI), the Internet of Things (IoT), and blockchain, offer great potential in the pursuit of further enhancing energy efficiency in computing [1].

2.5.12.1 Artificial Intelligence (AI) Potential Contributions to Energy Efficiency

AI algorithms analyze data patterns and forecast resource demands, refining the efficient allocation of computing resources and dropping the energy waste level. AI techniques, such as machine learning, improve algorithms to perform tasks using minimal computational resources, thereby reducing energy consumption. AI-driven predictive maintenance systems identify potential equipment failures in data centers, enabling proactive maintenance to prevent downtime and improve energy usage.

2.5.12.1.1 Case Studies and Examples

Google DeepMind applied AI algorithms to enhance data center cooling systems, resulting in a 30% reduction in power consumption. IBM Watson utilizes its AI capabilities for energy optimization in buildings, helping organizations reduce energy consumption and carbon emissions. AI-powered smart grid systems optimize energy distribution, predict demand patterns, and integrate renewable energy sources for more efficient energy management [12].

2.5.12.2 Internet of Things (IoT) Potential Contributions to Energy Efficiency

IoT sensors gather data on energy usage, environmental conditions, and equipment performance in real time, allowing organizations to detect inefficiencies and optimize energy consumption. IoT devices and systems automate building operations such as lighting, HVAC, and energy management based on occupancy and environmental conditions, thereby enhancing energy management. IoT devices employ energy harvesting methods like solar or kinetic energy to self-power, reducing reliance on external energy sources as well as power consumption.

2.5.12.2.1 Case Studies and Examples

Siemens provides IoT solutions that optimize energy usage, advance occupant comfort, and lower operational costs in smart buildings. Schneider Electric's EcoStruxure platform utilizes IoT technology for comprehensive energy management across buildings, data centers, and industrial facilities. IoT-enabled smart grid deployments use sensors and smart meters to monitor energy distribution, identify faults, and improve energy flows, enhancing energy competence and grid steadiness [14].

2.5.12.3 Blockchain Potential Contributions to Energy Efficiency

Blockchain technology facilitates peer-to-peer energy trading and decentralized markets, promoting efficient use of renewable energy resources and reducing dependence on centralized energy systems [1]. Blockchain platforms provide transparent and immutable records of energy transactions, enabling consumers to trace the origin of their energy and encouraging the adoption of renewable energy sources. Blockchain-based smart contracts automate energy efficiency agreements, such as demand response programs and conservation incentives, fostering energy-saving behaviors and optimizing energy use.

2.5.12.3.1 Case Studies and Examples

Power Ledger uses blockchain for peer-to-peer energy trading and renewable energy certificate trading, enabling direct energy transactions between consumers [4]. WePower utilizes blockchain to crowdfunding and trade renewable energy projects, enhancing transparency and liquidity in renewable energy markets. LO3 Energy Brooklyn Microgrid project employs blockchain for peer-to-peer energy trading among residents, encouraging a local renewable consumption approach [7].

2.5.13 Regulatory Compliance and Green Computing Standards

Safeguarding regulatory compliance and adherence to green computing standards are a few of the requirements for facilities striving to minimize their environmental impact while maintaining applicable laws and regulations [1, 3].

2.5.13.1 Regulatory Frameworks and Industry Standards

The Energy Star is an Environmental Protection Agency (EPA) voluntary program that certifies energy-efficient products such as computers, servers, and other IT products. Compliance with Energy Star guarantees that the products are assured to meet or exceed specific energy efficiency requirements [4].

European Union: The EU Eco-Design Directive requires energy performance criteria for energy-using products placed on the market within the European Union. The purpose is to lead to decreased higher use and greenhouse emissions by establishing minimum efficiency requirements for things like computers and servers.

Energy efficiency standards for computers and monitors shall be based at a minimum on California Energy Commission (CEC) Standards for computing products sold or for use in California. Compliance with the above shall be required for all products sold into the State, thereby allowing for reduced energy consumption and reduced carbon impact.

The ISO 14001 Environmental Management System is that international standard that concerns the independent establishment of an environmental management system. The standards provide a framework by which establishments can formulate, implement, maintain, and significantly improve their environmental performances. Therefore, ISO 14001 implies dedication to environmental responsiveness and sustainable work practice.

Carbon Disclosure Project (CDP) is a global system facilitating companies to disclose their environmental impacts and carbon emissions. Participating in CDP and reporting carbon emissions data would actually help establishments be transparent and show accountability in environmental performance.

2.5.13.2 Ensuring Compliance in Software Development and Deployment

Throughout the software development lifecycle, integrated environmental issues, such as power management, resource optimization, and sustainable design principles, incorporate energy-efficient algorithms and optimize code performance with minimal resource consumption to decrease the environmental footprint of software applications [8, 29].

Implement energy-efficient technologies and best practices during software development and deployment, including virtualization, cloud computing, and server consolidation. Improve server configurations, utilize energy-saving functionalities, and deploy power management approaches lessening energy consumption across data centers and IT infrastructure.

Verify that software products adhere to relevant energy efficiency standards and regulations, as Energy Star certification criteria or specifications outlined in the EU Eco-Design Directive. Conduct energy efficiency testing on software applications and validate compliance with these standards formerly.

Establish monitoring and measurement protocols to track the environmental performance of software applications and IT infrastructure. Gather data on energy usage, carbon emissions, and other environmental impact indicators to evaluate conformity with regulatory mandates and pinpoint areas for enhancement, Figure 2.3 depicts green computing in IT [31].

Embrace a continuous improvement approach in green computing constantly evaluating and refining environmental routines. Identify prospects for efficiency enhancements, implement energy-conservation trials, and update software applications to incorporate cutting-edge technologies and best practices for enhanced power management and efficiency [21, 30].

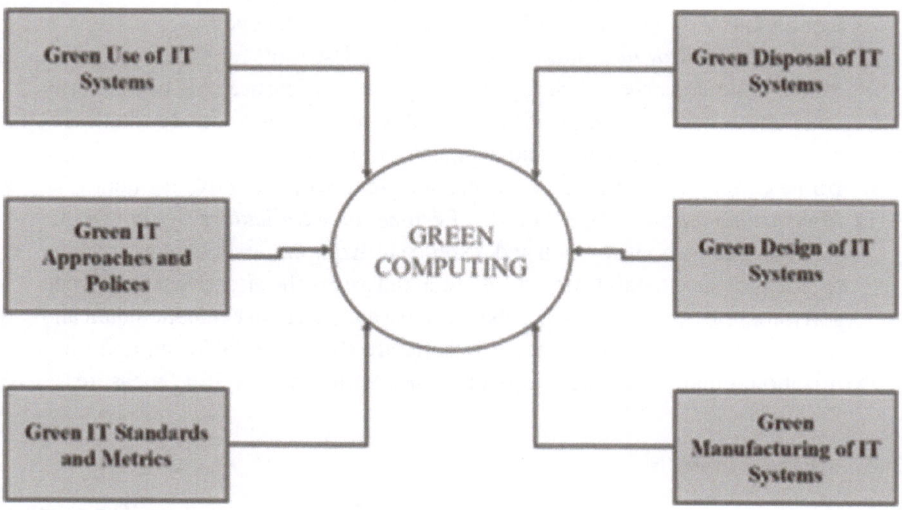

FIGURE 2.3 Green computing in IT.

2.6 FRAMEWORK FOR SOFTWARE APPROACH FOR GREEN COMPUTING

Green computing aims to minimize the environmental impact of IT. Software plays an essential role in attaining this objective in optimizing resource utilization with minimal consumption. Below is a framework outlining an approach for software in green computing approach:

A. ***Software Development Phase***: Green design principles focus on algorithms with lower computational complexity. Use data structures that optimize memory usage. Design software to lessen resource (CPU, memory, network) utilization during idle periods [19]. Thus, there is a need to implement power management features for background processes and idle states. Green coding practices avoid redundant code and unnecessary calculations. Optimize loops and conditional statements for efficiency. Utilize energy-efficient libraries and frameworks. Ensure proper resource cleanup and efficient garbage collection.

   Perform energy consumption profiling to identify areas for optimization. Conduct load testing to guarantee efficient resource usage during peak demand.

B. ***Software Deployment and Use Phase, Power Management Features***: Utilize built-in power-saving modes and sleep states on devices. Implement dynamic CPU clock scaling based on workload. Enable power management for peripherals like displays and storage drives. Employ server consolidation and virtualization techniques to make the most of resource utilization. Enhance software for distributed processing to leverage cloud resources. Educate users on power-saving options and eco-friendly settings [2, 24]. Deploy software for real-time energy consumption on one-to-one care at both application and system levels. Use analytics to identify resource usage patterns and trends. Continuously refine software for enhanced energy efficiency.

C. ***Tools and Techniques, Static Code Analysis***: Use tools for identifying inefficient code constructs. Energy Profiling Tools: Measure real-time energy consumption of software. Cloud-based Green Tools: Utilize platform-specific features for power management and resource optimization. Adopt frameworks promoting best practices for green software advancement.

D. ***Measurement and Evaluation, Key Performance Indicators (KPIs)***: Define KPIs for energy consumption and resource utilization. Conduct regular audits to assess environmental IMPACT. Monitor and assess the effectiveness of green software practices. Iteratively enhance software based on evaluation data and develop strategies to green existing software through refactoring and optimization. Finally, balance energy efficiency with robust security measures.

2.7 CONCLUSION

The present chapter proposes a software approach for green computing. The chapter studied the key software-centric strategies for achieving green computing objectives. The research highlights the foundation for feasible solutions by reviewing relevant literature, and highlighting the significance of sustainability in software advancement. The chapter emphasizes methods for code optimization, such as minimizing senseless computations, and draws attention to the substantial power management as energy savings that can be achieved via effective coding strategies. Strategically construct an optimized and efficient software procedure from the foundation conceivable by examination of energy-aware design perceptions, such as modularization, design patterns, and dynamic resource management using virtualization. The chapter scrutinized approaches for developing green software and how they support sustainability. It studied sequentially the strategies employed collaboratively in an innovation and open-source relevant contribution to green computing, using successful open-source projects as examples. Techniques for managing and processing energy-efficient data were presented, in addition to a more sustainable and prospective future. Finally, a framework for a software approach to green computing is presented, highlighting vital considerations for application. The chapter attempts to enhance the sustainable IT landscape, encouraging power-efficient software advancement practices.

REFERENCES

1. Soomro, T. R., & Sarwar, M. (2012). Green computing: From current to future trends. *International Journal of Humanities and Social Sciences*, *6*(3), 326–329.
2. Wisdom, D. D., Ajayi, A. E., Arinze, C. U., Idris, H., Bello, U. M., & Aladesote, I. O. (2022). An optimized TWIN battery resource management scheme in IEEE 802.16 e networks. In *Proceedings of Sixth International Congress on Information and Communication Technology: ICICT 2021, London, Volume 4* (pp. 73–95). Springer Singapore.
3. S Bijapur, C., & Sai, P. (2023). Green Computing Approaches for Data Centers and Storage Systems: A Survey of Green Computing Strategies for Resource Efficiency. *Gnanesh and Sai, G Pramod, Green Computing Approaches for Data Centers and Storage Systems: A Survey of Green Computing Strategies for Resource Efficiency (September 19, 2023).*
4. Kocak, S. A. (2013, October). Green software development and design for environmental sustainability. In *11th International Doctoral Symposium an Empirical Software Engineering (IDOESE 2013). Baltimore, Maryland* (Vol. 9).
5. Saraiva, J., Zong, Z., & Pereira, R. (2021, June). Bringing green software to computer science curriculum: perspectives from researchers and educators. In *Proceedings of the 26th ACM Conference on Innovation and Technology in Computer Science Education V. 1* (pp. 498–504).
6. Kaur, A., & Kaur, S. (2019). Green computing: Emerging issues in IT. *International Journal of Trend in Scientific Research and Development (IJTSRD)*, *3*(5), 438–440.
7. Kazandjieva, M., Heller, B., Gnawali, O., Hofer, W., & Kozyrakis, P. L. C. (2011). Software or hardware: The future of green enterprise computing. *Computer Science Technical Report CSTR*, *2*.
8. Ketankumar, D. C., Verma, G., & Chandrasekaran, K. (2015). A green mechanism design approach to automate resource procurement in cloud. *Procedia Computer Science*, *54*, 108–117.
9. Nyabuto, G. M. (2024). A review of current research trends in green computing. *East African Journal of Information Technology*, *7*(1), 51–59. https://doi.org/10.37284/eajit.7.1.1707

10. Ciocoiu, C. N. (2011). Integrating digital economy and green economy: Opportunities for sustainable development. *Theoretical and Empirical Researches in Urban Management*, *6*(1), 33–43.
11. Deng, J., Hu, J., Li, W., & Wu, J. (2011). *Trends and Development on Green Computing. In International Workshop on Computer Science for Environmental Engineering and EcoInformatics* (pp. 281–286). *Berlin, Heidelberg*: *Springer Berlin Heidelberg*..
12. Visalakshi, P., Paul, S., & Mandal, M. (2013, May). Green computing. In *International Journal of Modern Engineering Research (IJMER). Proceedings of the National Conference on Architecture, Software systems and Green computing (NCASG), Paiyanoor (India)* (pp. 63–69).
13. Appasami, G., & Joseph, K. S. (2011). Optimization of operating systems towards green computing. *International Journal of Combinatorial Optimization Problems and Informatics*, *2*(3), 39–51.
14. Taruna, S., Singh, P., & Joshi, S. (2014). Green computing in developed and developing countries. *arXiv preprint arXiv:1406.2773*.
15. Castillo, O., & Melin, P. (2021). Review on the interactions of green computing and computational intelligence techniques and their applications to real-world problems. *Journal of Smart Environments and Green Computing*, *1*(2), 103–119.
16. Verdecchia, R., Lago, P., Ebert, C., & De Vries, C. (2021). Green IT and green software. *IEEE Software*, *38*(6), 7–15.
17. Ghansawant, V. (2020). Green computing: Current research trends. *International Journal of Science and Research (IJSR)*, 2319–7064. DOI: 10.21275/MR21709173309.
18. Wisdom, D. D., Ahmed, M. A., Farouk, N., Isaac, S., Idris, H., & Hassan, J. B. (2020). An enhanced power saving scheme (EPSS) in IEEE 802.16 e networks. *International Journal of Information Processing and Communication IJIPC*, *8*(2).
19. Wisdom, D. D., Saidu, I., Tambuwal, A. Y., Isaac, S., Ahmad, M. A., & Faruk, N. (2019, December). An efficient sleep-window-based power saving scheme (ESPSS) in IEEE 802.16 e networks. In *2019 15th International Conference on Electronics, Computer and Computation (ICECCO)* (pp. 1–6). IEEE.
20. Benamer, W. H., Elberkawi, E. K., Neihum, N. A., Anwiji, A. S., & Youns, M. A. (2021). Green Computing case study: calls for proposing solutions for the Arabian Gulf Oil Company. In *E3S Web of Conferences* (Vol. 229, p. 01063). EDP Sciences.
21. Haron, H., Ahmaro, I. Y., Ahmad Aljunid, S., & Bakri, M. (2015). Software reusability in green computing. *Advanced Science Letters*, *21*(10), 3283–3287.
22. Priya, S., Kumari, R., Shruthi, R., Sumana, P., & Harish, G. (2024). Green computing: A case study on the holistic approach of innovative computing. Unpublished manuscript, R.V. College of Engineering, Bangalore, India.
23. Isaac, S., Wisdom, D. D., Nigeria, S., Ahmad, M. A., & Christian, A. U. (2020). Battery-life management with an efficient sleep-mode power saving scheme (BM-ESPSS) in IEEE 802.16 e networks. *International Journal of Mechatronics, Electrical and Computer Technology (IJMEC)*, *7*(2).
24. Wisdom, D. D., Christian, A. U., Hyacinth, E. A., Odunayo, O. E., Igulu, K., & Umar, B. (2023). IoT devices battery life energy management scheme. In *Accra Espoke Innovations Conference and Africa AI Stakeholders Summit*.
25. Rao, T. V. N., Rani, M. J., Swetha, C., & Satyam, A. (2015). Sustainable environment friendly green computing for futuristic technologies. *Journal of Information Sciences and Computing Technologies*, *2*, 128–132.
26. Naeem, B. (2021). *Green Computing: Analysis of Power and Energy Consumption of Personal Computers* (Doctoral dissertation, CAPITAL UNIVERSITY).
27. Pillai, A. S., Vessly, R. A., & Joseph, R. (2022). Green cloud computing: A greener approach to IT. *International Journal of Research in Engineering and Science (IJRES)*, *10*(4), 42–48. ISSN (Online): 2320-9364, ISSN (Print): 2320-9356

28. Nagaraju, V. (2013). Green computing a modern approach to information technology. *BEST: International Journal of Management, Information Technology and Engineering*, *1*(1), 23–28.
29. Hema, K., Subhashini, P., & Lakshimi, S. V. (2017). Emerging issues of green computing in IT. *International Journal of Scientific & Engineering Research*, *8*(5), 52.
30. Thomas, R., Manjaly, F. J., & Mala, T. (2015). Approaches in green computing. *International Journal of Engineering Research & Technology (IJERT) NSRCL*, *3*(28).
31. Mehtälä, H. E. J. (2023). *Green in software engineering: Tools, methods and practices for reducing the environmental impacts of software use—A literature review.*

3 Green Computing and Wildlife Conservation

Javier Prieto

3.1 INTRODUCTION

In an age marked by escalating concerns over environmental sustainability and biodiversity loss, the convergence of green computing and wildlife conservation emerges as a beacon of hope. As our planet grapples with the repercussions of rapid technological advancement and habitat degradation, the imperative to harness innovative solutions becomes increasingly urgent. This introduction sets the stage for a profound exploration into the pivotal role of green computing in fostering sustainable development and safeguarding Earth's diverse ecosystems.

The contemporary landscape of environmental conservation is fraught with challenges, from habitat fragmentation to climate change-induced disruptions. Amidst these complexities, the burgeoning field of green computing offers a glimmer of optimism. Green computing, characterized by the efficient utilization of IT resources to minimize environmental impact, represents a paradigm shift in our approach to technology. It transcends mere efficiency gains to embrace a holistic ethos of ecological responsibility and resource stewardship [1].

At the heart of this discourse lies the symbiotic relationship between green computing and wildlife conservation. By leveraging cutting-edge technologies and innovative methodologies, green computing holds the potential to catalyze transformative change in how we perceive and protect the natural world. From optimizing energy consumption in data centers to harnessing the power of big data analytics for biodiversity monitoring, the possibilities are as vast as they are promising.

Against this backdrop, this chapter embarks on a journey of discovery, elucidating the multifaceted intersections between technology and ecology. Through a nuanced exploration of case studies, best practices, and forward-thinking initiatives, it endeavors to unravel the intricacies of this dynamic relationship. By illuminating the synergies between green computing and wildlife conservation, it seeks to inspire collaboration and innovation among diverse stakeholders.

As we stand at the crossroads of technological advancement and environmental stewardship, the need for proactive engagement has never been more pressing. By embracing the principles of green computing and embracing a conservation-oriented mindset, we have the opportunity to forge a path toward a more sustainable future—one where the harmonious coexistence of humanity and nature is not just an aspiration, but a tangible reality.

In the subsequent sections that follow, we will delve into the myriad ways in which green computing can be harnessed to advance wildlife conservation goals. From the optimization of sensor networks to the development of eco-friendly computing

DOI: 10.1201/9781003471356-3

architectures, each facet of this discourse offers a glimpse into the transformative potential of technology. Together, let us embark on a journey of exploration and discovery, guided by the shared vision of a world where technology and ecology converge for the greater good.

The world is facing unprecedented environmental challenges, and nowhere are these challenges more acute than in the fragile habitats that support wildlife populations. From the dense rainforests of the Amazon to the vast savannas of Africa, ecosystems are under siege from a myriad of threats, ranging from habitat destruction to climate change-induced disruptions. This introduction shines a spotlight on the urgent need to address these challenges and protect the invaluable biodiversity that sustains life on Earth.

At the heart of the environmental crisis lies the relentless encroachment of human activity into natural habitats. Rapid urbanization, industrialization, and agricultural expansion have led to widespread deforestation, fragmentation of ecosystems, and loss of critical habitats. As a result, countless species are facing extinction, with alarming declines in populations observed across a wide range of taxa [2].

Moreover, climate change looms as a specter over wildlife habitats, exacerbating existing threats and introducing new challenges. Rising temperatures, shifting precipitation patterns, and extreme weather events are disrupting ecosystems and pushing species beyond their tolerance limits. The consequences are dire, with cascading impacts on food webs, migration patterns, and reproductive cycles.

Compounding these challenges are the myriad indirect effects of human activity, from pollution to invasive species introduction. Pollution from industrial runoff, plastic waste, and chemical contaminants is poisoning waterways and soil, wreaking havoc on aquatic and terrestrial ecosystems alike. Meanwhile, the introduction of invasive species threatens native biodiversity, outcompeting native species and altering ecosystem dynamics.

In the face of these mounting threats, the imperative to act is clear. The survival of countless species, as well as the health and resilience of ecosystems, hangs in the balance. Conservation efforts must be intensified, and innovative solutions must be embraced to address the multifaceted challenges facing wildlife habitats.

However, amidst the gloom and doom, there are glimmers of hope. Across the globe, dedicated individuals and organizations are working tirelessly to protect and restore wildlife habitats. From grassroots conservation initiatives to large-scale restoration projects, there is a growing recognition of the need to prioritize the conservation of biodiversity and safeguard the natural heritage of our planet.

In the next section, we will delve into the intersection of green computing and wildlife conservation, exploring how innovative technologies can be harnessed to address the challenges facing wildlife habitats. By leveraging the power of data analytics, remote sensing, and energy-efficient computing, we have the potential to revolutionize conservation efforts and drive positive change for the future of our planet's precious biodiversity.

3.2 GREEN COMPUTING: CONCEPTS AND PRACTICES

As the world grapples with the urgent need to mitigate the environmental impact of human activity, the concept of green computing emerges as a beacon of sustainability in the realm of technology. In this chapter, we embark on a journey to explore the core principles of green computing and delve into the innovative practices that underpin its transformative potential.

At its essence, green computing represents a paradigm shift in our approach to technology—a shift from resource-intensive, environmentally harmful practices to sustainable, eco-friendly alternatives. Central to the concept of green computing is the recognition that the IT industry, while indispensable in driving innovation and progress, also carries a significant ecological footprint. From energy consumption in data centers to the disposal of electronic waste, the environmental impacts of IT infrastructure are far-reaching and profound.

To address these challenges, green computing embraces a holistic approach that encompasses the entire lifecycle of IT resources, from design and manufacturing to use and disposal. At its core, green computing seeks to optimize resource utilization, minimize energy consumption, and reduce environmental pollution through the adoption of eco-friendly technologies and practices [3].

Key principles that underpin green computing include energy efficiency, resource conservation, and waste reduction. Energy efficiency lies at the heart of green computing, with a focus on optimizing the performance of hardware and software to minimize energy consumption. This includes the use of energy-efficient components, power management techniques, and the adoption of renewable energy sources to power data centers and IT infrastructure.

Resource conservation is another cornerstone of green computing, emphasizing the importance of maximizing resource utilization and minimizing waste. This involves strategies such as virtualization, which allows multiple virtual machines to run on a single physical server, thereby reducing the need for additional hardware and conserving resources. Additionally, recycling and proper disposal of electronic waste are essential components of green computing, ensuring that end-of-life IT equipment is handled in an environmentally responsible manner.

Furthermore, green computing embraces the concept of sustainable design, advocating for the development of eco-friendly products and technologies that minimize environmental impact throughout their lifecycle. This includes the use of recyclable materials, energy-efficient manufacturing processes, and the incorporation of end-of-life considerations into product design.

In practice, green computing encompasses a wide range of initiatives and practices aimed at reducing the environmental footprint of IT infrastructure. From data center optimization and server consolidation to cloud computing and virtualization, there are numerous strategies that organizations can employ to embrace green computing principles and drive positive environmental change.

Now, we will explore how green computing can be leveraged to advance wildlife conservation efforts, examining the innovative ways in which technology can be harnessed to protect and preserve the natural world. By embracing the principles of green computing and integrating them into conservation practices, we have the potential to usher in a new era of sustainability—one where technology and ecology converge for the greater good of our planet and its inhabitants [4].

In the ever-evolving landscape of technology, the imperative to address environmental concerns has propelled the emergence of green computing—a paradigm that advocates for energy-efficient design, manufacturing, and usage of IT resources. In this section, we delve into the fundamental principles and innovative practices that define green computing, with a specific focus on its role in mitigating the environmental impact of information technology (IT).

Energy efficiency lies at the forefront of green computing, representing a foundational principle that guides the design, manufacturing, and usage of IT resources. At its core, energy-efficient design entails the development of hardware and software solutions that optimize performance while minimizing energy consumption. This encompasses a spectrum of strategies, ranging from the selection of energy-efficient components to the implementation of power management techniques that reduce energy waste during idle periods.

In the realm of hardware design, energy efficiency manifests through the use of low-power components, such as processors, memory modules, and storage devices, that prioritize performance per watt. Manufacturers are increasingly incorporating energy-efficient design principles into the development of IT equipment, leveraging advancements in semiconductor technology and circuit design to minimize power consumption without compromising performance.

Moreover, energy-efficient manufacturing practices play a pivotal role in reducing the environmental footprint of IT resources. From the selection of eco-friendly materials to the optimization of production processes, manufacturers are exploring innovative approaches to minimize energy consumption and waste generation throughout the manufacturing lifecycle. This includes the adoption of sustainable sourcing practices, the use of renewable energy in manufacturing facilities, and the implementation of waste reduction strategies to minimize environmental impact.

In addition to energy-efficient design and manufacturing, the adoption of green computing practices extends to the usage phase of IT resources. Organizations are increasingly embracing strategies to optimize energy consumption in data centers, server farms, and computing infrastructure, with a focus on maximizing resource utilization and minimizing waste. This includes the deployment of energy-efficient servers, the implementation of virtualization and cloud computing technologies, and the adoption of power management techniques that dynamically adjust energy usage based on workload demands.

Furthermore, end-users play a crucial role in driving energy efficiency in IT usage, with individuals and organizations encouraged to adopt sustainable computing practices that minimize energy consumption and environmental impact. This includes strategies such as turning off unused devices, optimizing power settings on computers and peripherals, and utilizing energy-efficient software applications that prioritize resource efficiency.

Green computing represents a holistic approach to addressing environmental concerns in the realm of IT. By prioritizing energy-efficient design, manufacturing, and usage of IT resources, organizations can significantly reduce their environmental footprint while simultaneously driving innovation and progress in the technology sector. In the following section, we will explore how green computing can be leveraged to advance wildlife conservation efforts, highlighting the transformative potential of technology in safeguarding our planet's precious biodiversity.

At the forefront of this global challenge lies the realm of IT, where the adoption of green IT practices holds immense potential to mitigate environmental impact and drive positive change. Here, we delve into the critical role of green IT in reducing greenhouse gas emissions, exploring innovative strategies and initiatives that can help pave the way toward a more sustainable future.

The IT sector is a significant contributor to greenhouse gas emissions, with data centers, computing infrastructure, and electronic devices collectively accounting for a substantial portion of global energy consumption. As the demand for digital services continues to grow exponentially, the environmental footprint of IT operations is projected to increase unless proactive measures are taken to address energy efficiency and sustainability.

One of the key pillars of green IT is energy efficiency, which plays a pivotal role in reducing greenhouse gas emissions associated with IT operations. By optimizing the design, manufacturing, and usage of IT resources, organizations can minimize energy consumption and carbon emissions while maximizing performance and productivity. This includes the adoption of energy-efficient hardware components, the implementation of power management techniques, and the deployment of renewable energy sources to power data centers and computing infrastructure.

Furthermore, the transition toward cloud computing and virtualization represents a transformative shift in IT infrastructure management, offering opportunities to consolidate resources, optimize energy usage, and reduce carbon emissions. By leveraging virtualization technologies to consolidate server workloads and maximize resource utilization, organizations can achieve significant energy savings and carbon footprint reductions, while also improving scalability and agility in IT operations.

Moreover, green IT extends beyond the confines of data centers and computing infrastructure to encompass the entire lifecycle of IT products and services. From sustainable design and manufacturing practices to responsible end-of-life disposal and recycling, green IT principles guide organizations in minimizing environmental impact and promoting resource conservation throughout the IT lifecycle. This includes the adoption of eco-friendly materials, the reduction of electronic waste through recycling and refurbishment programs, and the implementation of circular economy initiatives to promote resource reuse and recovery.

In addition to technological solutions, green IT also emphasizes the importance of raising awareness and fostering a culture of sustainability within organizations and communities. By promoting eco-friendly behaviors and encouraging stakeholders to adopt sustainable computing practices, organizations can amplify the impact of green IT initiatives and drive meaningful change toward reducing greenhouse gas emissions.

Green IT plays a critical role in reducing greenhouse gas emissions and advancing climate action goals. By prioritizing energy efficiency, embracing sustainable practices, and fostering a culture of environmental responsibility, organizations can harness the transformative power of technology to create a more sustainable and resilient future for generations to come. In the section that follows, we will explore how green IT can be leveraged to address specific environmental challenges, including wildlife conservation and biodiversity preservation, highlighting the synergies between technology and environmental sustainability.

3.3 WILDLIFE CONSERVATION: CHALLENGES AND OPPORTUNITIES

The conservation of wildlife and biodiversity stands as one of the paramount challenges of our time, as the delicate balance of ecosystems is threatened by a myriad of anthropogenic pressures. We delineate the pressing challenges facing wildlife conservation, while also illuminating the opportunities that exist for innovative solutions and concerted action.

At the forefront of wildlife conservation efforts lies the pervasive issue of habitat loss and degradation. Human activities such as deforestation, urbanization, and agricultural expansion continue to encroach upon natural habitats, fragmenting ecosystems and displacing countless species from their native habitats. As pristine wildernesses diminish and fragmented habitats become increasingly isolated, biodiversity loss accelerates, with species facing heightened risks of extinction due to reduced gene flow and increased vulnerability to environmental stressors.

Furthermore, climate change emerges as a potent threat to wildlife populations, exacerbating existing challenges and introducing new complexities to conservation efforts. Rising temperatures, altered precipitation patterns, and extreme weather events disrupt ecosystems and push species beyond their climatic tolerances, forcing range shifts and altering the timing of critical life cycle events such as migration and reproduction. For many species, these rapid environmental changes outpace their capacity to adapt, leading to population declines and heightened extinction risks.

The illegal wildlife trade represents another formidable challenge to conservation efforts, driven by demand for exotic pets, traditional medicines, and luxury goods. Poaching and trafficking of endangered species decimate populations, destabilize ecosystems, and fuel organized crime networks, posing a grave threat to global biodiversity. Despite concerted efforts to combat illegal wildlife trade through legislation, enforcement, and public awareness campaigns, the illicit market persists, driven by lucrative profits and persistent demand.

Moreover, invasive species emerge as a significant driver of biodiversity loss, as non-native species outcompete native flora and fauna, disrupt ecological processes, and alter ecosystem dynamics. Invasive species introductions, whether intentional or accidental, wreak havoc on native ecosystems, leading to declines in biodiversity, loss of ecosystem services, and economic damages. Controlling invasive species and mitigating their impacts represent formidable challenges for conservationists, requiring coordinated management efforts across international borders and ecosystems [5].

In addition to these challenges, wildlife conservation efforts are further hampered by inadequate funding, limited resources, and competing interests. As conservation organizations grapple with dwindling budgets and increasing demands, prioritizing conservation actions and allocating resources effectively becomes a formidable task. Furthermore, conflicting land use interests, political instability, and socio-economic pressures often impede conservation efforts, complicating the already complex landscape of wildlife conservation.

Amidst these challenges, however, lie opportunities for innovative solutions and collaborative action. Advances in technology, such as remote sensing, data analytics, and genetic monitoring, offer unprecedented insights into wildlife populations and ecosystems, enabling more targeted and effective conservation strategies. Moreover, the growing awareness of the intrinsic value of biodiversity, coupled with increased public engagement and advocacy, provides a powerful catalyst for conservation action and policy change.

Wildlife conservation faces formidable challenges, ranging from habitat loss and climate change to illegal wildlife trade and invasive species. However, by leveraging technological innovations, fostering international cooperation, and mobilizing public support, there exist opportunities to address these challenges and safeguard the future of Earth's precious biodiversity. We will explore how green computing can be harnessed to advance wildlife conservation efforts, highlighting the synergies between technology and conservation in addressing these pressing challenges and seizing opportunities for positive change.

In the ongoing battle to conserve wildlife and protect biodiversity, technological interventions offer a promising avenue for innovation and progress. Here, we identify key opportunities for leveraging technology to address pressing challenges in wildlife conservation, while also highlighting the transformative potential of these interventions in driving positive change.

One of the most significant opportunities for technological intervention in wildlife conservation lies in the realm of data analytics and remote sensing. Advances in satellite imagery, drones, and sensor networks enable conservationists to gather vast amounts of data on wildlife populations, habitat dynamics, and ecosystem health with unprecedented detail and accuracy. By harnessing the power of big data analytics and machine learning algorithms, researchers can analyze these data to identify patterns, trends, and correlations that inform conservation decision-making and management strategies.

Furthermore, technological innovations such as GPS tracking devices and radio telemetry enable researchers to monitor animal movements, behavior, and population dynamics in real time, providing valuable insights into species' ecology and informing conservation strategies. By tracking the movements of endangered species and identifying key habitat corridors and migration routes, conservationists can develop targeted conservation interventions to mitigate human-wildlife conflicts, protect critical habitats, and promote landscape connectivity.

Another promising avenue for technological intervention in wildlife conservation lies in the development of bioacoustic monitoring systems and acoustic sensors. These systems enable researchers to monitor wildlife populations and detect species' presence based on their vocalizations and other acoustic signals. By deploying acoustic monitoring networks in remote and inaccessible areas, conservationists can gather data on elusive and endangered species, assess population trends, and identify priority areas for conservation action.

Moreover, advances in genetic technologies, such as DNA barcoding and non-invasive genetic sampling techniques, offer powerful tools for monitoring wildlife populations and combating illegal wildlife trade. DNA analysis enables researchers to identify species, track individual animals, and assess genetic diversity with high precision, facilitating conservation genetics studies and informing breeding and reintroduction programs. Additionally, non-invasive genetic sampling techniques, such as scat analysis and hair trapping, enable researchers to collect genetic data from wildlife populations without the need for direct contact, minimizing disturbance and stress to animals.

In addition to these technological innovations, the advent of citizen science platforms and mobile applications provides opportunities for public engagement and crowd-sourced data collection in wildlife conservation. Citizen scientists can contribute valuable observations and data on wildlife sightings, habitat conditions, and environmental changes, augmenting traditional research efforts and expanding the reach of conservation initiatives. By harnessing the collective power of citizen scientists, conservationists can gather data on a scale and scope that would be otherwise unattainable, fostering public awareness, engagement, and stewardship of natural resources [6].

Technological interventions offer immense opportunities for advancing wildlife conservation efforts, from data analytics and remote sensing to genetic technologies and citizen science platforms. By harnessing the power of technology, conservationists can gather data, monitor wildlife populations, and inform conservation strategies with unprecedented precision and effectiveness. In the following section, we will explore how green computing can be leveraged to support and enhance these technological interventions, highlighting the synergies between technology and conservation in addressing the pressing challenges facing wildlife and biodiversity conservation.

3.4 GREEN COMPUTING SOLUTIONS FOR WILDLIFE CONSERVATION

In the quest to conserve wildlife and protect biodiversity, the integration of green computing solutions offers a promising avenue for innovation and sustainability. We delve into the application of energy-efficient computing in remote wildlife monitoring, exploring how technology can be harnessed to advance conservation efforts while minimizing environmental impact.

Remote wildlife monitoring plays a crucial role in conservation biology, enabling researchers to gather data on wildlife populations, behavior, and habitat use with minimal disturbance to animals and ecosystems. Traditional monitoring methods often involve manual observations, camera traps, and field surveys, which can be labor-intensive, time-consuming, and logistically challenging, particularly in remote and inaccessible areas.

Energy-efficient computing technologies offer a transformative solution to these challenges, enabling researchers to remotely monitor wildlife populations and ecosystems with unprecedented efficiency and precision. By leveraging a combination of sensor networks, remote sensing technologies, and data analytics, conservationists can gather real-time data on wildlife movements, habitat conditions, and environmental changes, facilitating evidence-based decision-making and targeted conservation interventions.

One of the key applications of energy-efficient computing in remote wildlife monitoring lies in the deployment of sensor networks and IoT (Internet of Things) devices. These devices, equipped with a range of sensors such as motion detectors, temperature sensors, and GPS trackers, enable researchers to collect continuous data on wildlife activity and environmental parameters in remote and challenging environments. By wirelessly transmitting data to centralized servers or cloud-based platforms, these sensor networks enable researchers to monitor wildlife populations and habitat conditions in real time, without the need for constant human presence in the field.

Moreover, advances in energy-efficient computing architectures, such as edge computing and fog computing, offer additional benefits for remote wildlife monitoring. Edge computing enables data processing and analysis to be performed closer to the source of data generation, reducing latency and bandwidth requirements while also minimizing energy consumption. Fog computing extends this concept further by distributing computing tasks across a network of edge devices, enabling distributed data processing and analysis in remote and resource-constrained environments.

In addition to sensor networks and edge computing, the integration of renewable energy sources such as solar and wind power offers opportunities to further reduce the environmental footprint of remote wildlife monitoring systems. By powering sensor networks and IoT devices with renewable energy sources, conservationists can minimize reliance on fossil fuels and reduce greenhouse gas emissions associated with data collection and transmission.

Furthermore, energy-efficient computing technologies enable researchers to optimize data collection and analysis workflows, maximizing the value of data collected from remote wildlife monitoring systems. By leveraging data analytics techniques such as machine learning and predictive modeling, researchers can extract valuable insights from large volumes of data, identify patterns and trends, and inform conservation strategies with unprecedented accuracy and efficiency [7].

Energy-efficient computing solutions offer a powerful toolkit for advancing remote wildlife monitoring and conservation efforts. By leveraging sensor networks, edge computing, renewable energy sources, and data analytics techniques, conservationists can gather real-time data on wildlife populations and ecosystems, inform evidence-based conservation decisions, and minimize environmental impact. In the section that follows, we will explore practical examples and case studies of energy-efficient computing solutions applied in wildlife conservation, highlighting the transformative potential of technology in safeguarding Earth's precious biodiversity.

In the realm of wildlife conservation, data analytics has emerged as a powerful tool for informing conservation decision-making, enabling researchers and practitioners to glean valuable insights from complex datasets and guide strategic interventions. In the next section, we showcase case studies that demonstrate the application of data analytics in wildlife conservation, highlighting innovative tools and applications that bridge green computing and wildlife protection.

3.5 CASE STUDIES BASED ON DATA ANALYTICS

3.5.1 Monitoring Elephant Movements in Africa

In Africa, the conservation of elephant populations is a critical priority, as these iconic megafaunas face numerous threats, including habitat loss, poaching, and human-wildlife conflicts. To address these challenges, conservationists have deployed GPS tracking collars on elephants to monitor their movements and behavior in real time. By collecting and analyzing GPS data, researchers can identify key habitat areas, migration routes, and hotspots of human-wildlife conflicts, enabling informed conservation decisions and targeted interventions to protect elephant populations and mitigate human-wildlife conflicts [8].

3.5.2 Protecting Endangered Species in the Amazon Rainforest

The Amazon rainforest harbors unparalleled biodiversity, but it is also under constant threat from deforestation, illegal logging, and land conversion for agriculture. To protect endangered species such as jaguars and giant river otters, conservationists have developed camera trap networks that capture images and videos of wildlife in their natural habitat. By analyzing camera trap data using machine learning algorithms, researchers can estimate population sizes, assess species distributions, and monitor changes in wildlife abundance over time. These insights inform conservation strategies and support efforts to safeguard the biodiversity of the Amazon rainforest [9].

3.5.3 Combatting Illegal Wildlife Trade in Southeast Asia

In Southeast Asia, illegal wildlife trade poses a significant threat to endangered species such as tigers, pangolins, and rhinoceros. To combat this illicit activity, conservation organizations have developed predictive analytics models that analyze large volumes of data, including market trends, social media posts, and online advertisements, to identify potential hotspots of illegal wildlife trade and trafficking. By leveraging these insights, law enforcement agencies can target their efforts more effectively, intercept illegal shipments, and dismantle criminal networks involved in wildlife trafficking, ultimately reducing the demand for illegal wildlife products and protecting vulnerable species from exploitation.

3.5.4 Monitoring Marine Protected Areas with Satellite Imagery

Marine protected areas (MPAs) play a crucial role in conserving marine biodiversity and supporting ecosystem health, but monitoring these vast and remote ocean environments poses logistical challenges. To overcome these challenges, researchers have developed remote sensing technologies that use satellite imagery to monitor changes in coral reef health, sea surface temperatures, and marine biodiversity in MPAs. By analyzing satellite data using machine learning algorithms, researchers can detect coral bleaching events, track the movement of marine species, and assess the effectiveness of conservation measures in MPAs, informing adaptive management strategies and ensuring the long-term sustainability of marine ecosystems [10].

Data analytics represents a powerful tool for informed conservation decision-making, enabling researchers and practitioners to extract valuable insights from complex datasets and guide strategic interventions to protect wildlife and biodiversity.

By showcasing case studies that highlight the application of data analytics in wildlife conservation, we demonstrate the transformative potential of technology in bridging green computing and wildlife protection, ultimately advancing efforts to safeguard Earth's precious biodiversity for future generations.

3.6 RAISING ENVIRONMENTAL AWARENESS

In the global effort to conserve wildlife and protect biodiversity, raising environmental awareness stands as a crucial pillar of action. Here, we delve into the role of green computing in educating and mobilizing communities for wildlife conservation, exploring innovative approaches that leverage technology to foster environmental stewardship and drive positive change.

Green computing offers a unique opportunity to engage and empower individuals and communities in conservation efforts through education, outreach, and advocacy. By harnessing the power of technology, conservation organizations can reach a broader audience, disseminate information effectively, and inspire collective action toward the protection of wildlife and ecosystems.

One of the key ways in which green computing facilitates environmental awareness is through the development of online educational resources and digital learning platforms. Conservation organizations, educational institutions, and government agencies can leverage digital technologies to create engaging and interactive educational materials, including webinars, e-learning courses, and virtual field trips, that raise awareness about wildlife conservation issues and inspire individuals to take action.

Moreover, social media platforms provide a powerful tool for mobilizing communities and amplifying conservation messages. By harnessing the reach and influence of social media networks, conservation organizations can engage with diverse audiences, share inspiring stories and conservation success stories, and encourage individuals to participate in conservation initiatives such as citizen science projects, community clean-up events, and fundraising campaigns.

Furthermore, green computing enables organizations to reduce their environmental footprint and model sustainable practices, thereby inspiring individuals and communities to adopt more eco-friendly behaviors in their own lives. By implementing energy-efficient computing technologies, reducing paper consumption, and minimizing waste generation, conservation organizations can demonstrate their commitment to environmental stewardship and encourage others to follow suit.

In addition to education and outreach efforts, green computing can also facilitate citizen science initiatives that empower individuals to contribute to wildlife conservation efforts in meaningful ways. By developing mobile applications and online platforms that enable users to report wildlife sightings, monitor environmental changes, and participate in research projects, conservation organizations can harness the collective power of citizen scientists to gather data, monitor wildlife populations, and inform conservation strategies.

Moreover, green computing can facilitate community-based conservation initiatives that empower local communities to take ownership of conservation efforts in their own backyard. By providing communities with access to technology and training in green computing practices, conservation organizations can support grassroots conservation projects, promote sustainable livelihoods, and foster a sense of stewardship and pride in local natural resources.

Green computing plays a vital role in raising environmental awareness and mobilizing communities for wildlife conservation. By leveraging technology to educate, engage, and empower individuals and communities, conservation organizations can inspire collective action toward the protection of wildlife and ecosystems, ultimately contributing to the long-term sustainability of our planet's precious biodiversity. In the following section, we will explore practical examples and case studies of green computing initiatives that are driving environmental awareness and community mobilization for wildlife conservation, highlighting the transformative potential of technology in fostering environmental stewardship and creating a more sustainable future for generations to come.

In today's interconnected world, digital platforms have emerged as powerful tools for disseminating information, fostering dialog, and mobilizing communities around pressing global issues. Among these issues, environmental conservation and sustainability stand as urgent priorities, requiring widespread awareness and collective action to address them effectively. Now, we explore the potential for digital platforms to serve as vehicles for environmental awareness, examining their capacity to reach diverse audiences, engage stakeholders, and catalyze positive change.

Digital platforms encompass a wide range of online channels, including social media networks, websites, blogs, podcasts, and mobile applications, each offering unique opportunities for communicating environmental messages and engaging audiences. These platforms provide a dynamic and interactive space where individuals can access information, share experiences, and participate in discussions related to environmental conservation and sustainability.

Social media networks, in particular, play a central role in disseminating environmental awareness to a global audience. Platforms such as Facebook, Twitter, Instagram, and LinkedIn enable organizations, activists, and individuals to share news, stories, images, and videos related to environmental issues, reaching millions of users around the world. By leveraging the viral nature of social media, environmental messages can quickly gain traction and reach audiences beyond traditional communication channels.

Moreover, digital platforms provide opportunities for two-way communication and engagement, allowing organizations to interact directly with their audience, respond to questions and concerns, and solicit feedback and input on conservation initiatives. This interactive dialog fosters a sense of community and collaboration among stakeholders, empowering individuals to become active participants in environmental conservation efforts.

Websites and blogs offer additional avenues for disseminating environmental awareness, providing organizations with a platform to publish articles, reports, infographics, and multimedia content that educate and inform audiences about environmental issues and solutions. Through search engine optimization (SEO) techniques and content marketing strategies, organizations can increase the visibility and reach of their online content, ensuring that it reaches a broader audience of interested individuals.

Podcasts have also emerged as popular channels for delivering environmental messages, offering audiences a convenient and accessible way to consume information while on the go. Environmental podcasts cover a wide range of topics, including climate change, biodiversity conservation, sustainable living, and environmental activism, providing listeners with insights, interviews, and stories that inspire and inform.

Mobile applications represent another powerful tool for disseminating environmental awareness, offering users interactive and engaging experiences that educate, motivate, and empower them to take action for the planet. Environmental apps cover diverse topics, from wildlife identification and habitat mapping to carbon footprint tracking and eco-friendly shopping, providing users with tools and resources to make informed decisions and live more sustainably.

Digital platforms hold immense potential for disseminating environmental awareness and mobilizing communities for action. By harnessing the reach, interactivity, and engagement capabilities of social media networks, websites, blogs, podcasts, and mobile applications, organizations can effectively communicate environmental messages, inspire behavioral change, and catalyze collective action toward a more sustainable future. In the sections that follow, practical examples are explored, and case studies are presented about digital platforms that are driving environmental awareness and mobilizing communities for environmental conservation, highlighting the transformative potential of technology in addressing the urgent challenges facing our planet.

3.7 COLLABORATIVE INITIATIVES

In the pursuit of effective wildlife conservation and environmental sustainability, collaborative initiatives that bring together diverse stakeholders from the IT industry, conservation organizations, and government bodies have emerged as a cornerstone of success. In this section, we showcase successful partnerships that exemplify the power of multi-stakeholder collaborations in driving positive change for the environment and biodiversity.

3.7.1 Partnership for Sustainable Cloud Computing

In recent years, the IT industry has increasingly recognized the importance of sustainability and environmental responsibility. Leading tech companies have forged partnerships with conservation organizations and government bodies to promote sustainable practices in cloud computing, one of the largest consumers of energy in the IT sector. Through initiatives such as the Partnership for Sustainable Cloud Computing, companies commit to reducing their carbon footprint, increasing energy efficiency, and investing in renewable energy sources to power data centers and cloud infrastructure. By collaborating with conservation organizations and government bodies, the IT industry can leverage its technological expertise and resources to drive innovation and promote environmental sustainability in the digital age [11].

3.7.2 Smart Parks Initiative

The Smart Parks Initiative represents a collaborative effort between conservation organizations, government agencies, and technology companies to leverage cutting-edge technologies such as sensor networks, remote sensing, and data analytics to enhance the management and protection of national parks and protected areas. By deploying sensor networks and IoT devices, park managers can monitor wildlife populations, detect illegal activities such as poaching and deforestation, and assess environmental conditions in real time. By partnering with technology companies and government bodies, conservation organizations can leverage technological innovations to improve conservation outcomes, enhance park management efficiency, and safeguard biodiversity for future generations.

3.7.3 Digital Conservation Platforms

Digital conservation platforms such as Earth observation satellites, biodiversity databases, and online mapping tools provide valuable resources for conservationists, researchers, and policymakers to monitor environmental changes, track wildlife populations, and prioritize conservation actions. These platforms are often developed through collaborative efforts between the IT industry, conservation organizations, and government bodies, leveraging expertise and resources from each stakeholder group. By sharing data, knowledge, and technology, collaborative initiatives such as digital conservation platforms enable stakeholders to make informed decisions, allocate resources effectively, and coordinate conservation efforts at local, regional, and global scales.

3.7.4 Public-Private Partnerships for Sustainable Supply Chains

Public-private partnerships play a crucial role in promoting sustainability and responsible sourcing practices in global supply chains. By collaborating with governments, conservation organizations, and industry partners, companies can develop and implement sustainability standards, certifications, and best practices to ensure that products are produced in an environmentally and socially responsible manner. Through initiatives such as the Roundtable on Sustainable Palm Oil (RSPO) and the Marine Stewardship Council (MSC), companies commit to sourcing raw materials such as palm oil and seafood from sustainable and certified sources, thereby reducing environmental impacts and supporting conservation efforts in ecologically sensitive areas.

Collaborative initiatives between the IT industry, conservation organizations, and government bodies represent a powerful force for driving positive change in environmental conservation and sustainability. By leveraging their respective expertise, resources, and networks, stakeholders can work together to develop innovative solutions, implement best practices, and achieve shared conservation goals. In the section that follows, we will explore additional examples and case studies of collaborative initiatives that demonstrate the transformative potential of multi-stakeholder collaborations in advancing environmental conservation and sustainability on a global scale.

3.8 CASE STUDIES BASED ON GREEN COMPUTING INITIATIVES

Now, some real-world case studies of green computing initiatives that have been implemented in wildlife conservation efforts are presented. These initiatives showcase the intersection of technology and environmental conservation, demonstrating how innovative solutions can drive positive outcomes for wildlife and ecosystems while minimizing environmental impact. Through these case studies, we aim to highlight the successes, challenges, and lessons learned from these projects, providing valuable insights for future conservation efforts.

3.8.1 SMART (Spatial Monitoring and Reporting Tool) Technology in Elephant Conservation

In the forests of Southeast Asia, elephants face numerous threats, including habitat loss, poaching, and human-wildlife conflicts. To address these challenges, conservation organizations have deployed SMART (Spatial Monitoring and Reporting Tool) technology, a suite of software tools that integrate GPS tracking, camera trap data, and remote sensing to monitor elephant movements, detect poaching activities, and assess habitat quality in real time. By analyzing data collected through SMART technology, conservationists can identify key conservation priorities, allocate resources effectively, and implement targeted interventions to protect elephant populations and their habitats.

Outcome: The use of SMART technology has led to significant improvements in elephant conservation efforts, including the identification of critical habitat areas, the detection of poaching incidents, and the implementation of anti-poaching patrols. By leveraging technology to monitor and protect elephants more effectively, conservation organizations have achieved measurable successes in reducing human-elephant conflicts and conserving vital habitat areas.

Lessons learned: The successful implementation of SMART technology highlights the importance of integrating data-driven approaches into wildlife conservation efforts. However, challenges remain, including the need for ongoing training and capacity building for field staff, ensuring data accuracy and reliability, and addressing technological limitations in remote and rugged environments. Moving forward, collaboration between conservation organizations, technology developers, and local communities will be essential to maximize the effectiveness of SMART technology in elephant conservation.

3.8.2 Satellite Monitoring of Marine Protected Areas

In the vast and remote ocean environments of the world's MPAs, monitoring and enforcement present significant challenges for conservationists. To address these challenges, researchers have turned to satellite monitoring technology, using high-resolution satellite imagery to assess changes in coral reef health, detect illegal fishing activities, and monitor marine biodiversity in MPAs. By analyzing satellite data, conservationists can identify areas of concern, prioritize conservation actions, and evaluate the effectiveness of MPA management strategies.

Outcome: Satellite monitoring has provided valuable insights into the health and status of marine ecosystems in MPAs, enabling researchers to detect coral bleaching events, track the movement of fishing vessels, and assess the impact of human activities on marine biodiversity. By leveraging satellite technology, conservation organizations have been able to make informed decisions and implement targeted interventions to protect and restore marine ecosystems in MPAs.

Lessons learned: While satellite monitoring offers immense potential for marine conservation, challenges remain, including the need for improved data resolution and accuracy, the development of standardized protocols for data analysis and interpretation, and the integration of satellite data with ground-truthing efforts and local knowledge. Moving forward, collaboration between researchers, government agencies, and local stakeholders will be critical to overcome these challenges and maximize the effectiveness of satellite monitoring in MPAs.

3.8.3 Energy-Efficient Computing in Wildlife Monitoring

In remote and inaccessible habitats, traditional methods of wildlife monitoring can be costly, time-consuming, and logistically challenging. To overcome these limitations, researchers have turned to energy-efficient computing technologies, using low-power sensors, drones, and remote cameras to collect data on wildlife populations and behavior. By deploying energy-efficient computing solutions, conservationists can monitor wildlife more effectively, reduce the environmental impact of monitoring efforts, and gather valuable data for conservation decision-making [12].

Outcome: Energy-efficient computing has revolutionized wildlife monitoring efforts, enabling researchers to collect vast amounts of data on wildlife populations and behavior with minimal environmental impact. By deploying low-power sensors and remote cameras, conservation organizations have been able to monitor wildlife more cost-effectively, gather data on rare and elusive species, and inform conservation strategies with unprecedented accuracy and efficiency.

Lessons learned: While energy-efficient computing offers significant benefits for wildlife monitoring, challenges remain, including the need for standardized protocols for data collection and analysis, the development of user-friendly interfaces for data visualization and interpretation, and the integration of technology with traditional ecological monitoring methods. Moving forward, collaboration between researchers, technology developers, and conservation practitioners will be essential to overcome these challenges and maximize the effectiveness of energy-efficient computing in wildlife conservation.

The case studies presented in this section, demonstrate the transformative potential of green computing initiatives in wildlife conservation efforts. By leveraging technology to monitor and protect wildlife more effectively, conservation organizations can achieve measurable successes in conserving biodiversity and safeguarding ecosystems for future generations. However, challenges remain, and ongoing collaboration between stakeholders will be essential to address these challenges and drive continued progress in environmental conservation.

3.9 CONCLUSION

In this exploration of the symbiotic relationship between green computing and wildlife conservation, we have uncovered a wealth of opportunities and potential for driving positive change. As we conclude our journey, let us summarize the key takeaways and emphasize the profound impact that green computing can have as a catalyst for sustainable development and wildlife protection.

Throughout this discourse, we have witnessed how green computing offers innovative solutions to address pressing environmental challenges while advancing wildlife conservation efforts. From energy-efficient computing technologies to data analytics and digital platforms, green computing empowers conservationists with tools and resources to monitor, protect, and restore ecosystems with unprecedented efficiency and precision.

One of the central themes that emerged from our exploration is the interconnectedness of technology and nature, and the transformative potential that arises when these two realms converge. By harnessing the power of technology, conservation organizations, government bodies, and the IT industry can collaborate to develop innovative solutions that address the complex and interconnected challenges facing wildlife and ecosystems.

Moreover, green computing not only enhances the effectiveness of conservation efforts but also promotes sustainability and environmental stewardship in the broader context of human development. By reducing energy consumption, minimizing environmental impact, and promoting responsible resource management, green computing serves as a driving force for sustainable development, ensuring that future generations inherit a healthy and vibrant planet.

As we look to the future, it is clear that the integration of green computing principles into wildlife conservation efforts will play a pivotal role in shaping the trajectory of environmental sustainability. By embracing technology as a tool for positive change and fostering collaboration among stakeholders, we can unlock new opportunities for innovation, resilience, and progress in safeguarding Earth's precious biodiversity.

The symbiotic relationship between green computing and wildlife conservation represents a paradigm shift in our approach to environmental stewardship. By recognizing the potential of technology as a catalyst for sustainable development and wildlife protection, we can harness its transformative power to create a more resilient, equitable, and sustainable future for all life on Earth. As stewards of this planet, let us commit to harnessing the power of green computing to protect and preserve the natural world for generations to come.

REFERENCES

1. Lannelongue, L., Aronson, H.E.G., Bateman, A. et al. (2023). GREENER principles for environmentally sustainable computational science. Nature Computational Science 3, 514–521. https://doi.org/10.1038/s43588-023-00461-y
2. Egoh, B.N., Nyelele, C., Holl, K.D., Bullock, J.M., Carver, S., Sandom, C.J. (2021). Rewilding and restoring nature in a changing world. PLoS ONE, 16(7), e0254249. https://doi.org/10.1371/journal.pone.0254249
3. Pazienza, A., Baselli, G., Vinci, D.C. et al. (2024). A holistic approach to environmentally sustainable computing. Innovations in Systems and Software Engineering 20, 347–371. https://doi.org/10.1007/s11334-023-00548-9
4. Awasthi, K., Awasthi, S. (2023). Green Computing: A Sustainable and Eco-friendly Approach for Conservation of Energy (A Contribution to Save Environment). In: Awasthi, S., Sanyal, G., Travieso-Gonzalez, C.M., Kumar Srivastava, P., Singh, D.K., Kant, R. (eds) Sustainable Computing. Springer, Cham. https://doi.org/10.1007/978-3-031-13577-4_20
5. Combating Poaching and Wildlife Trafficking, March 2, 2015: https://www.undp.org/publications/combating-poaching-and-wildlife-trafficking
6. Front. Ecol. Evol., 15 June 2021. Sec. Conservation and Restoration Ecology, Volume 9 - 2021 | https://doi.org/10.3389/fevo.2021.682124
7. Long, L.D., Toan, H.L., Binh, T.T., Trung, N.Q., Truong, N.S. (2024). Machine Learning-Based Predictive Models for Energy Consumption Estimation in Energy-Efficient Building Envelope Design. In: Reddy, J.N., Wang, C.M., Luong, V.H., Le, A.T. (eds) Proceedings of the Third International Conference on Sustainable Civil Engineering and Architecture. ICSCEA 2023. Lecture Notes in Civil Engineering, vol 442. Springer, Singapore. https://doi.org/10.1007/978-981-99-7434-4_58
8. 2022 ELEPHANT CONSERVATION REPORT, African Wildlife Foundation, https://www.awf.org/sites/default/files/202208/2022%20Elephant%20Conservation%20Progress%20Report.pdf
9. Sala, O.E., et al. (2000). Global biodiversity scenarios for the year 2100. Science, 287(5459), 1770–1774.
10. Halpern, B.S., et al. (2010). Global map of human impact on marine ecosystems. Science, 319(5865), 948–952.
11. Dangelico, R.M., Vocalelli, D. (2017). "Green" practices and corporate performance: An empirical analysis of the IT industry. Journal of Business Ethics, 140(2), 365–385.
12. Roy, S., Le, C. (2014). Energy-efficient computing in wildlife monitoring. Environmental Monitoring and Assessment, 186(2), 861–873.

4 Role of Remote Sensing and GIS in Sustainable Computing Practices

Greetta Pinheiro, Aditya Raj, and Ishfaq Hussain Rather

4.1 INTRODUCTION

Sustainable computing, commonly called green computing, focuses on the development and optimization of computer networks, systems, chips, and software to improve efficiency by effectively utilizing energy, sustainable recycling, and reducing adverse environmental impacts. "Sustainable computing" encompasses green practices for mitigating the detrimental effects of technological footprints on the environment. Due to rapid technological advancements, numerous mechanisms, software solutions, and devices are being developed, and extensive research efforts are being carried out to enhance their green computing capabilities. In contrast, the increasing number of cloud data centers presents a major challenge due to their exorbitant energy consumption and significant CO_2 emissions, compelling enterprises to adopt sustainable production paradigms.

The international plan "Transforming Our World: The 2030 Agenda for Sustainable Development (Agenda, 2030)," as illustrated in Figure 4.1, was introduced by the United Nations (UN) during the 2014 UN Sustainable Development Summit to tackle global issues. To address problems such as inequality, climate change impact, and poverty, 17 sustainable development goals (SDGs) were proposed. These SDGs gained widespread global recognition, and in September 2015, most organizations officially adopted them. The efficient and effective progress of the different indicators of the SDGs is monitored using geospatial technologies. Geospatial technologies include technological frameworks integrating location data, i.e., spatial information. The data generation using a wide range of sensors and monitoring the various sustainable development-related measures are encompassed in these technologies. Typically, geospatial technologies are a collection of three distinct systems, namely geospatial information system (GIS), global positioning system (GPS), and remote sensing (RS) [1]. In RS, the information extraction is performed using electromagnetic sensors that sense the spectral and spatial features of the land cover. In comparison to ground-based techniques, RS is cost-effective and rapid. Integrating in-situ monitoring with RS data provides reliable geospatial information, which helps comprehensively assess disasters, change detection, risks, and natural resources. This information helps in informed decision-making, project operations, and policy formulation related to sustainable development.

 DOI: 10.1201/9781003471356-4

FIGURE 4.1 Sustainable Development 2030 Agenda includes the 17 SDGs.

The RS images are the primary data source that provides the earth observation (EO) data [2], containing diverse spatial [3], spectral [4], and temporal [5–7] resolutions. The satellite or airborne platforms mounted with LiDAR or optical sensors acquire the images [5, 8], which help monitor atmospheric and surface phenomena. However, there are various challenges in leveraging RS imagery for EO and monitoring applications. For example, real-time and continuous monitoring data is required in disaster mitigation and monitoring applications. However, the long intervals between the orbital revisiting times of RS satellites impede their applicability for such applications [9]. Conversely, while RS excels in delineating natural and physical geographical attributes, it fails to capture the socioeconomic environment patterns, such as human activity patterns or socioeconomic interconnectivity between urban centers [10]. GIS is an ideal platform for integrating spatial and attribute data related to environment and natural resources, facilitating optimal land use plan generation at a micro-watershed scale. Moreover, GPS technology enables precise in-situ measurements of different terrain parameters, which creates baseline and derivative information on natural resources for different developmental initiatives. Weather forecasting and advances in telecommunication further enhance the effectiveness of optimal land use and action plans. RS functions as a pivotal application for geospatial data acquisition, while the spatial location on Earth's surface is obtained using GPS, and the GIS is responsible for the complete management of the acquired geospatial data, consisting of tasks such as data acquisition, preprocessing, storage, manipulation, and dissemination [1].

Geospatial technologies provide invaluable data for various applications, including but not limited to land use land cover (LULC) mapping [11, 12], disaster monitoring [13], and change detection [13]. Due to the rapid technological advancements in recent decades, there was an exponential surge in data generated from various sensors, giving rise to the term RS big data [14]. The geographic location coordinates integrated with the generated big RS data from smart devices and handheld GPS modules have been part of our daily lives. They are efficient in practical domains like environmental monitoring and disaster response [15].

Sustainability encompasses qualitative and quantitative continuity in resource utilization, reflecting a state of equilibrium between human activities influenced by technological advancements, knowledge acquisition, social behavior, and food production [16]. Various perspectives on sustainability, including ecological, economic, and social viewpoints, necessitate an optimal balance between ecological and socioeconomic considerations. Sustainability applications address global challenges such as ozone layer depletion, deforestation, resource degradation, and local concerns about maintaining socioeconomic systems.

To achieve sustainable development objectives, it is imperative to understand the status, dynamics, and constraints of natural resources. Spaceborne multispectral measurements provide a comprehensive overview of large regions at regular intervals and hold significant potential for providing reliable information on diverse natural resources such as minerals, soils, groundwater, forest cover, and marine resources in a cost-effective and timely manner.

Today, RS and GIS, considered a scientific cornerstone, find applications across nearly every facet of Earth and environmental phenomena. In the 21st century, given the paramount importance of sustainable development, this chapter provides a concise overview and discussion of the applications and opportunities associated with RS and GIS technology integration for monitoring and extracting information on Earth's observation data to support SDGs. Additionally, we address emerging challenges and future directions, which hold significance for practitioners, researchers, and professionals involved in decision-making across sectors such as urban development, environment, resource management, mining, forestry, and agriculture aligned with SDGs.

4.2 REMOTE SENSING

RS involves detecting and monitoring Earth's surface features and geo-bio-physical characteristics using electromagnetic radiation (EMR) as interaction and without direct contact. Analysis of propagated signals' characteristics, such as wavelength and frequency of EMR, facilitates the study of various objects on Earth's surface, atmosphere, or oceans. Typically, RS uses artificial satellites or airborne sensors to detect Earth's surface features. Besides satellites, geospatial data collection methods include aerial photography employing unmanned aerial vehicles (UAVs), balloons, and aircraft. RS involves recording emitted or reflected energy (i.e., EMR), followed by data processing and analysis. Based on the source of EMR, there are two categories of RS: "active" or "passive." Passive RS predominates in contemporary RS systems, where solar energy is used as the EMR source. Passive remote sensors consist of spectroradiometers, radiometers, spectrometers, and imaging radiometers. In contrast, active RS systems illuminate the observed object or scene by incorporating an inherent source of EMR, including scatterometers, LiDAR, radar, and laser altimeters. In contrast to in-situ observation methods, RS does not require physical contact with the objects under study. RS applications span various fields such as geography, hydrology, geology, natural resource management, land surveying, LULC monitoring, and [18–22]. While the advent of artificial satellites marked a significant milestone in RS, its use predates the launch of the first artificial satellite [17].

Moreover, RS applications are essential in commerce, intelligence, military, planning, economics, etc. [17]. Over recent years, RS has experienced remarkable development, attributable to the proliferation of EO satellites, advancements in tools and processing techniques, and vast amounts of RS big data availability for novel applications [15, 18].

In recent decades, RS tools have been extensively utilized across various temporal, spectral, and spatial scales for different applications [19]. Due to the technological advancements in RS and the availability of extensive datasets, it was widely used for assessing sustainable development initiatives [20–24]. RS offers archived and near-real-time data on Earth systems, contributing to widespread adoption [19]. It finds application across various domains within Earth system science to procure spatial information, enabling its application in addressing global socioeconomic, ecological, and environmental challenges. RS facilitates the acquisition of synoptic views of spatial information at different local, regional, and global levels, thereby expediting decision-making processes [19]. RS is the primary surveying technology, particularly in inaccessible or remote locations, due to its ability to gather information directly.

Various research studies have explored how RS can assist in sustainable development, covering areas such as natural hazards, environmental assessments, and socioeconomic progress [23, 25–27]. For instance, [28], in his research on sustainable forest management, used RS, while [29] developed a global vegetation index for monitoring plant growth dynamics. Moreover, the authors in [30] have used RS data to investigate the impact of zoning on vegetation indices and urban ecosystem temperatures and [25] used RS as the primary data source for mapping water resources across different terrains. In his research, Van Westen [31] reviewed the use of RS in natural disaster management, highlighting its contribution to disaster prevention, mitigation, and post-disaster assistance.

Machine learning (ML) and deep learning (DL) techniques, such as decision trees, random forests, support vector machines, and convolutional neural networks, have enhanced RS data analysis for socioeconomic monitoring and environmental assessments since the early 1990s. Despite earlier limitations due to RS image resolution, recent developments in platforms and interfaces, including cloud platforms like Google Earth Engine and graphics processing units, have significantly enhanced the monitoring and mapping of sustainable development applications.

Moreover, the surge in global collaborations within the RS community and various social media platforms has propelled the increased usage of RS for sustainable development assessments. The proliferation of open-source RS software and sophisticated analytical tools further contributes to the expanded use of RS for monitoring the environment and natural resources.

4.3 GEOGRAPHIC INFORMATION SYSTEMS

GIS denotes a computerized system designed to acquire, analyze, store, query, manage, and visualize spatial or geographic data [1]. GIS's ability to integrate diverse data types with geographic location information makes it a powerful decision-making tool [32–35]. Geospatial data consists of the attributes of spatial features and geographic location features. Besides geospatial data, GIS includes additional parts such as hardware, software, personnel, and organizational structures. The GIS system is illustrated in Figure 4.2. It finds utility across diverse sectors, including individuals, organizations, research institutions, scholars, healthcare entities, corporations, and governmental bodies at various levels. The applications of GIS are multifaceted, ranging from RS, wildlife management, natural hazard assessment, waste management, natural resource management, hydrology, land-use planning, and regulation of riparian zones.

Furthermore, GIS applies to public health, emergency planning, military operations, and transportation. In water resources studies, owing to the spatial nature of data involved, GIS has garnered widespread adoption for hydrological modeling [36]. It facilitates the digital depiction of watershed features through LULC maps, soil maps, and digital elevation models (DEMs). GIS has become indispensable due to the prevalence of geographic attributes in most information in water resources planning and management concerning wastewater, groundwater, surface water, or stormwater systems [37]. According to the American Water Works Association (AWWA), in 2000, various GIS technologies were utilized by approximately 90% of water-related projects in the USA. The GIS practices have been on an upward trajectory with a significant increase in users. Shamsi [37] delineate several advantages of GIS, including its speediness compared to traditional tools, leading to enhanced productivity and efficiency, thereby saving time and costs.

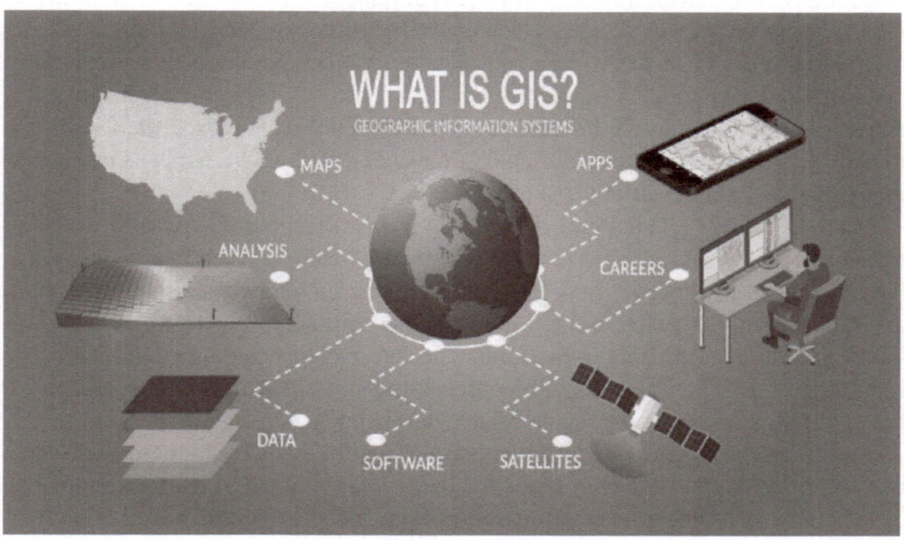

FIGURE 4.2 GIS system. (Source: https://gisgeography.com/what-is-gis/.)

Furthermore, GIS fosters improved communication, stakeholder cooperation, and project management [38–41]. Shamsi [37] expound on various GIS applications in water resource systems. At the same time, the authors in [39, 40] portray GIS as a medium for communication, highlighting its evolution into a tool for disseminating information to the public. The myriad applications and advantages of GIS permeate various disciplines.

GIS is crucial in decision-making across physical, social, and economic realms. These tools facilitate the acquisition of spatial data from diverse sources, enabling swift data processing and customization to meet the requirements of multidisciplinary analyses, studies, and forecasts [42]. GIS tools are pivotal in collecting, organizing, editing, processing, updating, and disseminating spatial data. They prove particularly valuable in amalgamating input data from various origins, employing diverse methodologies and techniques, ranging from initial field data collection to fully automated systems devoid of human intervention. Through data processing from multiple sources, GIS tools yield novel information and products [36].

Maintaining a delicate equilibrium between spatial organization, ecological sustainability, societal acceptance, and economic viability poses significant challenges in land management. This complexity is amplified in rural areas, where development objectives should prioritize spatial, social, economic, and environmental considerations. Achieving these objectives necessitates active engagement of local communities. Adopting advanced GIS tools facilitates the dissemination of accurate information and enhances the community's awareness. Spatial Information Infrastructure is implemented to foster integration and ensure widespread access to various geospatial information maintained and updated by public administrative bodies. This framework directly manifests the INSPIRE Directive, which promotes interoperability and harmonizes European spatial data [43].

4.4 SUSTAINABILITY

The "sustainability" concept originated in 1713 when the German equivalent term "nachhaltigkeit" was introduced by German scientist Hans Carl von Carlowitz, specifically within the forestry domain [44]. Sustainability has been considered a guiding principle in forestry since the 18th century [45]. Since the publication of the Brundtland Report in 1987, sustainability has been formalized as a policy concept. Sustainable development was defined in this report as "development that meets the needs of the present without compromising the ability of future generations to meet their own needs" [46]. Subsequently, the sustainable development principle gained global attention to form better policies. Since then, sustainability has become a ubiquitous concept across diverse fields of science and technology, including agriculture [47], hydrology and water resource management [48, 49], socio-ecological systems [50], business and marketing [51], and tourism [52].

Sustainability entails qualitative and quantitative continuity in resource utilization [53]. Gallopín [54] defines sustainability as a function of the system's outputs over time. The scope of sustainability consists of global challenges such as deforestation, climate change, ozone layer depletion, natural resource depletion, and local and regional concerns related to ecosystem and socio-ecosystem maintenance [53, 55]. It is necessary to examine sustainability at finer spatial scales, such as regional or local levels, to advance the objective of global sustainability [55]. Nidumolu et al. [56] describe the irreplaceable nature of sustainable development in their research paper. The critical role of science and technology in sustainability has been identified and studied to ensure the needs of future generations. Over time, the technological advancements and contributions of numerous scientific academies, research organizations researchers, and practitioners worldwide have contributed toward sustainability [57]. Different initiatives have immensely promoted sustainability, spanning industrial ecology, energy systems, and ecosystem resilience [57].

4.5 ROLE OF RS AND GIS

The main aim of sustainable development lies in achieving social and economic progress while concurrently managing and preserving natural resources [26]. In this context, the applications combining RS and GIS have gained paramount importance for EO, aiding in comprehending Earth surfaces' geological, ecological, hydrological, environmental, and physical attributes in alignment with SDGs. The availability of tools and information is crucial for strengthening the capabilities of national statistical offices and data systems. This will enable them to provide accurate, detailed, and timely access to high-quality data. The primary objective of these tools and information is to enhance data capabilities in developing countries, including landlocked and small island developing states, African nations, and least-developed countries.

RS provides impartial data, while GIS is crucial in decision support systems for spatial analysis and managing natural resources databases. RS and GIS have been used in cartography for a long time, but the first artificial satellite, Sputnik 1, launched by the Soviet Union on October 4, 1957, marked the beginning of satellite RS [58]. Over time, there have been many remote sensors created with different abilities that have greatly improved our understanding of the Earth's surface for a variety of purposes. These sensors have given us regional and global views that have helped us identify, understand, and solve environmental problems on an unprecedented scale. In recent years, there have been advancements in remote sensors, such as the deployment of satellites that can capture higher frequency and resolution images across different dimensions like spectral, radiometric, and spatial aspects compared to their earlier versions.

A notable example is the Landsat mission, which has been providing satellite imagery since 1972, primarily for public welfare. The Landsat program has undergone significant advancements over the years. It has transitioned from Landsat-MSS data that had a spatial resolution of 60–80 meters and four spectral bands to Landsat-TM data that offers a higher spatial resolution of 30 meters and seven spectral bands, covering a broader range of the electromagnetic spectrum. The Landsat 8 satellite orbits 438 miles above Earth, completing 14 orbits daily and capturing 400 scenes using infrared sensors, facilitating an entire Earth scan every 16 days [59].

Landsat imagery has been crucial in various research studies for agriculture, disaster management, forestry, hydrology, and land use/land cover change.

Furthermore, the advent of high-spatial-resolution satellites such as Worldview, RapidEye, Sentinel, KompSat, TripleSat, ALOS, GeoEye, Pléiades, SkySat, and SPOT has augmented efforts to generate information on natural resources in recent years. Additionally, advancements in hyperspectral sensing and microwave remote sensors have provided opportunities to glean finer details on natural resources and overcome challenges posed by adverse weather conditions. Polarimetric images derived from microwave energy offer insights into vegetation structure, soil properties, and geological features. At the same time, radar interferometry enables the generation of DEMs to monitor phenomena such as glaciers, volcanic eruptions, and land subsidence.

Moreover, the emergence of satellites like Suomi-NPP VIIRS enables global measurements of near-infrared and nocturnal visible light, which are invaluable for climate studies and Earth science [60, 61]. Beyond scientific research, such data aids in monitoring nighttime phenomena, anthropogenic light emissions, and humanitarian efforts such as assessing demographic changes associated with conflicts and mapping poverty.

In addition to satellite-based data collection, the Global Navigation Satellite System (GNSS) has emerged as a vital tool for data acquisition [62–63]. Initially pioneered by the USA, GNSS technology is now adopted globally, with many countries operating satellite constellations. These systems provide precise location data and support various applications ranging from navigation in smartwatches to safe navigation for aircraft, drones, and autonomous vehicles. Regional augmentation systems further enhance precision and safety in navigation and are utilized for monitoring atmospheric conditions, precision agriculture, landslides, and structural deformation.

RS and GPS technologies-based data are amalgamated with various spatial and non-spatial attributes within GIS, thereby facilitating their utilization in the formulation of action plans or developmental strategies aimed at fostering sustainable development. The usability of combined data is subject to the particular information needs of a community. These needs may encompass different tasks, such as resource identification, pollution modeling, water management, traffic or sewer management, and disaster prediction. These tasks aim to reduce risks and build resilience in the community. The TIGER system, developed by the US Census and Geological Survey, stands as a prominent example of GIS technology. It integrates data and map formats containing land features such as buildings, roads, water bodies, political boundaries, and administrative divisions. This integration enables the overlaying of demographic data for various applications, thus facilitating spatial analysis. These technologies are essential in helping stakeholders understand the complex relationships and dependencies involved in achieving the SDGs. They are important because they improve the capabilities of national statistical offices and data systems to ensure access to timely, accurate, detailed, and high-quality data. These resources are mainly focused on developing countries, including landlocked and small island developing states, African nations, and least-developed countries [65].

The prominence of geospatial data has emerged in recent times as a critical and influential factor with direct and indirect implications for the developmental efforts of nations. Consequently, with geospatial technologies and RS, policymakers, including governmental bodies, are empowered to make informed decisions about agriculture, forestry, mining, land management, urban development, environmental conservation, and water resource management. Notably, research conducted in Namibia demonstrates that EO-derived outcomes hold considerable potential for supplementing national statistics or serving as primary data sources following validation through ground-truthing [66]. Against the backdrop of the SDGs, the subsequent discourse delves into various practical implementations of geospatial technologies and RS.

Addressing poverty is a significant challenge in pursuing development and sustainability. Different communities necessitate tailored approaches for upliftment. The integration of remotely sensed satellite data with state-of-the-art machine-learning techniques has facilitated the task of global mapping and prediction of poverty. Using indicators such as deforestation, environmental variables, and night lights captured via satellite imagery aids in delineating the geographical prevalence of poverty and its interplay with factors like public health and food security.

Developed countries are implementing zero-emission mandates to combat climate change. However, RS combined with geospatial analysis provides a way to assess the suitability of sites for solar and wind energy generation [67, 68]. Moreover, national-level studies have the potential to pinpoint high-priority investment prospects for clean energy initiatives [69] and have extensively examined global offshore and onshore wind energy potentials concerning topographic features, land use patterns, and environmental constraints.

Integrated sensors measure various environmental parameters, generate new information, and facilitate data sharing through WebGIS, emphasizing the importance of deriving actionable insights beyond mere sensor concatenation [70]. A comprehensive review is required to integrate geospatial technologies with various sensors in order to understand urban systems better [71]. Responsible consumption and production are integral to maintaining sustainability, with RS proving invaluable in monitoring the exploitation beyond sustainable levels of other natural resources, water, grasslands, and forests [72–74]. A holistic approach is essential given the interconnectedness of SDGs. Monitoring climate alongside Earth's surface resources is crucial for sustainable environmental management. Both microwave and optical RS systems monitor climatic factors, while geospatial technologies like Google Earth facilitate web-based visualization [75].

The aquatic ecosystem holds significant importance in maintaining the equilibrium of Earth's ecosystem. Continuous monitoring of sea temperature, coastal eutrophication levels, and plastic debris accumulation in oceans is imperative. Satellite imagery has become crucial for mapping sea surface temperature and evaluating seagrass thermal dynamics [76]. Moreover, the concentration of chlorophyll-a, a key regulator of eutrophication, can be assessed through satellite imagery [44]. Satellite data has also facilitated the identification of major plastic pollutants contributing to debris formation, prompting the development of observation systems based on satellite tracking [77].

4.6 APPLICATIONS OF RS AND GIS IN ACHIEVING SUSTAINABILITY GOALS

Integrating RS and geographic information systems (GIS) into sustainable computing practices enhances data-driven decision-making and presents a significant opportunity to address critical social, environmental, and economic challenges outlined in the 17 SDGs and are illustrated in Figure 4.3.

Here is a detailed elaboration on how RS and GIS contribute to achieving specific SDGs:

Goal 2: Ensuring food security represents a crucial aspect of sustainable development, epitomized by SDG 2, "Zero Hunger." RS technology not only helps map and estimate crop yields but also assesses land suitability for agriculture based on geo-climatic parameters. Additionally, micro-level geospatial tools' implementation is pivotal for drainage pattern analysis, groundwater mapping, variable rate application, and the efficient management of agricultural inputs. Generally, high-resolution satellites are more conducive to local-level applications, whereas mid-resolution satellites offer insights at regional or continental scales.

FIGURE 4.3 Applications of GIS and RS.

Goal 6: Geospatial analysis has long been leveraged in public health, notably for mapping disease outbreaks and identifying their sources. Advanced satellite imagery has enabled scientists to map vector habitats and track disease outbreaks with greater accuracy. By analyzing various geospatial variables, researchers can identify disease hotspots and understand how poverty and other factors affect disease spread. These findings are vital for disease elimination efforts and improving public health outcomes. Vector-borne diseases, in particular, are closely intertwined with access to clean water and sanitation, aligning with the objectives of SDG 6. RS techniques have been instrumental in monitoring changes in water quality, surface water mapping, and supporting water resource management initiatives in both regional and long-term contexts. Efforts have been made to use European satellite data, notably through the Sentinel-1 Program, to aid water management in low-income countries. Different methods have been explored to support water and sanitation goals [67].

Goal 7: Affordable and Clean Energy: RS and GIS technologies offer valuable insights for optimizing energy infrastructure and facilitating the transition toward renewable energy sources. Through advanced spatial analysis and modeling, these tools aid in identifying suitable locations for solar, wind, and hydroelectric installations. Furthermore, GIS-based energy modeling facilitated effective energy planning and management, resulting in improved energy efficiency and decreased dependency on fossil fuels. By leveraging RS and GIS, stakeholders contribute indispensably to advancing SDG 7 objectives by promoting the adoption of clean and affordable energy solutions.

Goal 8: Gives the importance of eradicating forced labor, modern slavery, and child labor. RS observations can help identify modern slavery within industries, countries, or regions, facilitating preventive and eradication efforts. Examples include mapping industries such as fish processing or fishing, crop harvesting, and mining [42, 78]. In some cases, RS can also map environmental degradation like deforestation, encroachment, and pollution, highlighting the environmental dimensions of contemporary enslavement.

Goal 9: Industry, Innovation, and Infrastructure: Sustainable computing practices empowered by RS and GIS technologies stimulate innovation within the IT sector. These practices drive the development of eco-friendly hardware, energy-efficient software, and sustainable data center designs. By promoting green computing initiatives, stakeholders contribute to establishing resilient infrastructure and sustainable industrialization, aligning with the objectives of SDG 9. RS and GIS provide critical support in optimizing resource allocation, enhancing operational efficiency, and minimizing environmental impacts across various industries.

Goal 11: Sustainable Cities and Communities: RS and GIS have a pivotal role in the planning and managing of sustainable urban environments. These technologies support informed decision-making processes by providing detailed insights into land use, transportation networks, and infrastructure development. GIS-based urban planning tools enable stakeholders to optimize resource allocation, improve disaster resilience, and enhance access to essential services, creating inclusive, safe, and sustainable cities as envisioned in SDG 11.

Goal 12: Responsible Consumption and Production: Green computing practices facilitated by RS and GIS technologies promote responsible consumption and production patterns within the IT sector. These practices focus on reducing energy consumption, minimizing electronic waste, and optimizing resource utilization. By adopting sustainable procurement policies and lifecycle assessment methodologies, stakeholders can minimize the environmental footprint of computing activities and promote sustainable consumption patterns, thereby contributing to the objectives of SDG 12.

Goal 13: Climate Action: RS and GIS technologies provide valuable tools for monitoring and addressing the impacts of climate change. By enabling the monitoring of deforestation, land degradation, and urban sprawl, RS data facilitates informed decision-making processes—GIS-based spatial analysis and modeling support climate change adaptation and mitigation strategies by identifying climate-related risks and vulnerabilities. By integrating RS and GIS technologies, stakeholders can contribute to SDG 13 objectives by enhancing resilience, reducing emissions, and promoting sustainable land use and resource management practices.

Goal 15: Life on Land: RS and GIS are critical in monitoring and conserving terrestrial ecosystems, biodiversity hotspots, and natural habitats. GIS-based land use planning tools aid in identifying ecologically sensitive areas, prioritizing conservation efforts, and mitigating deforestation and habitat loss. By leveraging RS and GIS technologies, stakeholders contribute to preserving biodiversity and conserving terrestrial ecosystems, thereby supporting the objectives of SDG 15. RS technologies offer vital ground truth evidence concerning land surface dynamics. Forest cover, a significant indicator of land surface conditions, undergoes changes in total area and proportion of degraded land, which is essential for SDG monitoring. Utilizing EO data enables the mapping of land cover changes, leveraging the advantages of broad temporal and spatial coverage, standardized data production, frequent updates, and cost-effectiveness of open EO solutions [66]. Actions for restoration can be formulated based on estimated natural resource losses [28, 45, 73, 79, 80]. However, challenges persist in satellite monitoring, particularly in terms of temporal resolution and data availability [81]. The emergence of UAVs as viable alternatives for environmental monitoring offers improved spatial and temporal resolutions at a lower cost than conventional methods, which is particularly beneficial for biomass, forest, and vegetation monitoring.

Goal 17: Partnerships for the Goals: Collaboration and partnerships between governments, academia, industry stakeholders, and civil society organizations are essential for leveraging RS and GIS technologies to achieve the SDGs. Stakeholders maximize the impact of sustainable computing practices on SDG implementation by fostering multi-stakeholder partnerships, sharing knowledge and best practices, and promoting technology transfer and capacity-building initiatives. Through collective action and collaboration, stakeholders accelerate progress toward a more sustainable future.

The final two SDGs focus on fostering peace and partnerships to bolster SDGs. Recognizing the interconnectedness between human societies and the environment, collaborative efforts among stakeholders are essential. Examples such as the Himalayas providing freshwater to neighboring countries like India and Bangladesh and the Amazon rainforest spanning multiple nations in South America underscore the need for international cooperation in natural resource conservation and disaster prevention [82].

In addition to SDG applications, numerous studies delve into specific aspects of geospatial technology. Organizations such as the Committee on EO Satellites and Group on EOs highlight the importance of EO in supporting the global indicator framework for SDGs. Research studies shed light on the critical role of EO in aligning with the 2030 Agenda and monitoring progress toward associated targets. Additionally, they establish detailed connections between RS data and essential variables for SDGs. Likewise, Holloway and Mengersen [26] review statistical machine-learning methods and SDG RS applications. A wealth of information on SDG technology applications can be found across various scholarly publications.

4.7 CONCLUSION

The technological advancements in computing technologies over the past decade have brought forth various environmental challenges, necessitating the adoption of sustainable practices in the computing realm. The emergence of green computing as a strategic response underscores the importance of integrating environmental considerations into computing practices. In this context, the convergence of GIS and RS offers promising avenues for addressing these challenges. By leveraging the analytical capabilities of GIS and the rich data provided by RS, stakeholders can develop innovative solutions to monitor and manage environmental resources effectively. This chapter highlights the transformative potential of GIS and RS in advancing sustainable computing practices. These technologies can contribute significantly to environmental conservation efforts through interdisciplinary collaboration and innovative applications, such as climate change modeling and deforestation monitoring. Moreover, it emphasizes the need for a holistic approach considering technological advancements and broader societal and environmental implications. By integrating environmental considerations into decision-making processes, stakeholders can work toward achieving a harmonious balance between technological innovation and environmental stewardship. GIS and RS are potent tools for promoting sustainable development and environmental conservation. By harnessing their capabilities and fostering interdisciplinary collaboration, stakeholders can pave the way for a more sustainable future.

REFERENCES

1. K.-T. Chang, "Geographic Information System," *International Encyclopedia of Geography*, pp. 1–10, Mar. 2019, doi: 10.1002/9781118786352.WBIEG0152.PUB2
2. G. M. Buchanan, A. Nelson, P. Mayaux, A. Hartley, and P. F. Donald, "Delivering a global, terrestrial, biodiversity observation system through remote sensing," *Conservation Biology*, vol. 23, no. 2, pp. 499–502, 2009, [Online]. Available: http://www.jstor.org/stable/29738753
3. F. Li, W. P. Kustas, M. C. Anderson, J. H. Prueger, and R. L. Scott, "Effect of remote sensing spatial resolution on interpreting tower-based flux observations," *Remote Sensing of Environment*, vol. 112, no. 2, pp. 337–349, Feb. 2008, doi: 10.1016/J.RSE.2006.11.032
4. S. Asadzadeh and C. R. de Souza Filho, "A review on spectral processing methods for geological remote sensing," *International Journal of Applied Earth Observation and Geoinformation*, vol. 47, pp. 69–90, May 2016, doi: 10.1016/J.JAG.2015.12.004
5. M. Stellmes, A. Röder, T. Udelhoven, and J. Hill, "Mapping syndromes of land change in Spain with remote sensing time series, demographic and climatic data," *Land Use Policy*, vol. 30, no. 1, pp. 685–702, Jan. 2013, doi: 10.1016/J.LANDUSEPOL.2012.05.007
6. G. Pinheiro and S. Minz, "Image Quality Evaluation of Various Pan-Sharpening Techniques Using Landsat-8 Imagery," pp. 391–403, 2023, doi: 10.1007/978-981-99-1620-7_31
7. G. Pinheiro and S. Minz, "Image Quality Assessment of Spatiotemporal Image Fusion: A Case Study Approach using Landsat-8 and Sentinel-2," in *43rd Asian Conference on Remote Sensing 2022 (ACRS2022)*, Mongolia: Asian Association on Remote Sensing (AARS), 2022. Accessed: Mar. 16, 2023. [Online].
8. G. P. Asner *et al.*, "Carnegie Airborne Observatory-2: Increasing science data dimensionality via high-fidelity multi-sensor fusion," *Remote Sensing of Environment*, vol. 124, pp. 454–465, Sep. 2012, doi: 10.1016/J.RSE.2012.06.012
9. E. Schnebele and G. Cervone, "Improving remote sensing flood assessment using volunteered geographical data," *Natural Hazards and Earth System Sciences*, vol. 13, no. 3, pp. 669–677, Mar. 2013, doi: 10.5194/NHESS-13-669-2013
10. Y. Liu *et al.*, "Social sensing: A new approach to understanding our socioeconomic environments," *Annals of the Association of American Geographers*, vol. 105, no. 3, pp. 512–530, May 2015, doi: 10.1080/00045608.2015.1018773
11. N. Joshi *et al.*, "A review of the application of optical and radar remote sensing data fusion to land use mapping and monitoring," *Remote Sensing*, vol. 8, no. 1, p. 70, Jan. 2016, doi: 10.3390/RS8010070.
12. B. L. Turner, E. F. Lambin, and A. Reenberg, "The emergence of land change science for global environmental change and sustainability," *Proceedings of the National Academy of Sciences of the United States of America*, vol. 104, no. 52, pp. 20666–20671, Dec. 2007, doi: 10.1073/PNAS.0704119104
13. F. Wang and Y. J. Xu, "Comparison of remote sensing change detection techniques for assessing hurricane damage to forests," *Environmental Monitoring and Assessment*, vol. 162, no. 1–4, pp. 311–326, Mar. 2010, doi: 10.1007/S10661-009-0798-8/METRICS.
14. X. Cui and X. Wang, "Review on studies of urban spatial behavior and urban planning from the perspective of big data," *ICCREM 2015 - Environment and the Sustainable Building - Proceedings of the 2015 International Conference on Construction and Real Estate Management*, pp. 521–531, 2015, doi: 10.1061/9780784479377.060
15. S. Li *et al.*, "Geospatial big data handling theory and methods: A review and research challenges," *ISPRS Journal of Photogrammetry and Remote Sensing*, vol. 115, pp. 119–133, May 2016, doi: 10.1016/J.ISPRSJPRS.2015.10.012

16. A. Farshad and J. A. Zinck, "Seeking agricultural sustainability," *Agriculture, Ecosystems & Environment*, vol. 47, no. 1, pp. 1–12, Oct. 1993, doi: 10.1016/0167-8809(93)90132-9
17. J. B. Campbell and R. H. Wynne, "Chapter 1: History and scope of remote sensing," *Introduction to Remote Sensing*, pp. 3–30, 2011, Accessed: Aug. 25, 2024. [Online]. Available: https://books.google.com/books/about/Introduction_to_Remote_Sensing_Fifth_Edi.html?id=NkLmDjSS8TsC
18. P. Liu, L. Di, Q. Du, and L. Wang, "Remote sensing big data: Theory, methods and applications," *Remote Sensing*, vol. 10, no. 5, p. 711, May 2018, doi: 10.3390/RS10050711
19. J. R. Jensen and D. C. Cowen, "Remote Sensing of Urban/Suburban Infrastructure and Socio-Economic Attributes," *The Map Reader: Theories of Mapping Practice and Cartographic Representation*, pp. 153–163, Apr. 2011, doi: 10.1002/9780470979587.CH22
20. D. J. Lary, A. H. Alavi, A. H. Gandomi, and A. L. Walker, "Machine learning in geosciences and remote sensing," *Geoscience Frontiers*, vol. 7, no. 1, pp. 3–10, Jan. 2016, doi: 10.1016/J.GSF.2015.07.003
21. S. K. Singh, P. K. Srivastava, S. Szabó, G. P. Petropoulos, M. Gupta, and T. Islam, "Landscape transform and spatial metrics for mapping spatiotemporal land cover dynamics using Earth Observation data-sets," *Geocarto International*, vol. 32, no. 2, pp. 113–127, Feb. 2017, doi: 10.1080/10106049.2015.1130084
22. A. Merghadi *et al.*, "Machine learning methods for landslide susceptibility studies: A comparative overview of algorithm performance," *Earth-Science Reviews*, vol. 207, p. 103225, Aug. 2020, doi: 10.1016/J.EARSCIREV.2020.103225
23. R. Avtar *et al.*, "Assessing sustainable development prospects through remote sensing: A review," *Remote Sensing Applications*, vol. 20, p. 100402, Nov. 2020, doi: 10.1016/J.RSASE.2020.100402
24. M. Paganini, I. Petiteville, S. Ward, G. Dyke, M. Steventon, and J. Harry, "→ Satellite Earth Observations in Support of the Sustainable Development Goals Special 2018 Edition ESA-EOGB (Earth Observation Graphic Bureau) Satellite Earth Observations in Support of the Sustainable Development Goals Part I: Satellite Data Supporting the SDGs," 2018.
25. S. Dudhani, A. K. Sinha, and S. S. Inamdar, "Assessment of small hydropower potential using remote sensing data for sustainable development in India," *Energy Policy*, vol. 34, no. 17, pp. 3195–3205, Nov. 2006, doi: 10.1016/J.ENPOL.2005.06.011
26. J. Holloway and K. Mengersen, "Statistical machine learning methods and remote sensing for sustainable development goals: A review," *Remote Sensing*, vol. 10, no. 9, p. 1365, Aug. 2018, doi: 10.3390/RS10091365
27. L. García, J. D. Rodríguez, M. Wijnen, and I. Pakulski, "Earth Observation for Water Resources Management: Current Use and Future Opportunities for the Water Sector," *Earth Observation for Water Resources Management: Current Use and Future Opportunities for the Water Sector*, Apr. 2016, doi: 10.1596/978-1-4648-0475-5.
28. S. E. Franklin, *Remote Sensing for Sustainable Forest Management*. CRC Press, 2001.
29. A. R. Huete, H. Q. Liu, K. Batchily, and W. Van Leeuwen, "A comparison of vegetation indices over a global set of TM images for EOS-MODIS," *Remote Sensing of Environment*, vol. 59, no. 3, pp. 440–451, Mar. 1997, doi: 10.1016/S0034-4257(96)00112-5
30. J. S. Wilson, M. Clay, E. Martin, D. Stuckey, and K. Vedder-Risch, "Evaluating environmental influences of zoning in urban ecosystems with remote sensing," *Remote Sensing of Environment*, vol. 86, no. 3, pp. 303–321, Aug. 2003, doi: 10.1016/S0034-4257(03)00084-1
31. C. Van Westen, "Remote sensing for natural disaster management," *International Archives of Photogrammetry and Remote Sensing.*, vol. Vol. XXXIII, no. Part B7, 2000.

32. M. D. M. Kadiyala, S. Nedumaran, P. Singh, C. S., M. A. Irshad, and M. C. S. Bantilan, "An integrated crop model and GIS decision support system for assisting agronomic decision making under climate change," *Science of The Total Environment*, vol. 521–522, pp. 123–134, Jul. 2015, doi: 10.1016/J.SCITOTENV.2015.03.097
33. J. Malczewski, "A GIS-based approach to multiple criteria group decision-making," *International Journal of Geographical Information Systems*, vol. 10, no. 8, pp. 955–971, 1996, doi: 10.1080/02693799608902119
34. J. Malczewski, "GIS-based multicriteria decision analysis: A survey of the literature," *International Journal of Geographical Information Science*, vol. 20, no. 7, pp. 703–726, Aug. 2006, doi: 10.1080/13658810600661508
35. J. M. C. Pereira, and L. Duckstein, "A multiple criteria decision-making approach to GIS-based land suitability evaluation," *International Journal of Geographical Information Science*, vol. 7, no. 5, pp. 407–424, 1993, doi: 10.1080/02693799308901971
36. M. K. Goyal, A. Sharma, and R. Y. Surampalli, "Remote sensing and GIS applications in sustainability," *Sustainability: Fundamentals and Applications*, pp. 605–626, Jan. 2020, doi: 10.1002/9781119434016.CH28
37. U.M. Shamsi, *GIS Applications for Water, Wastewater, and Stormwater Systems - U.M. Shamsi - Google Books*. CRC Press, 2005.
38. M. F. Goodchild, "Geographical information science," *International Journal of Geographical Information Systems*, vol. 6, no. 1, pp. 31–45, 1992, doi: 10.1080/02693799208901893
39. M. F. Goodchild, "Geographic information systems and science: Today and tomorrow," *Annals of GIS*, vol. 15, no. 1, pp. 3–9, 2009, doi: 10.1080/19475680903250715
40. T. Blaschke and H. Merschdorf, "Geographic information science as a multidisciplinary and multiparadigmatic field," *Cartography and Geographic Information Science*, vol. 41, no. 3, pp. 196–213, May 2014, doi: 10.1080/15230406.2014.905755
41. G. Lü, M. Batty, J. Strobl, H. Lin, A. X. Zhu, and M. Chen, "Reflections and speculations on the progress in Geographic Information Systems (GIS): a geographic perspective," *International Journal of Geographical Information Science*, vol. 33, no. 2, pp. 346–367, Feb. 2019, doi: 10.1080/13658816.2018.1533136
42. G. M. Foody, F. Ling, D. S. Boyd, X. Li, and J. Wardlaw, "Earth observation and machine learning to meet sustainable development goal 8.7: Mapping sites associated with slavery from space," *Remote Sensing*, vol. 11, no. 3, p. 266, Jan. 2019, doi: 10.3390/RS11030266
43. Geobuiz (2019). "Geospatial industry and readiness index. Geospatial media and communications." https://geobuiz.com/geobuiz-report-2019/
44. B. Bendix Bad Schmiedeberg, "HANS CARL VON CARLOWITZ SYLVICULTURA OECONOMICA," *Stud. Mater. Ośr. Kult. Leśn*, vol. 13, pp. 29–40, 2014.
45. K. F. Wiersum, "200 years of sustainability in forestry: Lessons from history," *Environmental Management*, vol. 19, no. 3, pp. 321–329, May 1995, doi: 10.1007/BF02471975/METRICS
46. G. Harienbrundtland, "World Commission on environment and development," *Environmental Policy and Law*, vol. 14, no. 1, pp. 26–30, Mar. 1985, doi: 10.1016/S0378-777X(85)80040-8
47. D. Tilman, K. G. Cassman, P. A. Matson, R. Naylor, and S. Polasky, "Agricultural sustainability and intensive production practices," *Nature*, vol. 418, no. 6898, pp. 671–677, Aug. 2002, doi: 10.1038/nature01014
48. N. K. Ajami, G. M. Hornberger, and D. L. Sunding, "Sustainable water resource management under hydrological uncertainty," *Water Resources Research*, vol. 44, no. 11, p. 11406, Nov. 2008, doi: 10.1029/2007WR006736
49. D. P. Loucks, "Sustainable water resources management," *Water International*, vol. 25, no. 1, pp. 3–10, 2000, doi: 10.1080/02508060008686793

50. E. Ostrom, "A general framework for analyzing sustainability of social-ecological systems," *Science (1979)*, vol. 325, no. 5939, pp. 419–422, Jul. 2009, doi: 10.1126/SCIENCE.1172133
51. K. P. Frank-Martin Belz, *Sustainability Marketing: A Global Perspective*, Second. 2012.
52. M. Mowforth and I. Munt, "Tourism and sustainability: Development, globalisation and new tourism in the Third World: Fourth edition," *Tourism and Sustainability: Development, globalisation and new tourism in the Third World: Fourth Edition*, pp. 1–456, Dec. 2015, doi: 10.4324/9781315795348/TOURISM-SUSTAINABILITY-MARTIN-MOWFORTH-IAN-MUNT.
53. D. P. Rao, "Role of Remote Sensing and Geographic Information System in Sustainable development". International Archives of Photogrammetry and Remote Sensing. Vol. XXXIII, Part B7. Amsterdam, 2000.
54. G. C. Gallopín, "Environmental and sustainability indicators and the concept of situational indicators. A systems approach," *Environmental Modeling & Assessment*, vol. 1, no. 3, pp. 101–117, Sep. 1996, doi: 10.1007/BF01874899
55. M. L. M. Graymore, N. G. Sipe, and R. E. Rickson, "Regional sustainability: How useful are current tools of sustainability assessment at the regional scale?," *Ecological Economics*, vol. 67, no. 3, pp. 362–372, Oct. 2008, doi: 10.1016/J.ECOLECON.2008.06.002
56. R. Nidumolu, C. K. Prahalad, and M. R. Rangaswami, "Why sustainability is now the key driver of Innovation," *Harvard Business Review*, pp. 57–64, September 2009.
57. W. C. Clark and N. M. Dickson, "Sustainability science: The emerging research program," *Proceedings of the National Academy of Sciences of the United States of America*, vol. 100, no. 14, pp. 8059–8061, Jul. 2003, doi: 10.1073/PNAS.1231333100/ASSET/C184054C-5298-49A6-A0FB-9A0E212771A3/ASSETS/PNAS.1231333100.FP.PNG
58. A. J. Tatem, S. J. Goetz, and S. I. Hay, "Fifty years of earth observation satellites: Views from above have lead to countless advances on the ground in both scientific knowledge and daily life," *American Scientist*, vol. 96, no. 5, p. 390, Sep. 2008, doi: 10.1511/2008.74.390
59. T. Dev Acharya, I. Yang, and G. Student, "Exploring Landsat 8," *International Journal of IT, Engineering and Applied Sciences Research*, vol. 4, no. 4, pp. 2319–4413, 2015, Accessed: Feb. 29, 2024. [Online]. Available: http://earthobservatory.nasa.gov/IOTD/
60. K. Shi *et al.*, "Modeling and mapping total freight traffic in China using NPP-VIIRS nighttime light composite data," *GIScience & Remote Sensing*, vol. 52, no. 3, pp. 274–289, May 2015, doi: 10.1080/15481603.2015.1022420
61. K. Shi *et al.*, "Evaluating the ability of NPP-VIIRS nighttime light data to estimate the gross domestic product and the electric power consumption of China at multiple scales: A comparison with DMSP-OLS data," *Remote Sensing*, vol. 6, no. 2, pp. 1705–1724, Feb. 2014, doi: 10.3390/RS6021705
62. J. Guo *et al.*, "Multi-GNSS precise point positioning for precision agriculture," *Precision Agriculture*, vol. 19, no. 5, pp. 895–911, Oct. 2018, doi: 10.1007/S11119-018-9563-8/FIGURES/9
63. J. Xin, J. Zhou, S. X. Yang, X. Li, and Y. Wang, "Bridge structure deformation prediction based on GNSS data using Kalman-ARIMA-GARCH Model," *Sensors*, vol. 18, no. 1, p. 298, Jan. 2018, doi: 10.3390/S18010298
64. T. Bellone, P. Dabove, A. M. Manzino, and C. Taglioretti, "Real-time monitoring for fast deformations using GNSS low-cost receivers," *Geomatics, Natural Hazards and Risk*, vol. 7, no. 2, pp. 458–470, Mar. 2016, doi: 10.1080/19475705.2014.966867

65. T. Dev Acharya and D. Ha Lee, "Remote sensing and geospatial technologies for sustainable development: A review of applications," *Sensors and Materials*, vol. 31, no. 11, pp. 3931–3945, 2019, doi: 10.18494/SAM.2019.2706
66. V. Mariathasan, E. Bezuidenhoudt, and K. R. Olympio, "Evaluation of earth observation solutions for Namibia's SDG monitoring system," *Remote Sensing*, vol. 11, no. 13, p. 1612, Jul. 2019, doi: 10.3390/RS11131612
67. L. Andres, K. Boateng, C. Borja-Vega, and E. Thomas, "A review of in-situ and remote sensing technologies to monitor water and sanitation interventions," *Water*, vol. 10, no. 6, p. 756, Jun. 2018, doi: 10.3390/W10060756
68. S. J. Lee, B. Bush, and R. George, "Analytic science for geospatial and temporal variability in renewable energy: A case study in estimating photovoltaic output in Arizona," *Solar Energy*, vol. 85, no. 9, pp. 1945–1956, Sep. 2011, doi: 10.1016/J.SOLENER.2011.05.005
69. J. Bosch, I. Staffell, and A. D. Hawkes, "Temporally-explicit and spatially-resolved global onshore wind energy potentials," *Energy*, vol. 131, pp. 207–217, Jul. 2017, doi: 10.1016/J.ENERGY.2017.05.052
70. P. McCord, F. Tonini, and J. Liu, "The Telecoupling GeoApp: A Web-GIS application to systematically analyze telecouplings and sustainable development," *Applied Geography*, vol. 96, pp. 16–28, Jul. 2018, doi: 10.1016/J.APGEOG.2018.05.001
71. T. Blaschke, G. J. Hay, Q. Weng, and B. Resch, "Collective sensing: Integrating geospatial technologies to understand urban systems—An overview," *Remote Sensing*, vol. 3, no. 8, pp. 1743–1776, Aug. 2011, doi: 10.3390/RS3081743
72. J. Crespo Cuaresma *et al.*, "Economic development and forest cover: Evidence from satellite data," *Scientific Reports*, vol. 7, no. 1, pp. 1–8, Jan. 2017, doi: 10.1038/srep40678
73. J. Reiche *et al.*, "Combining satellite data for better tropical forest monitoring," *Nature Climate Change*, vol. 6, no. 2, pp. 120–122, Jan. 2016, doi: 10.1038/nclimate2919
74. S. Al-Zyoud, W. Rühaak, E. Forootan, and I. Sass, "Over exploitation of groundwater in the Centre of Amman Zarqa Basin—Jordan: Evaluation of well data and GRACE satellite observations," *Resources*, vol. 4, no. 4, pp. 819–830, Nov. 2015, doi: 10.3390/RESOURCES4040819
75. F. J. Wentz, "A 17-Yr climate record of environmental parameters derived from the tropical rainfall measuring mission (TRMM) microwave imager," *Journal of Climate*, vol. 28, no. 17, pp. 6882–6902, Sep. 2015, doi: 10.1175/JCLI-D-15-0155.1
76. S. R. Phinn, E. M. Kovacs, C. M. Roelfsema, R. F. Canto, C. J. Collier, and L. J. McKenzie, "Assessing the potential for satellite image monitoring of seagrass thermal dynamics: For inter- and shallow sub-tidal seagrasses in the inshore Great Barrier Reef World Heritage Area, Australia," *International Journal of Digital Earth*, vol. 11, no. 8, pp. 803–824, Aug. 2018, doi: 10.1080/17538947.2017.1359343
77. N. Maximenko *et al.*, "Towards the integrated marine debris observing system," *Frontiers in Marine Science*, vol. 6, no. JUL, p. 437964, Aug. 2019, doi: 10.3389/FMARS.2019.00447/BIBTEX.
78. D. S. Boyd, B. Jackson, J. Wardlaw, G. M. Foody, S. Marsh, and K. Bales, "Slavery from space: Demonstrating the role for satellite remote sensing to inform evidence-based action related to UN SDG number 8," *ISPRS Journal of Photogrammetry and Remote Sensing*, vol. 142, pp. 380–388, Aug. 2018, doi: 10.1016/J.ISPRSJPRS.2018.02.012.
79. S. Turubanova, P. V. Potapov, A. Tyukavina, and M. C. Hansen, "Ongoing primary forest loss in Brazil, Democratic Republic of the Congo, and Indonesia," *Environmental Research Letters*, vol. 13, no. 7, p. 074028, Jul. 2018, doi: 10.1088/1748-9326/AACD1C
80. Y. Qin *et al.*, "Improved estimates of forest cover and loss in the Brazilian Amazon in 2000–2017," *Nature Sustainability*, vol. 2, no. 8, pp. 764–772, Jul. 2019, doi: 10.1038/s41893-019-0336-9

81. Pinheiro, G., & Minz, S. (2024). Granular computing based segmentation and textural analysis (GrCSTA) framework for object-based LULC classification of fused remote sensing images. *Applied Intelligence*, vol. 54, no. 7, pp. 5748–5767.
82. D. C. Dunn *et al.*, "Empowering high seas governance with satellite vessel tracking data," *Fish and Fisheries*, vol. 19, no. 4, pp. 729–739, Jul. 2018, doi: 10.1111/FAF.12285

5 Role of ICT in Good Health and Well-Being

Sakshi Gupta, Ankita Verma, and Deepti Singh

5.1 INTRODUCTION

Information and communication technology (ICT) has expeditiously advanced right into a tremendous catalyst for the development of society. Consequently, individuals' techniques of working, socializing, and acquiring statistics have been transformed at the same time. The term "Information and Communication Technology" refers to a big group of systems and technology that make it easier to acquire, organize, and proportion information. They also make it simpler to talk across a huge variety of structures [1]. ICT has created a power in nearly every facet of modern life. This is obvious from how fast social networks and smartphones have become popular, as well as how far cloud computing and artificial intelligence (AI) have come. As a result, corporations and social norms were modified.

ICT is being used in an increasing manner in various regions of existence, which is having a large effect on society as an entire. Davis et al. [2] explored that the adoption of ICT has altered how individuals achieve knowledge. ICT provides them power to access a large quantity of facts and makes gaining knowledge more personalized and flexible. E-commerce and digital bills have revolutionized how companies function, permitting clients globally to connect and conduct transactions without difficulty [3]. Technology has also modified how the public and authorities interact, giving human beings more freedom and making it less difficult to recognize what is happening within the globe [4].

ICT has a huge effect on many components of lifestyles and enhancing fitness and well-being throughout all social businesses is becoming increasingly vital. A lot of different web and mobile applications and equipment are being used to enhance the speed, response-time, and accessibility of medical services in the healthcare industry by the usage of ICT [5]. These advancements include but are not limited to telemedicine for remote medical advice, electronic health facts (EHRs) for better statistics control, cellular health apps (mHealth) for tracking fitness, and AI for higher assessment and remedy.

In the field of healthcare, ICT refers to the combination of digital technologies into operational systems and clinical exercise that allows humans to facilitate administrative responsibilities, improve clinical outcomes, and optimize the treatment of the patient [6]. This consists of the implementation of digital health records to save and retrieve details related to patients, telemedicine systems to facilitate virtual consultations, wearable era to monitor health position, and records analytics to adjust the health of a complete society.

DOI: 10.1201/9781003471356-5

ICT performs an essential role in the healthcare area for numerous motives, which is not limited to the development of the latest technologies. It signifies various outcomes such as better fitness effects and a change in the way in which healthcare is managed. ICT techniques allow healthcare employees to connect with individuals who are unnoticed and act quickly to assist them [6]. It helps them surmount barriers, which include distance and a shortage of health resources. Patients are also empowered to actively participate in the management of their own health, which improves fitness care, adherence to treatment, and prevention strategies. All these benefits are provided by the tools of ICT.

Overall, ICT helps to provide innovative ways to various persistent issues and guarantees that every individual has an equitable right of entry to superior clinical facilities. Hence, ICT in the long term contributes to the development of healthcare. By recognizing that ICT has the electricity to alternate matters, it might be stated that ICT is important to health and well-being [7].

5.2 ICT FOR IMPROVED HEALTHCARE ACCESS AND DELIVERY

The rapid advancement of ICT has significantly impacted various aspects of our lives. By providing new approaches to old problems, ICT has become an effective instrument to improve healthcare accessibility and delivery [8].

When it comes to healthcare, ICT has become the base for providing new ways to improve accessibility, efficiency, and quality of service. One potent tool to help underprivileged people get the treatment they need, regardless of where they live or their financial situation, is the use of ICTs in healthcare systems [9]. ICT has a huge influence on various aspects of healthcare. The following are the key areas of influence in healthcare, that is, telemedicine, electronic health records (EHRs), and mobile health applications.

5.2.1 Telemedicine

Telemedicine is an innovative application of the provision of healthcare services pertaining to the use of ICTs. It allows patients and healthcare practitioners to consult, diagnose, and treat illnesses remotely using telecom technology. Through video conferencing, telemedicine is able to provide effective communication between patients and healthcare specialists, regardless of their geographical location. There are no geographical constraints with telemedicine because the avenue that is made available lets a patient have access to medical expertise and support no matter where he/she might be physically located. It also helps the experts to develop their expertise and abilities where health facilities are poor and thus provides equal and non-discriminatory access to specialized healthcare services to all [10]. Telemedicine facilitates e-consultations and tele-appointments, thereby increasing the efficiency of health care and making access to health easier with a lesser load on the traditional infrastructural facilities in hospitals [8]. Telemedicine and remote consultation are modalities through which medical care and guidance are given to patients without necessarily needing to book appointments physically.

There are several benefits that telemedicine has for both patients and healthcare providers. Through telemedicine, patients are able to see or consult healthcare providers from the comfort of their own homes thereby saving on travel time, money, or hassle [11]. It can also accelerate access to timely healthcare by getting expert advice and treatment for patients in remote or disadvantaged regions. Telemedicine makes healthcare professionals more efficient by making them available to more patients in less time, hence reducing the waiting time in clinics and also utilizing resources to the fullest [11].

Telemedicine usually incorporates the following three aspects: live video consultation, store-and-forward telemedicine, and remote patient monitoring. Real-time video consultation allows patients to communicate directly with healthcare practitioners immediately, like a clinic face-to-face encounter. In store-and-forward telemedicine, physicians can view patients' data and discuss their opinions with the help of experts at convenient times; such instances are greatly helpful in subspecialty consultation matters like dermatology, radiology, or pathology when detailed scrutiny of images or data is required [12]. Remote patient monitoring involves the devices/sensors that the patient wears and collects data, which is then sent for monitoring of vital signs, medication adherence, and progression of disease by health professionals [13].

There are several challenges related to the practice of telemedicine, some of which include reimbursement problems, licensure, and regulation barriers, technological constraints—like access to high-speed internet in rural areas—and concerns with patient privacy and data security. For telemedicine to realize its full potential in improving access to and the delivery of health care, there must be all-inclusively coordinated and collaborative efforts by policymakers, healthcare providers, technology suppliers, and other stakeholders in surmounting these challenges.

As technology is constantly changing at a seriously rapid rate, telemedicine, as indicated, is going to play a significant role in how healthcare is provided. Virtual reality and augmented reality are growing technologies that allow further immersion between the patient and healthcare practitioners in telemedicine. Another frontier opened by the integration of AI and machine learning into telemedicine is letting these technologies analyze patient data to automatize processes such as classifying conditions, suggesting diagnoses, or even recommending treatment plans, which will further improve telemedicine [10].

Telemedicine, in general, is one of the effective strategies that look forward to improving access to health care and facilitating the delivery of care in economically disadvantaged and geographically remote areas. It uses telecommunications technology to break down geographical barriers and improve effectiveness by bringing the best possible care to the patient to enable them to receive better health and population health outcomes.

5.2.2 mHealth and Health Monitoring

The mHealth technologies form part of the result of the ICT revolution, which has greatly impacted how healthcare is accessed and delivered in modern times. People can use smartphones, wearable devices, and different mobile applications to track their health condition, monitor important indications, and receive personalized health suggestions in real time [9]. mHealth solutions enable patients to be engaged in the process of health management, encourage disease prevention practices, and facilitate the early identification and prevention of health issues. In addition, the mHealth treatments have significantly supported the self-management of chronic diseases and medication adherence, while leading to better health outcomes. The extensive use of current-generation mobile devices enables mHealth technology to harmonize with telehealth and telemedicine for health monitoring, disease management, and promotion of health activities. Consequently, mHealth employs smartphones, wearable sensors, and phone applications as the platform on which to affect an all-inclusive health management system. It enables them to be aware of their health data, access credible information about health, and be actively involved in preventive programs for better health outcomes.

5.2.2.1 Remote Monitoring and Personalized Care

One of the main uses of mHealth is in remote monitoring of health, which enables the users to monitor their health by simple measurement of the vital signs, symptoms, and health behaviors without visiting the hospitals or health centers. Wearable gadgets, including fitness trackers and smartwatches, are a lint at facilitating around-the-clock measurements related to, say, heart rate, blood pressure, and levels of physical activity [14]. The real-time data can easily be relayed to healthcare practitioners to offer timely interventions and customized care plans to meet specific requirements at an individual level [15].

5.2.2.2 Chronic Disease Management

mHealth contributes to a broader agenda of chronic disease management. It gives a hand to patients with conditions like diabetes, hypertension, and asthma because of health monitoring and provision of timely treatments. Diabetes management applications allow the ability to track your blood glucose, log meals, and prescriptions, and receive personalized advice for managing the disease. Asthma management applications provide access to symptom monitoring, medicine adherence, and identification of triggers in the environment, whereby an individual is empowered and can be in control of their illness so that the symptoms do not deteriorate [16].

5.2.2.3 Health Promotion and Behavior Change

It is about health promotion rather than the treatment of illness; it deals with the total wellness aspects, giving people and communities the knowledge and resources required for health. It centers on providing individuals as well as communities with the requisite knowledge and resources to be healthy and take the initiative, through informed decisions and healthy habits, to lead a proactive life. The main focus is placed on empowering an individual, as well as communities, with the basic tools to make healthy choices and take action with an outlook to better the general well-being. On the contrary, behavior change is the conscious, deliberate, or systematized effort at the alteration or modification of one's behavior to attain a desired behavioral outcome.

Over and above disorder management, mHealth allows for the implementation of initiatives and interventions that work toward the curbing and prevention of chronic diseases and enhance general well-being. The mHealth application delivers through its interactive attributes, personalized feedback loops, and gamification features that promote the adoption toward healthier practices, such as physical activity, healthy eating, smoking cessation, and stress coping. In addition, the mHealth interventions can be made available to targeted populations, specific health coverages, geographic locations, social status, and populations facing marginalization. This makes the reduction of health disparities possible and fosters the achievement of health equity [17].

Due to the ongoing technological possibilities, mHealth can continually change the provision of health care and hence produce better health outcomes in populations. Wearable sensor technologies, AI, and data analytics are in development and, therefore, likely to increase the potential of the mHealth solutions. This involves advanced tracking, predictive analytics, and personalized treatments [14]. The incorporation of mHealth into current health systems as well as in work practices can enhance smooth service provision `and support the portability and continuity of service in various settings [18].

Therefore, mHealth is a potent contribution to health monitoring, disease management, and behavioral change, which can lead to healthy outcomes and life. Through the use of mobile technology, mHealth can act, with great potential, to transform the healthcare system and empower people to gain control and manage their health and well-being with innovation.

5.2.3 Electronic Health Records

ICT has made it possible to transform traditional paper-based records of health into EHRs that help in improving coordination to ensure better healthcare provision services and management of information concerning health. EHRs give the medical care provider assured, secure access to the combined history of patient care, and they guarantee informed, intelligent clinical decision support to reduce the occurrence of errors during medical procedures [19]. Besides, EHRs allow for easy transfer of information between various healthcare organizations and providers, thus promoting interoperability. This, therefore, improves the end health outcome of a patient and secures the continuation of care.

EHRs are ways of storing, transmitting, and digitizing information on patients' health, an indispensable element in the delivery of modern health care. EHR systems have bigger and greater benefits compared to traditional paper record systems. Among the benefits named, there are improved accuracy, ease of accessibility, and capability of effortless data exchange between different systems. It really optimizes clinical decision-making and patient care.

Rather, a very crucial benefit related to the application of EHRs in the treatment procedure is the availability of complete and accurate information on patients. The EHR comprises all relevant information on patients from all sources put together into a single electronic medium, which includes medical history, laboratory test results, medication lists, and even imaging studies. From a different perspective, the paper records are likely to be erroneous and at times incomplete [19]. It enables professionals to make clinical decisions, identify possible drug interactions, and discover any allergies or diseases, providing consistency in care among different sites of health care.

5.2.3.1 Enhanced Coordination of Care

An EHR supports professional collaboration among the different professions giving care to the patient, providing enhanced care coordination and transition among different care settings. EHRs enable healthcare teams to share information and harmonize the treatment regime confidently through a secure electronic exchange of messages and a common repository for patient history. Enhanced communication facilitates better interdisciplinary teamwork, decreases unwanted exams and procedures, and lowers and eliminates medical errors—altogether, these improvements result in an elevated quality and safety of care to the patient.

5.2.3.2 Enhanced Data Analytics and Population Health Management

More so, EHRs provide large pools of data to be used toward quality improvement and population health management activities. HHS programs assist healthcare organizations by identifying patterns, tracking health status and outcomes, and applying evidence-based interventions to improve a population's health and analyze anonymous patient EHR data to track progress in meeting quality measures among others. All these are through the use of EHR systems [20]. For instance, there can be the use of EHRs for the tracking incidence of chronic conditions, determining the populations at more risk in a common trend of susceptibility, and, in turn, can establish more specific actions that influence the enhancement of control and prevention of the disease.

However, with the many benefits that could accompany the use of EHRs, there are unique challenges and considerations that also should be recognized. Among others, major issues exist in the domains of data privacy and security, interoperability of multiple EHR systems, and the increased burden on healthcare providers due to documentation obligations [19]. Moreover, the needed investments, training initiatives, and reorganizations of the workflows in order to implement and receive acceptability for EHRs are far-reaching. Smaller healthcare organizations and locations with fewer resources would likely struggle with the above issues [20]. Relentless teamwork between policymakers, healthcare givers, technology vendors, and patient advocates is needed to make the best solutions arise. This teamwork is only possible through the proper planning and utilization of EHR systems.

The ongoing development of EHR technology holds potential for future improvements in the quality of healthcare delivery and patient outcomes. Technological advances including application programming interfaces, machine learning algorithms, and standards to define interoperability can support more seamless clinical decisions and at the same time open the way for a more flexible, patient-centered healthcare delivery system [19]. More efforts, therefore, must be directed to increasing patients' involvement, empowering patients through accessible and controllable personal health information, and encouraging the sharing of information to truly experience the potential of EHRs in the modern age.

EHRs become a key element in care provision today because they enable data-driven decision-making, improve people's care coordination, and are a comprehensive source of a person's information. Through the application of digital technology, EHR systems have the potential to be transformative in nature with respect to the nature of healthcare delivery, population health outcomes, and the quality and efficiency of patient care.

5.2.4 Artificial Intelligence and Health Analytics

Healthcare is on the brink of a revolution, one that will be spoken about in the same vein as the Industrial Revolution, the introduction of penicillin, and the invention of the internet. From the prediction of diseases to tailoring treatment, AI algorithms can handle large amounts of medical data, revealing hidden patterns in predicting how diseases will progress and, in fact, even develop a tailored treatment strategy for an individual patient [21]. This brings out practicable insights from the data for optimal resource allocation and boosting patient outcomes. Healthcare analytics present such an opportunity for clinicians in practice [8]. Integration of ICT into the process of delivery and access to health reduces inconveniences in between information management processes, enhances patient empowerment without physical barriers, and increases the optimization of a new advanced technology in the decision-making process leading to better results. Continued advancement in ICT has unqualified potential for changing the nature of healthcare provisioning by successively increasing health outcomes in populations.

Just like eHealth, other advanced technologies such as the use of healthcare analytics and AI hold much potential in changing the ways of managing population health and making clinical decisions when delivering healthcare. In addition, because the approach to AI and healthcare analytics is built on data and state-of-the-art algorithms, it presents unparalleled opportunities for synthesis into actionable insights and escalation of service quality while pursuing adequate resource allocation at a reasonable cost [22].

5.2.4.1 Clinical Decision Support

One of the basic applications within medical science for AI is clinical decision support systems (CDSSs). The systems run on machine learning algorithms, scrutinize the patient data, develop diagnostic insights, recommend individual treatment plans, and reciprocate to the arising questions of health and medication. CDSS can help medical staff achieve better patient outcomes, reduce diagnostic errors, and make evidence-based decisions by being integrated with EHRs and other healthcare information systems [22]. AI systems can analyze medical images not only to identify any abnormalities but also to predict the development of diseases and support radiologists in better image study interpretations [23].

5.2.4.2 Predictive Analysis and Population Health Management

Healthcare analytics, which encompasses data mining and predictive modeling techniques, enables healthcare organizations to identify patterns, predict health outcomes, and further stratification of patient populations according to careful risk categorization [24]. By analyzing huge bundles of clinical and administrative information, healthcare analytics may enable the pinpointing of those people who are most at risk of experiencing negative health outcomes, specifically rehospitalizations and complications. This enables the use of tailored interventions seeking to reduce or prevent these risks [22]. In addition, healthcare analytics support population health management programs by enabling healthcare organizations to measure facility performance metrics, track health trends, and act using evidence-based interventions that result in better outcomes for population health [24].

5.2.4.3 Challenges with AIs and Healthcare Analytics

Though AI and healthcare analytics hold promise for great benefits, they are not short of their limitations and concerns worthy of mention. Concerns arising out of AI include ethical implications, fairness and bias of algorithms, integrity and quality of data, and lastly, regulatory compliance, as elucidated by [22]. These substantial challenges hold up the broad spread of most implementations and adoption of AI and healthcare analytics solutions. These barriers include concerns over issues on interoperability, security, and data privacy [22]. Over and above, concerns over algorithmic transparency, accountability, and undesired consequences point to areas where regulatory oversight and ethical framing in design and deployment should occur in AI-supported healthcare solutions [25].

Analytics and AI have the potential to significantly alter ways of delivering healthcare and achieving outcomes for patients. Three such technological advancements are blockchain, federated learning, and explainable AI, which can enable a more conscientious and ethical application of AI in health care by solving concerns regarding privacy, transparency, and sharing of data [25]. There will also be a need to augment data standardization, governance, and interoperability so that the full benefits of healthcare analytics are realized, where relevant valuable insights are driven from data into the hands of healthcare providers and patients. What applies today, with greater opportunity than ever before, is the ability of healthcare analytics and AI to allow the transformation of population health management, augmentations of clinical decision-making, and optimization of healthcare delivery. AI-powered solutions can change the face of healthcare delivery, more effectively apportion and use resources, and improve the health status of both populations and individuals using data and advanced algorithms that control the new technology.

5.3 ICT ENSURING ENHANCED PREVENTION ON DISEASES AND THEIR CONTROL

Application of digital tools and platforms, the ICT programs being implemented offer leading solutions on surveillance, response strategies, health education, and outbreak response. In total, it is easier to carry out early detection of the disease and containment by a general strategy, and this gives the ability to prevent the disease and make informed health decisions for the community and individuals. This section portrays a wide range of the application of ICT in controlling and preventing diseases with some concentration on the key technologies, challenges, and the likely advancements in the future.

5.3.1 Early Warning and Digital Surveillance

The digital surveillance systems facilitate real-time monitoring of disease trends and early epidemic detection and are increasingly ICT-enabled. Chretien et al. [26] identified unusual patterns or concentrations of disease and analyzed health data from multiple relevant sources, including laboratory results and social media sites, among other types of surveillance networks. A case in point would be the health alert systems, including for instance ProMED and HealthMap, that track news articles, social media posts, and official health notifications, with the aim of detecting emerging health risks in a timely manner and notifying the public, public health authorities, and the public at large in the same regard [26]. In addition to that, combining the digital surveillance tools and the conventional surveillance systems will enhance the capabilities and, as a result, it would be easy to note and act on bioterrorism incidents, infectious disease outbreaks, and other public health emergencies [27].

5.3.2 Health Education and Communication

When public health officials employ ICT for health communication and education programs, they are better able to engage with communities and spread correct information. Websites, smartphone apps, and social media channels are examples of digital platforms that can be utilized to refute myths and disinformation, promote preventative measures, and disseminate health-related messages [28]. During public health emergencies or disease outbreaks, for example, social media campaigns and online forums offer timely information, recommendations for preventative measures, and avenues for discussion with subject matter experts. Additionally, to empower users to take control of their own health, mobile health (mHealth) applications feature self-assessment tools, reminders for vaccinations or preventative tests, and customized health education content [14].

5.3.3 Digital Contact Tracing and Case Management

ICT is essential for managing cases and locating contacts during disease outbreaks because it facilitates the rapid identification and disruption of transmission networks. Digital contact tracing systems monitor people's locations and interactions using Bluetooth, GPS, or proximity sensing. Wearable technology and smartphone apps are some of these instruments [29]. Contact tracking programs alert individuals who might have been in contact with the virus, offer advice on testing and quarantine procedures, and allow communication with public health authorities to request more assistance after a confirmed case has been identified [29]. Additionally, teleconsultations and remote case management are made possible by digital platforms, allowing medical practitioners to keep an eye on patients' symptoms and offer vital services like medication administration and mental health support to those in isolation or quarantine [29].

5.3.4 Digital Tools for Immunization and Preventive Care

ICT is essential for measuring vaccination coverage rates, developing immunization and preventive care programs, and supporting vaccination campaigns. Healthcare professionals can use digital immunization registries and monitoring systems to keep track of immunization status, record vaccine administrations, and provide notifications about upcoming vaccinations or booster doses [30]. Additionally, ICT platforms give healthcare providers access to decision support tools that make it easier to identify people who have not received their vaccines on time, determine a person's eligibility for vaccinations based on age, health, and risk factors, and ease vaccine reluctance through customized communication [30]. Furthermore, telemedicine and telehealth services enable remote consultations for immunization, educational sessions, and follow-up therapy for marginalized and rural areas [10].

5.3.5 Challenges with ICT-based Disease Prevention and Control Programs

Despite their potential advantages, ICT-based disease prevention and control programs face a variety of concerns and problems. Improving digital literacy, equitable access to technology, and data security and privacy are essential for increasing the efficacy and inclusivity of digital interventions [29]. Furthermore, for seamless integration and collaboration across health systems and jurisdictions, coordination among stakeholders, standardization of data formats and protocols, and interoperability between diverse ICT platforms and systems are essential [27]. Concerns regarding algorithmic bias, misrepresentation, and confidence in digital technologies underscore the significance of including community involvement, transparency, and ethical considerations in the design and implementation of ICT solutions [26].

However, as ICT continues to advance, there is an opportunity to bolster activities related to disease prevention and control. Technological developments, digital health programs, and data analytics will assist with this. Improved disease prognosis, risk prediction, and targeted therapeutics are possible thanks to the rapidly developing disciplines of AI, machine learning, and predictive analytics [25]. Additionally, there has to be more collaboration between academic institutions, community organizations, public health agencies, and technology developers in order to use ICT to reduce new health risks, promote health equity, and create robust health systems [27]. Thus, among the creative ways that ICT might support efforts linked to disease prevention and control are proactive communication, real-time surveillance, and customized interventions. By utilizing digital tools and platforms, public health officials may effectively engage the community, stop the spread of infectious diseases, and identify epidemics early. They can save lives and safeguard public health by doing this.

5.4 ICT FOR SUPPORTING HEALTHY LIFESTYLES AND BEHAVIORS

In today's world, ICT is becoming increasingly important in encouraging and supporting healthy behaviors. ICT projects, that make use of digital platforms and technologies, make it easier to use creative methods for behavior change interventions, illness prevention, and health promotion. This section looks at the various ways that ICT can be used to support and encourage healthy habits and lifestyles. It highlights the most important technologies, difficulties, and potential future paths.

5.4.1 Mobile Health Applications

Applications for mobile health are among the most popular and easily available types of ICT. Numerous features, such as stress management, fitness tracking, diet tracking, and help quitting smoking, are available to users of smartphone applications. These features enable people to take charge of their personal well-being and general health. Fitness applications include tools for activity tracking, personalized training programs, and progress tracking [14]. These characteristics are meant to encourage customers to engage in regular exercise and physical activity. Nutrition apps enable users to track what they eat, establish goals for their diet, and receive customized meal recommendations based on their current health status and preferences [31].

5.4.2 Wearable Devices and Activity Trackers

Wearable technology, such as fitness trackers and smartwatches, enables real-time monitoring of vital signs, physical activity, and sleep patterns, which is beneficial for mobile health apps. These devices use sensors and algorithms to track several health variables in order to provide users with useful advice and assessments regarding their lifestyle choices [32]. These metrics consist of, but are not restricted to, the number of steps taken, the distance traveled, the number of calories burned, and more. Moreover, wearable technology may include features like stress detection, sleep tracking, and heart rate monitoring. According to [32], these characteristics enable users to keep a more thorough record of their general health and well-being. According to [31], the implementation of wearable technology enables individuals to adopt healthier habits and accomplish their wellness goals. This is accomplished by encouraging self-awareness and changing behavior through regular observation and feedback.

5.4.3 Social Media and Online Communities

Social media platforms and online communities present significant opportunities for health promotion, peer support provision, and community activity engagement. Laranjo et al. [33] posit that individuals possess the capacity to engage in virtual interactions with peers who share similar interests, exchange personal experiences, and obtain information and resources pertaining to an extensive array of health-related subjects via social networking sites, health-focused groups, and online forums. According to [33], organizing health campaigns and challenges through social media platforms can improve participation, create a sense of community, and motivate people to adopt healthier habits like quitting smoking, exercising frequently, and maintaining a balanced diet. Furthermore, health advocates and social media influencers use their platforms to promote healthy lifestyle changes, clear up misconceptions, and spread health-related messaging. This gives them the ability to successfully impact a wide range of people's behavior changes.

5.4.4 Gamification and Behavior Change Techniques

ICT components like gamification and behavior change tactics are meant to boost interest and drive in implementing healthy habits. According to [34], gamified health applications integrate components of games, such as leaderboards, challenges, and awards, to encourage users to participate in activities that promote health and meet predetermined objectives. Using fitness applications, users may be able to obtain virtual badges or awards for completing workouts, hitting activity goals, or maintaining regular exercise schedules. According to [35], digital treatments use behavior change techniques such as goal-setting, self-monitoring, giving feedback, and enlisting social support to promote long-term adherence to wholesome habits and sustain behavior improvement. By making health-related activities more entertaining, engaging, and motivating, behavior change methods and gamification increase user engagement and encourage positive behavior change. This is accomplished by making health-related actions more satisfying.

ICT programs that promote healthy lifestyles and behaviors face several problems and considerations, even with the potential benefits they may offer. Several issues need to be resolved in order to maximize the effectiveness and inclusivity of digital interventions. These issues include digital disparities, fair access to technology, privacy and data security, and the accuracy and integrity of health information [33]. Furthermore, user engagement, intervention sustainability, and long-term behavior modification are concerns that highlight the significance of using evidence-based design, user-centered approaches, and continuous assessment and enhancement of ICT solutions [31]. Furthermore, while designing and implementing ICT solutions meant to improve health and alter behavior, ethical factors including informed permission, transparency, and autonomy must be carefully considered.

As we consider the future, ICT's ongoing development has the potential to improve support for healthy behavior and way of life. Technological developments, user experience design, and innovations based on behavioral research are what drive this potential. According to [36], the development of technologies like machine learning, AI, and tailored digital health interventions presents opportunities for more customized, adaptable, and successful behavior modification interventions. To guarantee that ICT fosters positive health outcomes and encourages healthy habits among all parts of society, it is also crucial to address digital divides, advocate for health equality, and involve various populations in digital health projects.

ICT provides users with strong tools that enable them to support and encourage the adoption of healthy lifestyle choices, leading to good changes in their general well-being. ICT efforts use social media platforms, wearable technology, mobile applications, and gamification techniques to motivate and involve consumers in adopting better habits. In the end, these modifications result in better health and a higher standard of living.

5.5 ICT FOR EMPOWERING INDIVIDUALS TO MANAGE THEIR HEALTH

By enabling people to take responsibility for their own health and well-being, the use of ICT has fundamentally altered the healthcare industry. ICT projects facilitate access to health information, resources, and assistance for people by means of digital tools and platforms. This endows people with the ability to manage their own health, make informed decisions, and monitor their metrics. The various ways that ICT can assist people in taking control of their own health are covered in this section. It focuses on significant instruments, issues, and potential advancements in the future.

5.5.1 Personal Health Records (PHRs)

PHRs, or personal health records, are computerized platforms that enable individuals to securely manage and access health-related data. According to [37], patient health records (PHRs) allow individuals to store all their medical history in one location, including diagnoses, prescriptions, allergies, and vaccination information. Through their PHRs, individuals may view their health records, track changes over time, and communicate pertinent information with their healthcare providers. This facilitates continuity of treatment and facilitates decision-making. PHRs may also include healthcare tools, such as appointment scheduling, medication reminders, and health education materials, to support patients in following their treatment regimens and taking care of their health.

5.5.2 Patient Portals and Telehealth Platforms

Remote patient consultations, medical service delivery, and communication between patients and healthcare providers are all facilitated via patient portals and telehealth platforms. Patients can request medicine refills, schedule appointments, view test results, and securely communicate with the care team, among other things, with the aid of digital platforms [38]. Using secure messaging, the phone, or video conferencing, telehealth technologies enable remote consultations between patients and medical professionals without the need for physical presence. Remote access to healthcare services improves consistency, accessibility, and convenience of care, particularly for those unable to travel due to physical restrictions, chronic illnesses, or limited mobility.

5.5.3 Health Monitoring Devices and Sensors

With the use of health monitoring gadgets and sensors, people may view their blood pressure, blood sugar levels, pulse rate, and activity levels in real time, among other health parameters. According to [39], wearable technology, smartphone apps, and home tracking systems provide consumers with actionable health-related information that they may utilize to identify changes or issues early on. Wearable fitness trackers that monitor sleep habits and daily activity levels and provide users with information on their sleep quality and amount of activity are helpful examples [40]. In a similar vein, by pairing smartphone apps with Bluetooth-enabled devices, consumers may monitor long-term health issues including diabetes and high blood pressure as well as their food, medication compliance, and other lifestyle factors.

5.5.4 Health Information and Decision Support Tools

ICT provides people with access to a wealth of health information and decision-making tools, enabling them to make informed decisions about their health and well-being. You can discover evidence-based information on a variety of health-related issues, including how to manage diseases, implement preventative measures, and locate alternative therapies, via websites, mobile applications, and other internet resources [41]. Additionally, people can utilize symptom checks, risk calculators, and treatment decision aids to assess their symptoms, determine the likelihood that they will develop specific medical illnesses, and balance the advantages and disadvantages of various treatment options.

By providing them with trustworthy information and decision-making tools, ICT empowers people to take charge of their own healthcare, promotes health literacy, and facilitates group decision-making. ICT's ongoing development holds promise for empowering individuals to take charge of their own health. New technology, improved user interfaces, and customized medical care make this feasible. It is imperative to ensure that ICT fosters empowerment and enhances health outcomes for all individuals [36]. To this end, it will be critical to reduce the digital divide, promote health equity, and involve a range of groups in digital health projects. But they also come with a lot of difficulties and things to think about, like what is covered in the next part.

5.6 CHALLENGES AND CONSIDERATIONS

ICT has a great deal of potential to enable people to take control of their own health. However, in order to ensure that ICT use is beneficial, equitable, and available to all, issues related to digital literacy, technology accessibility, health disparities, and privacy must be addressed [42]. In order to maintain public confidence in digital health solutions, legal compliance, data security and privacy, interoperability between various ICT platforms, and the security of people's health information must be prioritized. The necessity for situation-specific, individualized advice, potential biases in decision support system, and uncertainties over the reliability and correctness of health information all underscore the significance of creating and continuously testing evidence-based ICT solutions. Therefore, it is critical to address the ICT difficulties in the healthcare industry.

5.6.1 Factors to Be Considered

It is imperative to address these concerns in order to optimize the effectiveness and equality of digital health interventions. The main issues and concerns surrounding the use of ICT to improve healthcare are covered in this section, along with some possible solutions.

5.6.1.1 Digital Divide and Health Inequities

Leveraging ICT for health improvement is significantly hampered by the "digital divide," which is the term for unequal access to and use of digital technology among different demographic groups. According to [43] those who are elderly, have few financial means, live in rural areas, or have little computer literacy may find it challenging to accurately access and use digital health solutions. Health disparities could be exacerbated by the fact that those who stand to gain the most from digital health interventions might also be the least likely to use them.

5.6.1.2 Health Literacy and Technological Complexity

One more problem stems from the requirement for people to have a deep understanding of both technology and health in order to use and navigate digital health technologies efficiently. According to [44], a sizeable section of the populace might not have the requisite knowledge or experience to interpret health information, use sophisticated digital tools or applications, or make the best decisions regarding their health. Furthermore, the wealth of health information available online can cause confusion, the spread of false information, and elevated stress, especially for those with limited health knowledge. In order to address these issues, it is imperative to develop digital health solutions that are user-friendly, accessible to all individuals, and culturally sensitive.

5.6.1.3 Data Privacy and Security Concerns

Digital health professionals should prioritize data security, encryption, user permission, and adherence to privacy regulations in order to address the prevalence of privacy and security issues, which pose significant barriers to the widespread adoption and acceptance of digital health solutions. People may be reluctant to disclose confidential medical data or utilize online platforms if they perceive a potential threat to their privacy or security [45]. Data breaches, third-party misuse, and unauthorized access to personal health information can undermine the credibility and efficacy of digital health interventions.

5.6.1.4 Integration and Interoperability

Integrating and establishing interoperability between digital health systems and platforms poses a significant technical challenge. The absence of standardized data formats, the division of health information among several systems, and the lack of interoperability among technologies create obstacles in data sharing and care coordination. The presence of fragmentation not only poses challenges in delivering healthcare, but it also hinders the use of data insights for informed health decision-making and enhancing outcomes [46]. Facilitating interoperability is crucial for enabling health systems and partners to effortlessly exchange and merge data. For instance, it is necessary to establish health information interchange standards and interoperability frameworks.

5.6.1.5 Ethical and Legal Considerations

When designing, deploying, and utilizing digital health tools, ethical and legal considerations are of the highest relevance. In order to ensure that digital health interventions preserve users' rights and encourage ethical conduct, it is necessary to thoroughly ponder elements such as informed consent, autonomy, data ownership, and responsibility. The legal frameworks governing the production and implementation of digital health solutions, including regulations for medical equipment, laws safeguarding data, and requirements for telehealth permits, varied from one country to another. Regulation compliance may present difficulties for developers and suppliers, according to [47]. It is imperative to establish clear directives, benchmarks, and moral frameworks to guarantee the proper planning and application of digital health treatments.

5.6.2 Strategies for Mitigation

The best way to solve these issues is to work together with legislators, medical experts, technology developers, researchers, and community stakeholders. This should be a multidisciplinary effort. A number of approaches to solving the problem include:

1. *Advancing digital inclusion*: Programs targeted at closing the digital divide and giving marginalized people better access to digital health technologies. These initiatives could involve funding gadget purchases, developing internet infrastructure, and delivering computer literacy instruction.
2. *Health literacy and user education*: Programs and materials designed to improve people's comprehension of health and technology so they can use digital health tools wisely and make well-informed decisions.
3. *Implementing privacy-enhancing technologies*: Utilizing privacy-enhancing technology, like encryption, anonymization, and secure data storage, to protect users' confidence and privacy, maintain data integrity, and guarantee adherence to privacy laws.
4. *Interoperability standards*: The creation and application of data exchange protocols and interoperability standards to enable the sharing and fusion of health data among various systems. This facilitates the smooth delivery of healthcare services and the ability to make well-informed decisions based on empirical evidence.
5. *Ethical guidelines and governance*: Adherence to ethical principles, regulatory structures, and governance frameworks is essential to guaranteeing the conscientious creation, distribution, and application of digital health instruments. These policies should also protect user rights and advance accountability and openness.

Through tackling these problems and putting in place practical measures to lessen their effects, ICT can give people the tools they need to improve their general well-being, advance health equity, and improve their quality of life.

5.7 CONCLUSION

In conclusion, ICT has revolutionized the healthcare industry by offering cutting-edge methods that enhance accessibility, availability, preventative care, and patient empowerment. ICT has revolutionized the provision, management, and access to healthcare services through telemedicine, mobile health apps, EHRs, AI, and other advancements.

ICT has not only made it possible for people to live without boundaries imposed by geography, but it has also enabled them to take charge of their own health and well-being. Through the use of telemedicine, patients can receive medical consultations remotely, eliminating the need for in-person visits and opening up access to healthcare in underserved or remote areas. Mobile health applications provide users with an easy way to track their health indicators, access health-related information, and utilize their phones to engage in preventive behaviors. EHRs give healthcare providers access to complete, up-to-date patient data, which improves patient outcomes, speeds up clinical procedures, and facilitates care coordination. The amalgamation of AI with healthcare analytics enables personalized treatment plans, data-driven decision-making, and predictive modeling, ultimately enhancing the effectiveness and efficiency of healthcare delivery.

Despite the amazing advancements made possible by ICT, challenges like the digital divide, obstacles to health literacy, data privacy concerns, interoperability issues, and ethical considerations still exist. In order to ensure equitable and impartial use and access to digital health technologies, safeguard patient privacy and confidentiality, enable data exchange and integration, uphold ethical principles and user rights, and more, it is critical to address these issues and close these gaps.

ICT in healthcare has a bright future ahead of it that holds enormous promise for further advancement and innovation. The fields of wearable sensors, genomics, machine learning, AI, and wearable sensors will all continue to drive advances in personalized medicine and therapy optimization. The delivery of healthcare will be expanded by combining ICT with cutting-edge paradigms like virtual reality, digital therapies, and precision public health. This will improve patient experiences and health outcomes.

In this rapidly changing environment, sustained investment in ICT innovation, stakeholder collaboration, and a resolute devotion to solving issues and inequities will be essential. By leveraging ICT, healthcare systems can improve their resilience, responsiveness, and patient-centeredness, ultimately achieving their mission of universal access to high-quality treatment.

REFERENCES

1. Castells, M. (2011). *The Rise of the Network Society*. John Wiley & Sons.
2. Davis, N., Preston, C., & Sahin, I. (2009). *ICT and the Literacy Practices of Student Writing. In the Handbook of Research on New Literacies* (pp. 359–388). Routledge.
3. OECD. (2019). *Digitalization and Productivity: In-Depth Analysis on the ICT Sector and Its Impacts*. https://www.oecd.org/sti/ieconomy/digitalization-and-productivity-in-depth-analysis-on-the-ict-sector-and-its-impacts-6d1c8e7a-en.htm
4. Norris, P. (2001). *Digital Divide: Civic Engagement, Information Poverty, and the Internet Worldwide*. Cambridge University Press.
5. . World Health Organization (WHO). (2020). *Digital Health. https://www.who.int/health-topics/digital-health#tab=tab_1*
6. Coye, M. J., Kvedar, J. C., & Everett, W. (2014). Connected health: A review of technologies and strategies to improve patient care with telemedicine and telehealth. *Health Affairs*, 33(2), 194–199.

7. World Health Organization (WHO). (2019). *Classification of digital health interventions v1.0: A shared language to describe the uses of digital technology for health.* https://www.who.int/reproductivehealth/publications/mhealth/classification-digital-health-interventions/en/
8. Wickramasinghe, N., & Goldberg, S. (2016). Health information technology as a universal equalizer for healthcare access: Promise and pitfalls. *Journal of Medical Internet Research*, 18(2), e47.
9. World Health Organization (2020). *Digital health*. Retrieved from https://www.who.int/health-topics/digital-health#tab=tab_1
10. Bashshur, R. L., Doarn, C. R., Frenk, J. M., Kvedar, J. C., Shannon, G. W., & Woolliscroft, J. O. (2018). Telemedicine and the COVID-19 pandemic, lessons for the future. *Telemedicine and e-Health*, 26(5), 571–573.
11. Wade, V. A., Karnon, J., Elshaug, A. G., & Hiller, J. E. (2014). A systematic review of economic analyses of telehealth services using real-time video communication. *BMC Health Services Research*, 14(1), 443.
12. Krupinski, E. A., Antoniotti, N., Burdick, A., & Weinstein, R. S. (2017). Telemedicine in dermatology: Findings and experiences worldwide—A systematic literature review. *Telemedicine and e-Health*, 23(6), 453–466.
13. Ohannessian, R., Duong, T. A., & Odone, A. (2019). Global telemedicine implementation and integration within health systems to fight the COVID-19 pandemic: A call to action. *JMIR Public Health and Surveillance*, 6(2), e18810.
14. Free, C., Phillips, G., Galli, L., Watson, L., Felix, L., Edwards, P., ... & Haines, A. (2013). The effectiveness of mobile-health technologies to improve health care service delivery processes: A systematic review and meta-analysis. *PLoS Medicine*, 10(1), e1001363.
15. Chib, A., van Velthoven, M. H., Car, J., & Majeed, A. (2016). mHealth adoption in low-resource environments: A review of the use of Mobile healthcare in developing countries. *Journal of Health Communication*, 20(1), 4–34.
16. Marcano Belisario, J. S., Huckvale, K., Greenfield, G., Car, J., & Gunn, L. H. (2014). Smartphone and tablet self-management apps for asthma. *Cochrane Database of Systematic Reviews*, (11). Art. No. CD010013.
17. Harris, L. T., Tufano, J., & Le, T. (2016). *An integrative review of technology to support health promotion efforts. Computational and mathematical methods in medicine*, 2016.
18. Labrique, A. B., Vasudevan, L., Kochi, E., Fabricant, R., & Mehl, G. (2013). mHealth innovations as health system strengthening tools: 12 common applications and a visual framework. *Global Health: Science and Practice*, 1(2), 160–171.
19. Adler-Milstein, J., & Jha, A. K. (2017). HITECH act drove large gains in Hospital electronic health record adoption. *Health Affairs*, 36(8), 1416–1422.
20. Buntin, M. B., Burke, M. F., Hoaglin, M. C., & Blumenthal, D. (2011). The benefits of health information technology: A review of the recent literature shows predominantly positive results. *Health Affairs*, 30(3), 464–471.
21. Topol, E. J. (2019). High-performance medicine: The convergence of human and artificial intelligence. *Nature Medicine*, 25(1), 44–56.
22. Obermeyer, Z., & Emanuel, E. J. (2016). Predicting the future—Big data, machine learning, and clinical medicine. *New England Journal of Medicine*, 375(13), 1216–1219.
23. Esteva, A., Kuprel, B., Novoa, R. A., Ko, J., Swetter, S. M., Blau, H. M., & Thrun, S. (2019). Dermatologist-level classification of skin cancer with deep neural networks. *Nature*, 542(7639), 115–118.
24. Halamka, J. D., & Tripathi, M. (2012). The HITECH era in retrospect. *New England Journal of Medicine*, 366(24), 2249–2251.

25. Rajkomar, A., Dean, J., Kohane, I., & Butte, A. (2019). Machine learning in medicine. *New England Journal of Medicine*, 380(14), 1347–1358.
26. Chretien, J. P., Rivers, C. M., Johansson, M. A., & Mayer, A. J. (2014). Google flu trends: The limits of big data for predicting epidemics. *American Journal of Public Health*, 104(10), 372–379.
27. Friedman, D. J., Parrish, R. G., & Ross, D. A. (2015). Electronic health records and US public health: Current realities and future promise. *American Journal of Public Health*, 105(3), 498–502.
28. . World Health Organization. (2013). *mHealth: New horizons for health through mobile technologies*. https://www.who.int/goe/publications/goe_mhealth_web.pdf
29. Ferretti, L., Wymant, C., Kendall, M., Zhao, L., Nurtay, A., Abeler-Dörner, L., … & Fraser, C. (2020). Quantifying SARS-CoV-2 transmission suggests epidemic control with digital contact tracing. *Science*, 368(6491), eabb6936.
30. Wilson, K., Atkinson, K. M., & Westeinde, J. (2015). Apps for immunization: Leveraging mobile devices to place the individual at the center of care. *Human Vaccines & Immunotherapeutics*, 11(10), 2395–2399.
31. Coughlin, S. S., Whitehead, M., Sheats, J. Q., Mastromonico, J., & Smith, S. (2016). A review of smartphone applications for promoting physical activity. *Health Informatics Journal*, 22(3), 393–410.
32. Patel, M. S., Asch, D. A., & Volpp, K. G. (2015). Wearable devices as facilitators, not drivers, of health behavior change. *JAMA*, 313(5), 459–460.
33. Laranjo, L., Arguel, A., Neves, A. L., Gallagher, A. M., Kaplan, R., Mortimer, N., & Lau, A. Y. (2015). The influence of social networking sites on health behavior change: A systematic review and meta-analysis. *Journal of the American Medical Informatics Association*, 22(1), 243–256.
34. Cugelman, B. (2013). Gamification: What it is and why it matters to digital health behavior change developers. *JMIR Serious Games*, 1(1), e3139.
35. Michie, S., Richardson, M., Johnston, M., Abraham, C., Francis, J., Hardeman, W., … & Wood, C. E. (2013). The behavior change technique taxonomy (v1) of 93 hierarchically clustered techniques: Building an international consensus for the reporting of behavior change interventions. *Annals of Behavioral Medicine*, 46(1), 81–95.
36. Bakker, D., Kazantzis, N., Rickwood, D., & Rickard, N. (2016). *Mental health smartphone apps.*
37. Tang, P. C., Ash, J. S., Bates, D. W., Overhage, J. M., & Sands, D. Z. (2006). Personal health records: Definitions, benefits, and strategies for overcoming barriers to adoption. *Journal of the American Medical Informatics Association*, 13(2), 121–126.
38. Irizarry, T., Shoemake, J., Nilsen, M. L., & Czaja, S. (2015). Patient portals as a tool for health care engagement: A mixed-method study of older adults with varying levels of health literacy and prior patient portal use. *Journal of Medical Internet Research*, 17(3), e50.
39. Steinhubl, S. R., Muse, E. D., & Topol, E. J. (2015). The emerging field of mobile health. *Science Translational Medicine*, 7(283), 283rv3–283rv3.
40. Bakker, J. P., Ford, E. S., Mohlman, G. J., & Li, C. (2016). Predictors of obstructive sleep apnea risk among patients with type 2 diabetes mellitus. *Therapeutic Advances in Endocrinology and Metabolism*, 7(3), 85–92.
41. Wang, Y. C., Lee, C. M., Lew-Ting, C. Y., Hsu, H. T., & Tsai, C. C. (2011). Establishment of decision aids in Taiwan. *Journal of Evidence-Based Medicine*, 4(1), 34–40.
42. Alami, H., Gagnon, M. P., Fortin, J. P., Légaré, F., & Fadden, G. (2016). Implementation of a web-based intervention to improve patient healthcare empowerment: The development and preliminary testing of a usability questionnaire. *Journal of Medical Internet Research*, 18(11), e281.

43. Viswanath, K., & Kreuter, M. W. (2007). Health disparities, communication inequalities, and eHealth. *American Journal of Preventive Medicine*, 32(5), S131–S133.
44. Berkman, N. D., Sheridan, S. L., Donahue, K. E., Halpern, D. J., & Crotty, K. (2011). Low health literacy and health outcomes: An updated systematic review. *Annals of Internal Medicine*, 155(2), 97–107.
45. Hutton, L., & Henderson, J. (2017). privacy concerns and privacy-related behavior on Facebook. *Telecommunications Policy*, 41(5–6), 1–14.
46. Jha, A. K., Doolan, D., Grandt, D., Scott, T., & Bates, D. W. (2018). The use of health information technology in seven nations. *International Journal of Medical Informatics*, 102, 50–58.
47. Kerr, C., Nixon, G., & Wild, D. (2020). Ethical and legal considerations for digital health technologies. *Journal of Medical Internet Research*, 22(7), e18614.

6 Green Computing and Sustainability

Y. Lalitha Kameswari

6.1 INTRODUCTION

The globe has seen an extraordinary upsurge in technical development in the last few years, which has resulted in a significant rise in the use of electronic devices and digital infrastructure [1]. Although these technological advancements have transformed many facets of human existence, they have also presented serious obstacles to sustainability and the environment. The idea of "green computing," sometimes referred to as "sustainable computing" or "eco-friendly computing," aims to solve these issues by encouraging the environmentally responsible design, production, use, and disposal of computing systems and devices [2]. It includes a broad range of actions meant to lessen the effects of information technology (IT) activities on the environment and guarantee the long-term viability of digital technologies. Green computing's main objective is to reduce the amount of energy and other resources, decrease the amount of electronic garbage (e-waste), and lessen the carbon footprint that comes with computing. This includes implementing recycling and waste management programs, adopting energy-efficient hardware and software, streamlining data center operations, and encouraging eco-friendly computing behaviors among people and businesses. One of the main tenets of green computing initiatives is sustainability. It highlights how important it is to strike a balance between social, economic, and environmental factors when designing, implementing, and managing IT services and systems. The architecture of cloud computing is shown in Figure 6.1.

Through the assimilation of sustainability ideas into computing procedures, entities can attain financial benefits, augment operational efficacy, and facilitate environmental preservation initiatives [3]. Green computing is a multidisciplinary field that involves environmental science, engineering, economics, and policy-making in addition to the IT business. It emphasizes how technology and the environment are intertwined, underscoring the significance of using comprehensive strategies to handle challenging sustainability issues [4]. Against the backdrop of both environmental degradation and rapid technological advancement, green computing has become a crucial paradigm for building a more sustainable future. People, companies, and governments may leverage the power of technology while reducing its negative environmental effects and laying the groundwork for a more robust and sustainable digital ecosystem by adopting green computing ideas and practices [5].

DOI: 10.1201/9781003471356-6

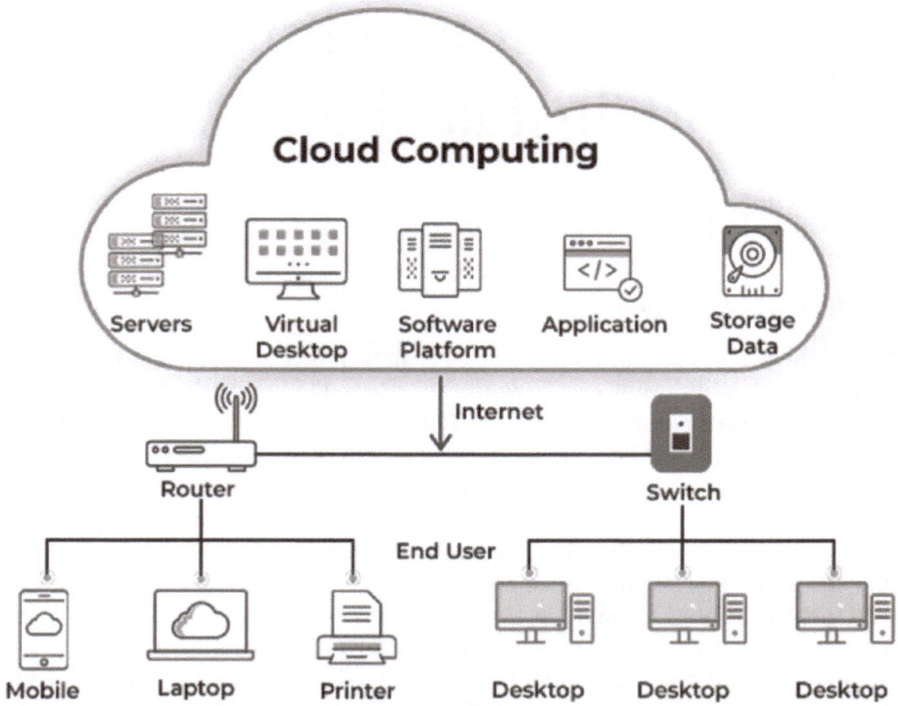

FIGURE 6.1 Cloud computing. (Source: https://www.spiceworks.com/tech/cloud/articles/what-is-cloud-computing/.)

6.2 LIFE CYCLE ASSESSMENT IN GREEN COMPUTING

In the fields of sustainability and green computing, life cycle assessment (LCA) is an essential instrument. It allows for a thorough assessment of the environmental effects related to the whole life cycle of computer goods and services, including the extraction of raw materials, production, distribution, usage, and disposal [6]. LCA helps to minimize the overall environmental footprint of computing systems by offering insightful information about environmental hotspots and facilitating well-informed decision-making. Determining the scope of the assessment, including its borders, functional units, and system boundaries, is the first step in LCA. This entails figuring out which crucial phases of the computer product or service life cycle need to be examined. Data on resource use, energy use, emissions, and trash generation are gathered and quantified during the inventory analysis stage [7]. Information about the extraction of raw materials, manufacturing procedures, transportation, energy consumption during usage, and disposal at the end of life are all part of this process. Impact assessment is analyzing how the activities found in the inventory analysis will affect the environment. This entails evaluating the effects on ecosystems, human health, resource depletion, climate change, and other pertinent environmental categories. LCA is shown in Figure 6.2.

During the inventory analysis stage, information is collected and quantified on the use of resources, energy, emissions, and garbage generation [7]. This process includes information on raw material extraction, manufacturing processes, transportation, energy consumption during use, and disposal at the end of life. Analyzing the potential environmental effects of the activities identified in the inventory analysis is known as impact assessment. This comprises assessing how it will affect human health, ecosystems, resource depletion, climate change, and other relevant environmental categories. Information on resource consumption, energy use, emissions, and rubbish generation is gathered and quantified during the inventory analysis stage [7]. Information about the extraction of raw materials, manufacturing procedures, transportation, energy consumption during usage, and disposal at the end of life are all covered by this process. Impact assessment is the process of examining the possible environmental impacts of the activities found in the inventory analysis. Estimating the effects on ecosystems, public health,

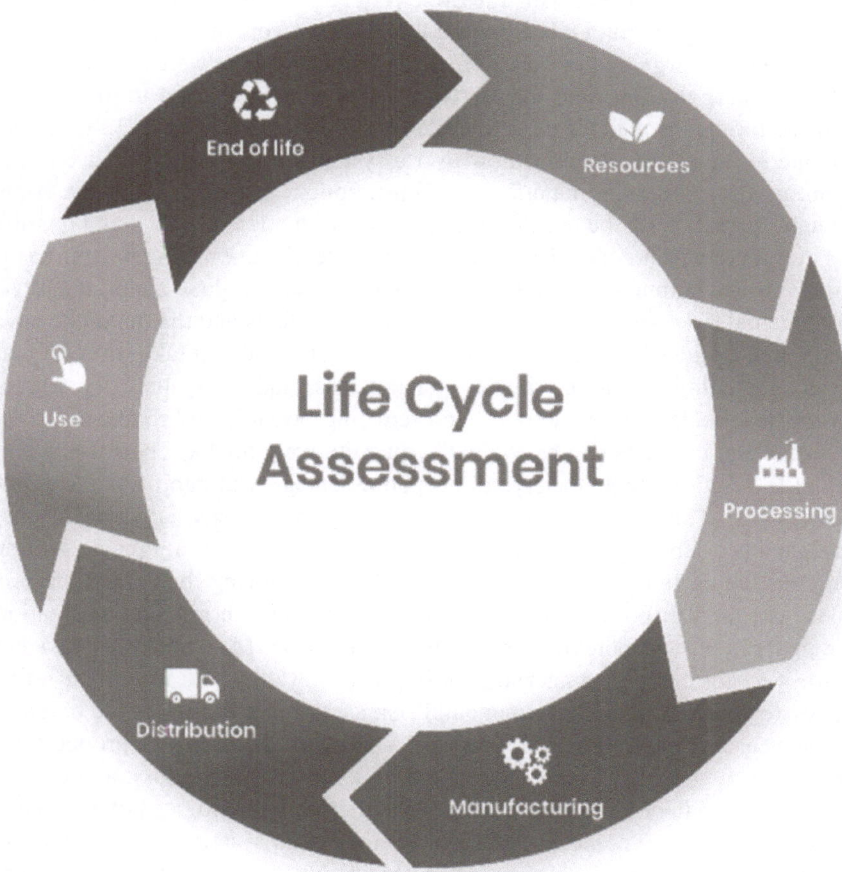

FIGURE 6.2 Life cycle assessment. (Source: https://oneclicklca.com/en/resources/articles/life-cycle-assessment-for-green-building-experts.)

resource depletion, climate change, and other relevant environmental aspects is part of this process [8]. Stakeholders can help shift the computer ecosystem toward one that is more environmentally conscious and sustainable by including LCA in decision-making processes. The full assessment and analysis of the environmental impact of IT products and systems across their life cycle necessitates the utilization of many approaches and tools [9]. Throughout a product or service's whole life cycle, the environmental consequences it has on the environment are measured and evaluated using the LCA approach [10]. It considers every phase, which includes extraction of raw materials, manufacturing, transportation, usage, and disposal at the end of life. By giving stakeholders information on resource consumption, energy use, emissions, and waste generation, LCA enables them to pinpoint environmental hotspots and possible areas for development. Measuring the greenhouse gas emissions (such as carbon dioxide, methane, and nitrous oxide) connected to a good, service, or company is the main goal of carbon footprint analysis. It evaluates emissions from energy use, transportation, and waste management, among other sources, across the course of their life cycle [11]. Analyzing one's carbon footprint can assist find ways to cut emissions and lessen the effects of climate change. An examination of energy and resource efficiency measures how well IT systems and goods use energy, water, and materials. MFA is a method used to analyze the flow of materials throughout the life cycle of a product or system [12]. MFA is a technique for analyzing material flow over a system's or product's life cycle [12]. It monitors the extraction, manufacture, consumption, and disposal of materials, offering information on the use of resources, the production of waste, and possible effects on the environment. MFA facilitates the identification of opportunities to minimize waste output, enhance recycling and reuse, and reduce material use. An environmental risk assessment looks at the possible effects and threats to the environment that could arise from using IT systems and products. It takes into account elements including pollution, toxicity, habitat loss, and ecosystem degradation to assist stakeholders in recognizing and reducing possible environmental risks. IT systems and products can be evaluated quantitatively for their performance in terms of the environment, society, and economy using sustainability metrics and indicators [13]. These measurements could be carbon intensity, energy efficiency ratings, and eco-labeling standards. MFA is a method for examining material flow during the life cycle of a system or product [12]. Monitoring the extraction, production, use, and disposal of materials, it provides data on resource utilization, waste generation, and potential environmental impacts. MFA makes it easier to find ways to cut down on material use, improve recycling and reuse, and minimize waste generation. An environmental risk assessment examines the potential consequences and environmental risks associated with the use of IT products and systems [14]. It considers factors like toxicity, pollution, habitat loss, and ecosystem deterioration in order to help stakeholders identify and mitigate potential environmental risks [15]. The performance of IT goods and systems in relation to the economy, society, and environment can be objectively assessed. Making informed decisions, encouraging creativity, and accelerating the shift to a more environmentally conscious and sustainable IT ecosystem are all made possible by effective environmental assessment.

6.3 ENERGY-SAVING PROCESSOR ARCHITECTURE

An essential component of green computing is energy-efficient CPU design, which aims to reduce power consumption without sacrificing performance. The total energy footprint of computer systems, such as servers, desktops, laptops, mobile devices, and embedded systems, can be significantly decreased with the help of energy-efficient processors [16]. Processors that are energy-efficient are made to use the least amount of electricity possible when doing calculations. To reduce energy waste and increase energy efficiency, this entails refining the processor's circuitry, architecture, and microarchitecture. Advanced semiconductor manufacturing processes, like lower transistor sizes and low-power design methodologies, are utilized by energy-efficient CPUs [17]. These procedures make it possible to produce processors with lower dynamic power consumption and leakage currents, which saves energy. Dynamic Voltage and Frequency Scaling (DVFS) is a method that dynamically modifies the processor's operating voltage and frequency in response to workload needs. DVFS mechanisms are included in energy-efficient processors to lower voltage and frequency during periods of low activity. This reduces power consumption without compromising performance. Two power-saving methods that are used to cut off power to underutilized functional units and clock signals within the processor are power gating and clock gating. Power gating and clock gating are two techniques used by energy-efficient processors to turn off inactive parts and lower power consumption when the CPU is idle or under low demand. Multicore architectures and parallel processing are two features that energy-efficient processors use to increase performance without sacrificing efficiency. Through the distribution of computational tasks compared to single-core architectures, energy-efficient CPUs with many cores can achieve improved throughput and efficiency [18]. Green Cloud Computing Architecture is shown in Figure 6.3.

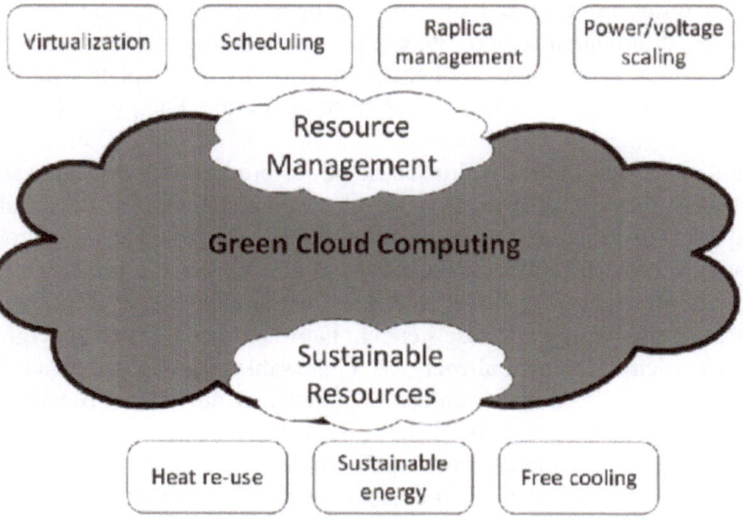

FIGURE 6.3 Green cloud computing. (Source: https://www.researchgate.net/figure/Green-Cloud-Computing-Techniques_fig3_318117091.)

Energy-efficient CPUs use instruction set architectures optimized for minimal power consumption. By reducing the number of instructions performed per task and streamlining instruction pipelines to use less energy, these ISAs promote power efficiency. On-chip power management functions including dynamic power allocation, thermal monitoring, and power budgeting are present in energy-efficient processors. These characteristics allow the processor to dynamically adjust its power usage in response to changes in workload, temperature, and power limitations. Specialized accelerators and units for certain tasks, such as graphics processing, encryption, and machine learning, may be included in energy-efficient processors [19]. Through the delegation of specific tasks to specialized units, energy-efficient processors can maximize energy efficiency and enhance system performance in general. Energy-efficient processor design seeks to balance power and performance by using these ideas and techniques, allowing the creation of computer systems that provide high performance with the least amount of energy usage and environmental effect possible [20].

6.4 RENEWABLE ENERGY SOURCES FOR DATA CENTERS

Given that data centers are notorious for consuming large amounts of energy, renewable energy sources are essential for mitigating the environmental impact of these facilities [21]. Long-term sustainability is enhanced by incorporating renewable energy into data center operations in addition to lowering carbon emissions [22]. One of the most popular renewable energy sources for data centers is solar energy. Data centers can have solar panels mounted on their grounds or roofs that collect solar radiation and turn it into electricity. Developments in solar panel technology and falling prices have made solar energy a more attractive choice for data center operations. Another well-liked renewable energy source for data centers is wind energy. Wind turbines capture the wind's kinetic energy and transform it into electrical power. Information centers situated in regions with reliable and strong wind patterns can profit from using wind energy to partially or completely replace their energy requirements [23]. Common sources of Renewable Energy for Data Centers are shown in Figure 6.4.

Some data centers use the hydroelectric power produced by flowing water, particularly those that are close to rivers or other bodies of water. A dependable and sustainable energy source for data center operations is provided by hydroelectric dams and turbines, which harness the energy of flowing water to produce electricity [24]. Geothermal energy produces electricity by harnessing heat from the Earth's crust. Geothermal power plants use steam or hot water that is stored underground to generate electricity. Geothermal energy is a renewable resource that data centers in geothermal resource-rich areas can use to power their operations. Biomass energy is the process of turning organic materials into heat or electricity, such as wood waste, biogas, and agricultural wastes [25]. Anaerobic digestion, gasification, and combustion are only a few of the processes used by biomass power plants to provide renewable energy. Data center operations can incorporate biomass energy as a sustainable substitute for conventional fossil fuels. In order to maintain resilience and dependability, a lot of data centers use hybrid renewable energy systems, which

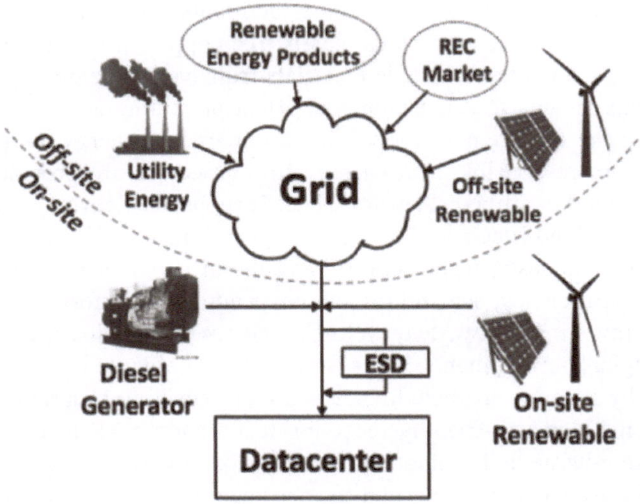

FIGURE 6.4 Sources of renewable energy for data centers. (Source: https://www.researchgate.net/figure/Various-energy-integration-option-in-data-center-RWUS12_fig25_320491323.)

integrate several renewable energy sources. Data centers can reduce the erratic and unpredictable nature of individual renewable sources and maximize energy production according to regional needs by varying their renewable energy mix. Power purchase agreements with renewable energy providers or utilities are another way that data centers might obtain renewable energy [26]. PPAs eliminate the need for on-site renewable infrastructure by allowing data centers to access renewable energy produced off-site, such as from sizable solar or wind farms. Data centers may minimize their dependency on fossil fuels, drastically lower their carbon footprint, and support international efforts to mitigate climate change by utilizing renewable energy sources. Furthermore, incorporating renewable energy into data center operations can boost company sustainability programs, promote brand recognition, and draw in stakeholders and customers who care about the environment.

6.5 RECYCLING PROGRAMS FOR E-WASTE

The management of the disposal and recycling of electronic trash, or "e-waste," is the goal of e-waste recycling programs. Electronic items that have been abandoned, including televisions, tablets, laptops, cell phones, and other consumer electronics, are referred to as e-waste. Because of its hazardous components and inappropriate disposal methods, e-waste has grown to be a major global environmental and health concern in light of the quick speed at which technology is developing and the shorter product lifecycles. To reduce dangers to the environment and public health, proper handling and recycling procedures should be given top priority in e-waste recycling initiatives. This entails making certain that electronic equipment are disassembled, separated, and processed correctly in order to salvage valuable materials and reduce exposure to potentially harmful compounds including lead, mercury, cadmium, and brominated flame retardants. The goal of e-waste recycling programs is to collect precious metals like copper, silver, and gold as well as plastics, glass, and other valuable materials from electronic gadgets. Recycling these materials lessens the environmental effect of mining and extraction while also reducing the requirement for virgin resources and energy. Guidelines and requirements for responsible e-waste recycling processes are provided by certifications and standards like e-Stewards, R2 (Responsible Recycling), and WEEE (Waste Electrical and Electronic Equipment) compliance. Following these guidelines guarantees honesty, responsibility, and moral behavior all along the recycling process. Efficiency, scalability, and environmental performance can all be enhanced by investing in e-waste recycling processes through research, innovation, and technological developments. The sustainability of e-waste recycling programs is enhanced by innovations including closed-loop recycling programs, automated sorting systems, and eco-friendly recycling techniques. Stakeholders can effectively manage e-waste and promote a circular economy, where electronic devices are reused, refurbished, and recycled to minimize waste and conserve resources by putting in place comprehensive e-waste recycling programs that address collection, awareness, regulation, collaboration, safe handling, resource recovery, certification, and innovation (Figure 6.5).

FIGURE 6.5 E-Waste recycling programs. (Source: https://www.lg.com/in/recycling/.)

6.6 CLOUD COMPUTING FOR GREEN IT

Consolidating computing resources into centralized data centers is made possible by cloud computing. In comparison to typical on-premises IT infrastructures, cloud providers can achieve economies of scale and lower overall energy usage by pooling resources and maximizing utilization rates. Energy efficiency is a key consideration in the construction of cloud data centers, which includes sophisticated cooling systems, power-saving technology, and power-saving structures. The energy overhead associated with idle servers and underutilized hardware is decreased by the more effective use of computer resources made possible by virtualization and resource pooling approaches. Platforms for the cloud allow for resource allocation and dynamic scalability in response to variations in demand. Because of its elasticity, businesses can instantly scale up or down their computing power to maximize resource efficiency and prevent over-provisioning [27]. Consequently, energy usage can be aligned with actual workload requirements, improving overall efficiency. Cloud computing relies heavily on virtualization technologies, which allow actual servers to be divided into numerous virtual machines (VMs) or containers. Through server consolidation and workload optimization, server virtualization lowers the number of physical servers needed, boosts hardware utilization rates, and results in energy savings. To reduce their environmental impact, cloud companies invest in green data center design practices. This entails utilizing sustainable building materials and techniques, putting in place energy-efficient cooling systems, optimizing server technology, and employing renewable energy sources. Green data centers lessen environmental damage and carbon emissions related to IT infrastructure. The necessity for business travel and commuting is decreased by telecommuting and remote collaboration made possible by cloud-based collaboration tools and remote work platforms. Cloud computing makes it possible to have virtual meetings, share documents, and communicate in real time. This lowers transportation-related carbon emissions and promotes sustainable work habits. By digitizing documents and workflows, cloud-based document management and storage solutions encourage paperless operations. Businesses can use document management systems and cloud storage services to cut down on paper use, generate less waste, and expedite corporate operations in an eco-friendly way. All things considered, cloud computing provides a strong foundation for developing green IT projects, improving energy efficiency, and fostering sustainability in a number of industries. Organizations may lessen their energy use, environmental impact, and resource optimization by utilizing the scalability, flexibility, and resource optimization features of cloud platforms. Energy efficiency in Cloud Computing is shown in Figure 6.6.

6.7 SUSTAINABLE IT ARCHITECTURE

The design, implementation, and administration of IT systems and infrastructure in a way that supports social responsibility, environmental sustainability, and economic viability is referred to as sustainable IT architecture. In order to reduce adverse effects on the environment and increase beneficial social and economic results, it incorporates sustainability concepts into the planning, development, and operation of IT systems.

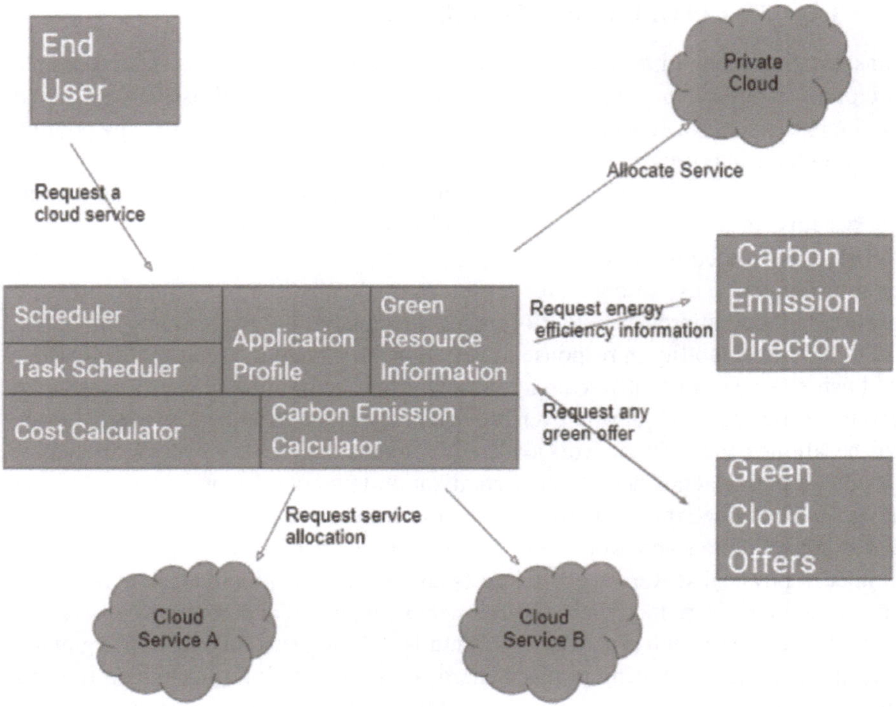

FIGURE 6.6 Energy efficiency in cloud computing. (Source: https://www.geeksforgeeks.org/energy-efficiency-in-cloud-computing/.)

Energy efficiency is given top priority in sustainable IT architecture for all parts of IT systems, including data centers, networking technology, software, and hardware. In data centers, it entails the selection of energy-efficient hardware components, low-power software application optimization, and the installation of effective cooling and power management systems. Sustainable IT architecture lessens its negative effects on the environment and greenhouse gas emissions by using less energy. This entails putting in place effective processes for resource allocation and provisioning, encouraging the reuse and recycling of IT gear and components, and applying virtualization and consolidation approaches to optimize server and storage use. Sustainable IT architecture decreases costs, cuts resource consumption, and lessens environmental impact by optimizing resource utilization [28]. Sustainable IT architecture places a strong emphasis on lifecycle management techniques to reduce environmental effects and encourage ethical IT asset disposal at the end of its useful life. This entails evaluating the effects that IT goods and services have on the environment at every stage of their lifecycle, from installation and purchase to use and disposal. In order to minimize e-waste and conserve resources, sustainable IT design includes techniques for prolonging product lifespans, upgrading and repairing equipment, and putting in place appropriate recycling and disposal procedures. Renewable energy sources, including solar, wind, and hydroelectric power, are included in sustainable IT architecture to support IT operations and infrastructure. To support clean and sustainable energy sources, this entails

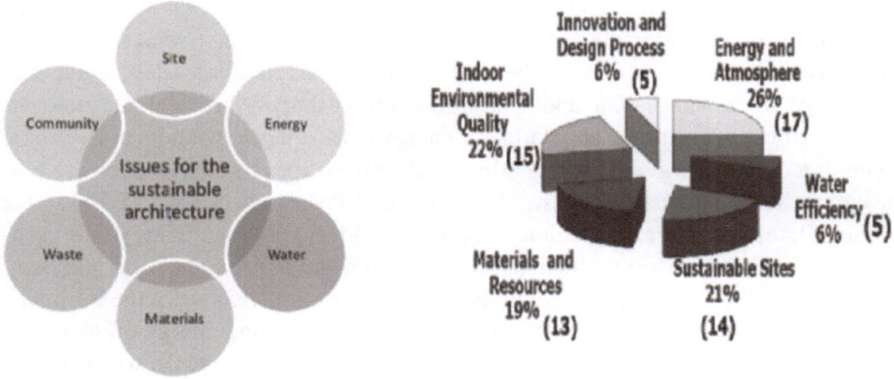

FIGURE 6.7 Sustainable IT architecture. (Source: https://www.researchgate.net/figure/Outlines-six-issues-for-the-sustainable-architecture-and-sustainable-building-Source-By_fig2_322833852.)

making investments in renewable energy generation technology, acquiring renewable energy credits, and forming partnerships with renewable energy suppliers. Sustainable IT architecture lowers carbon emissions, encourages environmental sustainability, and lessens dependency on fossil fuels by incorporating renewable energy into IT processes. Energy efficiency, resource conservation, and environmental sustainability are given top priority in the design and management of green data centers, which is a component of sustainable IT architecture. In order to reduce energy consumption and carbon footprint, green data center design integrates energy-efficient cooling systems, effective power distribution and management technologies, and renewable energy generation. Sustainable IT Architecture is shown in Figure 6.7.

Additionally, in order to reduce ecological footprint and encourage responsible environmental stewardship, sustainable IT architecture takes into account elements like water usage, facility location, and environmental impact evaluations. Social responsibility factors such as labor rights, diversity and inclusion, ethical sourcing, and community involvement are all included in sustainable IT architecture. It entails collaborating with vendors and suppliers who uphold social responsibility, advocating for human rights and fair labor practices throughout the supply chain, encouraging inclusion and diversity in the IT workforce, and funding community development projects. Prioritizing the welfare of individuals and communities affected by IT operations, sustainable IT architecture aims to produce favorable social results. Through the incorporation of these concepts and practices into IT architecture and operations, entities can establish IT systems that are sustainable, generating economic, social, and environmental advantages while bolstering long-term corporate goals.

6.8 GREEN COMPUTING POLICIES BESIDES REGULATIONS

Green computing policies and laws are actions taken by organizations or governments to encourage environmentally friendly practices in the IT sector. The main objectives of these laws and rules are usually to minimize electronic waste, cut down on energy use, and promote the use of environmentally friendly technologies. Energy efficiency guidelines for electronic devices, such as computers, servers, displays, and networking equipment, have been set by numerous nations. These guidelines encourage the advancement and widespread use of energy-efficient technologies while establishing minimal standards for energy performance. Numerous electronic items can obtain energy efficiency ratings and certifications through the Energy Star program, which is overseen by the Environmental Protection Agency (EPA) in the United States and other international agencies. Products with the Energy Star certification fulfill strict energy efficiency requirements and assist consumers and companies in finding energy-saving solutions. The Eco-design Directive of the European Union establishes standards for the environmental impact and energy efficiency of energy-related devices, such as servers and PCs. The directive seeks to encourage the development and manufacture of goods with reduced resource consumption, energy consumption, and environmental impact over the course of their life cycles. The European Union also enacted the Waste Electrical and Electronic Equipment (WEEE) Directive, which requires the collection, recycling, and safe disposal of electronic waste. The directive promotes recycling and the recovery of valuable materials while requiring manufacturers to assume accountability for the end-of-life management of their products. Certain hazardous compounds, including lead, mercury, and cadmium, are prohibited from being used in electrical and electronic equipment that is sold in the European Union under the Restriction of Hazardous Compounds (RoHS) Directive. The goal of the directive is to encourage the employment of safer substitutes while lowering the dangers that hazardous substances pose to human health and the environment. Numerous governments have put in place green procurement policies that give preference to the acquisition of environmentally friendly and energy-efficient goods and services, including IT services and equipment. These regulations promote the development of green markets and push government organizations to take environmental factors into account when purchasing IT equipment. Guidelines and criteria for evaluating the environmental performance of electronic items are provided by a number of voluntary certification programs and labels, such as EPEAT (Electronic Product Environmental Assessment Tool) [27]. In order to satisfy consumer demand for sustainable products and prove that their products comply with environmental regulations, manufacturers might choose to voluntarily pursue certification for their goods. Guidelines are provided by agencies such as the U.S. Department of Energy and The Green Grid. Data center operators can lower energy consumption and operating costs by using energy-saving technologies, optimizing cooling systems, and improving server utilization. Governments, organizations, and companies may encourage sustainable practices, lessen their negative effects on the environment, and aid in the shift of the IT sector toward a more sustainable one by putting green computing laws and regulations into place.

6.9 SOCIAL IMPACT OF GREEN IT PRACTICES

The social impact of green IT practices covers a range of social well-being, equity, and community development issues in addition to environmental considerations. Adoption of green IT practices, like the use of energy-efficient technologies, renewable energy deployment, and sustainable IT infrastructure, can lead to the creation of new jobs in environmentally friendly businesses. Green IT initiatives improve employment opportunities and strengthen community economic resilience by promoting economic growth, igniting innovation, and aiding in the development of sustainable technology industries. By lowering air and water pollution, avoiding environmental risks, and limiting exposure to hazardous chemicals and pollutants related to traditional IT operations, green IT practices can enhance public health and well-being. Green IT practices boost community health, lower healthcare expenses, and increase quality of life by encouraging cleaner and healthier settings. By developing digital literacy campaigns, extending broadband infrastructure, lowering the cost, and improving the accessibility of IT services, green IT projects can advance digital inclusion and technology access. Green IT practices support social justice, equitable opportunity, and inclusive economic development by bridging the digital divide and providing underprivileged communities with access to ICT resources. Green IT practices promote participation in environmental sustainability initiatives, community engagement, and teamwork. Green IT promotes community engagement, environmental stewardship, and group action toward common sustainability objectives through programs including electronic trash recycling schemes, energy efficiency awareness campaigns, and community-based renewable energy projects. Through the promotion of environmental awareness, sustainability education, and technological training programs, green IT practices assist in education and capacity building. Green IT initiatives enable people and communities to take an active role as change agents and innovators by incorporating sustainability principles into educational curricula, developing skills in green technologies, and offering training opportunities in sustainable IT practices. By lowering carbon emissions, lessening the effects of climate change, and supporting sustainable resource management techniques, green IT practices help to increase climate resilience and adaptation. Communities may strengthen their resistance to climate-related risks and disruptions by making investments in climate-smart technologies, disaster recovery plans, and robust IT infrastructure. This will protect infrastructure and livelihoods from environmental threats. By reducing their negative effects on natural resources, sacred locations, and cultural landscapes, green IT practices can aid in cultural preservation and heritage conservation efforts. Through the use of sustainable IT solutions, enterprises can reduce their environmental impact, safeguard, and encourage eco-friendly travel strategies that honor regional customs, values, and indigenous knowledge systems. A vast array of advantages are included in the social effect of green IT practices, such as the creation of jobs, the promotion of health, digital inclusion, community participation, education, climate resilience, and cultural preservation. Organizations may optimize good social outcomes, advance social justice, and support sustainable development goals by incorporating social concerns into green IT plans and initiatives, evaluating how sustainable IT methods affect society, especially as it relates to community awareness and corporate social responsibility.

6.10 ECONOMIC BENEFITS OF GREEN COMPUTING

There are numerous financial advantages to green computing for organizations, governments, and people. Saving money is one of the main economic advantages of green computing. Energy-efficient strategies can drastically lower an organization's energy usage and utility costs. Examples of these practices include virtualization, server consolidation, and optimized cooling systems. Furthermore, implementing green IT solutions frequently results in cheaper running costs for waste disposal, energy use, and hardware maintenance. Green computing projects optimize IT infrastructure and streamline procedures to increase productivity and efficiency. Organizations may increase workflow automation, optimize system performance, and consolidate resources with the use of virtualization, cloud computing, and energy-efficient technology. Improved company agility, quicker reaction times, and more productivity all follow from this, improving operational performance and giving businesses a competitive edge. Investing in green computing can save money in the long run by lowering the need for expensive infrastructure expansions and upgrades. Organizations can minimize capital costs, future-proof their IT infrastructure, and adjust to changing business requirements without making large upfront investments by implementing scalable solutions and energy-efficient technologies. Green computing reduces the need for periodic hardware refresh cycles and infrastructure overhauls by enabling businesses to achieve cost-effective scalability and flexibility in resource allocation. To promote the use of green computing technologies and sustainable behaviors, governments and regulatory organizations frequently provide tax breaks, subsidies, and refunds. These monetary benefits encourage businesses to invest in and assist defray the initial expenses of adoption. Organizations can lower the total cost of ownership for green IT expenditures and hasten return on investment by utilizing tax incentives and rebates. Through their demonstration of environmental responsibility and business sustainability leadership, green computing projects can improve brand reputation and market differentiation. Customers and stakeholders are beginning to place a higher value on environmentally conscious businesses and favor goods and services from sustainable businesses. Organizations can improve their brand image, draw in eco-aware clients, and obtain a competitive advantage in the market by supporting green IT efforts. Green computing assists businesses in reducing the risks of environmental liabilities, regulatory non-compliance, and reputational harm. Organizations can reduce the risk of fines, penalties, and legal liabilities resulting from environmental infractions by following green computing standards, regulations, and best practices. A corporate culture of responsibility and accountability is promoted, environmental standards are adhered to, and regulatory compliance is supported by green IT initiatives. The financial advantages of green computing include lower costs, more output and efficiency, avoiding long-term expenses, tax breaks and rebates, improving brand reputation, standing out in the market, and reducing risk. Organizations can attain notable financial benefits and simultaneously support environmental sustainability and social responsibility objectives by adopting green computing principles and allocating resources toward sustainable IT solutions.

6.11 CHALLENGES AS WELL AS INNOVATIONS IN SUSTAINABLE IT

6.11.1 Challenges

The IT infrastructure uses more energy as a result of the growing demand for processing power, which raises carbon emissions and degrades the environment. Fast technological change generates electronic garbage (e-waste), which makes handling hazardous materials, recycling, and disposal difficult. Because of multinational supply chains and intricate logistics, ensuring sustainability throughout the IT supply chain including raw material extraction, manufacture, transportation, and end-of-life disposal remains a challenge. Data centers have significant energy consumption for server power and cooling, which makes it difficult to maximize efficiency and minimize environmental effects. Underprivileged communities and developing regions, where infrastructure and resources may be few, present problems in closing the digital gap and guaranteeing fair access to technology.

6.11.2 Innovations

Low-power CPUs, solid-state drives, and energy-efficient cooling systems are examples of energy-efficient hardware innovations that assist cut down on energy use and lessen the environmental effects. Increasing the use of renewable energy sources to power data centers and IT infrastructure such as solar, wind, and hydroelectric electricity promotes sustainability and lessens dependency on fossil fuels. By encouraging sustainable patterns of consumption and production, the use of circular economy principles such as product lifespan extension, reuse, repair, and recycling helps reduce e-waste and conserve resources. The utilization of virtualization and cloud computing technologies facilitates shared infrastructure, dynamic scaling, and resource consolidation, which enhances efficiency and lowers carbon emissions and energy usage. Modular infrastructure, sophisticated cooling systems, and the incorporation of renewable energy sources are examples of innovations in green data center design that maximize environmental sustainability and energy efficiency while improving data center performance and reliability. IT goods and packaging can lessen their environmental effect and encourage sustainable consumption habits by utilizing recyclable materials, biodegradable components, and eco-friendly packaging materials. Community technology centers, public access programs, and inexpensive broadband efforts are examples of digital inclusion initiatives that bridge the digital divide and provide equitable access to technology, hence promoting social inclusion and economic empowerment. Blockchain technology makes supply chains more transparent, traceable, and accountable. This helps companies keep an eye on and validate sustainable practices, moral sourcing, and ethical production all the way through the supply chain. The IT sector may advance sustainability goals, reduce environmental impact, and foster social responsibility throughout the entire technology ecosystem by tackling these issues and utilizing technologies. Driving significant change requires stakeholder collaboration, research and development spending, and a dedication to sustainable practices.

6.12 CONCLUSION AND FUTURE SCOPE

In order to address the environmental impact of IT and to promote responsible resource management in the digital era, green computing and sustainability are essential building blocks. The IT industry has made great progress in lowering its carbon footprint and environmental impact through programs including energy efficiency, electronic waste management, renewable energy integration, and sustainable IT practices. Green computing places a strong emphasis on cutting down on energy use, eliminating electronic waste, and implementing sustainable practices all the way through the lifecycle of an IT system. Businesses can lessen their environmental impact and support global sustainability goals by making environmental responsibility a top priority. Through encouraging the adoption of energy-efficient technologies, renewable energy sources, and circular economy concepts, sustainable IT practices foster innovation and efficiency. Green data center architecture, virtualization, cloud computing, and environmentally friendly materials are examples of virtualization, cloud computing, and environmentally friendly materials all help to increase environmental performance, lower costs, and improve efficiency in green data center architecture. Collaboration amongst stakeholders, including governments, business executives, academic institutions, and civil society, is necessary to address the issues of sustainability and green computing. Through collaboration, information exchange, and group efforts, interested parties can promote systemic change and a business and environmental stewardship culture. Initiatives related to green computing have a lot of social and economic ramifications, including the creation of jobs, the improvement of health, digital inclusion, and economic growth. Green computing programs can foster inclusive growth and shared prosperity by placing a high priority on social fairness, technology access, and community engagement.

Future prospects for sustainability and green computing are bright, with plenty of chances for influence, innovation, and cooperation. In the IT industry, more research and development into cutting-edge technologies like blockchain, the Internet of Things (IoT), and artificial intelligence (AI) can open up new possibilities for improving sustainability and solving environmental issues. By utilizing these technologies, resource management may become more intelligent, energy efficiency can be increased, and environmental performance can be optimized for a range of applications. It is possible to promote investment in clean technologies and wider adoption of sustainable practices by fortifying legislative frameworks and policy incentives for sustainability and green computing. Establishing standards, encouraging best practices, and fostering environments that support sustainable innovation and development are all important tasks for governments and regulatory agencies. Resource efficiency, waste reduction, and product lifespan extension can all be facilitated by advancing circular economy concepts and principles in the IT sector. Throughout the course of a product's lifecycle, companies can reduce waste production, conserve resources, and optimize value by designing products with durability, repairability, and recycling in mind. To encourage sustainable consumption habits and drive behavior change, stakeholders including businesses, consumers, and policymakers need to be better informed about green computing and sustainability. Capacity-building programs, awareness campaigns, and educational activities can enable people and organizations to make well-informed decisions and take significant steps toward sustainability. Improving international cooperation and knowledge sharing on sustainability and green computing concerns can stimulate innovation, hasten the transfer of technology, and advance best practices globally. Beyond national borders and encouraging a common commitment to sustainability, international collaborations, research networks, and multi-stakeholder platforms can promote cooperation and group action on urgent environmental issues. The development of a more robust and ecologically conscious IT sector depends on green computing and sustainability. Stakeholders can embrace the revolutionary potential of green computing to create a more fair and sustainable future for future generations by embracing innovation, cooperation, and collective action.

REFERENCES

1. Waas, T., Hugé, J., Block, T., Wright, T., Benitez-Capistros, F., & Verbruggen, A. (2014). Sustainability assessment and indicators: Tools in a decision-making strategy for sustainable development. *Sustainability, 6*(9), 5512–5534.
2. United, N. (2018). Revision of world urbanization prospects. *United Nations,. Retrieved October17*, 2020..
3. López, C. D., Carpio, M., Martín-Morales, M., & Zamorano, M. (2019). A comparative analysis of sustainable building assessment methods. *Sustainable Cities and Society, 49*, 101611.
4. Awadh, O. (2017). Sustainability and green building rating systems: LEED, BREEAM, GSAS and Estidama critical analysis. *Journal of Building Engineering, 11*, 25–29.
5. Guzmán, P. C., Roders, A. P., & Colenbrander, B. J. F. (2017). Measuring links between cultural heritage management and sustainable urban development: An overview of global monitoring tools. *Cities, 60*, 192–201.
6. Daoudi, N. S., Mestoul, D., Lamraoui, S., Boussoualim, A., Adolphe, L., & Bensalem, R. (2019). Vernacular architecture in arid climates: Adaptation to climate change. In: Guedes, M., Cantuaria, G. (eds), *Bioclimatic Architecture in Warm Climates*. Springer, Cham. https://doi.org/10.1007/978-3-030-12036-8_4
7. Dessein, J., Soini, K., Fairclough, G., Horlings, L., Battaglini, E., Birkeland, I., …, & Reimer, M. (2015). *Culture in, for and as Sustainable Development: Conclusions from the COST Action IS1007 Investigating Cultural Sustainability*. University of Jyväskylä.
8. Wu, S. R., Fan, P., & Chen, J. (2016). Incorporating culture into sustainable development: A cultural sustainability index framework for green buildings. *Sustainable Development, 24*(1), 64–76.
9. Banani, R., Vahdati, M. M., Shahrestani, M., & Clements-Croome, D. (2016). The development of building assessment criteria framework for sustainable non-residential buildings in Saudi Arabia. *Sustainable Cities and Society, 26*, 289–305.
10. Zarghami, E., Fatourehchi, D., & Karamloo, M. (2017). Impact of daylighting design strategies on social sustainability through the built environment. *Sustainable Development, 25*(6), 504–527.
11. Moore, T., & Doyon, A. (2018). The uncommon nightingale: Sustainable housing innovation in Australia. *Sustainability, 10*(10), 3469.
12. Ameen, R. F. M., Mourshed, M., & Li, H. (2015). A critical review of environmental assessment tools for sustainable urban design. *Environmental Impact Assessment Review, 55*, 110–125.
13. Mattoni, B., Guattari, C., Evangelisti, L., Bisegna, F., Gori, P., & Asdrubali, F. (2018). Critical review and methodological approach to evaluate the differences among international green building rating tools. *Renewable and Sustainable Energy Reviews, 82*, 950–960.
14. Awadallah, T., Habet, S., Mahasneh, A., & Adas, H. (2011). Green building guideline of Jordan. *Green Building, 20*(6).
15. Ali, H. H., & Al Nsairat, S. F. (2009). Developing a green building assessment tool for developing countries—Case of Jordan. *Building and Environment, 44*(5), 1053–1064.

16. Hadi Zare, M., & Kazemian, F. (2015). Reviewing the role of culture on formation of vernacular architecture. *European Online Journal of Natural and Social Sciences*, *3*(4 (s)), 547.
17. Maleki, B., Rubio, M. D. M. C., Hosseini, S. M. A., & De La Fuente Antequera, A. (2019, June). Multi-criteria decision making in the social sustainability assessment of high-rise residential buildings. In *IOP Conference Series: Earth and Environmental Science* (Vol. 290, No. 1, p. 012054). IOP Publishing.
18. Mangut, B., & Ozsoy, F. A. (2020). Housing neighborhoods as an interaction of enclosure and disclosure. *Archnet-IJAR: International Journal of Architectural Research*, *14*(1), 45–59.
19. Akadiri, P. O., Chinyio, E. A., & Olomolaiye, P. O. (2012). Design of a sustainable building: A conceptual framework for implementing sustainability in the building sector. *Buildings*, *2*(2), 126–152.
20. Eizenberg, E., & Jabareen, Y. (2017). Social sustainability: A new conceptual framework. *Sustainability*, *9*(1), 68.
21. Abel, C. (1993). Eco-culture, development, and architecture. *Knowledge and Policy*, *6*(3), 10–28.
22. Abel, C. (2012). *Architecture and Identity*. Routledge.
23. Rapoport, A. (2019). Culture and built form—A reconsideration. In *Culture-Meaning-Architecture* (pp. 175–216). Routledge.
24. Atanda, J. O. (2019). Developing a social sustainability assessment framework. *Sustainable Cities and Society*, *44*, 237–252.
25. Jenkins, P., Smith, H., & Wang, Y. P. (2006). *Planning and Housing in the Rapidly Urbanising World*. Routledge.
26. Moore, K. D. (Ed.). (2019). *Culture-Meaning-Architecture: Critical Reflections on the Work of Amos Rapoport*. Routledge.
27. Sayigh, A., & Marafia, A. H. (1998). Vernacular and contemporary buildings in Qatar. *Renewable and Sustainable Energy Reviews*, *2*(1–2), 25–37.
28. Brown, R., & Maudlin, D. (2012). Concepts of vernacular architecture. *The SAGE Handbook of Architectural Theory*, 340–355. Sage.

7 Sustainable Agriculture

Gopal Singh Rawat, Aditya Raj, and Akshay Dheeraj

7.1 INTRODUCTION

Throughout history, limited resources have been overcome by technological advancements, leading to increased agricultural production. Yet, the ever-growing population and climate change present a risk to both the supply and demand of food. By the year 2050, it is estimated that the world's population is projected to reach 9 billion, representing a 25% growth from the current population [1]. Nevertheless, population expansion will predominantly occur in emerging nations like Mexico, India, China, and more [2]. Moreover, developing countries are projected to experience an acceleration in the urbanization trend by 2050. Because of the ongoing growth in the world population, we need to be more careful about nutrition and food quality. Doubling food production by 2050 is necessary to meet future food demands [3, 4]. There is a need to raise grain crops and meat production to 3 billion tons and 470 million tons, respectively, by 2050 to meet global food demand [5].

The agriculture industry is witnessing a general trend towards information-driven smart farming (SF). Measures that are ecologically and economically meaningful are implemented in SF to boost productivity. The technique utilizes precision farming principles, specifically GPS guidance for targeted agricultural practices.

There have been different views on the definition of sustainable agriculture. As per MacRae et al. [6], sustainable agriculture emphasizes resilient management practices, waste minimization, and sustained production for nourishment and fulfilment. The term "sustainable agriculture" is vague, covering a wide range of approaches. There are two distinct concepts known as "goal-prescribing" and "system-describing" concepts that represent differences. These approaches have the advantage of being implemented more easily, depending on the established standards. In the realm of system description, sustainability is an inherent quality of an agricultural system, which strives to achieve various and sometimes contradictory objectives over time. A continuous optimization process enables sustainable development; however, implementing it is challenging and restricted by numerous obstacles and barriers. The Food and Agriculture Organization (FAO) has identified the three pillars of sustainable agriculture such as social, environmental, and economic accountability. In this regard, the five principles of sustainable agriculture, identified by FAO, are enhancing the efficient utilization of resources, improving the life and well-being of people living in rural areas, conserving natural resources, practising better governance, and improving the strength of people, community, and ecosystem. In its report on approaches to sustainable agriculture, the International Union for Conservation of Nature has identified 14 approaches to

DOI: 10.1201/9781003471356-7

achieve sustainable agriculture, namely, organic farming, climate-smart agriculture, nature-inclusive agriculture, permaculture, agroecology, biodynamic agriculture, sustainable intensification, ecological intensification, carbon farming, circular agriculture, low external input agriculture, high nature value farming, conservation, and regenerative agriculture.

The term "Smart agriculture" or "Agriculture 4.0" signifies the utilization of advanced technologies to improve agricultural yield while reducing both water and energy consumption [7]. SF has revolutionized agriculture by boosting productivity and conserving resources. Various technologies and platforms are utilized in SF to help farmers benefit from innovative ideas. In cyber-physical farm management, SF utilizes artificial intelligence (AI) and the Internet of Things (IoT), as stated by Bacco et al. [8]. The surveillance of climate variables, soil attributes, and moisture levels in smart agriculture addresses various crop production issues. Smart agriculture tackles crop production issues by monitoring climate factors, moisture, and soil characteristics. IoT has provided a diverse set of tools for farmers to make farming more responsive and technology-driven where farmers can provide inputs to intelligent systems to get knowledge about optimal use of inputs to get maximum yields. IoT has played a significant role in the management of water, soil, irrigation, weather, nutrient, waste, livestock monitoring, and farm management. Further, blockchain has emerged as a major milestone in making farming smart. It establishes a trust network regarding the agreements in agriculture, inventory, and conditions of farm; often here data gathering is extremely expensive.

Precision agriculture (PA) utilizes enhanced technological sensors and analysis tools to increase crop yields and help in better management decisions. The concept of PA has been adopted worldwide to increase production, improve fertilizer, and irrigation management, and reduce labour [9]. The utilization of extensive data and information results in improved agricultural resource usage, crop yields, and crop quality. The data from heterogeneous sources is used in PA to achieve the optimal utilization of fertilizers, insecticides, and water for irrigation so that the yield of the crops from the field can be optimized. The use of technology in agriculture, such as satellite imaging, drones, and sensors, reduces farmers' workload and increases the productivity of farms [9]. The concept of smart agriculture empowers farmers to manage crop diversity, address potential intrusions, and monitor real-time data. SA relies on digital automation, along with the foundation of data collection, processing, analysis, transmission, and decision-making [10]. However, there is a major gap, in terms of achieving the goal of sustainability in agriculture, between the three categories of the economy of the world, namely, developed, developing, and under-developed countries. The developed economies have a high rate of adoption of existing and the development of new innovative technologies, thus contributing to a higher rate of practising sustainable agricultural practices. On the contrary, under-developed economies have various socioeconomic challenges, like poverty, crime, illiteracy, infrastructure, poor governance, and poor health, which hinder their technological innovation and thus adaptation to sustainable practices in agriculture. The developing countries have an increasing trend of adoption of precision agricultural technologies, where agricultural practitioners are adapting to the technology and utilizing it to improve their crop yields.

As this process poses challenges or may be unfeasible for individuals, it is imperative to automate it through techniques and tools to ensure streamlined decision-making. Developments in machine learning (ML), deep learning, and computer vision can help diagnose various crop diseases swiftly and accurately in large farms. This technology offers quick and precise outcomes through computerized analysis using image processing techniques. The use of computer vision and precision enhancements can decrease labour costs and waste of time while enhancing crop quality and overall output.

The work will provide a reference for the researchers to understand the concepts of SF, PA, and animal farming concepts in Section 7.2. The work contributes to exploring various datasets that have been used by researchers. Further, Section 7.3 focusses on various cutting-edge technologies used to achieve sustainable agriculture practices. Section 7.4 presents the technical challenges in practising SF methodologies, which could be a source of light for future researchers. Finally, Section 7.5 presents the conclusion of the chapter.

7.2 LITERATURE REVIEW

Over the years, researchers and scientists have used the technology to enhance agricultural productivity, keeping in mind the sustainability factor. In their study, Velten et al. [11] aimed to improve understanding of sustainable agriculture through an analysis of its social science and governance elements. They also highlighted areas of consensus and concern in emerging definitions. A literature review utilizing cluster analysis was undertaken to explore comprehensive insights into sustainable agriculture, discern patterns, and identify distinctions in the application of ideas and aspects associated with it. This section discusses some of the most extensively contributed agricultural areas where technology has proven effective.

The study by Akkem et al. [12] offered a detailed overview of deep learning and ML techniques applied in SF. In addition, they have examined various time series algorithms and relevant techniques for recommending the ideal crop yield. Moysiadis et al. [13] offered an extensive review of SF, encompassing various technologies and referencing best practices in Europe. By their work, two-fold benefits have been brought to European researchers. Firstly, it presents the research efforts of SF practitioners across. In Europe, the practitioners adopt innovative technological trends across diverse crops. Furthermore, it sheds light on the foremost SF initiatives in the European context. Mohamed et al. [14] concentrated on innovative approaches related to SF between 2019 and 2021, emphasizing the gathering of data, storage, transmission, analysis, and also, suitable solutions using the IoT. The application of UAVs and robots was demonstrated, showcasing their ability to perform various tasks in agriculture, including irrigation, seedling, weed detection, harvesting, pest control, and livestock management, using IoT, AI, DL, ML, and wireless communications in real time. Furthermore, they highlighted the significance of incorporating a 5G mobile network in the development of smart systems. Idoje et al. [15] discussed the challenges of incorporating smart technology into agriculture and highlighted issues with the current framework of smart agriculture. The application of IoT in SF revealed numerous research gaps, leading to recommendations for additional studies to enhance worldwide food production. Researchers developed a multi-layer SF architecture that showcases various entities relevant to real-time applications, utilizing both edge and cloud environments. It then examines the associated security and privacy concerns, detailing potential attack scenarios within SF architecture and throughout the food supply chain [16]. Agricultural IoT (AIoT) framework was presented along with the mechanism to send the data to servers over Wi-Fi networks [17]. Farooq et al. [18] highlighted dimensions and various components of AIoT systems and integration with cloud computing technology with various data analytics facilities that can enhance crop yield. They also highlighted the policies and standards for AIoT defined by various countries. Sishodia et al. [19] presented the overview of remote sensing techniques used for PA along with the work done during 2015–2020. Authors explored different vegetation indices used for remote sensing applications along with the challenges. They also explored the applications of remote sensing for irrigation water management, soil moisture, water stress, evapotranspiration (ET), management of disease, nutrient and weed, crop yield estimation. Cisternas et al. [20] provided the systematic review of PA implementations in various crops. They also focussed on comparison criteria and selection of appropriate PA technology. Sharma et al. [21] reviewed ML applications in the agriculture domain such as crop disease identification, weed detection, moisture content, and crop yield prediction. These collected information can help reduce labour cost, allow farmers to take intelligent decisions which can enhance crop yield, and improve crop quality. Radoglou-Grammatikis et al. [22] explored the applications of UAV in PA and technology used for each application. They detailed the role of GPS and GIS along with different techniques like soil mapping and listed 20 applications of UAVs. Coulibaly et al. [23] identified three key challenges with applications of DL techniques in agriculture. They also reviewed the DL applications in agriculture for crop disease and weed recognition, pest identification, etc.

Bao and Xie [24] presented a systematic review of the assessment of AI in the field of solving problems related to animals and other livestock. Since the year 2016, there has been a notable rise in the number of related studies, emphasizing the detection and recognition of animal behaviour. The majority of these studies have concentrated on poultry (16.92%), cattle (37.44%), and pigs (37.95%). At the experimental stage, sensors and AI models predominantly concentrated on collecting, processing, assessing, and analysing data in animal farming research. Ulian et al. [25] highlighted the potential of fungi to support SA and protect the environment, drawing on traditional knowledge about their uses and practices. Diversity and global distribution of edible plants along with the ecosystem services provided by these plants were also presented. They reported the biodiversity importance along with crops and the role of fungi for sustainable agriculture. Singh et al. [26] investigated the dilemma of balancing food demand and the preservation of natural heritage. Solutions put forward involve market-based incentives, sustainable farming practices, and community engagement in land conservation. Gomiero et al. [27] presented a review of the impact of agricultural practices on the environment such as water demand, pollution, and greenhouse gas emission. They also presented various agricultural practices which cause less pollution and degradation of these natural resources and preserve soil fertility. Soumare et al. [28] presented the biological nitrogen fixation

(BNF) process which is an alternative to reduce the excessive use of chemicals for fulfilment of required nitrogen. A comprehensive examination of the BNF process was conducted, accompanied by a brief overview of BNF's history, nitrogen fixation's cycle and mechanisms, the market value of bio-fertilizers, and their implementation in agriculture. In their research, Yadav et al. [29] explored the positive impact of organic farming on sustainable agriculture in northern India.

7.2.1 Datasets Used for the Study

Researchers primarily used digital images to explore how technology affected agriculture. However, a few researchers have either employed synthesized data or built their own databases to achieve their aims, with a focus on expert systems, agriculture robots, and sensor technology for data collection and transmission. By utilizing IoT-enabled sensors on devices like UAVs, satellites, tractors, or irrigation platforms, real-time data can be continuously pooled. In this subsection, various types of data or technology used to create the databases to study the impact of technology on various phases of agriculture have been presented in Table 7.1. The ImageNet dataset revolutionized the field of computer vision by providing millions of labelled images serving as the basis and benchmark for the advancement of sophisticated models.

TABLE 7.1
Dataset Used in Various Studies

Areas of Farming	Dataset Used
Soil parameter estimation	Public reports (2014–2017) [30]
Soil classification	LUCAS topsoil dataset [31]; COCO and cityscape data [32]
Fertilizers and pesticide optimization	Digital images of pests, sensor data
Crop recommendation system	Soil testing lab dataset [33]; climate and previous crop production data [34]
Feature selection and classification	Benchmark dataset of soya bean and mushroom [35]
Crop detection	Time series Landsat data [36]
Plant health analysis	PlantVillage [37]; plant shoot images for water stress classification [38]; PlantDoc [39]; rice and cassava dataset [40]; 236 leaf picture data [41]
Disease identification	Hold-out test dataset [42]; apple leaf disease dataset [43]; citrus disease image gallery dataset [44]
Yield prediction	RGB and multispectral datasets [45]; SAR data [46]
Behaviour classification	Calf and cow datasets of 30-frame video length [47]
Weed detection	Images from crop fields of Belgium and Spain [48]; South China [49]; Shiraz University (Iran) [50]; Sâa Josě farm, Brazil [51]
Irrigation task	Sensor data; crop, weekday, bank holiday, Julian day, and climatic data [52]; meteorological station data, historical sensor data, and actual irrigation records [53]
Land cover mapping	Landsat 5 TM images [54]; Riverina region images in NSW, Australia [55]

Several researchers have suggested using large-scale image datasets to overcome the limitations of agricultural datasets. Examples include NBAIR, AgriPest, DeepWeeds, PlantVillage, IP102, and web repositories like plant leaf disease. The usual format of these images is RGB, captured under varied environmental conditions, and accompanied by annotated files for object detection.

Karnott Systems manufactures a control device tailored to meet the requirements of farmers. This device collects and shares real-time data, incorporates geo-fencing, and utilizes geographic information to enhance its functionalities. The data can be shared using services available on the internet, such as the agroAPI platform designed for information reception. Several farms are granted access to the data, functioning as a valuable research library [56]. Tarris employs AI as a foundation to provide images captured using UAVs and satellites for precision farming. AgriOpenData has developed a decision support system (DSS) that utilizes blockchain technology. This system offers additional services to its users. With robotic agriculture, the entire process from seeding to harvesting is streamlined, reducing water consumption.

7.3 STATE-OF-THE-ART TECHNIQUES AND CONCEPTS

ML and deep learning techniques can be applied in farming for selecting seeds and soils, detecting and predicting crop diseases, identifying pests and managing them, phenotyping crops, optimizing fertilizers and pesticides, managing weeds, analysing water and irrigation, and predicting crop yields. Table 7.2 displays a range of cutting-edge techniques employed in agricultural research. Data mining techniques are crucial for data analysis. Patterns are an integral part of big data analysis, necessitating various approaches to uncover them. Several agricultural tasks, including pest identification, disease detection, yield prediction, and fertilizer and pesticide planning, have benefited from the application of data mining techniques [8]. Besides crop management, they can also explore other models to measure farm organization.

7.3.1 Machine Learning

The classification process involves the identification and categorization of input data into known classes. This critical step in computer vision involves detecting and segmenting incoming data into multiple classes to signify its significance. In the context of plant leaf categorization, plant images are categorized based on identified diseases.

In Supervised techniques, the data's final label is already known in this category, and the models are trained to determine the class label for each data point. Some techniques in this category include genetic algorithm (GA), decision tree, random forest (RF), support vector machine (SVM), KNN, fuzzy logic, and more.

In unsupervised techniques, the data's final label is unknown. Within this category, models are designed to automatically identify clusters using distance metrics that match the data type. Fuzzy C-means, artificial neural networks (ANN), and k-means are the primary classifier techniques used in this category. Below, we provide an explanation of various unsupervised ML techniques.

TABLE 7.2
Various State-of-the-Art Techniques for Sustainable Agriculture [57]

Sl. No.	Farming Steps	Techniques/Models Used
1	Soils and seeds	Extreme learning machine (ELM), logistic regression, cubist regression model (Cubist), support vector machine (SVM), partial least squares regression (PLSR), least-squares support vector machines (LS-SVM), Cubist, principal component regression (PCR), k-nearest neighbour (KNN), ensemble learning, multilayer perceptron (MLP), and speeded up robust features (SURF) algorithm
2	Pest detection	UAV-based computer vision system, CapsNet, IoT-based drone implementation system, VGG model (deep learning model), CNN model
3	Crop phenotyping	Deep phenomics (pre-trained neural networks), robotized imagery characterization techniques, Gaussian mixture models, simplex volume maximization approach, AN, k-means clustering
4	Crop disease detection, prediction, and monitoring	Multiple linear models, support vector machines (SVM), deep convolutional neural networks (DNNs), principal component analysis (PCA), ANN, KNN classifier, random forest, decision tree, CNN, naïve Bayesian, stochastic gradient descent (SGD), AlexNet precursor, VGG 19, inspection, FRADD, propagation-based neural networks (BPNN), faster region-based convolutional neural networks (faster R-CNN), independently recurrent neural network (IndRNN)
5	Input fertilizers and pesticide management	Pattern recognition, image-based pest control apps, NeuroPIpred (ML tool-based technology), neural networks, random forest, DCNN, naïve Bayes algorithm, time series analysis, VGG-19, VGGNet, ResNet-50, CAE+CNN
6	Weed detection and management	IoT-controlled flying machines NB-IoT, RF, KNN, NVIDIA digit, YOLO-v3 detector, SVM, unmanned aerial mapping machines
7	Water analysis and optimal irrigation	Naive Bayes technique, decision tree, fog computing-based architecture, genetic algorithm, IoT-based smart irrigation system, fuzzy logic, LoRaWAN, boosted trees classifier (BTC), SVM, support vector regression, gradient boosted regression trees (GBRT), and linear regression models
8	Crop yield management	Convolutional neural networks (CNN), deep neural network (DNN), long short-term memory (LSTM), RNN, fuzzy neural networks system (FNN), CNN-LSTM model, YOLO model, deep belief network (DBN), SSTNN (spatial-spectral-temporal neural network), Bayesian regularization BP (backpropagation), stacked-sparse autoencoder (SSAE), random forest, support vector machine

Huang et al. [58] and Zhu et al. [59] demonstrated the utilization of various ML, computer vision, and convolutional neural network (CNN) algorithms for tasks such as automated seed sorting and estimations of soil quality. CNN-based deep neural network (DNN) model was applied to count soybean seeds and classify haploid seeds based on embryo position, phenotypic expression, and form by Veeramani et al. [60]. The ELM classifier, employing various activation functions, is applied for the prediction of fertility levels categorized as low, medium, and high. This prediction is based on input values derived from soil parameters. Additionally, the ELM classifier is utilized to forecast the pH levels of the associated soil, employing diverse activation functions.

The integration of ML with analysis software ensures efficient evaluation of the health of the crops. By analysing the data, it becomes possible to identify the most critical areas affected by infestations allowing farmers to optimize pesticide usage, concentrating their efforts on those specific locations.

In the context of SF, alternative models such as SVMs [61], principal component analysis (PCA) [62], and multiple linear models are commonly utilized. The use of colour and texture in disease detection techniques in agriculture and horticulture helps improve the identification and classification of visually similar diseases.

Researchers [63] focussed their study on grape leaf disease detection by applying an SVM classifier. Gavhale et al. [64] successfully identified two grape plant diseases, powdery mildew and downy mildew, achieving an accuracy rate of 88.89%. In the research by Sreedhar and Kumar [65], crop diseases such as canker and anthracnose affecting citrus trees, including oranges, limes, lemons, and grapefruits, were detected with an accuracy rate of 95%. Kaur et al. [66] achieved a 90% accuracy in classifying soybean diseases, including *Septoria* leaf blight, frog eye, and downy mildew, using a large dataset. With the help of techniques such as spatial neighbourhood, granular computing, clustering, and dimensionality reduction, Raj and Minz [67] addressed the challenge of classifying the remote sensing images. In a previous study, Raj and Minz [54] presented a technique of grouping similar pixels called spatial rough k-means, which aims to classify mixed pixels based on their spatial neighbourhood relationship. A comparative analysis was conducted by the authors to evaluate the performance of various existing clustering algorithms and compare them with the proposed algorithm for image partitioning and map-reduce methods.

7.3.2 Deep Learning

Non-contact and efficient technology-driven solutions are offered by computer vision techniques in agriculture. By integrating remote cameras for high-quality image acquisition, these techniques deliver effective solutions driven by technology. In their review, Dhanya et al. [68] discuss how deep learning computer vision can aid farmers in various tasks. Unal [69] explains that incorporating advanced IT tools and techniques into agricultural production leads to "smart farming," a groundbreaking agricultural method that enhances productivity and profitability. Farmers can now apply treatments with the same accuracy as humans, thanks to advancements in connectivity, automation, and AI [70]. Methods are being developed to optimize human labour in agriculture by farmers, data scientists, and engineers. SF has become increasingly intelligent as crucial information resources are collected and improved daily. Deep learning is an ML technique that draws inspiration from ANN. Deep learning networks are primarily characterized by their depth, which differentiates them from neural networks. Deep learning networks can uncover hidden structures in unlabelled and unstructured data because of this characteristic.

Algorithms developed in the past are at a disadvantage compared to deep learning networks, which can autonomously extract features.

Guo et al. [71] demonstrated that the utilization of deep convolutional neural networks (DNNs) proved instrumental in achieving a diagnostic accuracy of 99.53% for plant diseases. In the context of rice-related challenges [72], neural networks have been effectively employed for tasks such as disease identification. As per Istanbul Technical University 2017's findings [73], CNN algorithms outperformed feature-based learning algorithms when discriminating phenological stages. Namin et al. [74] introduced a novel deep learning model tailored for plant phenotype analysis, incorporating innovative LSTM designs by integrating CNNs. Notably, CNNs are better when used for sensor readings in time series data format as they reduce the errors and recurrent neural network (RNN) finds applications in crop yield prediction leveraging time series approach to mitigate biases derived from sensor data. SF encompasses the analysis of seeds as well. According to a study conducted by Qiu et al. [75] in 2018, computer vision techniques that utilize deep learning have significantly improved the performance limitations of traditional computer vision. This improvement has led to the expansion of the technology's application in the identification of seed varieties. Various spectral imaging techniques are often combined with these methods to achieve precision. In a study conducted by Zhu et al. [59], it was observed that spectroscopy and ML-based CNN models exhibited strong performance. This study aimed to document different seed variations. ML models achieved a classification accuracy of more than 80% for cotton seeds by utilizing the features extracted by CNN and ResNet models. Plants use the soil as a medium to root and grow. A consistent supply of major and microelements is essential for crop plants to maximize their production and productivity. Continuous cultivation on the same plot of land has led to a decrease in its fertility and productivity. Land deterioration has negatively impacted crop production. A study on the soil's health, specifically focussing on inorganic nutrient concentration and microbiological state, will assist in understanding its limitations and suggesting remedial actions. The analysis of soil is a must for classifying the soil taxonomically. Yu et al. [76] used CNN and ConvLSTM to predict the soil temperature (ST). Shi et al. [77] presented a ConvLSTM model that makes use of CNN architectures for transitioning between input and state. By analysing spatiotemporal data from the past ten days, the model predicts future ST at one-, three-, and five-day intervals. Two distinct input channels were utilized to train each model. The raw data from the ST was first entered into the model and then processed using empirical mode decomposition (EMD). Alibabaei et al. [78] utilized LSTM, CNN-LSTM, and BiLSTM to simulate soil-water content and daily reference ET. They used the FAO Penman-Monteith equation, weather data, and ERA5 land to calculate ET and collect information on soil-water content. The BiLSTM model achieved an MSE ranging from 0.014 to 0.056. In performance tests, BiLSTM outperformed traditional ML techniques like RF and SVR.

The challenge of crop and weed classification was addressed by Dheeraj and Chand by presenting a deep learning-based classification system that utilized RGB images to distinguish weeds and crops [79]. The authors explored the effectiveness of popular deep learning-based transfer learning models, MobileNetV2 and

DenseNet169, by evaluating their performance in the context of crop and weed recognition. In a separate study, the authors presented a transfer learning-based deep learning model to EfficientNet B0 for the identification and classification of plant leaf diseases in pepper, potato, and tomato plants. Utilizing images sourced from the well-known plant disease dataset "PlantVillage," the EfficientNet B0 model was trained, and its performance was compared with other CNN-based deep learning models [80]. The WheatRust21 dataset was prepared by Nigam et al. [81], comprising 6556 images depicting both healthy and diseased leaves under natural field conditions. Their study involved the application of classical CNN-based models such as MobileNetV2, InceptionNetV3, DenseNet169, ResNet152, and VGG19 for the identification of wheat rust disease. The results indicated an accuracy range between 91.2% and 97.8%. Dheeraj and Chand developed the modified CNN model named LWDN by utilizing the DenseNet121 architecture for disease identification [82]. Their presented model is lightweight with 1.5M parameters and reached 99.37% accuracy on the PlantVillage dataset.

In addition to the methods discussed, a range of commercially accessible AI-based tools can be applied to the domain of smart agriculture. Notable examples include Trace Genomics, PEAT, FarmShots, Blue River Technologies, AGEYE Technologies, VineView, and Fasal. These tools play a pivotal role in advancing PA and optimizing farming practices.

7.3.3 Remote Sensing Technologies and IoT

Smart framing and sustainable agriculture require such information and an intelligent system that is driven by data to support cost-effective and sustainable agricultural practices. Utilizing data from earth observation (EO) and navigation satellites in conjunction with ground sensor data, these services assist farmers in making informed decisions about resource allocation, resulting in improved economic and ecological outcomes. Since the 1980s, EO has been used in agriculture. However, the Copernicus program, which has been operational since 2015, has significantly improved the availability and quality of satellite data. Sentinel-1 and 2 satellites contribute valuable time series data, enabling accurate derivation of information such as calamities, biomass development, crop types [83], and farming practices like ploughing and seeding. The Copernicus program, coupled with the easily accessible Landsat complete data archive, along with Sentinel-2, has opened avenues for innovative data analysis techniques leveraging data-intensive exploration and fusion for more robust insights. Khan et al. [84] highlighted the potential of IoT in advancing agriculture, identifying the issues faced while integrating advanced technologies with existing agricultural systems focussing primarily on activities such as sowing, harvesting, packaging, transportation, and throughout the cropping process. Effective application timing and irrigation rates are key to minimizing crop water stress and maximizing crop productivity. Uniform irrigation is commonly practised by farmers based on their understanding of farming, soil, and climate. Almost all traditional farming methods neglect the differences within fields and apply a uniform irrigation rate. Utilizing remote sensing data allows for identifying variations in the field and implementing variable rate irrigation using common systems like a centre pivot.

By adjusting application rates based on field conditions, variable rate application can minimize water stress and maximize yields [85, 86]. Crop water demand indicators such as crop water stress, ET, and soil moisture can be analysed by examining remote sensing images taken at various points during the growing season. Farmers use indicators to measure the amount of water needed for their crops and create accurate irrigation schedules. Remote sensing products have ensured development and testing of several techniques and indices for effective water management [87]. Remote sensing data is extensively utilized to calculate ET, necessary for irrigation scheduling and determining crop water needs [88].

7.4 CHALLENGES

Numerous security challenges persist within the agricultural domain, owing to inherent factors such as compatibility issues, heterogeneity, and the management of extensive datasets. With the advent of Agriculture 4.0, it is imperative to achieve security against potential cyber threats while accurately generating, transmitting, and processing data [89]. The seamless operation of data-related technologies such as smart systems and analytics is only possible with managing data integrity. The diverse resources when pooled together may result in various security concerns such as privacy infringement, preservation of trust, and resource availability.

In the contemporary agricultural setup, where food production is continually expanding, the need for addressing environmental issues becomes immensely important. Presently, in Europe agriculture consumes 44% of water resources and contributes to over 10% of greenhouse gas emissions [90]. Thus, these environmental implications need to be recognized when coming up with a security measure within the agricultural framework to address data-related challenges which will ensure that the broader ecological impact of farming practices does not get undermined. Pesticides or chemical treatments are extensively used to increase the market reach of fruit crops, with consequential effects on pollinators and the broader environmental landscape.

The application of deep learning suffers from the limitation of small-size databases leading to the predominant usage of large datasets during the training phase [91]. In addition, the images in the database are typically acquired under highly constrained environmental conditions. The deep learning models when provided with data encounter various challenges, including indefinite persistence, uncertainty, and incapability, necessitating comprehensive data processing both in terms of geographically and temporally. Ensuring reliable data transmission is a crucial issue for IoT devices. Extraneous elements such as unnecessary noise and background in crop are required to be eliminated so that the desired segments are available in the image. It is challenging to obtain a similar image owing to environmental factors such as moisture and light intensity.

Other challenges include hardware-related issues while capturing authentic images, difficulties in selecting classification modules appropriately, scalability concerns with data mining algorithms, and issues pertaining to available feature extraction methods. Furthermore, it is imperative to address challenges related to data security, privacy, ownership, and right to use. The challenges associated with selection and deployment of analytical tools and intelligence present various sets of obstacles in information gathering and analysis.

Thus, in terms of information, agriculture faces multifaceted challenges. Monitoring systems often are required to meet high spatial and temporal demands, given the small size of food production plots. The dynamic variables such as crop growth and human-made changes require the information update very frequently. Particularly challenging updates are based on complex information requirements such as yield and nitrogen uptake. Ongoing research and development efforts are essential to enhance EO capabilities and services, aiming for a comprehensive sustainable farm management approach. Such an approach will ensure efficient, water-conserving irrigation, fertilizer optimization, robust, limited, and timely plant protection, as well as stable vegetation cover to mitigate erosion and ensure both high quantity and high-quality yields. The potential obstacles that limit the implementation of sustainable agriculture in practice were addressed by Siebrecht [92] proposing strategies to minimize or eliminate such issues, thus bridging the implementation gap. These obstacles were categorized into theoretical, methodological, personal, and practical impediments, emphasizing the need for a holistic approach to overcome challenges across diverse domains.

Theoretical challenges emerge from the inherent nature of sustainable agriculture, including issues arising from its conceptualization, definitions, and varied interpretations. Methodological obstacles arise in the context of evaluating and implementing sustainable agricultural practices. Personal challenges arise from individuals such as farmers, and their characteristics, their influence on the sustainability of agricultural practices. Practical hurdles are linked with constraints that hinder the initiation and adaptation to more sustainable agricultural approaches. The challenges were addressed by [92, 93] with pivotal actions such as assessment, institutionalization, and system development, along with initiatives in education and capacity building, as well as garnering social and political support.

7.5 CONCLUSION

AI is widely recognized and valued across many research domains, especially agriculture. The business decisions in farming rely heavily on data; thus, business survival in the agricultural sector is immensely dependent on evolving technologies to make best use of the data available. In this context, ML is anticipated to play a vital role in not only enhancing resource efficiency and facilitating resource utilization but also unlocking substantial environmental benefits. Stakeholder's perception, attitude, and availability of funding are crucial in realizing the transformative impact of ML on agriculture. ML solutions such as remote sensor-based soil moisture detection, GPS-assisted automatic irrigation, and precision weeding offer a pathway to overcoming challenges such as absence of irrigation systems, weed-related issues, crop yield fluctuations, plant monitoring challenges, thus improving the overall performance in the agriculture sector by effectively reducing crop losses. In addition, self-driving robots not only boost productivity but also minimize dependence on pesticides and herbicides. Furthermore, the adoption of drones for precise pesticide and herbicides spraying streamlines the farming practices by eliminating the burden of plant monitoring.

AI solutions prove to be invaluable in addressing resource and labour shortages associated with traditional agriculture setup. Conventionally agricultural activities rely heavily on labour-intensive activities which are time intensive. Thus, the integration of AI ensures flexibility, non-invasive and quick phenotyping, and on-demand information access with spatial precision in addressing agricultural challenges.

REFERENCES

1. Union Nations. *World Population Projected to Reach 9.8 Billion in 2050, and 11.2 Billion in 2100.* Retrieved March 21, 2024, from https://www.un.org/en/desa.
2. McNabb, D. E., & McNabb, D. E. (2019). The population growth barrier. *Global Pathways to Water Sustainability*, 67–81. Palgrave Macmillan.
3. Ayaz, M., Ammad-Uddin, M., Sharif, Z., Mansour, A., & Aggoune, E. H. M. (2019). Internet-of-Things (IoT)-based smart agriculture: Toward making the fields talk. *IEEE Access*, *7*, 129551–129583.
4. Zhang, X., & Davidson, E. A. (2018, December). Improving nitrogen and water management in crop production on a national scale. In *AGU Fall Meeting Abstracts* (Vol. 2018, pp. B22B–01).
5. Elder, M., & Hayashi, S.. (2018). A regional perspective on biofuels in Asia. *Biofuels and Sustainability: Holistic Perspectives for Policy-making*, 223–246.
6. MacRae, R. J., Hill, S. B., Henning, J., & Mehuys, G. R. (1989). Agricultural science and sustainable agriculture: A review of the existing scientific barriers to sustainable food production and potential solutions. *Biological Agriculture & Horticulture*, *6*(3), 173–219.
7. Pathan, M., Patel, N., Yagnik, H., & Shah, M. (2020). Artificial cognition for applications in smart agriculture: A comprehensive review. *Artificial Intelligence in Agriculture*, *4*, 81–95.
8. Bacco, M., Barsocchi, P., Ferro, E., Gotta, A., & Ruggeri, M. (2019). The digitisation of agriculture: A survey of research activities on smart farming. *Array*, *3*, 100009.
9. Mulla, D. J. (2013). Twenty five years of remote sensing in precision agriculture: Key advances and remaining knowledge gaps. *Biosystems Engineering*, *114*(4), 358–371.
10. Matei, O., Rusu, T., Petrovan, A., & Mihuţ, G. (2017). A data mining system for real time soil moisture prediction. *Procedia Engineering*, *181*, 837–844.
11. Velten, S., Leventon, J., Jager, N., & Newig, J. (2015). What is sustainable agriculture? A systematic review. *Sustainability*, *7*(6), 7833–7865.
12. Akkem, Y., Biswas, S. K., & Varanasi, A. (2023). Smart farming using artificial intelligence: A review. *Engineering Applications of Artificial Intelligence*, *120*, 105899.
13. Moysiadis, V., Sarigiannidis, P., Vitsas, V., & Khelifi, A. (2021). Smart farming in Europe. *Computer Science Review*, *39*, 100345.
14. Mohamed, E. S., Belal, A. A., Abd-Elmabod, S. K., El-Shirbeny, M. A., Gad, A., & Zahran, M. B. (2021). Smart farming for improving agricultural management. *The Egyptian Journal of Remote Sensing and Space Science*, *24*(3), 971–981.
15. Idoje, G., Dagiuklas, T., & Iqbal, M. (2021). Survey for smart farming technologies: Challenges and issues. *Computers & Electrical Engineering*, *92*, 107104.
16. Gupta, M., Abdelsalam, M., Khorsandroo, S., & Mittal, S. (2020). Security and privacy in smart farming: Challenges and opportunities. *IEEE Access*, *8*, 34564–34584.

17. Dagar, R., Som, S., & Khatri, S. K. (2018, July). Smart farming–IoT in agriculture. In *2018 International Conference on Inventive Research in Computing Applications (ICIRCA)* (pp. 1052–1056). IEEE.
18. Farooq, M. S., Riaz, S., Abid, A., Abid, K., & Naeem, M. A. (2019). A survey on the role of IoT in agriculture for the implementation of smart farming. *IEEE Access*, *7*, 156237–156271.
19. Sishodia, R. P., Ray, R. L., & Singh, S. K. (2020). Applications of remote sensing in precision agriculture: A review. *Remote Sensing*, *12*(19), 3136.
20. Cisternas, I., Velásquez, I., Caro, A., & Rodríguez, A. (2020). Systematic literature review of implementations of precision agriculture. *Computers and Electronics in Agriculture*, *176*, 105626.
21. Sharma, A., Jain, A., Gupta, P., & Chowdary, V. (2020). Machine learning applications for precision agriculture: A comprehensive review. *IEEE Access*, *9*, 4843–4873.
22. Radoglou-Grammatikis, P., Sarigiannidis, P., Lagkas, T., & Moscholios, I. (2020). A compilation of UAV applications for precision agriculture. *Computer Networks*, *172*, 107148.
23. Coulibaly, S., Kamsu-Foguem, B., Kamissoko, D., & Traore, D. (2022). Deep learning for precision agriculture: A bibliometric analysis. *Intelligent Systems with Applications*, *16*, 200102.
24. Bao, J., & Xie, Q. (2022). Artificial intelligence in animal farming: A systematic literature review. *Journal of Cleaner Production*, *331*, 129956.
25. Ulian, T., Diazgranados, M., Pironon, S., Padulosi, S., Liu, U., Davies, L., ... & Mattana, E. (2020). Unlocking plant resources to support food security and promote sustainable agriculture. *Plants, People, Planet*, *2*(5), 421–445.
26. Singh, M., Chaure, N. K., & Parihar, S. S. (2021). Organic farming for sustainable agriculture. *Indian Journal of Organic Farming*, *1*(1), 1–8.
27. Gomiero, T., Pimentel, D., & Paoletti, M. G. (2011). Is there a need for a more sustainable agriculture? *Critical Reviews in Plant Sciences*, *30*(1–2), 6–23.
28. Soumare, A., Diedhiou, A. G., Thuita, M., Hafidi, M., Ouhdouch, Y., Gopalakrishnan, S., & Kouisni, L. (2020). Exploiting biological nitrogen fixation: A route towards A sustainable agriculture. *Plants*, *9*(8), 1011.
29. Yadav, S. K., Babu, S., Yadav, M. K., Singh, K., Yadav, G. S., & Pal, S. (2013). A review of organic farming for sustainable agriculture in Northern India. *International Journal of Agronomy*, *2013*(1), 718145.
30. Cheng, X., Zhang, Y., Chen, Y., Wu, Y., & Yue, Y. (2017). Pest identification via deep residual learning in complex background. *Computers and Electronics in Agriculture*, *141*, 351–356.
31. Riese, F. M., & Keller, S. (2019). Soil texture classification with 1D convolutional neural networks based on hyperspectral data. *arXiv preprint arXiv:1901.04846*.
32. Zhang, Y., Chu, J., Leng, L., & Miao, J. (2020). Mask-refined R-CNN: A network for refining object details in instance segmentation. *Sensors*, *20*(4), 1010.
33. Rajak, R. K., Pawar, A., Pendke, M., Shinde, P., Rathod, S., & Devare, A. (2017). Crop recommendation system to maximize crop yield using machine learning technique. *International Research Journal of Engineering and Technology*, *4*(12), 950–953.
34. Mythili, K., & Rangaraj, R. (2021). Deep learning with particle swarm based hyper parameter tuning based crop recommendation for better crop yield for precision agriculture. *Indian Journal of Science and Technology*, *14*(17), 1325–1337.
35. Chouhan, S., Singh, D., & Singh, A. (2016). An improved feature selection and classification using decision tree for crop datasets. *International Journal of Computer Applications*, *142*(13).
36. Zheng, B., Myint, S. W., Thenkabail, P. S., & Aggarwal, R. M. (2015). A support vector machine to identify irrigated crop types using time-series Landsat NDVI

data. *International Journal of Applied Earth Observation and Geoinformation, 34*, 103–112.

37. Hughes, D., & Salathé, M. (2015). An open access repository of images on plant health to enable the development of mobile disease diagnostics. *arXiv preprint arXiv:1511.08060.*
38. Senthilnath, J., Kulkarni, S., Benediktsson, J. A., & Yang, X. S. (2016). A novel approach for multispectral satellite image classification based on the bat algorithm. *IEEE Geoscience and Remote Sensing Letters, 13*(4), 599–603.
39. Singh, D., Jain, N., Jain, P., Kayal, P., Kumawat, S., & Batra, N. (2020). PlantDoc: A dataset for visual plant disease detection. In *Proceedings of the 7th ACM IKDD CoDS and 25th COMAD* (pp. 249–253).
40. Hassan, S. M., & Maji, A. K. (2022). Plant disease identification using a novel convolutional neural network. *IEEE Access, 10*, 5390–5401.
41. Sengar, N., Dutta, M. K., & Travieso, C. M. (2018). Computer vision based technique for identification and quantification of powdery mildew disease in cherry leaves. *Computing, 100*(11), 1189–1201.
42. Ji, M., & Wu, Z. (2022). Automatic detection and severity analysis of grape black measles disease based on deep learning and fuzzy logic. *Computers and Electronics in Agriculture, 193*, 106718.
43. Li, X., & Li, S. (2022). Transformer help CNN see better: A lightweight hybrid apple disease identification model based on transformers. *Agriculture, 12*(6), 884.
44. Sannakki, S. S., Rajpurohit, V. S., Nargund, V. B., & Kulkarni, P. (2013, July). Diagnosis and classification of grape leaf diseases using neural networks. In *2013 Fourth International Conference on Computing, Communications and Networking Technologies (ICCCNT)* (pp. 1–5). IEEE.
45. Yang, Q., Shi, L., Han, J., Zha, Y., & Zhu, P. (2019). Deep convolutional neural networks for rice grain yield estimation at the ripening stage using UAV-based remotely sensed images. *Field Crops Research, 235*, 142–153.
46. Ranjan, A. K., & Parida, B. R. (2019). Paddy acreage mapping and yield prediction using sentinel-based optical and SAR data in Sahibganj district, Jharkhand (India). *Spatial Information Research, 27*(4), 399–410.
47. Qiao, Y., Guo, Y., Yu, K., & He, D. (2022). C3D-ConvLSTM based cow behaviour classification using video data for precision livestock farming. *Computers and Electronics in Agriculture, 193*, 106650.
48. Gao, J., Nuyttens, D., Lootens, P., He, Y., & Pieters, J. G. (2018). Recognising weeds in a maize crop using a random forest machine-learning algorithm and near-infrared snapshot mosaic hyperspectral imagery. *Biosystems Engineering, 170*, 39–50.
49. Zhang, X., Han, L., Dong, Y., Shi, Y., Huang, W., Han, L., …, & Sobeih, T. (2019). A deep learning-based approach for automated yellow rust disease detection from high-resolution hyperspectral UAV images. *Remote Sensing, 11*(13), 1554.
50. Bakhshipour, A., & Jafari, A. (2018). Evaluation of support vector machine and artificial neural networks in weed detection using shape features. *Computers and Electronics in Agriculture, 145*, 153–160.
51. Abouzahir, S., Sadik, M., & Sabir, E. (2018, December). Enhanced approach for weeds species detection using machine vision. In *2018 international conference on electronics, control, optimization and computer science (ICECOCS)* (pp. 1–6). IEEE.
52. Perea, R. G., Poyato, E. C., Montesinos, P., & Díaz, J. R. (2019). Prediction of irrigation event occurrence at farm level using optimal decision trees. *Computers and Electronics in Agriculture, 157*, 173–180.
53. Sengupta, A., Debnath, B., Das, A., & De, D. (2021). FarmFox: A quad-sensor-based IoT box for precision agriculture. *IEEE Consumer Electronics Magazine, 10*(4), 63–68.

54. Raj, A., & Minz, S. (2021). A scalable unsupervised classification method using rough set for remote sensing imagery. *International Journal of Software Science and Computational Intelligence (IJSSCI)*, *13*(2), 65–88.
55. Brinkhoff, J., Vardanega, J., & Robson, A. J. (2019). Land cover classification of nine perennial crops using sentinel-1 and-2 data. *Remote Sensing*, *12*(1), 96.
56. Reddy, K. S. P., Roopa, Y. M., LN, K. R., & Nandan, N. S. (2020, July). IoT based smart agriculture using machine learning. In *2020 Second international conference on inventive research in computing applications (ICIRCA)* (pp. 130–134). IEEE.
57. Shaikh, T. A., Rasool, T., & Lone, F. R. (2022). Towards leveraging the role of machine learning and artificial intelligence in precision agriculture and smart farming. *Computers and Electronics in Agriculture*, *198*, 107119.
58. Huang, S., Fan, X., Sun, L., Shen, Y., & Suo, X. (2019). Research on classification method of maize seed defect based on machine vision. *Journal of Sensors*, *2019*(1), 2716975.
59. Zhu, S., Zhou, L., Gao, P., Bao, Y., He, Y., & Feng, L. (2019). Near-infrared hyperspectral imaging combined with deep learning to identify cotton seed varieties. *Molecules*, *24*(18), 3268.
60. Veeramani, B., Raymond, J. W., & Chanda, P. (2018). DeepSort: Deep convolutional networks for sorting haploid maize seeds. *BMC Bioinformatics*, *19*, 1–9.
61. Schor, N., Bechar, A., Ignat, T., Dombrovsky, A., Elad, Y., & Berman, S. (2016). Robotic disease detection in greenhouses: Combined detection of powdery mildew and tomato spotted wilt virus. *IEEE Robotics and Automation Letters*, *1*(1), 354–360.
62. Mehra, T., Kumar, V., & Gupta, P. (2016, December). Maturity and disease detection in tomato using computer vision. In *2016 Fourth international conference on parallel, distributed and grid computing (PDGC)* (pp. 399–403). IEEE.
63. Ji, M., Zhang, L., & Wu, Q. (2020). Automatic grape leaf diseases identification via UnitedModel based on multiple convolutional neural networks. *Information Processing in Agriculture*, *7*(3), 418–426.
64. Gavhale, K. R., Gawande, U., & Hajari, K. O. (2014, April). Unhealthy region of citrus leaf detection using image processing techniques. In *International Conference for Convergence for Technology-2014* (pp. 1–6). IEEE.
65. Sreedhar, B., BE, M. S., & Kumar, M. S. (2020, October). A comparative study of melanoma skin cancer detection in traditional and current image processing techniques. In *2020 Fourth International Conference on I-SMAC (IoT in Social, Mobile, Analytics and Cloud)(I-SMAC)* (pp. 654–658). IEEE.
66. Kaur, S., Pandey, S., & Goel, S. (2018). Semi-automatic leaf disease detection and classification system for soybean culture. *IET Image Processing*, *12*(6), 1038–1048.
67. Raj, A., & Minz, S. (2022, October). Spatial granule based clustering technique for hyperspectral images. In *2022 IEEE 2nd Mysore sub section international conference (MysuruCon)* (pp. 1–6). IEEE.
68. Dhanya, V. G., Subeesh, A., Kushwaha, N. L., Vishwakarma, D. K., Kumar, T. N., Ritika, G., & Singh, A. N. (2022). Deep learning based computer vision approaches for smart agricultural applications. *Artificial Intelligence in Agriculture*, *6*, 211–229.
69. Ünal, Z. (2020). Smart farming becomes even smarter with deep learning—A bibliographical analysis. *IEEE Access*, *8*, 105587–105609.
70. Bhuyan, B. P., Tomar, R., Singh, T. P., & Cherif, A. R. (2022). Crop type prediction: A statistical and machine learning approach. *Sustainability*, *15*(1), 481.
71. Guo, Y., Zhang, J., Yin, C., Hu, X., Zou, Y., Xue, Z., & Wang, W. (2020). Plant disease identification based on deep learning algorithm in smart farming. *Discrete Dynamics in Nature and Society*, *2020*(1), 2479172.

72. Sharma, M., Kumar, C. J., Talukdar, J., Singh, T. P., Dhiman, G., & Sharma, A. (2023). Identification of rice leaf diseases and deficiency disorders using a novel DeepBatch technique. *Open Life Sciences, 18*(1), 20220689.
73. Yalcin, H. (2017, August). Plant phenology recognition using deep learning: Deep-Pheno. In *2017 6th International Conference on Agro-Geoinformatics* (pp. 1–5). IEEE.
74. Taghavi Namin, S., Esmaeilzadeh, M., Najafi, M., Brown, T. B., & Borevitz, J. O. (2018). Deep phenotyping: Deep learning for temporal phenotype/genotype classification. *Plant Methods, 14*, 1–14.
75. Qiu, Z., Chen, J., Zhao, Y., Zhu, S., He, Y., & Zhang, C. (2018). Variety identification of single rice seed using hyperspectral imaging combined with convolutional neural network. *Applied Sciences, 8*(2), 212.
76. Yu, F., Hao, H., & Li, Q. (2021). An Ensemble 3D convolutional neural network for spatiotemporal soil temperature forecasting. *Sustainability, 13*(16), 9174.
77. Shi, X., Chen, Z., Wang, H., Yeung, D. Y., Wong, W. K., & Woo, W. C. (2015). Convolutional LSTM network: A machine learning approach for precipitation nowcasting. *Advances in Neural Information Processing Systems, 28*.
78. Alibabaei, K., Gaspar, P. D., & Lima, T. M. (2021). Modeling soil water content and reference evapotranspiration from climate data using deep learning method. *Applied Sciences, 11*(11), 5029.
79. Dheeraj, A., & Chand, S. (2023). Using deep learning models for crop and weed classification at early stage. In Sentiment Analysis and Deep Learning: Proceedings of ICSADL 2022 (pp. 931–942). Singapore: Springer Nature Singapore.
80. Dheeraj, A., & Chand, S. (2024). LWDN: Lightweight DenseNet model for plant disease diagnosis. *Journal of Plant Diseases and Protection, 31*(3), 1043–1059.
81. Nigam, S., Jain, R., Marwaha, S., Arora, A., Haque, M. A., Dheeraj, A., & Singh, V. K. (2023). Deep transfer learning model for disease identification in wheat crop. *Ecological Informatics, 75*, 102068.
82. Dheeraj, A., & Chand, S. (2022, November). Deep learning model for automated image based plant disease classification. In International Conference on Intelligent Vision and Computing (pp. 21–32). Cham: Springer Nature Switzerland.
83. Choudhury, A., Biswas, A., Singh, T. P., & Ghosh, S. K. (Eds.). (2022). *Smart Agriculture Automation Using Advanced Technologies: Data Analytics and Machine Learning, Cloud Architecture, Automation and IoT.* Springer Nature.
84. Khan, N., Ray, R. L., Sargani, G. R., Ihtisham, M., Khayyam, M., & Ismail, S. (2021). Current progress and future prospects of agriculture technology: Gateway to sustainable agriculture. *Sustainability, 13*(9), 4883.
85. Evans, R. G., LaRue, J., Stone, K. C., & King, B. A. (2013). Adoption of site-specific variable rate sprinkler irrigation systems. *Irrigation Science, 31*, 871–887.
86. McDowell, R. W. (2017). Does variable rate irrigation decrease nutrient leaching losses from grazed dairy farming? *Soil Use and Management, 33*(4), 530–537.
87. Amani, M., Parsian, S., MirMazloumi, S. M., & Aieneh, O. (2016). Two new soil moisture indices based on the NIR-red triangle space of Landsat-8 data. *International Journal of Applied Earth Observation and Geoinformation, 50*, 176–186.
88. Mendes, W. R., Araújo, F. M. U., Dutta, R., & Heeren, D. M. (2019). Fuzzy control system for variable rate irrigation using remote sensing. *Expert Systems with Applications, 124*, 13–24.
89. Varga, P., Plosz, S., Soos, G., & Hegedus, C. (2017, May). Security threats and issues in automation IoT. In 2017 IEEE 13th International Workshop on Factory Communication Systems (WFCS) (pp. 1–6). IEEE.

90. Glaroudis, D., Iossifides, A., & Chatzimisios, P. (2020). Survey, comparison and research challenges of IoT application protocols for smart farming. *Computer Networks*, *168*, 107037.
91. Giua, C., Materia, V. C., & Camanzi, L. (2022). Smart farming technologies adoption: Which factors play a role in the digital transition? *Technology in Society*, *68*, 101869.
92. Siebrecht, N. (2020). Sustainable agriculture and its implementation gap—Overcoming obstacles to implementation. *Sustainability*, *12*(9), 3853.
93. Tripathi, A. D., Mishra, R., Maurya, K. K., Singh, R. B., & Wilson, D. W. (2019). Estimates for world population and global food availability for global health. In *The Role of Functional Food Security in Global Health* (pp. 3–24). Amsterdam, The Netherlands: Elsevier.

8 ICT in Education
A Bibliometric Analysis

Abhijit Vhatkar, Pravin Chavan, and Vilis Pawar

8.1 INTRODUCTION

Information and communication technology is commonly addressed as ICT. It has revolutionized the education sector [1]. It has had a positive impact on the teaching-learning method adopted by educational institutes. It has surpassed traditional classroom teaching methods [2].

ICT uses digital collaborative tools, online media, and multimedia content to enhance the teaching-learning process. Instructors have more opportunities to share content with learners with the help of ICT [3]. Educational institutes have significantly increased the use of ICT during the COVID-19 pandemic. ICT resources are used by most educational institutions today [4]. The use of ICT in the education sector is not only a technological shift but also a transformation of the methodological approach. The implementation of ICT in educational institutes resulted in an overall improvement in the teaching-learning process and overall understanding of the students. It provides ease of learning for students and reduces the burden on teachers [5]. ICT helps improve the overall outcome of education and prepares students for future competition [6].

The main objective of this chapter is to examine the use of ICT in the sphere of education. In doing so, it attempts to offer comprehensive explanations of ICT basics, applications, necessity, significance, the challenges associated with ICT adoption in the education sector, and upcoming ICT developments. This chapter highlights the current status of the research and directions for future research on the use of ICT in the education sector.

8.1.1 Definition and Conceptual Background

ICT is the collection and implementation of digital tools to create, store, and transfer information. It uses multiple technologies, including hardware and software, to create and store information, the Internet, and collaborative software tools to transfer the information [7].

As per the UNESCO learning portal, ICT is defined as a set of different tools used to create, store, and share information. These tools include computers, the Internet, and broadcasting tools.

ICT refers to a broad range of services and technologies related to computing, data management, telecommunications, and the Internet [8].

As per the Eurostat portal, all technological tools used to manage information and facilitate communication are referred to as ICT. This covers the hardware and software for computers and networks.

DOI: 10.1201/9781003471356-8

ICT has evolved and been integrated with new technologies to process, communicate, and share information. ICT represents a paradigm shift in the way people use technology and engage with one another, with roots in the integration of computing, telecommunications, and information systems.

The conceptual background of ICT dates back to the early stages of computers and digital technologies. The mid-20th century witnessed the introduction of computers, which laid the foundation for digital technologies and resulted in networks [9]. Next-generation computers and hardware devices have made it possible to connect with other computers and share data between them. Advances in telecommunication technologies have also played a crucial role in ICT development. The rise of telecommunication and advances in Internet facilities have helped people connect, collaborate, and share information [10]. Software systems and applications have enabled users to create, process, and utilize data. Innovation, decision-making, and productivity have all greatly benefited from the use of software [11].

ICT has been developed as a hardware, software, and network resource. Hardware, software, and network resources with the correct human resources and the implementation of technological tools create cohesive systems to meet a specific need for information processing and sharing. A holistic approach is required for the effective management of information in ICT [12].

ICT extends beyond traditional computing techniques. It also includes emerging technologies, such as artificial intelligence (AI), the Internet of Things (IoT), and blockchain. These cutting-edge technologies can enhance ICT by opening new avenues for automation and communication [13].

8.1.2 Relevance of ICT in Green Computing

ICT is becoming an integral part of modern educational systems. It is going to revolutionize the traditional education system and change teaching-learning methods. As the number of institutes using digital and ICT tools is increasing significantly, consideration of the environmental impact of ICT becomes critical and important. ICT is relevant to green computing, which is an eco-friendly technology. The use of ICT in education has the potential for technological advancement without compromising on environmental sustainability [14].

- *The impact of ICT on the environment*: The use of ICT in the education sector leads to ease of accessibility and increased efficiency but raises serious concerns about carbon emissions and energy usage.
- *Green infrastructure practices in ICT*: In ICT, green infrastructure focuses on the adoption of sustainable practices. The adoption of energy-efficient hardware, reduction in energy usage, and efficiency of data centers can reduce the carbon footprint [15].
- *Management of e-waste and the circular economy*: The issue of e-waste is becoming more significant in educational institutes because of the quick turnaround of electronic devices. Green computing promotes responsible e-waste management, which leads to recycling electronic devices and their disposal in ways that have less negative impact on the environment [16].

- *Energy-efficient classrooms*: Green computing also impacts how energy-efficient learning classrooms are built and run. Sustainable environments are supported by physical infrastructure in classrooms equipped with energy-efficient lighting, ventilation, air conditioning, and heating [17].
- *Integration of syllabi to teach sustainability*: Integration of syllabi with green computing methodology is also important. The effects of technology on the environment are taught to the students. With the integration of the curriculum with environmental sustainability principles, students will become more responsible for the environment.
- *Enabling remote learning to reduce carbon footprint*: Green computing offers the possibility of lowering carbon emissions by facilitating remote learning using these technologies. Educational institutes can reduce their dependence on physical infrastructure, paper usage, and transportation by using online technologies and tools. E-classrooms, collaborative tools, and online platforms help reduce the carbon footprint [18].
- *Awareness and involvement of stakeholders*: Educational institutes need to create awareness among stakeholders regarding the effect of ICT facilities on the environment. Stakeholders should be motivated by environmentally friendly behavior.

8.1.3 Need for ICT in Education

The traditional educational model emphasizes the physical delivery of knowledge by the teacher; reading textbooks and physical paper-based examinations make it less effective in the 21st century. Less active participation of students in teaching-learning methods is a serious problem in traditional learning methods. Not every student is equally affected by knowledge transfer, which takes the form of lectures in the classroom. Traditional teaching using a blackboard failed to get the attention of all students.

One of the main shortcomings of the traditional education paradigm is the limited availability of information based on students' expectations and convenience. Students are expected to attend regular physical classes, take notes in the classroom, and borrow hard-copy books to gain the necessary information. Different learning attitudes of different students create difficulties in understanding concepts. The speed of understanding among different students causes difficulties for many learners.

The shortcomings of existing conventional knowledge delivery methods have motivated ICT usage in the education sector. The convenience of information gathering, dependence on online collaborative tools for knowledge sharing, ease of availability of the study material, and scope of learning as per the attitude and learning speed of the students make ICT an important tool for the education sector [19].

8.1.4 Evolution of ICT in Educational Institutes

Traditionally, the education sector focuses on knowledge delivery by teachers in classrooms. The traditional media for the transfer of knowledge are blackboard teaching, classroom discussion, reading textbooks, and oral and written examinations [20]. The education sector has used these limited resources to disseminate knowledge almost until the last decade.

The evolution of the education sector began after the rise of computers. Computers have been used in universities since the beginning. Colleges and schools began using computers after the evolution of the computer hardware industry. Affordable pricing and the reduced size of computers have made it convenient to use in educational institutes [21]. Developments in system software and application software have made it easy for non-technical people to use computers. This leads to increased usage of computer hardware and software by teachers and students in the teaching-learning method. Application software helped teachers deliver information in the class in an eye-catching manner. This has improved students' attention and understanding during class. Application software is also useful for students to complete the tasks and assignments expected in the class [22].

Internet technology can be considered as the next milestone in ICT. Connectivity among the computers made it easy for teachers to share information with learners. Learner participation has also increased after the rise of Internet technology. An increase in the speed of the Internet has resulted in the sharing of information in multimedia formats. Sharing of educational videos, audio, e-books, images, etc. became possible after the improvement of Internet technology.

The learning management software (LMS) facilitates bidirectional communication between educators and students. The LMS created an opportunity for learners to actively participate in the teaching-learning process at their convenience, speed, and availability. LMS has also been very useful for the administrative tasks of educational institutes. The need for physical availability of students for necessary administrative tasks was reduced by the LMS [23].

The COVID-19 pandemic has acted as a catalyst for the rapid use of ICT in education in most parts of the world [24]. The availability of smart computer devices, smart mobile devices, high-speed Internet connectivity, cloud computing, virtual classrooms, online collaboration tools, online assessment, and information in multimedia formats have resulted in higher usage of ICT in the educational sector.

8.1.5 Trends of ICT Usage in Educational Institutes

ICT is continuously changing the education landscape. The introduction of innovative tools and recent teaching-learning methodologies has revolutionized the education sector. The changes and upgradation of overall technology have led to new trends in the education sector.

- *Blended learning*: This uses online platforms, information in multimedia formats, and collaborative tools. It creates flexibility for students to consume content at their convenience and pace. This reduces the burden on the teacher to deliver information inside the classroom from scratch. Higher educational program outcomes can be achieved through blended learning [25].

- *Personalized flexible education*: Personalized learning is becoming more popular because of technological advancements. AI is employed to understand the educational performance of each student. The difficulty and pace of learning can be adjusted according to each student's level of educational performance [26].
- *Virtual and augmented reality*: The use of various recent technologies such as augmented and virtual reality for the teaching-learning process results in improved engagement of the students. The creation of virtual models, simulations, and virtual trips can increase the learners' understanding of the concept. VR and AR technology are useful for understanding difficult, complex concepts and critical scenarios [27].
- *Gamification of learning*: Gamification of learning increases students' overall motivation and engagement in the learning process. This creates an enjoyable learning process for the students.
- *Collaborative learning experience*: LMS have enabled collaboration opportunities among various learners. Discussion forums, online document editing, and online classrooms encourage collaborative learning experiences among students. It prepares students for a collaborative work environment in real life [28].
- *Data-based decisions*: ICT generates a large amount of data that the education sector can utilize to make decisions. Students' achievements can be easily identified, and areas of improvement can be suggested based on the data generated. Pattern recognition for the use of ICT tools, engagement, preference for multimedia content, and so on can be analyzed. This has resulted in the development of evidence-based educational strategies.
- *Digital literacy and cybersecurity*: The growth of advanced ICT tools has led to the responsible and secure use of digital tools. Digital literacy has become increasingly important in ICT settings. Higher educational institutes incorporate cybersecurity as part of their curriculum [29].

8.1.6 Importance of ICT in Educational Institutes

Integrating ICT into education has been associated with several positive effects on the quality of education. Research indicates a direct positive association between ICT integration and enhanced educational outcomes. ICT integration results in increased productivity, enhanced student motivation, and expanded opportunities to access information and develop essential skills, such as critical thinking and collaboration. It is a thrust area for educational researchers to explore the impact and outcomes of ICT on education. The key areas of these findings are discussed below.

- *Enhanced student engagement*: Integrating ICTs in higher education significantly impacts the educational process and outcomes. The effective use of ICT facilitates educational access, equality, management, efficiency, pedagogy, and quality. The first and foremost important role played by ICT in education is to make education more interesting; infuse creativity that facilitates active, collaborative, creative, integrative, and evaluative learning; and improve the overall standard of education [30]. Enhanced productivity is the second-most significant benefit of ICT-based education. Several studies have also indicated that ICT-based learning is more effective for self-directed learning than traditional educational methods. Amutha [31] states that ICT-enabled education enhances student motivation and engagement. Kapur [32] asserted that ICT facilitates critical thinking and collaboration more effectively than traditional education. ICT-based learning also paves the way for autonomous learning and encourages creativity [33]. The use of ICT facilitates access to authentic learning materials that support out-of-class autonomous learning. Additionally, ICT-enabled education offers innovative tools for student assessment. They extended the possibilities of assessment far beyond the limits of conventional grading, offering a more current and adequate response to students. They represent varied solutions that can be more personalized and resonate with students' needs [34].

- *Conducive learning environment*: ICT is crucial in establishing a favorable learning environment. A conducive learning environment has task orientation, predictability, and consistency in engaging students in learning tasks [35]. Authors in [35] stated that the use of ICT in classrooms helps efficient classroom management. ICT facilitates the effective definition of classroom expectations, routines, and rules that foster productive behavior and minimize disruptions. Additionally, ICT enables active involvement and problem-solving among students that challenge their capabilities. However, Esfandiari and Gawhary [33] emphasized that technology alone is not sufficient; it is imperative to offer proper guidance to ensure that technological tools are effectively used to promote autonomy.
- *Collaborative learning*: Authors in [36] emphasized the collaborative learning benefits in education. ICT tools are equipped with the capabilities of real-time communication and interaction among students and teachers, resulting in synchronous collaboration. Furthermore, ICT provides resource-sharing and content-creating platforms, which are prerequisites of effective collaborative learning. Advanced ICT tools support educators in the coordination of group tasks; beyond student engagement, they enable collaborative project management. Well-designed ICT tools effectively collect and analyze data from collaborative processes and strengthen the feedback loop. ICT offers access to a wider range of information and expertise, broadening the scope of collaboration beyond the classroom.
- *Teacher-student interaction*: Quratulain et al. [37] underlined the role of ICT tools in teacher-student interaction and asserted that ICT-enabled education enhances communication between teachers and students. ICT is an ideal instrument for creating shared communicative spaces where many factors may come together and different methods and techniques can be used to enhance engagement and facilitate quick communication among users. The cooperation of various educational entities primarily enhances learning via collaborative efforts to facilitate mutual learning through reflective, critical, and independent means and fosters the enhancement of

collective knowledge production [38]. It has been discovered that ICT platforms, such as Moodle, enable significant teacher-student interaction and increase the motivation and engagement of education [39]. However, the success of ICT interventions in enhancing classroom interactions for constructivist learning relies on overcoming teachers' limitations and incorporating engaging features [40]. Besides, Gabelaia and Vasadze [41] argued that effective communication between teachers and students is a prerequisite for virtual student-teacher relationships in technology-mediated teaching and communication.

- *Integration of students' devices for learning*: Students are more adept at using technology, as they have been exposed to and familiar with ICT from a young age [42]. Research shows that smartphone use is practically universal in society, especially among teenagers, therefore it is common among young people [43]. Studies have shown that a considerable proportion of young individuals exhibit excessive smartphone use, exceeding 12 hours of online activities [44]. In addition, ICT-enabled education offers an opportunity to interlink students' digital devices such as smartphones and computers for better connection and engagement [45]. Teachers can interlink ICT with students' smartphones and other gadgets for educational purposes beyond the classroom. Instructors can produce, convey, disseminate, and retain materials that students can reevaluate in light of their learning requirements [46].
- *Equity in education*: Introducing ICTs in higher education has significant implications for the entire education process, particularly in addressing access, equity, management, efficiency, pedagogy, and quality, especially in developing countries such as India [47]. ICT-driven education has the potential to reach the masses with limited initial investment. The use of ICT helps children who cannot attend regular schools due to scheduling or location issues. Utilizing ICT in education has proven to be advantageous for students facing challenges in attending traditional schools because of geographical or time limitations. Research indicates that incorporating ICT into teaching and learning can help address obstacles and improve educational access [48].
- Integrating ICT into education offers endless opportunities for teachers and students to make education more engaging and accessible. Enhancing the learning experience with multimedia and smartphone applications to facilitate effective student learning. Teachers can utilize ICT tools creatively to enhance learners' skills and establish an engaging and cooperative learning atmosphere. It also contributes to literacy movements, enables mobile learning and inclusive education, and promotes research and communication.

8.1.7 Challenges for ICT in Educational Institutes

The integration of ICT into the educational sector has various benefits and challenges. Serval hurdles emerge as educational institutes and their stakeholders go through the transformation phase of ICT implementation. The key challenges faced by educational institutes are as follows.

- *Infrastructural limitations*: Most schools lack adequate ICT infrastructure. Institutes from urban areas may have high-speed Internet, whereas institutes from rural areas lack high-speed Internet connectivity. Outdated hardware, old networking devices, and a shortage of continuous power supply limit ICT in educational institutions [49].
- *Economic and social disparities*: Differences in the availability of digital devices based on economic and social factors still exist. Students from wealthier backgrounds had access to recent, fast, and personal gadgets in their homes. However, students from lower-income groups lack the availability of the basic and necessary information for ICT in education [50].
- *Preparedness of the educator*: The motivation and preparedness of educators to make efficient use of ICT tools are necessary. Many teachers may have a high learning curve for understanding ICT tools. Little or no exposure to ICT tools for teachers during their education and no incentives for adopting ICT methodology can be considered serious limitations [51].
- *Budget limitations*: The financial limitations faced by educational institutions are one of the basic barriers to ICT adoption. Modern computer devices, networking devices, system software, application software, collaborative tools, etc. require significant investment [52].
- *Security and privacy issues*: The implementation of ICT in educational institutions can cause serious security and privacy issues. Therefore, protecting students' educational data is important. Security against cyber threats must be seriously considered [53].
- *Pedagogical integration*: Seamless pedagogical integration is essential to successful ICT implementation. The focus on technology and tools should not change the focus of the teachers. ICT should supplement the teaching process, and human touch should not be considered less important in the teaching-learning process.
- *Impact on the environment*: ICT use in educational institutions has a substantial environmental impact. Electronic waste due to technological updates and carbon emissions from the smart classroom environment has become a major challenge [54].

8.2 METHODOLOGY

The bibliometric analysis method was used to analyze the data for this chapter. Bibliometric analysis allows researchers to identify the existing body of research and trends in research and to help draw meaningful insights from the research [55]. The bibliometric analysis methodology used in this chapter resulted in the identification of research trends and patterns in the field of 'ICT in education' (Figure 8.1).

- Research that led to the foundation of this chapter was identified from the Scopus database. The Scopus database is a well-known repository for high-quality research in any field [56]. A search was made on the Scopus

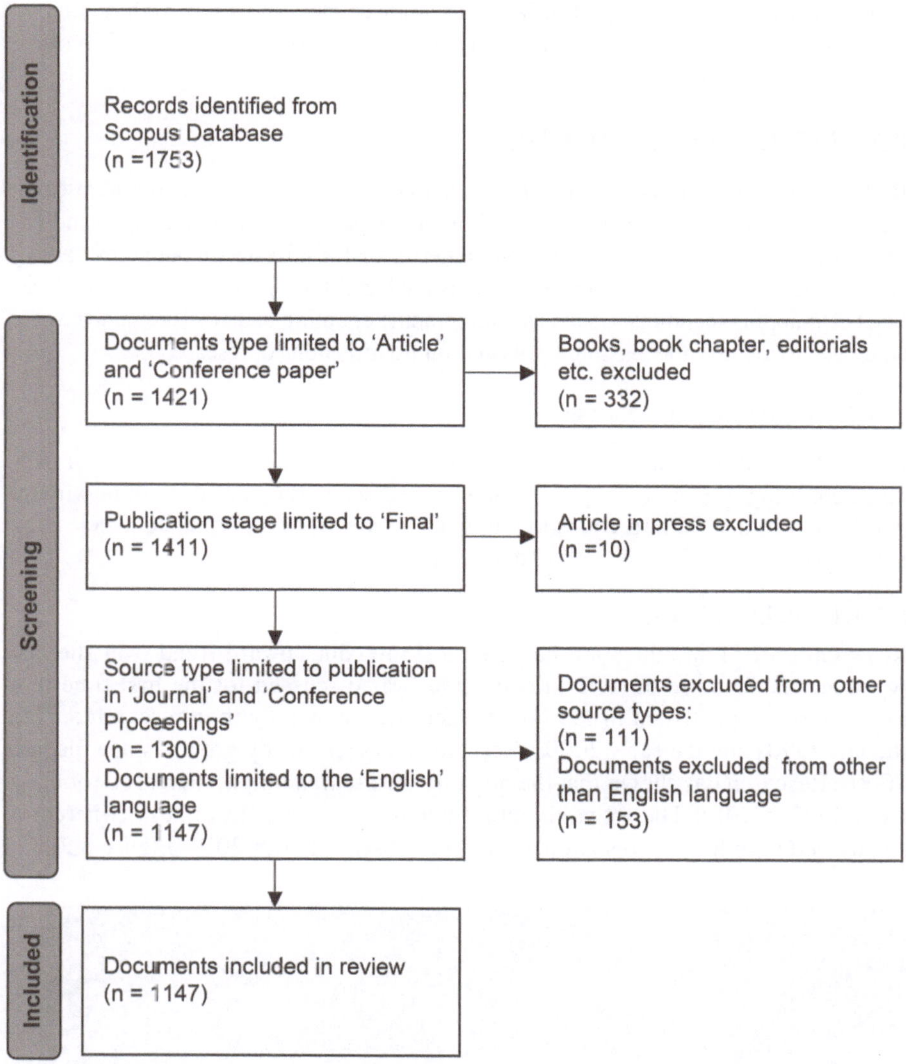

FIGURE 8.1 PRISMA flow diagram [57].

database with a search string as 'ICT' AND 'Education' OR 'Information and Communication Technology' AND 'Education.' The initial search resulted in the identification of 1753 research articles.

- Only 'articles' and 'conference papers' were considered for analysis, as they were peer-reviewed. Articles that had already been published were considered, whereas articles in press were excluded. The source types of articles were limited to 'journals' and 'conference proceedings.' Only articles from the 'English' language were considered, whereas articles from other languages were excluded.

- The rigorous screening criteria for research articles resulted in high-quality and relevant 1147 articles. These 1147 articles were considered for bibliometric analysis.

8.3 BIBLIOMETRIC ANALYSIS

Bibliometric analysis is used to identify the status of current research and future research direction in the field of 'ICT in education.' In this chapter, performance analysis and science mapping techniques are used in bibliometric analysis. Research output by various authors, institutes, countries, journals, etc. is analyzed through performance analysis. Science mapping techniques, such as bibliographic coupling and co-word analysis, are employed to identify the existing status and future directions of research [58].

8.3.1 Performance Analysis

It shows the publication trend over the years and identifies the top countries in ICT research. It highlights highly prolific authors and scholarly journals with maximum publication in the 'ICT in education' domain. It identifies highly-cited articles and keywords in the 'ICT in education' domain [59].

8.3.1.1 Publication Trend

Research on ICT in education has seen a significant upward trend over the last two decades. The use of 'ICT in education' was discussed for the first time in a research paper published in 1997 [60]. There was slow growth in research during the late 1990s and the early 2000s. Research has seen steady growth since the late 2000s. Research has shown that the quantity of research output increased robustly from 2007 to 2012. The research output fluctuated from 2013 to 2018, whereas a steady and high level of research output was observed after 2019 (Figure 8.2).

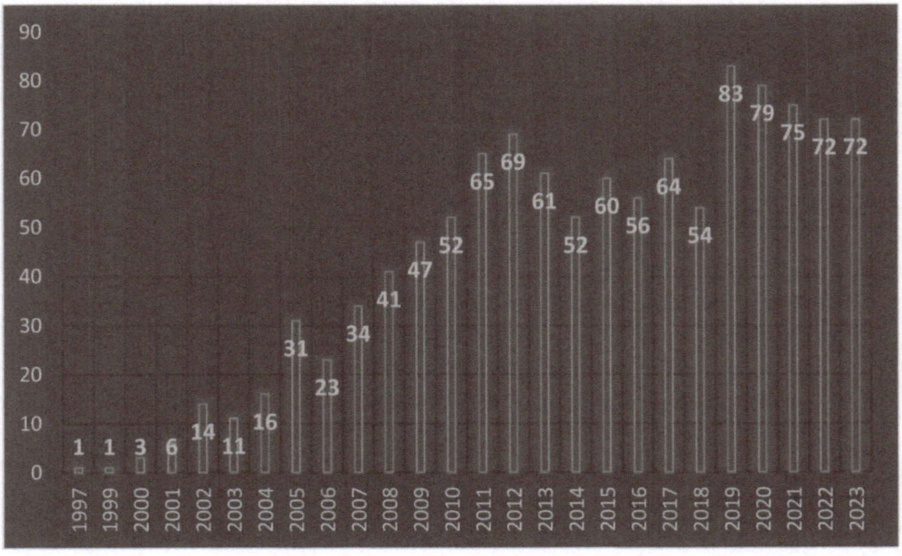

FIGURE 8.2 Publication trend.

TABLE 8.1
Top Contributing Countries

Sr. No	Country	Number of Research Articles	Citations
1	Spain	100	1541
2	India	84	445
3	Australia	73	853
4	United Kingdom	61	1805
5	China	51	422
6	Malaysia	51	321
7	United States	48	741
8	Indonesia	42	136
9	Greece	41	567
10	Japan	36	90

8.3.1.2 Top Contributing Countries

The 'ICT in education' domain has witnessed contributions in publications from all around the globe. Spain is the leader in research output, with 100 documents and 1541 citations. India has demonstrated a strong research culture, with 84 research papers and 445 citations. Australia made significant contributions to 73 research papers and 853 citations (Table 8.1). Significant contributions made by the United Kingdom, China, Malaysia, the United States, Indonesia, Greece, and Japan have demonstrated global cooperation and a variety of viewpoints in this research.

8.3.1.3 Highly Prolific Authors

The highly prolific authors Nurjanah, Santoso, and Hasibuan produced four research articles (Table 8.2) that revolve around ICT adoption in education [61], a framework of ICT adoption [62], and acceptance of ICT in education [63]. Another group of highly prolific authors, Rahmat and Au also published four research papers. Their research revolves around ICT integration among teachers [64], attitudes [65], and teachers' beliefs regarding ICT [66].

TABLE 8.2
Highly Prolific Authors

Sr. No	Author	Number of Research Articles
1	Nurjanah S.; Santoso H.B.; Hasibuan Z.A.	4
2	Rahmat M.K.; Au W.K.	4
3	Aoki K.	3
4	Hashim R.; Ahmad H.; Abdullah C.Z.	3
5	Mena J.; Singh B.; Clarke A.	3
6	Mooij T.	3

TABLE 8.3
Highly Prolific Journals

Sr. No	Source	Number of Research Articles
1	Education and Information Technologies	31
2	ACM International Conference Proceeding Series	26
3	Sustainability (Switzerland)	22
4	CEUR Workshop Proceedings	21
5	Computers and Education	17
6	Turkish Online Journal of Educational Technology	16
7	British Journal of Educational Technology	13
8	Journal of Physics: Conference Series	13
9	8th IFIP World Conference on Computers in Education, 2005	11
10	Australasian Journal of Educational Technology	11

8.3.1.4 Highly Prolific Journals

Few journals stand out as highly prolific in the 'ICT in education' research domain. 'Education and Information Technologies' leads the list with 31 research papers showcasing its central role in dissemination of the knowledge. The ACM International Conference Proceeding Series follows 26 research papers, indicating the significance of the research. Sustainability contributed to 22 articles and enriched the field of study (Table 8.3).

8.3.1.5 Highly Cited Articles

Research articles with a higher number of citations are considered important because of their quality of content and contribution to the body of existing research. The highest-cited article [67] received 533 citations. It focuses on the lack of ICT infrastructure, Internet facilities, student-computer ratios, and multimedia computer devices. The second most cited article [68] received 317 citations. It discusses the role of ICT in education, less evidence of the outcomes, and the desire to transform the educational system. The third most-cited article [69] received 227 citations. It discusses the significant variation in ICT use among various schools, the impact of software availability on ICT use, and collaboration among teachers as an important factor for ICT use (Table 8.4).

8.3.1.6 Highly Used Keywords

The research themes revolve around various keywords in the 'ICT in education' domain. 'ICT' is a highly used keyword with 276 times occurrence. It is followed by 'Education' and 'higher education' which has been appeared 108 and 96 times, respectively. 'E-learning' and 'ICT in education' have occurred 49 and 39 times, respectively (Figure 8.3).

8.3.2 Science Mapping

It includes bibliographic coupling to identify the existing status of research in the 'ICT in education' domain. It also has the co-word analysis to showcase the future

TABLE 8.4
Highly Cited Articles

Sr. No	Article Title	Citations
1	Obstacles to the integration of ICT in education: Results from a worldwide educational assessment [67]	533
2	Critical reflections on the benefits of ICT in education [68]	317
3	Factors that explain the use of ICT in secondary-education classrooms: The role of teacher characteristics and school infrastructure [69]	227
4	The use of ICT in education: A survey of schools in Europe [70]	209
5	Does ICT contribute to powerful learning environments in primary education? [71]	199
6	The role of ICT in modulating the effect of education and lifelong learning on income inequality and economic growth in Africa [72]	180
7	New technologies, new differences. Gender and ethnic differences in pupils' use of ICT in primary and secondary education [73]	179
8	Examining teachers' beliefs about ICT in education: Implications of a teacher preparation program [74]	175
9	Curricula and the use of ICT in education: Two worlds apart? [75]	138
10	What stimulates teachers to integrate ICT in their pedagogical practices? The use of digital learning materials in education [76]	131

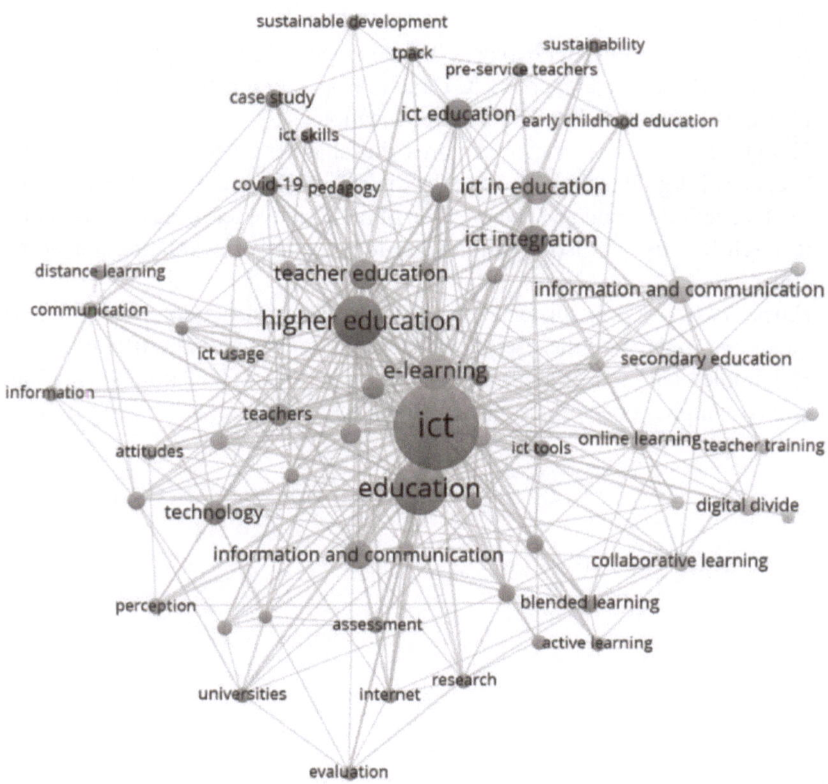

FIGURE 8.3 Highly used keywords.

direction for research in the 'ICT in education' domain. Data visualization under science mapping showcases various research themes with different colors [59].

8.3.2.1 Bibliographic Coupling

Bibliometric coupling is a useful technique in science mapping of bibliometric analysis. It evaluates the similarity between two research articles based on common references cited in these articles [55]. Articles with a higher number of common references had a common theme in research. Bibliographic coupling identifies various clusters with high degrees of similarity. Analysis of these clusters resulted in the identification of various themes and the status of existing research under these themes. Bibliographic coupling identifies the current status of research in the 'ICT in education' domain (Figure 8.4).

- *Red cluster*: This cluster focuses on the transformative effects of ICT in education. This study examines the motivating factors for ICT adoption among teachers. This highlights the importance of incorporating ICT into primary education. It provides a link between ICT technology, teaching pedagogy, and its impact on students.
- *Green cluster*: This cluster explores the effects of ICT integration in education and identifies the efficiency of ICT in the education sector. It highlights the impact of teachers' attributes and the school's infrastructure on ICT usage.
- *Blue cluster*: This cluster explores the influence of ICT on higher education. It considers the ongoing use of ICT and teachers' competency in ICT use. It identifies the motives for ICT use in education.
- *Yellow cluster*: This cluster explores the changes in teachers' education because of digital technology and the digital age. It focuses on ICT use during teacher education and the creation of an effective learning environment through ICT use. It also highlights the importance of evaluating teachers' education.
- *Purple cluster*: This cluster explores the views of professors from higher education, regarding the use of ICT in the 21st century and difficulties in ICT implementation. It focuses on the complexities of ICT implementation and how higher education professors deal with them.

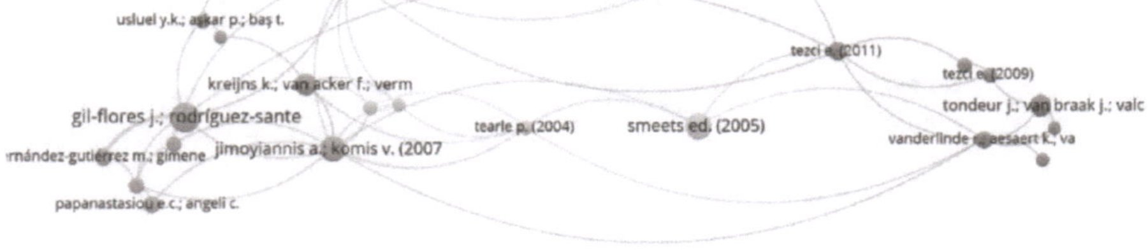

FIGURE 8.4 Bibliographic coupling.

- *Sky blue cluster*: This cluster explores various factors related to ICT in education and their effects. This cluster is focused on the influence of ICT on education. It considers the advantages and difficulties of ICT in education.

8.3.2.2 Co-Word Analysis

Co-word analysis is a science mapping technique used in bibliometric analysis. It focuses on the author's keywords [55]. It is assumed that the keywords used frequently together have a common theme. The co-word analysis helps identify future trends of research based on various identified clusters (Figure 8.5).

- *Implementation of ICT in the education sector*: This focuses on complex educational technology and the practical implementation of ICT in the educational sector. Future research should focus on innovative best practices for ICT implementation in the education sector. Case studies should be identified to explore the challenges associated with the ICT in education sector. Research on advanced pedagogical approaches to leveraging ICT has scope for future research.
- *Training in ICT*: It focuses on training, communication, and the perception of students toward ICT. An investigation can be conducted on communication technologies and their impact on productive learning environments.

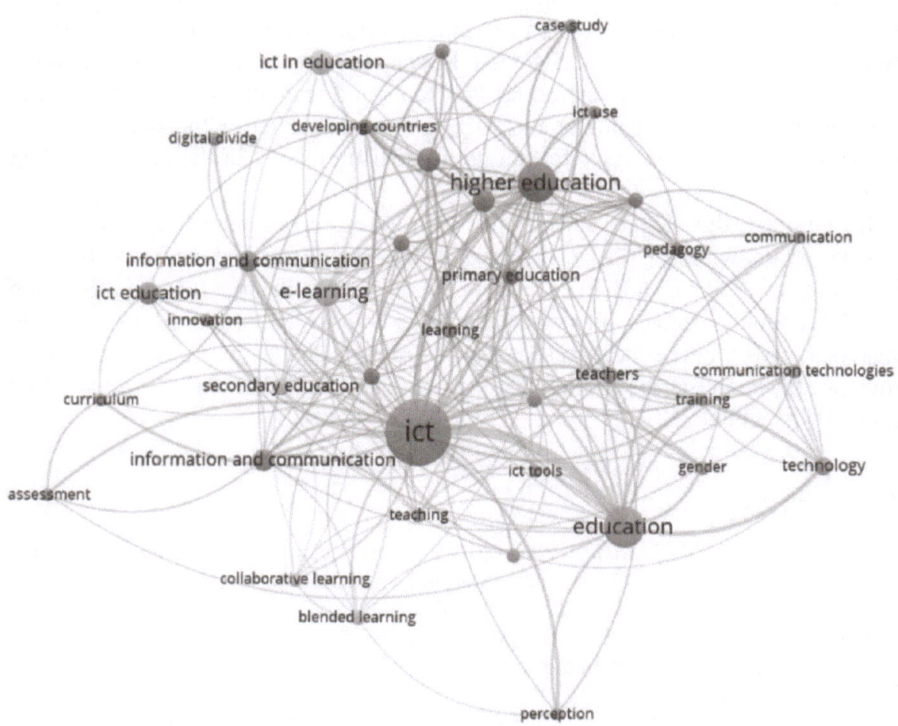

FIGURE 8.5 Co-word analysis.

Research can be conducted on the impact of gender and attitude on ICT use in education. The preparedness of teachers and new approaches to ICT implementation should be studied.

- *Technology upgrade and digital divide*: This has research potential in the development of assessment procedures in line with the use of ICT in the classroom. Research should be conducted in the field of curriculum development to promote digital literacy and ICT use. New technologies and their effects on curriculum development can provide a future scope for research. Research can be conducted to reduce the digital divide among students.
- *Mixed learning*: This has research potential for mixed learning models containing traditional and online learning approaches. A study can be conducted on how blended learning affects students' involvement and educational outcomes.
- *ICT in technical education*: Future research should focus on customizing ICT tools for higher education, including engineering education. Research can be conducted on emerging ICT technologies and their impacts on engineering education. Examining the changing role of ICT in technical education has scope for further research [77].

8.4 CONCLUSION

The theoretical viewpoints mentioned in this chapter highlight the importance of ICT use in the education sector. In the 21st century, traditional classroom instructions are inappropriate. Hence, it is not only necessary to adapt ICT in education but also to keep on constantly upgrading ICT tools and technology. The bibliometric analysis approach has provided the existing status of research in this domain. It has also offered recommendations for the future course of study in the field of 'ICT in education.'

In summary, this chapter adds significantly to the current knowledge corpus and lays the groundwork for further research. These theoretical and empirical findings help in the evolution of ICT in education. The chapter points out that the utilization of ICT is not only a choice but also a need for an hour for every educational institute. Stakeholders from the education sector might use this chapter as a guide, as it offers guidance toward a future in which ICT is an essential component of education rather than only a technology.

REFERENCES

1. Hoque, S. M. S., & Alam, S. M. (2010). The role of information and communication technologies (ICTs) in delivering higher education—A case of Bangladesh. *International Education Studies*, *3*(2).
2. Aina, J. K. (2013). Effective teaching and learning in science education through information and communication technology [ICT]. *IOSR Journal of Research and Method in Education*, *2*(5), 43–47.
3. Dlamini, P. N. (2020). Use of information and communication technologies tools to capture, store, and disseminate indigenous knowledge: A literature review. *Indigenous Studies: Breakthroughs in Research and Practice*, 325–347.

4. Arshad, M. (2020). COVID-19: It's time to be thankful to our ICT professionals. *Information Technology & Electrical Engineering*, *9*(2), 23–31.
5. Guma, A., Faruque, A. H., & Muhammad, K. (2013). *The role of ICT to make teaching-learning effective in higher institutions of learning in Uganda.*
6. Biagi, F., & Loi, M. (2013). Measuring ICT use and learning outcomes: Evidence from recent econometric studies. *European Journal of Education*, *48*(1), 28–42.
7. Bingimlas, K. A. (2009). Barriers to the successful integration of ICT in teaching and learning environments: A review of the literature. *Eurasia Journal of Mathematics, Science and Technology Education*, *5*(3), 235–245.
8. Mahan, J. (n.d.). *What Is ICT? Information and Communications Technology - C&C Technology Group*. https://cc-techgroup.com/what-is-ict/
9. Reinking, D., & Colwell, J. (2015). A brief history of information sources in the late 20th and early 21st century (A simulation).
10. Kim, B. (2019). ICT-based business communication with customers in the 4th industrial revolution era. *Business Communication Research and Practice*, *2*(2), 55–61.
11. Cox, M. J., & Marshall, G. (2007). Effects of ICT: Do we know what we should know? *Education and Information Technologies*, *12*, 59–70.
12. Ra, S., Chin, B., & Lim, C. P. (2016). A holistic approach towards information and communication technology (ICT) for addressing education challenges in Asia and the Pacific. *Educational Media International*, *53*(2), 69–84.
13. Trung, N. D., Huy, D. T. N., Le, T. H., Huong, D. T., & Hoa, N. T. (2021). ICT, AI, IOTs and technology applications in education—A case with accelerometer and internet learner gender prediction. *Advances in Mechanics*, *9*(3), 1288–1296.
14. Airehrour, D., Cherrington, M., Madanian, S., & Singh, J. (2019, August). Reducing ICT carbon footprints through adoption of green computing. In *10.12948/ie2019. 04.17. Academy of Economic Studies in Bucharest*. Department of Economic Informatics and Cybernetics.
15. Paul, P. K. & Ganguly, J. (2013). Green information infrastructure: Stakeholders-a study. *International Journal of Pharmaceutical and Biological Research (IJPBR)*, *4*(04), 159–164.
16. Heeks, R., Subramanian, L., & Jones, C. (2015). Understanding e-waste management in developing countries: Strategies, determinants, and policy implications in the Indian ICT sector. *Information Technology for Development*, *21*(4), 653–667.
17. Uddin, M., Okai, S., & Saba, T. (2017). Green ICT framework to reduce carbon footprints in universities. *Advances in Energy Research*, *5*(1), 1.
18. Versteijlen, M., Salgado, F. P., Groesbeek, M. J., & Counotte, A. (2017). Pros and cons of online education as a measure to reduce carbon emissions in higher education in the Netherlands. *Current Opinion in Environmental Sustainability*, *28*, 80–89.
19. Henderson, D. (2020). Benefits of ICT in education. *IDOSR Journal of Arts and Management*, *5*(1), 51–57.
20. Kaur, N., Dwivedi, D., Arora, J., & Gandhi, A. (2020). Study of the effectiveness of e-learning to conventional teaching in medical undergraduates amid COVID-19 pandemic. *National Journal of Physiology, Pharmacy and Pharmacology*, *10*(7), 563–567.
21. Horn, M. B., & Staker, H. (2011). The rise of K-12 blended learning. *Innosight Institute*, *5*(1), 1–17.
22. Campos, J. (2009). Development in the application of ICT in condition monitoring and maintenance. *Computers in Industry*, *60*(1), 1–20.
23. Pretorius, M., & van Biljon, J. (2010). Learning management systems: ICT skills, usability and learnability. *Interactive Technology and Smart Education*, *7*(1), 30–43.
24. Al-Ansi, A. M., Garad, A., & Al-Ansi, A. (2021). ICT-based learning during Covid-19 outbreak: Advantages, opportunities and challenges. *Gagasan Pendidikan Indonesia*, *2*(1), 10–26.

25. Dangwal, K. L. (2017). Blended learning: An innovative approach. *Universal Journal of Educational Research*, *5*(1), 129–136.
26. Gerbic, P. (2004, July). What about flexible learning and ICT? -A review of technology based flexible learning in tertiary education. In *Third Pan-Commonwealth Forum Conference, 4–8* July *2004*.
27. Raja, M., & Lakshmi Priya, G. G. (2022). Using virtual reality and augmented reality with ICT tools for enhancing quality in the changing academic environment in COVID-19 pandemic: An empirical study. In *Technologies, Artificial Intelligence and the Future of Learning Post-COVID-19: The Crucial Role of International Accreditation* (pp. 467–482). Cham: Springer International Publishing.
28. Balol, N. (2023). How the use of ICT encourages the students collaborative learning. *International Journal of Linguistics, Literature and Translation*, *6*(2), 42–49.
29. Chama, A. (2023). Digital literacy skills of teachers: A study on ICT use and purposes.
30. Nindhita, Y., Budiyanto, B., & Djarwoto, D. (2022). Do learning ICT usage affect the learning process quality? An empirical study in private university. *Technium Social Sciences Journal*, *37*, 24–36. https://doi.org/10.47577/tssj.v37i1.7567
31. Amutha, D. (2020). The Role and Impact of ICT in Improving the Quality of Education (SSRN Scholarly Paper 3585228). https://doi.org/10.2139/ssrn.3585228
32. Kapur, R. (2019). Use of ICT in Improving Quality of Education.
33. Esfandiari, M., & Gawhary, M. W. (2019). Is technology paving the way for autonomous learning? *World Journal of English Language*, *9*(2), 64. https://doi.org/10.5430/wjel.v9n2p64
34. Miranda, P., Isaias, P., & Pifano, S. (2019). *E-Assessment: Tools and Possibilities for Electronic Assessment in Higher Education.* 7431–7438. https://doi.org/10.21125/edulearn.2019.1778
35. Lim, C. P., Teo, Y. H., Wong, P., Khine, M. S., Chai, C. S., & Divaharan, S. (2003). Creating a conducive learning environment for the effective integration of ICT: Classroom management issues. *Journal of Interactive Learning Research*, *14*(4), 405+. Gale Academic OneFile.
36. Begum, R., & Naga Dhana Lakshmi, R. (2023). ICT-based collaborative learning approach: Enhancing students' language skills. In A. Kumar, G. Ghinea, S. Merugu, & T. Hashimoto (Eds.), *Proceedings of the International Conference on Cognitive and Intelligent Computing* (pp. 11–18). Springer Nature. https://doi.org/10.1007/978-981-19-2358-6_2
37. Quratulain, Parveen, Z., & Ghazanfar, S.. (2023). Role of ICT in teacher-student communication during Covid-19 in Pakistan. Pakistan *Journal of Humanities and Social Sciences*, *11*(1), Article 1. https://doi.org/10.52131/pjhss.2023.1101.0354
38. Sánchez Gómez, M. C., Rodríguez, A. I., & Muñoz, C. P. (2013). Collaborative work experiences in level 5 ICT primary schools. *Proceedings of the First International Conference on Technological Ecosystem for Enhancing Multiculturality*, 495–500. https://doi.org/10.1145/2536536.2536612
39. Yang, F., He, S., Qi, L., & Wen, J. (2020). Compliment response in teacher-student interaction: Examples from ICT platforms. *International Journal of Information and Education Technology*, *10*(10), 787–791. https://doi.org/10.18178/ijiet.2020.10.10.1459
40. Taduri, P., Chandhiramowuli, S., & Prakash, A. (2020). ICT and interactivity in the classroom: A case study of an ICT intervention in Indian rural public schools. In D. R. Junio & C. Koopman (Eds.), *Evolving Perspectives on ICTs in Global Souths* (pp. 17–30). Springer International Publishing. https://doi.org/10.1007/978-3-030-52014-4_2
41. Gabelaia, I., & Vasadze, N. (2021). The impact of technology-mediated interaction: Exploring new channels for effective student-lecturer communications in times

of disruption. In I. Kabashkin, I. Yatskiv, & O. Prentkovskis (Eds.), *Reliability and Statistics in Transportation and Communication* (pp. 804–813). Springer International Publishing. https://doi.org/10.1007/978-3-030-68476-1_74

42. Tariq, B., Dilawar, M., & Muhammad, Y. (2019). Innovative teaching and technology integration: Exploring elderly Teachers' attitudes. *International Journal of Distance Education and E-Learning*, *5*(1), Article 1. https://doi.org/10.36261/ijdeel.v5i1.789
43. Lee, Y., Blebea, J., Janssen, F., & Domoff, S. E. (2023). The impact of smartphone and social media use on adolescent sleep quality and mental health during the COVID-19 pandemic. *Human Behavior and Emerging Technologies*, *2023*, e3277040. https://doi.org/10.1155/2023/3277040
44. Wong, S. M., Chen, E. Y., Wong, C. S., Suen, Y., Chan, D. L., Tsang, S. H., Wong, T., Cheung, C., Chan, K., Lui, S. S., Wong, M. T., Chan, S. K., Lee, E. H., Myin-Germeys, I., & Hui, C. L. (2022). Impact of smartphone overuse on 1-year severe depressive symptoms and momentary negative affect: Longitudinal and experience sampling findings from a representative epidemiological youth sample in Hong Kong. *Psychiatry Research*, *318*, 114939. https://doi.org/10.1016/j.psychres.2022.114939
45. Madhushree L. M., Pradeep, M. D., & Aithal, P. S.. (2022). The Usage of Mobile Learning Technologies in Class Room - 21st Century. https://doi.org/10.5281/ZENODO.6593254
46. Vahedi, Z., Zannella, L., & Want, S. C. (2021). Students' use of information and communication technologies in the classroom: Uses, restriction, and integration. *Active Learning in Higher Education*, *22*(3), 215–228. https://doi.org/10.1177/1469787419861926
47. Singh Buttar, S. (2016). ICT in higher education. *PEOPLE: International Journal of Social Sciences*, *2*(1), 1686–1696. https://doi.org/10.20319/pijss.2016.s21.16861696
48. Saud, D. S. (2023). Teachers and students' perceptions towards using ICT in ELT in model schools. *Journal of Tikapur Multiple Campus*, 78–93. https://doi.org/10.3126/jotmc.v6i01.56347
49. Lomos, C., Luyten, J. W., & Tieck, S. (2023). Implementing ICT in classroom practice: What else matters besides the ICT infrastructure. *Large-Scale Assessments in Education*, *11*(1), 1–28.
50. Becker, B. (2023). Social disparities in adolescents' educational ICT use at home: How digital and educational inequalities interact. In *Research Handbook on Digital Sociology* (pp. 293–306). Edward Elgar Publishing.
51. Nawastheen, F. M., Palthamburaj, K., Shifaan, S., & Thannimalai, T. (2023). A study on the readiness and attitudes of Sri Lankan Tamil medium teachers towards the use of ICT in teaching and learning. *International Journal of Advanced and Applied Sciences*, *10*(6), 54–62.
52. Alisoy, H. (2023). Digital dynamics: Transforming classrooms with ICT. *Znanstvena Misel Journa*, *34*.
53. Kanvaria, V. K., & Yadav, A. (2024). integrating and innovating: The role of ICT in Education's evolution—An in-depth analysis of emerging technologies, current trends, challenges, and future directions in the digital age. *International Journal for Multidimensional Research Perspectives*, *2*(2), 33–48.
54. Appiah-Otoo, I., Acheampong, A. O., Song, N., & Chen, X. (2023). The impact of information and communication technology (ICT) on carbon dioxide emissions: Evidence from heterogeneous ICT countries. *Energy & Environment*, *34*(8), 3080–3102.
55. Lim, W. M., & Kumar, S. (2024). Guidelines for interpreting the results of bibliometric analysis: A sensemaking approach. *Global Business and Organizational Excellence*, *43*(2), 17–26.
56. Vhatkar, A., Patil, L., & Palav, M. R. (2023). A decade of distance education research in India a bibliometric review. *The Online Journal of Distance Education and e-Learning*, *11*(1).

57. Page, M. J., McKenzie, J. E., Bossuyt, P. M., Boutron, I., Hoffmann, T. C., & Mulrow, C. D., et al. (2021). The PRISMA 2020 statement: An updated guideline for reporting systematic reviews. *BMJ*, *372*, n71. doi: 10.1136/bmj.n71
58. Vhatkar, A., Pawar, V., Dash, S., Brahme, M., & Patil, L. (2023) Exploring the Impact of AI and Machine Learning Algorithms on Engineering Education: A Comprehensive Analysis of Research Articles in the Journal of Engineering Education. In *2023 12th International Conference on System Modeling & Advancement in Research Trends (SMART)*, Moradabad, India, 2023, pp. 449–453 IEEE.
59. Donthu, N., Kumar, S., Mukherjee, D., Pandey, N., & Lim, W. M. (2021). How to conduct a bibliometric analysis: An overview and guidelines. *Journal of Business Research*, *133*, 285–296.
60. Schie, J. V. (1997). A world-wide-web survey on the use of information and communication technology (ICT) in education. *European Journal of Teacher Education*, *20*(1), 85–92.
61. Nurjanah, S., Santoso, H. B., & Hasibuan, Z. A. (2017). An ICT adoption framework for education: A case study in public secondary school of Indonesia. *Journal of Physics: Conference Series*, *801*(1), 012029. IOP Publishing.
62. Nurjanah, S., Santoso, H. B., & Hasibuan, Z. A. (2017, November). ICT adoption for education: A proposed framework. In *2017 Second International Conference on Informatics and Computing (ICIC)* (pp. 1–6). IEEE.
63. Nurjanah, S., Santoso, H. B., & Hasibuan, Z. A. (2018, January). The user acceptance test of an "ICT Adoption for Education" framework. In *Proceedings of the 10th International Conference on Computer Modeling and Simulation* (pp. 129–133).
64. Rahmat, M. K., & AU, W. K. (2011). *ICT Integration among visual art education teachers: A study on Malaysian secondary school teachers* (Doctoral dissertation, ACARA-Australian Curriculum, Assessment & Reporting Authority).
65. Rahmat, M. K., & Au, W. K. (2012). Visual art education teachers' attitude toward incorporating ICT in arts classrooms. In *Workshop Proceedings of the 20th International Conference on Computer in Education* (pp. 119–126).
66. Rahmat, M. K., & Wing, K. A. (2018). Visual art education teacher's beliefs and attitudes toward incorporating ICT into art classrooms.
67. Pelgrum, W. J. (2001). Obstacles to the integration of ICT in education: Results from a worldwide educational assessment. *Computers & Education*, *37*(2), 163–178.
68. Livingstone, S. (2015). Critical reflections on the benefits of ICT in education. In *Digital Technologies in the Lives of Young People* (pp. 9–24). Routledge.
69. Gil-Flores, J., Rodríguez-Santero, J., & Torres-Gordillo, J. J. (2017). Factors that explain the use of ICT in secondary-education classrooms: The role of teacher characteristics and school infrastructure. *Computers in Human Behavior*, *68*, 441–449.
70. Wastiau, P., Blamire, R., Kearney, C., Quittre, V., Van de Gaer, E., & Monseur, C. (2013). The use of ICT in education: A survey of schools in Europe. *European Journal of Education*, *48*(1), 11–27.
71. Smeets, E. (2005). Does ICT contribute to powerful learning environments in primary education? *Computers & Education*, *44*(3), 343–355.
72. Tchamyou, V. S., Asongu, S. A., & Odhiambo, N. M. (2019). The role of ICT in modulating the effect of education and lifelong learning on income inequality and economic growth in Africa. *African Development Review*, *31*(3), 261–274.
73. Volman, M., Van Eck, E., Heemskerk, I., & Kuiper, E. (2005). New technologies, new differences. Gender and ethnic differences in pupils' use of ICT in primary and secondary education. *Computers & Education*, *45*(1), 35–55.
74. Jimoyiannis, A., & Komis, V. (2007). Examining teachers' beliefs about ICT in education: Implications of a teacher preparation programme. *Teacher Development*, *11*(2), 149–173.

75. Tondeur, J., Van Braak, J., & Valcke, M. (2007). Curricula and the use of ICT in education: Two worlds apart? *British Journal of Educational Technology*, *38*(6), 962–976.
76. Kreijns, K., Van Acker, F., Vermeulen, M., & Van Buuren, H. (2013). What stimulates teachers to integrate ICT in their pedagogical practices? The use of digital learning materials in education. *Computers in Human Behavior*, *29*(1), 217–225.
77. Kumar, M., Singh, T. P., Choudhury, T., & Gupta, S. C. (2019, December). ICT-the smart education system in India. In *2019 International conference on contemporary computing and informatics (IC3I)* (pp. 279–282). IEEE.

9 Integration of Green Computing and Economic Growth

Daniel Dauda Wisdom, Kingsley T. Igulu, Ezekiel Ebere Diri, Garba Alpha Baba, Isaac Oniovosah Ayetuoma, and Asanabe Michael Oltaunbosun

9.1 INTRODUCTION

Green computing denotes designing, manufacturing, using, and disposing of computing devices and systems in an ecologically accountable way (Figure 9.1). It involves reducing the ecological impact of activities in computing by reducing power consumption and making the best use of computing resources, as well as the reduction of electronic waste [1, 2]. Green computing is approaches, skills, technologies, and best practices that enable improved efficiency and sustainability and do not leave behind the carbon footprint reduction of ICT systems [3, 4].

It is relevant to the improvement of living standards as well as poverty alleviation. Economic growth refers to the long-term expansion in the production and consumption of goods and services in an economy. It is usually measured using gross domestic

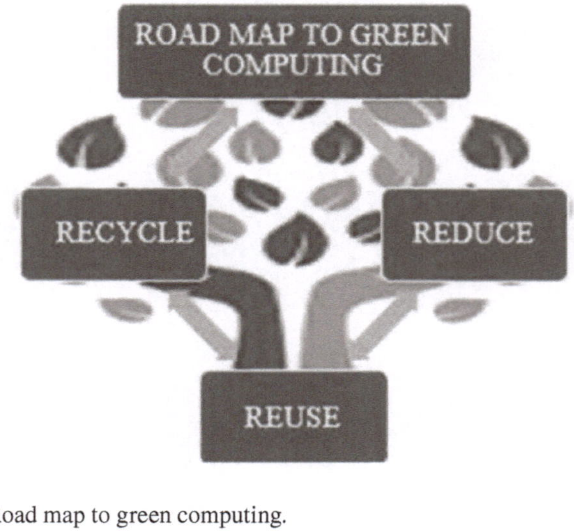

FIGURE 9.1 Road map to green computing.

DOI: 10.1201/9781003471356-9

product (GDP), employment rates, and income levels, among other indicators. This will cut down electricity bills, which will allow reinvestment of the money saved in innovation or expansion. Further, data center consolidation through virtualization and cloud computing reduces power consumption, hardware requirements, and associated costs [5]. Green computing requires people skilled in the design, implementation, and management of green computing IT solutions. This opens up new avenues of employment opportunities in energy-efficient hardware development, sustainable data center management, and green IT consulting. Moreover, due to the rise in demand from consumers for green products, the business enterprises that adapt green practices derive a competitive advantage and exploit new market opportunities [6]. Green computing enhances the innovative culture in companies to strive toward developing energy-efficient technologies and providing sustainable solutions. This novelty attracts investments in clean technologies and green infrastructure, further stimulating economic growth. This is further supported by governments in the form of tax breaks or subsidies to businesses when they apply green computing practices, hence making it possible for more industries to participate [7, 8]. Green computing further supports the Sustainable Development Goals (SDGs) because it engenders a positive brand image for companies and attracts environmentally responsible investors. Of these, policy and regulation turn out to be very instrumental in the full integration of green computing and economic growth. Supportive government policies are chief among these. Collaboration by industry leaders, policymakers, and research institutions is called for in developing efficient and less-costly green solutions. Additionally, raising awareness among consumers about issues concerning the environment arising from technology choices and advantages of green computing products can act as a way to a greener future. Businesses can support fewer carbon footprints; with the power of green computing, they can also unlock huge economic benefits. In a world increasingly focused on sustainability, green computing represents a sort of win-win situation, both for the environment and economic prosperity [9, 10].

9.2 LITERATURE REVIEW

To improve economic growth and recovery strategy, the study [1] suggests integrating the digital and green economies, specifically in light of recent crises. The research tries to survey the possibilities for workable economic growth and recovery present between the digital economy and the green economy. The results emphasize the need for more study in economic growth and strategies while investigating the collaborations between green and digital economies, which may further improve climate change and sustainable development.

In [2] the research presents a novel approach for minimizing data center power consumption which includes vigorously shortening services onto a portion of available servers and briefly stopping servers at intervals to conserve energy. Creating algorithms and methods for efficiency-related computer technologies is one of the goals, with an emphasis on creating computer systems that use less energy. The research paper does not specifically address the methodology that was used. A probabilistic service dispatch algorithm underpins the suggested strategy, which attempts to minimize the number of active servers while maintaining the degree of service quality mandated by service-level agreements. Potential avenues for future research could include determining whether the suggested strategy reduces energy use in data centers, gauging its effect on overall energy efficiency, and investigating.

Deng et al. in their paper [4] present a novel idea for green computing with a generic element to expand the typical responsibilities and connections of green computing research. It looks at the negative environmental effects of computer systems and suggests ways to mitigate them. The objectives are to expand on the discussion of generalized green computing based on hardware and software technologies, assess its indicative relevance, propose core ideas and methods for green computing, and establish the foundation needed for the methods and materials of green computing. Future research projects could include putting the recommended ideas and methods into practice in practical settings, evaluating how effective they are at reducing the environmental impact of computer systems, and developing further green computing approaches; additionally, examining various ways to lessen the unfavorable.

To address the growing issue of e-waste, especially in poor nations, the study [5] suggests adopting and implementing green computing methods. The study examined the increase in e-waste in developing nations, highlighted the unawareness of green computing regulations in these areas, and presented a strong case for the implementation of green IT laws. Further study will involve evaluating the efficacy of green computing policies in minimizing electronic waste and examining additional approaches that will improve and boost green computing adoption in developing nations.

In [6], an extensive study of the relationships and practical applications of green computing and computational intelligence approaches was examined. The research investigates the potential for a hybrid field fusing computational intelligence with green computing and tries to clarify the notions strongly. The study included a rapid examination of preceding research on the relationships between computational intelligence and green computing, as well as an investigation of current applications. The methodology involves a scientific study of research published in the area and a critical investigation of the body of literature currently available on computational intelligence and green computing practices. Overall, 80% of the growth in the studies on green computing used computational intelligence techniques within the last few years, based on this research.

To mitigate the emerging power consumption of software and IT systems that contribute to the overall power consumption, the research in [9] presents the implementation of green IT and green coding approaches. To discuss future trends in digital infrastructure to improve power effectiveness, increase the alertness of how much power software and IT systems consume, suggesting how software professionals can enhance environmentally friendly behavior via green IT and green coding practices. The procedure included investigating how much power software and IT systems consume, inspecting testing, and procedures, and signifying ways to minimize waste of energy using green coding techniques. To detect the main problems facing software and IT, the research further conducted an industry investigation.

A summary of recent developments in green computing research is provided in the publication [25]. It emphasizes the role that green computing plays in sustainable development; it describes the current state of the field's green computing research. The main objectives of green computing research, including lowering energy usage and e-waste, are covered in [25]. Future research topics that could be explored are listed in the study, such as cloud computing and data center energy efficiency improvements, encouraging businesses to take on more green projects, and assisting stakeholders in working together for a sustainable future.

9.3 IMPORTANCE OF INTEGRATING GREEN COMPUTING AND ECONOMIC GROWTH FOR SUSTAINABLE DEVELOPMENT

Synergy between green computing and economic growth cannot be overemphasized if we must achieve sustainable development. Sustainable development, among other aims, seeks to cater for the requirements of the current generation without jeopardizing the capacity of future generations to provide for themselves, and suffice it to note that through the alignment of green computing approaches, with goals related to economic growth, societies can reap the following benefits [11]. Figure 9.2 depicts the emerging green computing era.

1. *Environmental preservation*: Green computing contributes to reducing the negative impacts of ICT activities on the environment in so many ways, which include energy use, the production of electronic trash, and carbon emissions. By using energy-efficient technologies, optimizing the utilization of resources, and encouraging recycling and reuse, organizations can actually mitigate their ecological footprint and protect natural resources for future generations [12, 13].

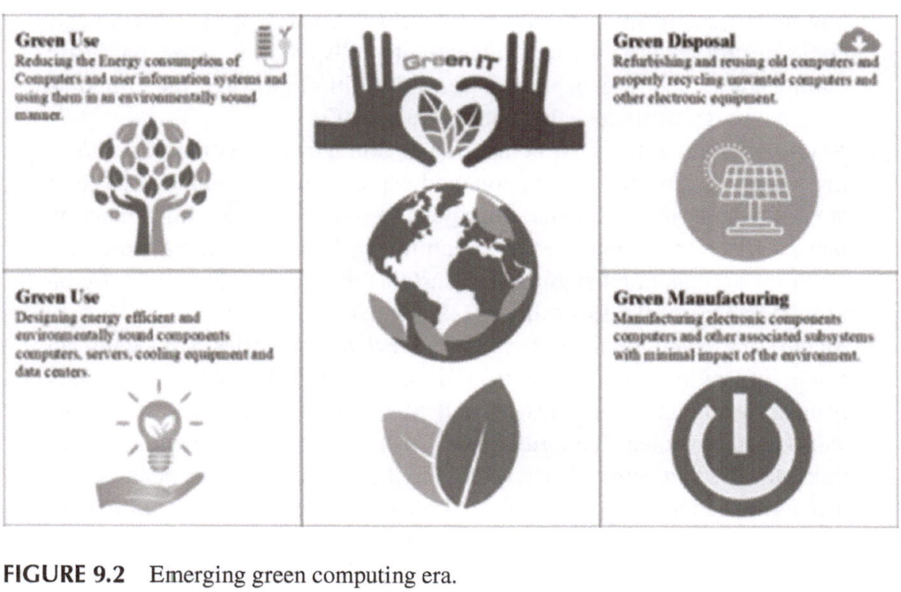

FIGURE 9.2 Emerging green computing era.

2. *Cost savings and efficiency*: Both public and private organizations can reduce cost, save money, and become more efficient by implementing green computing programs. These can be achieved by implementing sustainable practices, maximizing resource utilization, and reducing energy consumption [14].
3. The change to environmentally friendly computing boosts invention as well as releases fresh business opportunities in developing areas such as sustainable technology growth, efficiency, and renewable energy. The world can encourage entrepreneurship, job creation, and economic growth in sustainable industries by distributing resources toward green technology, research, and advancement [15, 16].
4. Green computing inspires flexibility as well as resistance to environmental challenges such as resource shortages, climate change, and environmental ruin. Societies can reduce risks and adjust to changing climatic conditions by building strong ICT infrastructure, lessening reliance on fossil fuels, and inspiring sustainable patterns of production and consumption [17].
5. Various organizations such as governments, corporations, academic institutions, and civil society groups must work in synergy to ensure the integration of green computing with economic advancement [17, 18].

9.3.1 The Role of Green Computing in Economic Growth

Green computing activities are necessary for improving financial growth. The ways green computing encourages economic expansion and the possible advantages are presented as follows:

1. *Cost savings*: Power consumption by businesses can be greatly reduced through the use of green computing techniques such as virtualization, power-efficient technology, as well as cloud computing. Establishments could minimize costs related to electricity bills, cooling costs, hardware maintenance, and organizational responsibilities in ways that improve resource usage while reducing energy waste [19].
2. *Resource efficiency*: Green computing encourages the economical use of raw materials, power consumption, and water. Businesses can lessen their environmental impact while improving resource use by implementing power-efficient technologies and streamlining data center operations. This encourages economic flexibility and sustainability as it reduces reliance on limited resources and saves money [19, 20].
3. *Regulatory compliance and risk moderation*: Industries are facing an expanding number of environmental rules and sustainability standards from government institutions as well as regulatory agencies around the world. Establishments can guarantee adherence to environmental regulations, minimalize supervisory risks, and prevent any fines or penalties by using green computing techniques. Companies that show a commitment to sustainability advance their standing with stakeholders, foster trust, and reduce the reputational risks related to ecological stewardship [21, 22].

4. *Job and economic development*: The shift to green computing opens up job prospects in numerous industries; it is therefore apt to say that participating in environmentally friendly IT infrastructure and labor force development will help countries create jobs, advance economic growth, and facilitate the shift to a low-carbon economy.
5. *Long-term cost avoidance*: The cost of setting up green computing innovations may be high; however, this cost is usually offset by long-term compensations frequently as the gains of the initiative begin to affect every aspect of the business or organization. Businesses can reduce the risk of growing energy cost and adjust to shifting regulatory atmospheres by making investments in power-efficient technologies. Green computing suggests long-term cost savings and durability, which support profitability, business continuity, and steady economic growth [23, 24].

9.3.2 Cost Savings and Efficiency Gains

The technical know-how and practices of green computing can culminate in cost reduction and efficiency for industries by improving resource utilization, minimizing energy consumption and waste, and streamlining operations [25].

Examples of establishment that have appreciated economic benefits through energy savings and resource optimization are the following:

1. *Virtualization and consolidation*: Virtualization technologies enable industries to consolidate multiple virtual servers onto a single physical server, minimizing hardware requirements, energy consumption, and space requirements in data centers. For instance, VMware's virtualization solutions helped in improving organization server sprawl, while enhancing resource utilization, with meaningful achieved cost savings through server consolidation and workload optimization [26].
2. *Cloud computing*: Cloud computing presents scalable, on-demand access to computing resources, allowing businesses to improve resource usage, while reducing idle capacity, and pay only for the resources they consume. Establishments such as Amazon Web Services (AWS), Microsoft Azure, and Google Cloud provide power-efficient data centers and infrastructure services, enabling businesses to leverage cloud computing for cost-effective and environmentally sustainable IT processes [27].
3. *Green data center design*: Focus on maximizing power efficiency, minimizing carbon emissions, and reducing environmental impact. Establishments such as Facebook and Apple have invested in green data center initiatives, incorporating renewable energy sources, advanced cooling technologies, and energy-efficient equipment to improve data center performance and achieve sustainable goals while minimizing operational costs.
4. *Remote work and telecommuting*: Green computing encourages remote labor and telecommuting practices, minimizing the need for computer systems, office space, and energy consumption associated with traditional office environments. Establishments such as Dell Technologies have

embraced remote work creativities, enabling employees to work from home using virtual partnership tools and teleworking technologies, resulting in cost savings, productivity gains, and minimizing environmental footprints.

5. *Lifecycle management and recycling*: Green computing promotes accountable lifecycle management of IT assets, along with renewal, reclamation, and disposal of outdated hardware and electronic waste. Organizations like HP and IBM have instituted environmentally friendly IT asset management programs that would help extend the life expectancy of IT machinery, recover precious materials, reduce landfill waste, and provide cost savings from asset re-purposing and recycling innovations [28].

9.3.3 Job Creation and Economic Opportunities

Although there may be upfront expenses associated with putting green computing initiatives into action, the benefits that accrue in the long run far outweigh the initial expenses. Businesses may future-proof their operations, reduce the risk of growing energy prices, and adjust to shifting regulatory environments by making investments in energy-efficient technologies. The shift to green computing boosts economic growth and opens up new job opportunities in several developing industries, such as sustainable technology development, energy efficiency, and renewable energy [29]. The use of green computing engenders employment growth and expansion of economic prospects through the following ways/sectors:

1. *Renewable energy sector*: The utilization of renewable energy sources, including solar, wind, and hydropower.
2. *Energy efficiency sector*: To cut down on electricity use and lessen its negative effects on the environment, green computing encourages the use of energy-efficient devices and procedures. Professionals with knowledge of sustainable IT solutions, energy management, and building efficiency are in high demand as a result. Energy auditors and consultants are among the employment options in the energy efficiency sector as well [30].
3. *Innovation and investment in sustainable technologies*, such as eco-friendly IT products, smart grids, energy-efficient hardware, and green data center solutions, are fueled by the trend toward green computing. This promotes the expansion of businesses that specialize in the development of sustainable technologies and opens doors for qualified individuals in a range of disciplines, such as sustainable product design and engineering, consultancy and advising services for green IT, research and development of sustainable materials, and initiatives for recycling and waste reduction [31].
4. *Green jobs in the IT sector*: The IT sector is experiencing a demand for individuals with experience in sustainable IT solutions, green data center management, and environmental stewardship as a result of the adoption of green computing methods. Green IT employment options include architects and engineers of green data centers, designers and producers of energy-efficient hardware, project managers for IT with an emphasis on green initiatives, and consultants and analysts for environmental sustainability [31, 32].

5. *Policy and advocacy roles*: The transition to green computing also creates opportunities for policymakers, regulators, and advocacy groups to support and promote sustainability initiatives at the local, national, and global levels. Job roles in this area include environmental policy analysts and researchers, advocates and campaigners for sustainability, renewable energy policy advisors, green technology lobbyists and activists, sustainability-focused nonprofit organizations and think tanks [33].

9.3.4 Market Demand and Consumer Preferences

Customers' increased awareness of environmental issues, worries about climate change, and desire for sustainable living are reflected in their growing demand for ecologically friendly goods and services. Businesses in many different areas, including the technology industry, will be significantly impacted by this shift in consumer tastes [33, 34]. Through the provision of eco-friendly IT practices, services, and products that support environmental sustainability and consumer values, green computing solutions address market desires.

How market development and innovation in green computing contribute to economic growth.

1. *Consumer awareness and demand*: As the awareness of consumers about the impact of their purchases on the environment increases, they dynamically look for goods and services that are sustainable, energy-efficient, and friendly to the environment. Due to this increased awareness level of consumers, the clamor for green technologies, such as eco-friendly devices, energy-efficient computers, and sustainable IT solutions, has begun to gain prominence [35].
2. *Regulatory pressures and compliance*: As a result of stricter environmental rules and sustainability requirements by relevant authorities, businesses are now required to reduce their carbon footprint, limit electronic waste, and embrace power-efficient technologies. Green computing solutions help organizations in meeting legal obligations, thereby avoiding fines and other punitive measures, and preserving their good rating with environmentally conscious customers [36].
3. *Cost savings and efficiency gains*: Green computing helps businesses to save money by reducing the following: energy usage, resource utilization, and operational costs. Further, virtualization technologies, cloud computing services, and power-efficient hardware empower businesses to cut carbon emissions, reducing electricity costs, ultimately realizing lasting cost profits.
4. *Innovation and differentiation*: Green computing results in the expansion of eco-friendly materials, sustainable technologies, and power-efficient solutions, which eventually leads to invention in the technology domain. Initiatives that allocate resources toward green IT invention stand out in the marketplace, draw in eco-aware customers, and outperform their rivals. For instance, to satisfy consumer demand, businesses such as Apple and Google have released energy-efficient devices, including laptops, cellphones, and data centers that run on renewable energy.

5. *Market expansion and global appeal*: Green computing solutions enable businesses to reach a wider audience and attract consumers from across the globe who care about the environment. Industries can reach new markets, draw in eco-aware clients, and grow their business globally by embracing eco-friendly possessions and services. Branch loyalty and customer trust can also be strengthened through the adoption of green computing innovations [37].

9.3.5 Investment and Financing for Green Computing Projects

Investment and financing are crucial for advancing green computing innovations that would enable industries to invest in workable technology projects and adopt eco-friendly practices.

1. *Capital investment*: Businesses allocate funds for power-efficient hardware, renewable energy systems, and eco-friendly IT solutions, which would result in lasting cost savings with eco-friendly profits [38].
2. *Venture capital and private equity*: Investors provide vital capital and support for green technology startups and workable IT establishments, fostering innovation and development in the area [39].
3. *Grants and incentives from governments*: Many government agencies provide a wide array of financial incentives, such as grants, tax holidays, and refunds, that not only spur investment in green computing but also increase the use of renewable energy and energy efficiency [40].
4. *Public-private partnerships*: Government-private sector-nonprofit linkage for green computing accelerates the mission by grabbing resources as well as expertise to report eco-friendly challenges.
5. *Green bonds and sustainable finance*: Economic instruments like green bonds increase the pool of funds for environmentally friendly projects and green computing by drawing in investors especially interested in sustainable growth and development projects.
6. *Corporate social responsibility (CSR) initiatives*: Industries and businesses therein take green computing initiatives as part of their CSR and bring eco-friendly factors into their operations to foster sustainability [40, 42].

9.3.6 Government Policies and Regulatory Support

Government regulations are very instrumental in evolving green computing and driving economic development by instituting environmental standards, with encouragement to set up a supporting governing atmosphere.

1. *Environmental regulations*: Governments worldwide advocate regulations in an endeavor to deal with the challenge of global warming by cutting carbon emissions and encouraging sustainability. It is these frameworks, standards, and power efficiency protocols which empower industries to adopt green computing practices and invest in renewable energy.

2. *Renewable energy mandates*: Governments implement renewable energy mandates to require services to generate a percentage of their electricity from renewable sources. This mandate at all levels enhances investment in green energy technologies, engendering the development of sustainable IT infrastructure and innovation [41].
3. *Energy efficiency standards*: It is the process by which governments establish rules for energy efficiency in electronic products and IT equipment to promote and encourage power conservation and at the same time slow down the rising rate of electricity consumption.
4. *Tax incentives and credits*: Governments give tax incentives and credits to businesses investing in power-efficient technologies and projects for renewable energy. Examples include investments like a tax waiver for renewable energy systems and accelerated depreciation allowances for energy-efficient equipment, tax deductions for energy efficiency improvements in commercial buildings, and tax credits for the purchase of electric vehicles and charging infrastructure.
5. *R&D funding*: The government provides funding and grants to R&D projects on green computing, renewable energy, and innovation in sustainable technologies. R&D funding programs encourage collaboration between academia, industry, and government agencies to advance scientific knowledge, develop cutting-edge technologies, and address environmental challenges, driving economic growth and job creation in the green technology sector [41, 42].
6. *Procurement policies*: Government procurement policies prioritize the purchase of environmentally friendly products and services, including energy-efficient IT equipment, eco-friendly office supplies, and sustainable technology solutions. By incorporating environmental criteria into procurement processes, governments demonstrate leadership in sustainability, stimulate demand for green products, and create market opportunities for businesses that prioritize environmental stewardship.
7. *Green building standards*: Governments establish green building standards, certification programs, and building codes to promote energy-efficient building design, construction, and operation. Green construction standards boost the approval of sustainable construction practices, energy-efficient building materials, and green IT solutions, resulting in minimized energy consumption, reduced operating costs, and better indoor environmental quality [40].

9.3.7 International Collaboration and Sustainable Development Goals

International collaboration is essential for advancing green computing and achieving SDGs by fostering knowledge sharing, technology transfer, as well as collective decision; this can be achieved through the following:

1. *Policy alignment and coordination*: Through the promotion of dialogue and cooperation among nations, policies and coordination that drive

environmental sustainability can be advanced and embraced by countries. Agreements such as the Paris Agreement on climate change provide a framework for countries to set emission reduction targets, implement mitigation measures, and enhance adaptation efforts to address the impacts of climate change while promoting sustainable development.

2. *Knowledge sharing and capacity building*: Through partnership between nations, expertise and best practices in green computing and sustainable technology can be shared, and this would result in the rapid adoption of green practices, improving technical skills as well as eliminating barriers to sustainable growth in many facets.
3. *Technology transfer and innovation*: Alliance and synergy among nations facilitate the transfer of green technologies and expand the frontier of green computing. As countries partner with each other, they will be able to access advanced technologies, collaborate on research, and develop innovative solutions to environmental impediments, resulting in environmental sustainability and economic development.
4. *Resource mobilization and investment*: International collaboration mobilizes financial resources, investment, and funding for green computing projects, renewable energy infrastructure, and sustainable development initiatives. Multilateral development banks, international organizations, and donor agencies provide financial assistance, grants, and loans to support green technology projects, capacity-building efforts, and policy reforms in developing countries [41, 42].
5. *United Nations SDGs*: The United Nations SDGs provide a global framework for addressing pressing environmental, social, and economic challenges, including poverty, inequality, climate change, and environmental degradation. The SDGs promote international collaboration and partnerships across sectors and stakeholders to achieve shared objectives, including Goal 7 (Affordable and Clean Energy), Goal 9 (Industry, Innovation, and Infrastructure), Goal 11 (Sustainable Cities and Communities), and Goal 13 (Climate Action) [42].
6. *Global climate action initiatives*: Clean Energy Ministerial (CEM), Mission Innovation, and the Global Green Growth Institute (GGGI) are some of the international collaborations and initiatives that promote global climate action, clean energy transition, and green growth; this is done by bringing together governments, businesses, civil society, and other stakeholders to catalyze collective action, scale up investment in renewable energy, and accelerate the transition to a low-carbon economy.

9.4 CASE STUDIES: SUCCESSFUL IMPLEMENTATION OF GREEN COMPUTING

The three case studies of establishments that have effectively employed green computing practices to drive economic development are presented in the following sections.

9.4.1 Google Data Center Efficiency Improvements

9.4.1.1 Strategy

Google employed various green computing initiatives to advance the power efficiency of its data centers. These creativities comprised enhancing server performance, encouraging cooling efficiency, as well as deploying renewable energy sources [38].

9.4.1.2 Challenges

Google handled encounters like harmonizing energy efficiency with data center performance, managing the complexity of extensive infrastructure, and ensuring compatibility with existing systems as well as processes.

9.4.1.3 Outcomes

Through improving data center operations and investing in renewable energy developments, Google realized important energy savings with a minimized cost. The establishment's data centers now operate at some of the maximum levels of energy efficiency in the business, contributing to environmental sustainability and economic development.

9.4.2 Facebook Open Compute Project (OCP)

9.4.2.1 Strategy

Facebook launched the Open Compute Project (OCP), an open-source hardware, and data center design enterprise focused on enhancing power efficiency, scalability, and sustainability. OCP encourages the growth and sharing of energy-efficient hardware designs, data center infrastructure inventions, and top practices.

9.4.2.2 Challenges

Facebook handled encounters such as overpowering resistance to change, addressing interoperability problems, and ensuring compatibility with existing hardware and software ecosystems [27].

9.4.2.3 Outcomes

Via OCP, Facebook and its traitors have developed state-of-the-art energy-efficient hardware designs, enhancing data center architectures, and sustainable IT solutions. OCP resulted in achieving a vital level of power savings, with a minimized cost, as well as ecological benefits for Facebook and its associates while driving invention and collaboration in the technology business.

9.4.3 Microsoft's Renewable Energy Procurement

9.4.3.1 Strategy

Microsoft, a multinational technology company, is committed to achieving carbon neutrality and transitioning to 100% renewable energy for its data centers and operations.

Microsoft invested in wind and solar farms, that is, renewable energy projects, and signed power purchase agreements (PPAs) to procure renewable energy at scale.

9.4.3.2 Challenges

Microsoft faced challenges such as navigating regulatory barriers, securing long-term renewable energy contracts, and managing the variability of renewable energy sources.

9.4.3.3 Outcomes

By investing in renewable energy procurement, Microsoft achieved its goal of carbon neutrality and made significant progress toward its commitment to operate carbon-negative by 2030. The company's renewable energy investments not only reduce its carbon footprint but also create economic opportunities, support local communities, and contribute to a more sustainable energy future [42].

9.5 ENTREPRENEURSHIP AND INNOVATION IN GREEN COMPUTING

Entrepreneurship and innovation are essential in driving economic growth through green computing by fostering the development of sustainable technology solutions, promoting energy efficiency, and addressing environmental challenges [2]. The role of entrepreneurship and innovation in green computing, along with examples of startups and technology companies that have innovated in this space and created economic value, are presented in the following sections.

9.5.1 Technology Innovation for Energy Efficiency

Entrepreneurs and startups are leveraging technology innovation to develop energy-efficient hardware, software, and IT solutions that reduce energy consumption, minimize environmental impact, and optimize resource utilization. Examples include Nvidia and Sonnen.

9.5.1.1 Nvidia

Nvidia, a leading graphics processing unit (GPU) manufacturer, developed energy-efficient GPUs optimized for data center workloads, enabling businesses to achieve high-performance computing with lower energy consumption.

9.5.1.2 Sonnen

Sonnen, a German energy storage company, developed smart battery systems and virtual power plants that optimize energy usage, reduce grid reliance, and enable homeowners to store and manage renewable energy more efficiently [4].

9.5.2 Renewable Energy Integration and Optimization

Startups and technology establishments are transforming renewable energy integration as well as optimization to accelerate the transition to clean energy and minimize reliance on fossil fuels. Examples include Enphase Energy and Nest Labs.

9.5.2.1 Enphase Energy

Enphase Energy, a solar energy company, developed microinverter technology that maximizes energy production from solar panels, improves system reliability, and simplifies installation, driving the adoption of residential solar power systems.

9.5.2.2 Nest Labs

Nest Labs, a subsidiary of Google, developed smart home devices, including thermostats and energy monitors, that optimize energy usage, reduce electricity bills, and promote energy conservation through data-driven insights and automation [6].

9.5.3 Data Center Efficiency and Green Infrastructure

Technology companies are innovating in data center efficiency and green infrastructure solutions to reduce energy consumption, minimize carbon emissions, and improve sustainability. Examples include CoolIT Systems and Verne Global.

9.5.3.1 CoolIT Systems

CoolIT Systems, a Canadian company, developed liquid cooling solutions for data centers that improve energy efficiency, reduce cooling costs, and enable high-density computing, contributing to environmental sustainability and cost savings for businesses.

9.5.3.2 Verne Global

Verne Global, a data center operator based in Iceland, leverages the country's abundant renewable energy resources and natural cooling environment to provide sustainable, low-carbon data center solutions to customers worldwide, attracting businesses seeking green computing options [8].

9.5.4 Circular Economy and Electronic Waste Management

Startups and technology companies are innovating circular economy models and electronic waste management solutions to minimize waste, extend product lifecycles, and promote sustainable consumption. Examples include Fairphone and Electronic Recyclers International.

9.5.4.1 Fairphone

Fairphone, a Dutch smartphone manufacturer, designs and produces modular smartphones with ethically sourced materials, repairable components, and a focus on longevity, enabling consumers to reduce electronic waste and support sustainable electronics manufacturing.

9.5.4.2 Electronic Recyclers International (ERI)

Electronic Recyclers International (ERI), a leading electronic waste recycling company, developed innovative recycling technologies and processes to recover valuable materials from electronic devices, reduce environmental pollution, and promote responsible e-waste management practices [10].

9.6 SKILLS DEVELOPMENT AND WORKFORCE TRAINING

There are a series of empowerments, collaborations, and partnerships that would drive technical know-how and capacity development toward addressing environmental problems and advancing green technology, thereby resulting in the attainment of sustainable development growth.

1. *Public-private partnerships*: Through the merging of the resources and strengths of both businesses, public-private companies promote environmental sustainability and economic development by simplifying technology transfer, knowledge sharing, and cooperative action on green computing projects. Engaging investors from diverse backgrounds fosters communication and consensus-building, resulting in inclusive and efficient solutions to environmental problems [2, 27].
2. Technical proficiency in green computing involves understanding eco-friendly IT practices, sustainable data center design, and energy-efficient hardware. Partnership across disciplines, involving computer science, engineering, and environmental science, supports addressing sustainability challenges comprehensively [28].
3. Leadership and management training permits individuals to drive organizational transformation resulting in sustainable technology creativities.
4. Practical training and hands-on experience enable the public to apply their knowledge in real-world settings and prepare for careers in sustainable technology [1].
5. *Industry credentials and certifications*: These certify and attest to an individual's proficiency in green computing as well as their dedication to sustainability and professional growth. In the field of green technology, certifications like LEED (Leadership in Energy and Environmental Design), CEM (Certified Energy Manager), and CSDP (Certified Sustainable Development Professional) offer credibility and recognition, improving people's employability and career possibilities [4].
6. *Academic and vocational training programs*: A variety of training courses, workshops, and programs on green computing, sustainable technology, and environmental management are offered by academic institutions, vocational training centers, and professional associations.

9.7 EFFICIENT ENERGY MANAGEMENT IN GREEN COMPUTING

Efficient energy management is one of the keystones of green computing (Figure 9.3). This reflects practices and technologies that can decrease the energy use of computers and related systems without loss of performance [16, 20]. Next is the consideration of a break-down of key issues in efficient energy utilization as it relates to green computing:

9.7.1 MAIN GOALS

a. Lowers the consumption of energy and the cost of electricity.
b. IT infrastructures' impacts on the environment are reduced.
c. Extend the lifespan of hardware by reducing heat generation [28, 30].

FIGURE 9.3 Efficient energy/battery management in green computing.

9.7.2 Strategies

9.7.2.1 Hardware

Utilize energy-efficient processors, memory, and other components; this can be achieved by the following:

- Implementing power management features like sleep modes and dynamic voltage/frequency scaling.
- Right-sizing hardware to meet actual computing needs [2, 32].
- Consolidating servers through virtualization.

9.7.2.2 Software

Develop and use software that is optimized for efficiency, avoiding unnecessary computations and resource usage.

- Implement power-saving settings on software and operating systems.
- Utilize cloud-based services that offer economies of scale in resource utilization [23, 32].

9.7.3 Data Center Management

- Optimize cooling systems to reduce energy consumption for temperature control.
- Utilize renewable energy sources where possible [34, 38].
- Implement monitoring and reporting systems to track energy usage and identify areas for improvement.

9.7.3.1 Emerging Trends

- Artificial intelligence (AI) for optimizing energy usage in data centers
- Internet of Things (IoT) for intelligent power management of devices
- Blockchain technology for secure and transparent energy trading [2, 38].

9.8 FUTURE TRENDS, OPPORTUNITIES, AND NEW DEVELOPMENTS IN GREEN COMPUTING TECHNOLOGIES

A. *Edge computing*: As edge computing gains traction, centralized data center latency and energy consumption are decreased by processing and analyzing data closer to the source.

B. *AI and Machine Learning*: These two fields of study have the potential to significantly improve efficiency and lessen environmental impact in data centers by optimizing energy usage, resource allocation, and system performance.
C. *IoT*: Smarter and more sustainable infrastructure is made possible by IoT devices and sensors, which allow for real-time monitoring and management of energy consumption, building operations, and environmental conditions.
D. *Blockchain technology*: By improving supply chains, renewable energy markets, and carbon trading, blockchain can increase accountability, transparency, and traceability. This will encourage more people to adopt sustainable practices and decentralized energy systems [2, 38].

Market developments and opportunities can be envisioned from the following perspectives:

Growth of the green data center market: As companies look to cut costs, improve performance, and achieve sustainability goals, there will likely be a large increase in demand for energy-efficient data centers. This will present a chance for infrastructure developers and providers of green technology.

Renewable energy integration: As renewable energy costs decline and as regulatory incentives and corporate commitments to carbon neutrality grow, so too will the integration of renewable energy sources, such as solar, wind, and hydroelectric power, into data center operations.

Eco-friendly consumer electronics: The desire of consumers for environmentally friendly devices, such as power-efficient computers and smartphones, is on the rise, encouraging manufacturers to innovate in sustainable product design, materials sourcing, and end-of-life recycling [23].

9.9 INTEGRATION OF GREEN COMPUTING AND ECONOMIC GROWTH ALGORITHM PROPOSED FRAMEWORK

A. **Data Collection and Analysis**
   a. *Economic data*: Collect data on various economic indicators like GDP, employment rates, energy prices, and investments in renewable energy.
   b. *Green computing data*: Collect data on data center energy consumption, energy efficiency of hardware and software, and adoption of green technologies (cloud computing, virtualization).
   c. *Analyze relationships*: Analyze the collected data to identify correlations between green computing practices and economic indicators. This could involve statistical modeling or machine learning techniques.

B. **Optimization Model Development**
   a. *Define an objective function*: This could be maximizing economic growth while minimizing environmental impact (energy consumption) or maximizing the ratio of economic growth to energy consumption.
   b. *Identify constraints*: These could include limitations in current technology, budget constraints for implementing green solutions, and user acceptance of certain practices.

c. *Develop an optimization algorithm*: This could involve linear programming, dynamic programming, or other optimization techniques to find the combination of green computing practices that best achieves the objective function within the defined constraints.

C. **Identify Constraints**

a. These may be technological, that is, constraints on the current technology, financial constraints for implementing green computing solutions, and user acceptance of some practices. Formulate an optimization algorithm: This could include the use of linear or dynamic programming for the solution methodology, or any other such optimization techniques to find a combination of green computing practices that maximize or minimize the objective function within given constraints.

D. **Policy and Incentives Design**

a. Based on the optimization model, design policies and incentives that will motivate businesses and individuals to put green computing into practice. Some policies and incentives for implementation include tax breaks for energy-efficient hardware and government investment in renewable energy infrastructure. This contribution thus aims to cause minimal environmental impact with the very wide dissemination of green computing. These measures, therefore, affect a large category of players involving industry, consumers, and the government, who have to be fairly competitive and effective to be participatory.

E. The changes occurring in economic indicators, rates of adoption of green computing, and environmental conclusions call for continuous monitoring and review of the executed policies.

F. The improvement model needs to be dynamic, iterative, and update in steps to correspond with the promotion of technology and economic conditions. In addition, it shall study multi-criteria optimization by balancing economic growth with environmental impact. Multi-criteria optimization has to consider the preferences of users so that it gains broader acceptance. To this end, successful implementation requires teamwork between economists, computer scientists, and policymakers. Algorithms are tailored to a specific set of economic and technological frameworks.

9.10 CONCLUSION

This chapter is a comprehensive analysis of the green computing practices-economic development relationship in the context of sustainable development. Drawing from the existing literature, this study is attempting to give many explanations as to why these seemingly very different elements need to be integrated. It contributes to economic development in such ways as simplifying cost savings through green computing, improving energy efficiency, creating employment opportunities, and meeting market demand. It also highlights the contribution of investment, financing instruments, enabling government policies, and international cooperation in scaling up SDGs. The case examples of real-life situations illustrate good practices in green computing applications. They are underway and demonstrate a transformation in the way the upcoming green computing is happening and, thus, an entrepreneurial advantage. The chapter, in relation, therefore, resonated with the development of skilled human resources that can understand the changing trend of green computing. The chapter finally proposed the framework of a multi-criteria optimization model that considers economic indicators, the adoption rate of green computing, and environmental impacts, hence setting a basis for future research aimed at developing decision algorithms comprehensive enough for policy and business applications. By embracing green computing practices, we will set our world on a course toward a prosperous economy thriving in harmony with a sustainable environment.

REFERENCES

1. Ciocoiu, C. N. (2011). Integrating digital economy and green economy: Opportunities for sustainable development. *Theoretical and Empirical Researches in Urban Management*, *6*(1), 33–43.
2. Kaur, N., & Mittal, P. (2013). Effective implementation of green computing. *International Journal of Computer Applications Technology and Research*, *2*(4), 465–473.
3. Benamer, W. H., Elberkawi, E. K., Neihum, N. A., Anwiji, A. S., & Youns, M. A. (2021). Green Computing case study: Calls for proposing solutions for the Arabian Gulf Oil Company. In *E3S Web of Conferences* (Vol. 229, p. 01063). EDP Sciences.
4. Deng, J., Hu, J., Li, W., & Wu, J. (2011, July). Trends and Development on Green Computing. In *International Workshop on Computer Science for Environmental Engineering and EcoInformatics* (pp. 281–286). Berlin, Heidelberg: Springer Berlin Heidelberg.
5. Appasami, G., & Joseph, K. S. (2011). Optimization of operating systems towards green computing. *International Journal of Combinatorial Optimization Problems and Informatics*, *2*(3), 39–51.
6. Taruna, S., Singh, P., & Joshi, S. (2014). Green computing in developed and developing countries. *arXiv preprint arXiv:1406.2773.*
7. Isaac, S., Wisdom, D. D., Nigeria, S., Ahmad, M. A., & Christian, A. U. (2020). Battery-life management with an efficient sleep-mode power saving scheme (BM-ESPSS) in IEEE 802.16 e networks. *International Journal of Mechatronics, Electrical and Computer Technology (IJMEC)*, *7*(2).
8. Castillo, O., & Melin, P. (2021). Review on the interactions of green computing and computational intelligence techniques and their applications to real-world problems. *Journal of Smart Environments and Green Computing*, *1*(2), 103–119.
9. Verdecchia, R., Lago, P., Ebert, C., & de Vries, C. (2021). Green IT and green software. *IEEE Software*, *38*(6), 7–15.
10. Wisdom, D. D., Tambuwal, A. Y., Mohammed, A., Audu, A., Soroyewun, M. B., & Isaac, S. (2019, October). A Delay Aware Power Saving Scheme (DAPSS) base on load in traffic IEEE 802.16 e networks. In *2019 2nd International Conference of the IEEE Nigeria Computer Chapter (NigeriaComputConf)* (pp. 1–8). IEEE.
11. Soomro, T. R., & Sarwar, M. (2012). Green computing: From current to future trends. *International Journal of Humanities and Social Sciences*, *6*(3), 326–329.
12. Wisdom, D. D., Isaac, S., Ahmed, M. A., Farouk, N., Magami, S., & Elijah, Y. (2020). An improved battery-life power saving scheme (IBPSS) in IEEE 802.16e networks. *International Journal of Information Processing and Communication IJIPC*, *8*(2).

13. S Bijapur, C., & Sai, P. (2023). Green Computing Approaches for Data Centers and Storage Systems: A Survey of Green Computing Strategies for Resource Efficiency. *Gnanesh and Sai, G Pramod, Green Computing Approaches for Data Centers and Storage Systems: A Survey of Green Computing Strategies for Resource Efficiency (September 19, 2023).*
14. Wisdom, D. D., Ajayi, E. A., Akindayo, S. O., Yanah, Y. M., Kwaido, E., & Shehu, S. A. (2019). An efficient automated revenue generation database management system. *Annals Journal of Computer Science Series. 17* (2), 201–215.
15. Kocak, S. A. (2013, October). Green Software Development and Design for Environmental Sustainability. In *11th International Doctoral Symposium an Empirical Software Engineering (IDOESE 2013).* Baltimore, Maryland (Vol. 9).
16. Ganya, A. H., Wisdom, D. D., Arinze, U. C., Ismail, A. B., Aliyu, M. M., & Ahmad, A. (2022): Predicting Various Diseases and Natural Changes in Groundnut Leaves from Early Stage to Maturity using Convolutional Neural Networks (CNN). In *Proceedings of the LASUSTECH 30th iSTEAMS Multidisciplinary Innovations Conference.* Lagos State University of Science & Technology, Ikorodu, Lagos State, Nigeria.
17. Saraiva, J., Zong, Z., & Pereira, R. (2021, June). Bringing Green Software to Computer Science Curriculum: Perspectives from Researchers and Educators. In *Proceedings of the 26th ACM Conference on Innovation and Technology in Computer Science Education V. 1* (pp. 498–504).
18. Wisdom, D. D., Ajayi, E. A., Arinze, U. C., Aladesote, O. I., Ganya, A. H., & Idris, H. (2020). A comprehensive survey on power saving scheme (CSPSS) in IEEE 802.16 e/m networks. *IEEE computer society, Nigeria, Technical Paper Series, Accra Ghana.*
19. Kaur, A., & Kaur, S. (2019). Green computing: Emerging issues in IT. *International Journal of Trend in Scientific Research and Development (IJTSRD), 3*(5), 438–440.
20. Wisdom, D. D., Ajayi, A. E., Arinze, C. U., Idris, H., Bello, U. M., & Aladesote, I. O. (2022). An Optimized TWIN Battery Resource Management Scheme in IEEE 802.16 e Networks. In *Proceedings of Sixth International Congress on Information and Communication Technology: ICICT 2021, London, Volume 4* (pp. 73–95). Springer Singapore.
21. Kazandjieva, M., Heller, B., Gnawali, O., Hofer, W., & Kozyrakis, P. L. C. (2011). Software or hardware: The future of green enterprise computing. *Computer Science Technical Report CSTR, 2.*
22. Wisdom, D. D., Tambuwal, A. Y., Chun, P. B., Adamu, H. K., & Ajayi, E. A. (2018). Enhanced model for computer viruses counter measures. In *1st International Conference on Education and Development ITED*, Baze University, Abuja, Nigeria.
23. Ketankumar, D. C., Verma, G., & Chandrasekaran, K. (2015). A green mechanism design approach to automate resource procurement in cloud. *Procedia Computer Science, 54*, 108–117.
24. Alhasan, S., Akinyemi, A. E., & Wisdom, D. D. (2020). A comparative performance study of machine learning algorithms, for efficient data mining management of intrusion detection systems. *International Journal of Engineering Applied Sciences and Technology, 5*(6), 2455–2143.
25. Ghansawant, V. (2020). Green computing: Current research trends. *International Journal of Science and Research (IJSR)*, 2319–7064. https://doi.org/10.21275/MR21709173309
26. Thomas, R., Manjaly, F. J., & Mala, T. (2015). Approaches in green computing. *International Journal of Engineering Research & Technology (IJERT) NSRCL, 3*(28).
27. Wisdom, D. D., Ahmed, M. A., Farouk, N., Isaac, S., Idris, H., & Hassan, J. B. (2020). An enhanced power saving scheme (EPSS) in IEEE 802.16 e networks. *International Journal of Information Processing and Communication IJIPC, 8*(2).

28. Mehtälä, H. E. J. (2023). Green in software engineering: Tools, methods and practices for reducing the environmental impacts of software use – A literature review.
29. Priya, S., Kumari, R., Shruthi, R., Sumana, P., & Harish, G.. (2024). *Green Computing: A Case Study on the Holistic Approach of Innovative Computing* (Unpublished manuscript, R.V. College of Engineering, Bangalore, India).
30. Ajayi, A. E., Idris, H., Wisdom, D. D., & Arinze, U. C. (2020). Quality of Service Aware Power Saving Scheme in IEEE 802.16e networks. *IEEE, Technical Paper Series, Ghana.*
31. Chawla, S., & Dalal, T. (2017). Challenges and proposed solutions to achieve green computing. *International Research Journal of Engineering and Technology (IRJET), 4*(4), 3657. https://doi.org/2395-0056
32. Igulu, K. T., Wisdom, D. D., Arowolo, M. O., & Singh, T. P., (2023). Computational Intelligence in big data analytics. CI-Industry-4.0: Computational Intelligence in Industry 4.0 and 5.0 Applications. *Taylor and Francis group.*
33. Rao, T. V. N., Rani, M. J., Swetha, C., & Satyam, A. (2015). Sustainable environment friendly green computing for futuristic technologies. *Journal of Information Sciences and Computing Technologies, 2*, 128–132.
34. Wisdom, D. D., Saidu, I., Tambuwal, A. Y., Isaac, S., Ahmad, M. A., & Faruk, N. (2019, December). An efficient sleep-window-based power saving scheme (ESPSS) in IEEE 802.16 e networks. In *2019 15th International Conference on Electronics, Computer and Computation (ICECCO)* (pp. 1–6). IEEE.
35. Naeem, B. (2021). *Green Computing: Analysis of Power and Energy Consumption of Personal Computers* (Doctoral dissertation, Capital University).
36. Wisdom, D. D., Vincent, O. R., Igulu, K., Hyacinth, E. A., Arinze, U. C., Oduntan, O. E., & Ganya, A. H. (2023). Industrial IoT Security Threats and Counter Measures, Book Chapter, Springer Nature. https://doi.org/10.1007/978-981-97-0052-3_20
37. Pillai, A. S., Vessly, R. A., & Joseph, R. (2022). Green cloud computing: A greener approach to IT. *International Journal of Research in Engineering and Science (IJRES), 10*(4), 42–48.
38. Eneh, A. H., Wisdom, D. D., Arinze, U. C., & Dazi, S. I. A., & Philibus, E. An Optimized Database Management System (ODMS). *Proceedings of the LASUSTECH 30th Multidisciplinary Innovation Conference 2020*, Series 30 Vol. 2, At: Lagos Nigeria.
39. Nagaraju, V. (2013). Green computing a modern approach to information technology. *BEST: International Journal of Management, Information Technology and Engineering, 1*(1), 23–28.
40. Wisdom, D. D., Christian, A. U., Hyacinth, E. A., Esther, O. O., Igulu, K., & Garba, A. B. (2022). IoT devices battery life energy management scheme. *Computology: Journal of Applied Computer Science and Intelligent Technologies, 2*(2), 1–13.
41. Hema, K., Subhashini, P., & Lakshmi, S. V. (2017). Emerging issues of green computing in IT. *International Journal of Scientific & Engineering Research (IJSER), 8*(5), 52.
42. Haron, H., Ahmaro, I. Y., Ahmad Aljunid, S., & Bakri, M. (2015). Software reusability in green computing. *Advanced Science Letters, 21*(10), 3283–3287.

10 Mobile Android-Based Applications Learning for Educating Women and Children for Law and Rights

Bhaveshkumar J Parmar and Hetal Thaker

10.1 INTRODUCTION

It is undeniable fact that every single human being's daily life is highly dependent on smartphone. In this chapter, we will look at the pros and cons of utilising information and communication technology (ICT) through smartphone to support gender equality and peace for children and women. When used constructively to address socio-legal concerns, smartphone/mobile technology can be a revolutionary force.

There can be many situations where the necessity to protect arise in case of women at large. For example, women going outside alone, domestic violence, marriage at a minor age, acid-attacks, and human trafficking are common situations where something need be done. What can we do? Where can we begin from? First and foremost, it may be the easiest thing to educate women about need for protection, how to stay safe, what to do in case of an emergency, and how to report violations to local authorities including police [1]. In addition to this, it is also impossible to exaggerate the importance of laws and safeguards in protecting children's rights. Differentiating between safe and unsafe forms of physical contact, the problem of child trafficking and strategies for finding lost children are all important topics for researchers. Smartphones and the internet have seen a dramatic increase in usage in our lives. Development of mobile applications that might increase awareness and assist preventive measures is, thus, one viable way to solve these difficulties.

The integration of audio, video, and graphics into the user interface of mobile applications facilitates the comprehension of legislation, information regarding violence, and the process of reporting violations of fundamental rights for children and women. Moreover, if these mobile applications are built as gamification platforms, they can effectively motivate more children to utilise the programme for self-protection. Gamification is the integration of game concepts into a context that is not a game. Rather it helps children learn at a faster pace.

DOI: 10.1201/9781003471356-10

Over the last decade, numerous apps have been created to address these social challenges.

A smartphone is crucial to a woman's safety in situations like these, as the number of crimes against women is rising. These days, Android comes with a number of apps that are useful in emergency. The "Raksha" app was introduced by the ruling party of India in 2014 with the goal of ensuring users' safety at all times. With a single tap, the button on the app can send a distress signal to registered contacts and a loud buzzer to those who are close to them. When there is no data connection, it sends an SMS alert to the contacts.

Gender-based violence and harassment on the internet can take many different forms, such as the uninvited sharing of sexually explicit recordings and images, digital surveillance, threats, cyberstalking, and more. When it happens to young individuals, there are frequently psychological and bodily aftereffects (such as migraines, extreme discomfort, elevated anxiety, sadness, embarrassment, and isolation). Furthermore, since it's not always feasible to remove abusive content entirely from the internet, children and young people who encounter online violence may have long-term effects. This chapter specifically examines mobile applications that offer an educational platform to teach children and women about safety, law, and rights.

10.2 CREATING A SAFE ENVIRONMENT FOR CHILDREN ON THE INTERNET

Addressing the distribution of detrimental and illicit content is a multifaceted endeavour. Effectively removing illicit material at its origin is inherently challenging due to the global distribution of websites hosting such content, often outside the reach of regulators.

Therefore, various countries adopt different approaches to combat the dissemination of illegal content, especially that which pertains to child/women abuse. One common tactic is the employment of filtering and banning suspicious lists. On the other hand, these technologies have the ability to place severe restrictions on freedom of speech, which is why their usage is controversial. This becomes much more troublesome when there is a lack of clear legal norms and concrete basis, further insufficient openness, and inadequate measures to avoid abuse, such as judicial review. Internet service providers have on rare occasions gone so far as to block access to sexual and reproductive health-related websites in addition to those pertaining to child abuse.

In addition, all local-level authorities may ignore their duty to address cases of child abuse if they are too busy banning and filtering of those contents. It is necessary to identify and penalise the real offenders responsible for child abuse, including those who make and disseminate unlawful content and materials linked to child abuse online.

It is imperative to identify and rescue individuals who have been subjected to abuse. It is more suitable to employ blocking and filtering techniques on private and school computers, utilising parental control, safe areas for children on the internet, and trustmarks and labels that differentiate between hazardous and non-harmful information. The German website "Netz für Kinder" serves as an exemplary platform where children can engage in safe browsing, learning, and playing activities.

10.2.1 Smartphone User Status

According to estimates, the number of mobile phone users in India has increased dramatically over time. Early in 2023, 1.10 billion real-time smartphones were connected through any of the mobile service providers in India, which is equal to estimate near to 77 percentage of the India's total population. Based on the 2011 census, women make up 48.4 per cent of India's population, while men make up 51.6 per cent. A third of the population, or 13.6 per cent, is thought to be between the ages of 13 and 17, and 13.6 per cent is between the ages of 5 and 12. Users of smartphones, who frequently use mobile devices for pleasure and information consumption, are affected by the low data rates. For e-shopping, e-wallets, online music, interactive gaming, education-entertainment, navigation, news updates, and communication, among many other uses, there are mobile apps accessible. The Google Play offers the majority of Android apps for free download. This may be done by utilising the various sensors and application programming interfaces (APIs)available in the Android operating system [2].

10.2.2 Smart Phone Applications and Safety Concern

Our society has long been deeply concerned with women's security. Women dislike travelling to abandoned locations and feel uneasy wandering alone at night. There are several instances of sexual and psychological harassment directed at women, making them fearful to work in an atmosphere where there are more male co-workers. With the use of technology, numerous developers have recently developed several ways to address these issues with continuous location tracking [3].

Location APIs on Android are used by child and woman security apps to track the user's location and alert them; the location is then shared with parents/guardians/trusted known ones. A music player API is also utilised by the app, which plays a help song to request assistance under harassing circumstances. These two represent the application's primary features. For young children, the application would continuously transmit the whereabouts of their gadgets to their parents' phones.

The messaging APIs can send SMS message which can be received by the parent's phone, which also allows them to follow their child's position. For female users, all they have to do is shake the phone in an emergency scenario to activate the programme. Once the girl's location has been determined, the app will notify her parents so they can notify the police station should the girl's condition worsen. The app will warn the girl's parents and request assistance via SMS. By playing a help tune, the rapid help feature allows you to ask for assistance from individuals around in the event of harassment of any kind. There is no way to modify the pre-set music tone thereafter.

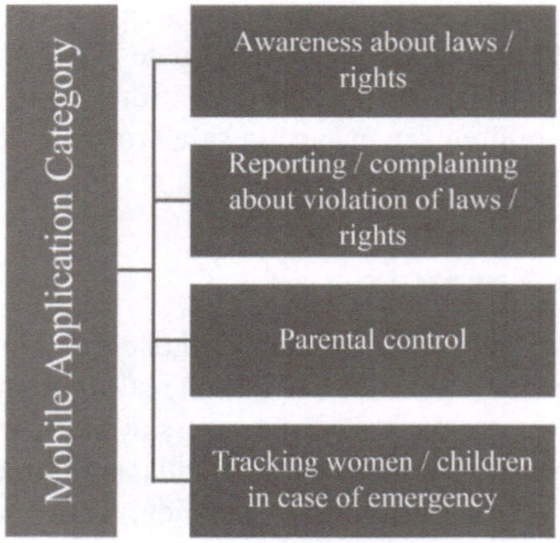

FIGURE 10.1 Mobile application categories. (Compiled by Authors.)

Broadly, mobile applications available in market can be categorised as in Figure 10.1 while Figure 10.2 shows the various categories of women safety applications.

10.3 GAMIFICATION TO UNDERSTAND CHILD LAWS

The integration of gamification into the legal framework represents a fundamental shift away from conventional wisdom and the introduction of practical acceptable methods with game-changing potential.

FIGURE 10.2 Category of women safety mobile applications.

The rise of digital media has given boost-up to gaming activity as a major influence in children's life, with many now identifying them as their principal form of joy. There is an ample research in the literature looking to the fact that games consistently and intriguingly engage players. In light of these possibilities, gamification has grown in popularity over the last decade as a potent method to enhance the user experience, engagement, and motivation. Several studies conducted over the past decade have examined the effects of games on children's motivation and engagement; one such study found that games with progress-based awards significantly increased players' interest and participation. Also, studies have demonstrated that kids who play games tend to retain more of what they learn. "The application of game design elements in non-gaming contexts" is how the term gamification is defined. The term "gamification" has a broader meaning when applied to non-game contexts; it describes an approach that attempts to imitate a game in some way. The main objective of gamification is to employ game design elements to encourage users to perform goal-oriented tasks, such as learning, behaviour, and user engagement, that they would not otherwise do. The gamification concepts can be applied to a wider variety of contexts, allowing education to reap the motivational benefits of games. Gamification has been popular in many other industries, and several studies have shown that it is effective in education.

A lot of studies in the last decade have concentrated on how digital educational games (DEGs) might be utilised to "gamify" learning for children. One may argue that scholars were piqued and professionals (teachers and game designers) were quick to adopt Marc Prensky's work when it came out at the turn of the millennium. However, gamifying research with children is an emerging trend that is relatively new. Both gamification initiatives are based on the idea that games are inherently engaging and inspiring, and they also account for the reality that the majority of children spend a considerable amount of time playing video games on their phones. When designed well, games may captivate children, encourage teamwork, and keep their attention while they work to fulfil objectives.

While the practice of gamifying research is still in its infancy, it has recently gained popularity. The "games with a purpose" (GWAP) initiative of 2006 could be considered the birthplace of gamified research. GWAPs may take the form of games with simple mechanics and an intentional aesthetic. A simple game like Tetris can be all it takes to keep your interest. However, it has shown to be a challenging problem to confront the necessity of combining domain-specific knowledge with talent in game design when a game is linked to a certain domain topic. This requires numerous viewpoints.

Incorporating gamification aspects into a learning environment makes it more interesting.

When kids aren't aware of and educated about their rights, it can greatly affect their daily lives. It's common knowledge that kids' use of computer games enhances their education. An integral aspect of the broader concept of gamification is the use of games as a motivator. Gamification has exploded in popularity over the past decade, finding applications in a wide variety of fields, including education.

The term "gamification" describes the practice of successfully engaging and inspiring people through the usage of game elements and concepts in contexts unrelated to gaming. The contemporary literature on game design provides the theoretical foundation for this method, which integrates mechanics, dynamics, and emotions

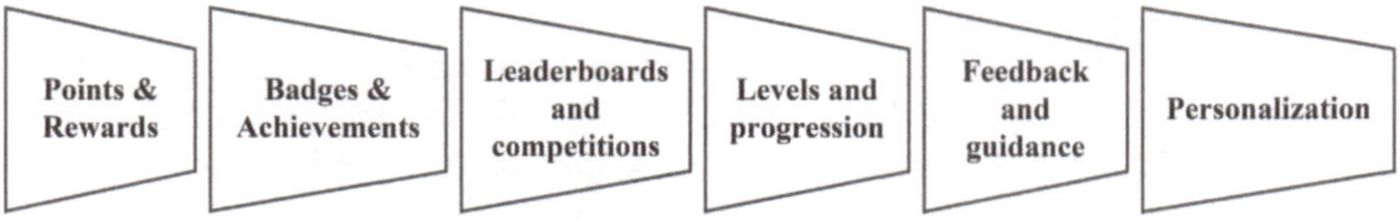

FIGURE 10.3 Children application development critical aspects.

to produce an enjoyable experience (Figure 10.3). Among the many parts that make up the aforementioned characteristics are point systems, incentives, aspects of competitiveness, and interface challenges.

10.3.1 App Search Procedure

This section of the chapter discusses mobile applications available in two application platforms: the Apple App Store and the Google Play Store. The stores can be searched specifically for two categories of mobile applications: those designed for woman and those designed for children. Various mobile applications pertaining to the domains of safety, legal rights, and reporting of violations against children and women were also investigated. The following are a few examples of these applications.

10.3.2 Mobile Applications for Child Right, Safety, and Laws Related to Children

There is a wide range of mobile applications in the market that focus on child rights and women's safety. The following section explores a handful of these applications. Tables 10.1 and 10.2 summarise these applications in tabular format.

UNICEF has just introduced a mobile application called ***Right Runner***. This game-based software aims to motivate gamers to actively engage in advocating for child rights. This programme educates, enables, and motivates children and young individuals about their entitlements. This programme serves as an exemplary model of gamification, providing a simple and effective means of educating and raising awareness among youngsters regarding their rights. The game comprises five unique stages. As the player advances through each level, they learn about different child rights, like the right to play, education, to comfortable stay in hygiene and harmless surroundings, importantly, to be free from any kind of violence, and the right to express their opinions.

Mobile applications designed for child safety aim to provide parents and caregivers with tools to monitor, track, and protect children in various situations. This literature explores the development, effectiveness, and challenges of such applications, emphasising their technological features, user experiences, and impact on child safety.

a. **Technological Features**
   1. *Location tracking and geofencing*: Mobile apps for child safety often incorporate GPS tracking and geofencing to monitor children's locations. For example, the app "Life360" provides real-time location tracking and

TABLE 10.1
Summary of Android Applications Focusing on Child Safety

Application Name	Downloads	Reviews	Ratings	Released on	Key Features
AI Child Rights	100+	8	4.4	Jun 18, 2023	• Child rights education • Safety tips and guidance • Child advocacy and support • Parenting resources • Child-friendly content • Child participation and empowerment • Legislation and policies
Child Rights *(Child Rights – Apps on Google Play)*	10k+	35	4.9	Sep 13, 2015	• Provides information about child rights
CHIRAG *(CHIRAG – Apps on Google Play)*	10T+	120	4.6	19 Aug, 2016	• CHIRAG is an Android application of MSCPCR
Child Rights Monitor *(Child Rights Monitor – Apps on Google Play)*	1K+	-NA-	-NA-	Feb 12, 2016	• Learn and practice child rights
Masoom *(Masoom – Apps on Google Play)*	1K+	39	4.6	Sep 19, 2017	• Examine, report, and review the safeguards • Inquire into violation of child rights • Inspect juvenile custodian home • Monitoring of child's right to education
Sishu Suraksha by ASCPCR	100+	-NA-	-NA-	Nov 9, 2019	• e-complaint box to lodge a complaint about violation of child rights
Child Abuse Prevention *(Child Abuse Prevention – Apps on Google Play)*	10T+	524	3.8	Apr 18, 2019	• 32 different covers life situations • Game based to learning, skill-enhancement

Source: Compilation by authors.

TABLE 10.2
Summary of Android Applications Focusing of Women Safety

Application Name	Downloads	Reviews	Ratings	Released on	Key Features
112 India App (112 India – Apps on Google Play)	1M+	5.56k	4.0	Nov 6, 2018	• Giving people all over the country a single panic tool • Sending field tools out on time • Integration with emergency and keep track of how events are going
Women Safety App	100k+	1.81k	4.0	Aug 28, 2015	• Awaken women for unsafe places • Deliver e-mail to their choice of ID(s) active present location map
I'm Safe – Women Safety App *(I'M SAFE – Women Safety App – Apps on Google Play)*	10K+	54	4.4	Oct 19, 2022	• Features of the app are as follows: Track me, SOS, helpline numbers, fake call, anonymous record, Org help
My Safetipin: Safety Companion App *(My Safetipin: Safety Companion – Apps on Google Play)*	50K+	365	3.9	Mar 9, 2016	• Features of the app are as follows: Safest route, quick audit, tacking, safety score, find support
bSafe – Never Walk Alone App (BSafe – Never Walk Alone – Apps on Google Play.)	1M+	8.96k	3.6	May 20, 2011	• Features of the app are as follows: Voice activation, live streaming, automatic recording, fake call
Smart 24×7 – Personal Safety App *(Smart24×7-Personal Safety App – Apps on Google Play)*	100K+	2.08k	2.6	May 27, 2013	• PANIC Button during emergency • Instant help from nearby police station
Shake2Safety – Personal Safety App	100k+	607	4.1	Jan 5, 2015	• Shaking the phone or by pressing power button four times sends messages • Saves a 4-second audio recording during an SOS event • Works even when there is no internet connection and locked screen

TABLE 10.2 ***(Continued)***
Summary of Android Applications Focusing of Women Safety

Application Name	Downloads	Reviews	Ratings	Released on	Key Features
Himmat Plus App *(Himmat Plus – Apps on Google Play)*	100K+	653	3.5	Jan 30, 2018	• Map with audio-video given to Delhi Police on emergency
Nirbhayam App *(NIRBHAYAM – Apps on Google Play)*	1L+	361	4.4	27 Feb, 2020	• Initiative by Kochi City Police • User can send location/ with message/photo/ audio/video with location
Safety-Help-SOS App	50k+	713	4.0	Dec 14, 2019	• Rapid active and deliver alerts • Conveyance of SMS to multiple contacts • Configure text SMS messages and continuous location updates
NCW – Her Legal Guide App *(NCW – Her Legal Guide App – Welcome to NEGD)*	500	7	5.0	Aug 12, 2023	• Contains details about the helplines pertaining to women
Hawk Eye – Telangana Police App	5L+	5.67T	3.2	Dec 30, 2014	• SOS function for assistance in emergencies • Report related to appreciating efforts by police register details of all migrants with police

allows parents to set up geofencing alerts, notifying them when a child enters or exits designated areas [4]. Similarly, "Glympse" allows for temporary location sharing and real-time tracking, which can be particularly useful for ensuring a child's whereabouts during activities [5].

2. *Emergency alerts and Save Our Soul (SOS) features*: Many safety apps feature emergency alerts and SOS functions. The app "Family Locator" includes an SOS button that sends immediate alerts to selected contacts, along with the child's location, in case of an emergency [6]. Another example is "bSafe", which offers an SOS button, automatic location sharing, and video recording during emergencies [7, 8].
3. *Parental controls and monitoring*: Applications like "Qustodio" and "Net Nanny" provide comprehensive parental controls, including web filtering, screen time management, and activity monitoring. These apps help parents manage their child's online presence and screen time [9, 10].

b. **Effectiveness**
   1. *Impact on safety and security*: Studies indicate that mobile safety apps can significantly enhance perceptions of safety among parents and children. According to a study by [11], parents using safety apps reported increased confidence in their ability to monitor and protect their children. However, the study also highlighted that while apps improve parental peace of mind, their effectiveness in preventing real-world incidents varies.
   2. *Effectiveness in emergency situations:* Research by [12] found that apps with real-time tracking and SOS features can be effective in emergency situations. The study emphasised that while these tools provide valuable support, their success depends on the promptness of response and the accuracy of location data.

c. **User Perception and Challenges**
   1. *Usability and user experience*: User experience plays a crucial role in the adoption of safety apps. A study [13] revealed that ease of use, intuitive design, and reliability are key factors influencing parents' satisfaction with child safety apps. Apps that are difficult to navigate or unreliable tend to see lower adoption rates.
   2. *Privacy and data security concerns*: Privacy concerns are significant when dealing with applications that track children's locations and activities. Research by [14] highlights that while parents appreciate the safety features, they are often worried about data security and the potential misuse of their child's personal information. Ensuring robust encryption and transparent data handling practices are essential for maintaining user trust.
   3. *Dependency and overreliance*: A potential drawback is the overreliance on technology for child safety. According to research [15], there is a risk that parents might become overly dependent on these apps, potentially neglecting other crucial aspects of child supervision and safety.

d. **Emerging Trends and Future Directions**
   1. *Integration with wearable technology*: The integration of mobile apps with wearable technology, such as smartwatches designed for children, is an emerging trend. Wearable devices equipped with GPS and communication features provide an additional layer of safety and real-time monitoring [16].
   2. *Advancements in artificial intelligence (AI)*: AI is being increasingly utilised to enhance safety features in mobile applications. AI algorithms can analyse patterns and provide predictive alerts or recommendations based on the child's behaviour and environmental context [17].

10.3.2.1 AI Child Rights

It is a specific application designed to protect the rights of children. The primary objective of this application is to enhance universal consciousness of the rights of children. This mobile application provides extensive information about the United Nations Convention on the Rights of the Child (UNCRC).

10.3.2.2 Child Rights

Child Rights – Apps on Google Play is an application that raises awareness about the rights of children. This application purports to facilitate children's awareness of their rights. This application offers information on various topics, including guiding principles, rights related to survival and growth, rights related to protection, and rights related to participation. This application provides diverse information pertaining to issues such as registration, nomenclature, citizenship, guardianship, parental separation, children without family support, refugee children, children with disabilities, and social welfare.

10.3.2.3 CHIRAG

The *Maharashtra Government (INDIA)*, in collaboration with the "State Child Rights Protection Commission", has developed an android-based application called ***CHIRAG*** ("Child Helpline for Information on their Rights to Address their Grievance") to facilitate the submission of complaints regarding violations of child rights. The inception of this application occurred in 2016. This application's main emphasis lies in displaying various activities involving youngsters through vibrant photographs showcasing their joyful expressions. This application contains information pertaining to many acts, including the RTE, POSCO ("Protection of Children from Sexual Offences"), CRC ("Convention on the Rights of the Child"), Child Labour Amendment Act 2016, Immoral Traffic, The Juvenile Justice, and Prohibition of Child Marriage. The platform offers the option to download PDFs containing information on kid rights. Additionally, it provides contact details for simple communication in the event of any rule violations.

10.3.2.4 The Child Rights Monitor (CRM)

Child Rights Monitor (CRM) application enables users to report cases of child abuse, request and provide support, and access information on child rights. Both the English and Tamil languages are supported by this application by default. One of the most important features of this application is that it gives users the option to either click on a picture or send a voice message if they come across a child who is being mistreated. Information provided by the user will be shared with the appropriate authorities and local volunteers in the area are indicated with the intention of rescuing the child that is the subject of the investigation. This application was developed with the intention of fostering and protecting youngsters, as well as providing them with possibilities to participate in activities. In addition to being able to search for relevant information, users of this programme are also able to report incidents, obtain support services, take part in campaigns, advocate for children, and report incidents.

10.3.2.5 The ReUnite

An app was made to make it easier to find and track down children who are lost. "Bachpan Bachao Andolan" came up with this technology to keep kids safe. Parents or people who know of children who have gone missing or been abandoned can give important details like the child's name, where they live, a scar, and what was done to try to find and identify the child. Any new information should be reported right away to the nearest police station. The database kept by the government with information about children who are reported missing is linked to this project. Face recognition technology, along with complex algorithms and analytics, is used in this app to help find lost children.

10.3.2.6 The Masoom

The application was launched with the intention of protecting the rights of children, and it received assistance from the Women and Child Development department of the Gujarat government. English, Gujarati, and Hindi are the three spoken languages that are supported by the application. Complaints can be submitted by users, and their status can be tracked. In addition to it, pictures, music, or video can all be included as part of the complaint data.

10.3.2.7 Shishu Suraksha by the Assam-State-Commission

Their app's creators hope that, while user using it, they will motivate users to take action in defence of the rights of future generations. Witnesses of a violation of a child's rights in Assam have the right to file a complaint. In order to bolster the Digital INDIA initiative, they developed an online platform where people may submit concerns about child protection.

10.3.2.8 Child Abuse Prevention

Child Abuse Prevention is a gamified platform that displays content in an animated format. It aims at strengthening children's understanding of child abuse and empowering them to protect themselves from potential offenders. This application employs an engaging and adaptable game approach to help youngsters effectively apply these concepts in their daily tasks. Children are taught many lessons on understanding their parents, which include learning about the anatomy of private body parts, identifying touch that may be dangerous, setting boundaries by saying no, and reporting any touch that is unclear or improper to their parents. In addition, children are informed about the existence of potential perpetrators in their environment. The first essential focusing area of the game is to recover children's abilities and increase their understanding of child abuse.

10.3.2.9 Kunjapp

The launch of *Kunjapp* in the state of Kerala aims to combat cybercrime targeting minors. This programme enables the reporting of child exploitation.

10.3.3 Mobile Applications for Women Rights, Safety, and Laws Related to Women

There are huge therapeutic, societal, and legal ramifications to the ever-increasing occurrence of violence against women. Efforts to control and manage the phenomena have thus intensified in the extra-legal sphere, such as through enforcement, new technology solutions, and security planning, in addition to the legislative initiatives undertaken in the past few years to avoid the phenomenon and enhance victim aid. Mobile phone applications aimed at preventing violence against women have proliferated in recent years, each with its own unique purpose and objective.

In addition to legislative initiatives aimed at preventing the phenomena and improving victim aid, there have been increased attempts in non-legislative domains to manage and limit it, such as through security planning and the adoption of new technological solutions. Applications for (possible) female victims of assault originated and expanded on this basis.

A personal safety app's usefulness in preventing and responding to violent incidents is practically endless; these apps can serve as a "virtual bodyguard" for their users. In the fight against gender-based violence, women have had a silent ally in the form of anti-violence apps for mobile devices since 2014. Some provide resources for learning about aggression and how to report it, while others help people find local anti-violence centres where they can get immediate, tangible help, and still others concentrate on education and prevention through listening desks and testing. These apps can basically be categorised into different groups based on the service they offer.

Apps that provide information: these apps may include emergency numbers, but their primary purpose is not to respond to emergencies; rather, they aim to raise awareness about important issues and help prevent dangerous situations; The "virtual guardian" can step in to respond to a distress signal by using tracking apps, which reveal the user's precise location. Not only may these applications be lifesavers in real emergencies, but they can also reassure loved ones whether you're away from home, hiking alone, or just out and about at night.

Finally, there is the category of emergency apps. These are the ones a person can use if she feels threatened and needs help right away, even if it's simply a phone call and not a police officer. Therefore, these apps make it possible to send the victim's location automatically, even in a crisis, and to sound an alarm that is both swift and effective.

One can find a plethora of similar apps, numbering in the hundreds, on both the domestic and international markets. The following is a summary of the roles played by these safety instruments for women.

Behavioural guidance: A number of applications serve as instructional resources, and among these are those that provide age-appropriate guidance to women. These are best practices for avoiding or effectively handling potentially harmful circumstances; apps aimed at ending violence against women often have pages detailing the relevant laws and regulations, as well as details on local resources for victims of domestic abuse, such as shelters and advocacy groups; noises and alarms: a lot of apps have buttons that press on signals (alarm noises, a constant or intermittent torch, etc.) that can be helpful to draw people's attention to the area, confuse or, better yet, frighten away any potential criminal; calls to emergency services: sometimes all it takes is pressing a button to dial 911.

In addition to virtual assistance, the most cutting-edge programmes have a genuine contact centre that is open all year round to give users the option to call in whenever they feel uneasy. One useful feature of many programmes is the ability to track and send your position in case of an emergency. By utilising GPS, you may geolocate yourself and notify rescue services or pre-set contacts of your whereabouts. As a community, you can sometimes warn other app users in the area about potential hazards, so they can either stay away from or cross the area carefully. Insurance in the event of damage: out of all the apps we looked at, one stood out because it addresses both preventative and remedial safety measures. Actually, it's insurance that pays for things like medical help, rekeying locks, and document restoration. Various smartphone applications are accessible to enhance women's confidence and sense of security, so empowering them with confidence and to live life without fear.

Mobile applications (apps) have emerged as crucial tools for enhancing women's safety in various contexts, from personal safety to emergency response.

a. **Technological Features**
   1. *Emergency alerts and tracking*: Many safety apps incorporate features like real-time location tracking and emergency alerts. For instance, the app "Circle of 6" allows users to quickly send their location to trusted contacts and alert them with a pre-set message (Circle of 6, 2023). Similarly, "SafeTrek" uses a simple interface to allow users to press and hold a button for safety, with automatic alerts sent if the button is released without a passcode [18].
   2. *Integrated safety networks*: Apps like "bSafe" offer integrated safety networks that include features like SOS signals, location tracking, and the ability to record audio and video during emergencies [7, 8]. These features aim to create a comprehensive safety net for users.

b. **Effectiveness**
   1. *Impact on safety perception*: Research shows that safety apps can significantly impact users' perception of safety. A study [19] found that users of safety apps reported higher feelings of security and greater confidence in managing potentially dangerous situations.
   2. *Real-world effectiveness*: However, the real-world effectiveness of these apps is mixed. A study [20] evaluated the effectiveness of safety apps in preventing violent crime and found that while apps provide valuable tools, their actual impact on crime rates is limited. The authors emphasise the need for integration with broader community safety initiatives.

c. **User Perception and Challenges**
   1. *User experience and accessibility*: User experience is critical for the adoption and effectiveness of safety apps. According to a study [21], factors such as ease of use, reliability, and user trust play significant roles in the perceived value of safety apps. Additionally, accessibility issues, such as app performance on different devices and compatibility with various operating systems, affect user satisfaction.
   2. *Privacy concerns*: Privacy is a significant concern for users of safety apps. Research [22] highlights that while users value safety features, they are also concerned about the collection and potential misuse of their personal data. Ensuring robust privacy policies and transparent data handling practices is crucial for maintaining user trust.

d. **Emerging Trends and Future Directions**
   1. *Integration with wearable technology*: The integration of safety apps with wearable technology, such as smartwatches and fitness trackers, is an emerging trend. This integration can enhance the functionality of safety apps by providing additional layers of monitoring and alert systems [23].

2. *Use of AI*: AI is being increasingly integrated into safety apps to improve predictive capabilities and response times. AI algorithms can analyse patterns and provide timely warnings or recommendations based on user behaviour and environmental data [24].

10.3.3.1 112 SOS Mobile App

The *112 SOS Mobile App* is an integral component of India's "Emergency Response Support System" (ERSS), enabling citizens in dire situations to request aid from nearby emergency service departments and volunteers. The application transmits notifications containing user particulars and position data and initiates calls to the Local Emergency Control Room and defined emergency contacts. When accessible, local volunteers are alerted, and the application strives to offer a solitary panic application, round-the-clock effective response, prompt deployment of field resources, and incorporation with current systems.

10.3.3.2 Women Safety App

The *Women Safety App* is a practical tool that allows individuals to inform and keep their trusted ones updated regarding their well-being in hazardous circumstances. The system transmits an email with the position coordinates and hyperlinks to Google Maps. Additionally, it captures two photographs and a video and provides a hyperlink to access the images or video. The application includes three distinct buttons of different colours: Green for indicating status updates, Orange for signalling caution, and Red for reporting instances of danger. Users have the option to select the button according to the gravity of the issue, allowing them to share a link to the images or video with their close ones.

10.3.3.3 I'm Safe

I'm Safe is based on intuition, reliable, and enormously secure software for women's safety. Features such as the Fake Call option to make phone calls more secure, the SOS tool to notify trusted contacts of possible danger, and the Track Me function to ensure daily safety are all part of the programme. In order to provide rapid assistance in dangerous situations, the software stores photos, recordings of sounds, and location data in a safe repository. In addition, users can practise escaping awkward situations by pretend to get a phone call. Among the many services provided by I'm Safe are emergency response simulations, secure audio recording, and simulated phone calls. This app allows users to store audio, images, and location data in a database securely, acquire helpline numbers, and make fake phone calls. In addition, the I'm Safe organisation offers female students and employees individualised security solutions, monitors compliance with POSH and NAAC rules, and serves as a conduit for anonymous reporting of internal difficulties.

10.3.3.4 Safetipin App

The *Safetipin App* is a unique app. With this technology, users will be able to find their way around unfamiliar towns and locations, learn about them, and get the support they need. The app's capabilities include encrypted routes, rapid evaluations of public areas, surveillance, and safety assessments. Members of the public can help by doing risk assessments and stepping up as safety supporters. Users can also check safety ratings before leaving and keep their networks active with this tool. You can only get it in India.

10.3.3.5 BSafe – Never Walk Alone – Apps

The idea behind ***bSafe App*** is in response to a sexual assault occurrence. Boasting millions of downloads and garnering over 10,000 media pieces, this technology effectively thwarts crimes such as violence, sexual assaults, and rape, while also providing valuable evidence for legal proceedings. The device has voice recognition, real-time broadcasting, audio and video capturing, simulated phone calls, and GPS monitoring to ensure user safety. This application features an SOS alert that can be activated by voice, enables live streaming, automatically records incidents, provides fake call functionality, and includes a social security network. The device can be conveniently stored in a jacket, pocket, or purse, enabling guardians to monitor your whereabouts and receive live audio updates. The alert additionally captures audio and video, transmitting them to the mobile device of your guardian. Additionally, it enables real-time GPS tracking, enabling guardians to safely monitor your journey home.

10.3.3.6 Smart24×7 App

Smart24×7 App has just introduced a personal safety and commute application for business organisations, which aims to improve the security of its employees. The application transmits distress signals to individuals of close emotional connection, produces short message service notifications in the event that the general packet radio service is non-functional, facilitates immediate assistance from the closest law enforcement agencies, medical facilities, and fire departments, and includes access to a call centre that operates continuously throughout the day and night.

10.3.3.7 Shake2Safety App

Shake2Safety App is an SOS application available on Google Play. It enables users to send text messages, share location-specific images, and record voice during emergency circumstances by either shaking their handsets or pressing power button four times. Further, it enables users to transmit numerous messages specific to a particular area, share photographs relevant to a location, capture audio, and utilise a siren button. This application operates independently and does not rely on an internet connection for its functionality.

10.3.3.8 Himmat App

The Delhi Police has just introduced a complimentary application named *Himmat App* specifically designed for ladies. Users must input a one-time password (OTP) and finish the registration procedure. The app immediately sends exact location data to the authorities after getting an SOS signal from a user.

10.3.3.9 Nirbhayam App

The *Nirbhayam App* provides women in critical and potentially dangerous situations with immediate access to law enforcement through a smartphone app. With the option to provide precise location coordinates, users may send area-specific help requests, messages, and photos. By pushing and holding the help button for five seconds, the user can activate an alarm through the program's emergency interface.

The next step is to notify the closest police command centre of this alarm. Users can quickly seek help by sending images along with their precise location using this tool. In addition to sharing their location, the software lets users upload media files like films, audio recordings, and images. The control room can receive images captured by the built-in camera. In addition to sharing one's current position, the app has an audio recording option that users can utilise to send voice messages. Basically, the video recorder lets users send recordings with their precise locations.

10.3.3.10 The Protection-Help-SOS

The application transmits SMS notifications containing the exact location coordinates to specified contacts. This characteristic ensures the safety of both elderly individuals and travellers. Individuals have the ability to augment their contact list with dependable contacts and, if required, transmit SMS messages to the entire group of chosen individuals. The functionalities include swift initialisation, the ability to support multiple contacts, a dark motif, customisable settings, continuous location updates, and an intuitive interface.

10.3.3.11 The NCW – Her Legal Guide

The purpose of this application is to provide women in India with a wealth of knowledge regarding their legal rights, including statutes, helplines, and more. This application functions as a dependable companion in the face of difficult situations. The mobile application is compatible with both the iOS and Android operating systems.

10.3.3.12 Hawk Eye

Hawk Eye is a Google Play app with various features, such as a way for people to report traffic violations, crimes, and police actions; a way to make sure ladies are safe when travelling; and an emergency SOS button. It also makes it easier to register renters, domestic workers, and labourers; enlist in community policing projects; and get the Telangana State Police contact information. Additionally, the application provides updates on the status of the inputted data. In case of an emergency, the SOS button enables quick communication with the police. To help loved ones and friends respond quickly in an emergency, the device can send a previously recorded message together with the user's present whereabouts.

It is important to address the issue of providing enough legal safeguards for the enormous number of women in India. To foster economic growth and public safety, Indian lawmakers have been hard at work on new legislation. The app Mahilao Ke Liye Kanoon (Mahilao Ke Liye Kanoon, 2019) summarises all the relevant statutes and norms regarding public safety and traffic violations. Laws that empower women are also highlighted, including those that ban dowry, safeguard married women from maltreatment, and put an end to domestic violence. The app is translated into Hindi to facilitate better understanding and usage.

10.4 CONCLUSION

Spread of mobile Android-based applications dedicated to educating women and children on safety, emergency assistance, and rights presents a significant change towards social empowerment and protection. These applications which are increasingly accessible even in rural areas due to widespread smartphone adoption prove to be useful resource for vulnerable section of people. They provide real-time assistance, educational content, and legal knowledge that can significantly enhance safety and well-being of women and children. Integration of local languages and culturally relevant content makes these applications more effective in their reach. These tools have potential to not only educate but also to exercise rights and take proactive steps in situations of distress. However, for these applications to realise their full potential, it is crucial to address challenges such as digital literacy, internet connectivity, and need for continuous updates to ensure content relevance and accuracy. Joint efforts involving government bodies, NGOs, and tech developers are essential to maximise the impact of these applications across the country. Mobile Android-based applications are bright sparks that promise for advancing safety, rights, and overall empowerment of women and children in India. With ongoing innovation and support, they can become a cornerstone of national strategies aimed at building a safer, more informed, and empowered society.

REFERENCES

1. Pawar, V., Wankhade, N. R., Nikam, D., Jadhav, K., & Pathak, N. (2014, March). SCIWARS android app for women safety. International Journal of Engineering Research and Applications, 4(3), 823–826. https://doi.org/10.1109/indicon.2015.7443652
2. Verma, S., Nakarani, B. S. P., & Rasaily, J. (2021). Advanced children and women security: An android mobile application. International Journal of Computer Science and Mobile Computing, 10(5), 87–94. https://doi.org/10.47760/ijcsmc.2021.v10i05.009
3. Yarrabothu, R. S., & Thota, B. (2015). Abhaya: An Android App for the safety of women. 2015 Annual IEEE India Conference (INDICON).
4. Life360. (2023). Life360: Family safety app. Retrieved from https://www.life360.com
5. Glympse. (2023). Glympse: Share your location in real-time. Retrieved from https://www.glympse.com
6. Family Locator. (2023). Family Locator: Keep your loved ones safe. Retrieved from https://www.familylocator.com
7. bSafe - Never Walk Alone - Apps on Google Play. (n.d.). bSafe – Never Walk Alone – Apps on Google Play. https://play.google.com/store/apps/details?id=com.bipper.app.bsafe&hl=en_US
8. bSafe. (2023). bSafe: Personal safety app. Retrieved from https://www.bsafeapp.com
9. Qustodio. (2023). Qustodio: Parental control app. Retrieved from https://www.qustodio.com
10. Net Nanny. (2023). Net Nanny: Internet safety for families. Retrieved from https://www.netnanny.com
11. Williams, R., & Carr, S. (2021). Parental perceptions of mobile safety applications: A survey study. Journal of Child Safety, 53(2), 142–157.
12. Anderson, T., & Miller, R. (2022). The efficacy of mobile safety applications in emergency situations. Journal of Safety Research, 74, 45–58.
13. Green, A., & Palmer, S. (2023). User experience and satisfaction with child safety applications. International Journal of Human-Computer Interaction, 89(4), 210–225.
14. Blackwell, L., & Smith, J. (2022). Privacy concerns and data security in child safety apps. Information Privacy Journal, 36(2), 123–139.
15. Johnson, P., & Lee, M. (2023). The impact of mobile technology on parental supervision: A critical review. Child Development Research, 48(3), 190–204.

16. Smith, A., & Roberts, J. (2024). Wearable technology and child safety: Future trends. Technology and Society Review, 43(1), 77–92.
17. Chen, L., Smith, R., & Johnson, K. (2024). Artificial intelligence in safety applications: Emerging trends and future directions. Journal of Mobile Technology, 58(2), 122–135.
18. SafeTrek. (2023). SafeTrek: Personal safety app. Retrieved from https://www.safetrekapp.com
19. Nhan, J., & Taylor, J. (2021). Perceptions of safety and the effectiveness of mobile safety applications. Safety Science, 139, 105–115.
20. Walker, R., & Koss, M. (2020). Evaluating the impact of safety apps on crime prevention. Journal of Crime Prevention, 32(4), 265–280.
21. O'Reilly, T., & Hunt, S. (2022). User experience in safety applications: Challenges and solutions. International Journal of Human-Computer Studies, 88, 45–60.
22. Roberts, M., & Davis, L. (2022). Privacy concerns in mobile safety apps: A user perspective. Information Privacy Journal, 35(1), 77–92.
23. Smith, A., & Adams, B. (2023). Wearable technology and Mobile safety apps: A synergistic approach. Technology and Society Review, 41(3), 150–164.
24. Chen, L., Wang, M., & Johnson, K. (2024). Artificial intelligence in child safety applications: Innovations and challenges. Journal of Mobile Technology, 60(1), 85–99.

11 ICT in Peace and Justice, Women and Children

Ankita Verma, Sakshi Gupta, and Deepti Singh

11.1 INTRODUCTION

We live in a diverse society, and the fundamental thread that has united the whole world is the principle of peace and justice. With around 10% of the global population living in extreme poverty[1] and 49.7% of the global population being women[2], it becomes crucial to establish a fair ecosystem with equal opportunities for all. However, several long-standing socio-economic, demographic, and political challenges are to be faced to create a just, resilient, and sustainable world. ICT can aid the judicial systems, healthcare, education, and government to address many pressing challenges with the help of innovations and apt applications of technology. With around 108 mobile subscriptions per 100 people in the world[3] and about 63% of the global population with affordable internet connections[3], communication technology has been revolutionized in this decade, leading to the ease of information dissemination and connectivity among the people. Information and communication technology (ICT) is essential to promoting peace, justice, and women's and children's empowerment in this age of technological deluge because it offers creative answers to persistent problems [1]. ICT helps stakeholders address issues like conflict resolution, access to justice, and the protection of rights more successfully by facilitating communication, collaboration, and advocacy efforts [1, 2]. Women and children can exercise their rights and actively engage in decision-making by using digital platforms to receive healthcare services, educational materials, and legal support [3]. ICT also gives voice to underrepresented groups, supporting campaigns to raise awareness, grassroots organizing, and policy advocacy efforts to advance child welfare and gender equality. We can build more just and inclusive communities where women's and children's rights are respected and safeguarded by utilizing the potential of ICT.

The inclusion of ICT in the administration of justice will enable the system to become more organized, efficient, transparent, and accessible. With the ubiquity of internet services all over the world, the entire judicial system needs to upgrade its existing working patterns. Digitization of case records maintenance, online access to laws and legislations, electronic filing of legal documents, virtual courtroom setup, and utilization of data analytics for aiding judicial decision-making are a few domains where ICT has assisted [2–5].

From a societal viewpoint, the usage of electronic media, communication systems, and social networking platforms has blurred the boundaries of the world. ICT has enabled various stakeholders to share their viewpoints and engage in

DOI: 10.1201/9781003471356-11

constructive dialogues that bust myths and create an environment of peace and harmony. Online social media platforms can be successfully employed as a tool for cross-cultural interactions, dispelling misconceptions, and creating acceptance of different religious, social, and political ideologies [6]. The power of social media can also be harnessed for mobilizing support for social causes, creating awareness for the human rights of underserved sections of society, and virtual protests against any power abuse [7].

For the development of a resilient, economically prosperous, and socially cohesive society, the empowerment of women and children plays a critical role. Despite many sincere efforts by governments and other social agencies, women still face multitudinous barriers that limit them from realizing their full potential. Crimes against women, legal and economic discrimination, regressive social practices, inaccessible healthcare, and less representation in power positions are only a few mention-worthy issues that exacerbate the conditions of women globally. ICT can act as a key enabler of education, healthcare, economic liberty, and leadership of women [8–10]. Along with the welfare of the women, ensuring the well-being of the children is also the biggest responsibility of the state. ICT plays a pivotal role in ensuring the welfare of children by providing avenues for education, protection, and empowerment. Through ICT, children gain access to quality educational resources, enabling them to learn and develop essential skills regardless of geographical constraints. ICT also facilitates communication and connectivity, allowing children to access support networks, report abuse, and seek assistance in times of need.

In this chapter, we will be discussing in depth the various facets of the application of ICT for ensuring peace and justice and for the empowerment of women and children. In Section 11.2, we will present how ICT has revolutionized the administration of justice and its employment in maintaining peace and harmony. Section 11.3 will emphasize the use of ICT for women's empowerment. In Section 11.4, the discussion of the role of ICT in children's welfare is presented. Along with the progress in the application of ICT, we have also discussed its perils and challenges. Section 11.5 concludes the chapter with some key insights.

11.2 ICT IN PEACE AND JUSTICE

ICT has emerged as a transformative force in promoting peace, justice, and human rights around the world. There are several ways through which ICT is revolutionizing conflict resolution, promoting access to justice, and advancing human rights. Some of the significant domains that have greatly benefited from the usage of technology are discussed in this section.

11.2.1 ICT for Justice

The introduction of ICT into the judicial process will rectify the stereotyped conceptions about our judicial system as inaccessible, conservative, sluggish, and discriminatory. Our judicial system is suffering from an access crisis due to the humongous volume of workload on the existing system. ICT will assist decision-makers with efficient tools and technologies for better management of legal resources, expedited information retrieval, reduced scope of human errors, and breaking geographical, demographical, and language barriers. This will greatly reduce, if not eliminate, sloppiness, inefficiencies, discrimination, and inaccessibility in the social justice system. Some of the state-of-the-art applications of ICT in justice are discussed below:

- *Digitization of court processes*: Introducing digital case management systems enables courts, law enforcement agencies, and legal practitioners to efficiently handle cases, documents, and schedules. This advancement simplifies case management, tracking, scheduling, and real-time transcription, thereby reducing paperwork, optimizing processes, and expediting case resolution. Electronic filing, which enables the filing of legal documents digitally, guarantees the utmost security of court records while also facilitating their effortless retrieval [10, 11]. A plethora of research and innovation has been done to create digital records of the existing cases and decisions [12–14]. Online dispute resolution platforms provide an online mechanism for resolving disputes, often through mediation or arbitration. These platforms can offer convenience, accessibility, and cost-effectiveness, especially for resolving low-value or non-complex disputes [11].[4]
- *Creating legal awareness*: Laws and legislations have been enacted to give the country's citizens the instruments to ensure equality, freedom of speech, and the protection of their fundamental human rights. It is vital to make these rules known to the larger public for whom they are intended. Since the introduction of communication technology, information has been predominantly disseminated through electronic media, online news outlets, social networking platforms, and microblogging websites. They are major instruments for raising knowledge about laws, legal cases, and significant judicial judgements, supporting individuals from diverse socio-economic strata in pursuing justice [15–17].
- *Assistance in courtroom proceedings*: Video conferencing, electronic evidence presentation, and digital record keeping have transformed the way courts work. These innovations have increased accessibility, simplified case administration, and improved the overall efficiency of judicial procedures. Furthermore, the introduction of computerized databases and forensic tools has greatly aided in the investigation and presentation of evidence, ensuring fair and transparent trials. The incorporation of ICT in judicial proceedings continues to expand and shape the future of the legal system [18–20].
- *Legal knowledge management systems*: There is a humongous volume of varied legal data available at our discourse consisting of case records, law amendments, policy data, etc. Artificial intelligence (AI) and data analytics can contribute significantly to refining and maintaining this data and knowledge extraction from this data for law researchers and practitioners. This gives the scope for streamlining the legal process by more informed decision-making and strategy development. Legal practitioners may discover patterns, trends, and correlations in large volumes of legal data by

efficiently using data analytics [21–23]. In the Indian context, various online repositories,[5] search engines specially designed for legal research are available to assist lawyers and the general public.

However, the adoption of ICT in justice presents several challenges, primarily due to the complex nature of legal documents, confidentiality concerns, technological limitations, and regulatory requirements.[6] Some of the key challenges are as follows:

- *Data security*: With the aid of technology, law firms and judicial institutions electronically retain crucial data including case documents, personally identifiable information, intellectual property like trade secrets or preliminary patent filings, financial account information, litigation strategies, and more [24, 25]. Consequently, ensuring data security emerges as a paramount concern in the digitalization of the legal sector, as breaches could significantly affect the interests of all stakeholders, including the judiciary and the public. It's imperative to promote awareness and offer education, training, and other support to safeguard these valuable digital assets [26].
- *Infrastructure setup and integration cost*: For the upgradation of the existing judicial system, costs will be incurred for infrastructure setup required for data storage, backup systems, access controls, and disaster recovery mechanisms [11]. Moreover, the courtrooms need to be equipped with high-speed internet, video, and audio devices. In many developing countries, most of the legal cases are stored physically in different formats, styles, and languages. Digitization of these records into a standard digital format for efficient indexing and retrieval is a cumbersome task [12, 13]. Lastly, these technologies have to be employed by humans; therefore, all legal professions must have digital literacy.
- *Media trial*: There is widespread agreement that media personnel possess both a legal and constitutional entitlement to report on court proceedings and share this information with the public, which fosters trust in the judicial process. However, this unrestricted freedom occasionally leads to a parallel criminal trial of suspects within the confines of news studios [27–29]. While it is legally and morally justified for media trials to ensure comprehensive investigation and impartial proceedings, they must be restricted by law when they veer into sensationalism and profit-driven motives, rather than serving the interests of justice.

11.2.2 ICT for Peace and Harmony

Creating a harmonious and peaceful society is the responsibility to be shared with the state and every individual. ICT plays an important role in maintaining societal peace and harmony by assisting in the following tasks:

- *Conflict prevention and resolution*: ICTs play a crucial role in conflict resolution and peacebuilding endeavours by facilitating a range of approaches. They assist in the detection and mapping of hate speech and rumours, implementing specific measures to combat them, and recognizing threats to livelihoods or factors that could incite conflict [30–32]. Moreover, ICTs streamline the gathering and evaluation of public opinions regarding risk and conflict dynamics, as well as mapping out instances of violence and monitoring armed groups, thereby enabling the provision of early warning systems to prevent conflicts [33, 34]. Additionally, ICT aids in the identification and amplification of instances showcasing peaceful behaviour, nurturing positive narratives, and fostering social unity within communities impacted by conflict [35].

- *Cultivating global harmony*: Social media's power should be harnessed to enhance unity within various religious communities, ethnic groups, genders, and races. Disseminating factual and scientific information instead of sensationalism should be the seminal objective of the various agencies engaging online. All need to address issues of intolerance legally and suitably while advocating for social harmony. Given the significant influence of social media in shaping public perspectives, it should be utilized to contribute to the well-being of society [36–38].
- *Human rights advocacy*: ICT has transformed human rights advocacy by allowing activists to document and expose injustices in real time. Smartphones, cameras, and social media platforms have enabled individuals to record and share evidence of abuse, resulting in increased responsibility and pressure for reform. Furthermore, social media has had a tremendous influence on public discourse and mobilization, making it an important tool for social and political participation [39–41].

Though ICT can assist in peacebuilding and the creation of social harmony, it comes with many of its perils. Some of the key hurdles posed by the non-judicious use of technology to societal harmony are discussed as follows:

- *Social media for false information spreading*: In the realm of breaking news, the proliferation of false information holds particular significance. As updates emerge incrementally, initial pieces of information often surface as unverified rumours. These rumours swiftly disseminate to a wide audience, shaping perceptions and interpretations of unfolding events. Social media serves as a primary platform for such rumours and has significant ramifications, fuelling communal tensions, ethnic conflicts, racial violence, and other societal repercussions that impact both individuals and communities [42–44].
- *Social media and polarization*: In recent years, there has been a growing apprehension regarding the adverse societal effects stemming from the online dissemination of misinformation and propaganda. Emerging technological advancements now enable individuals to effortlessly disseminate political content to extensive audiences, potentially enriching public discourse by incorporating diverse viewpoints. However, this accessibility also provides a platform for extremist elements and opportunistic actors aiming to sway the political narrative for their personal financial or political gain.

- *Ethical AI and autonomous weapons*: The development and deployment of AI technologies in conflict settings raise ethical concerns, particularly regarding the use of autonomous weapons systems. Establishing norms and regulations to govern the responsible use of AI in military and peacekeeping operations is critical for preventing unintended harm and preserving human dignity [45].

11.3 ICT FOR WOMEN

ICT has emerged as a transformative force in promoting peace, justice, and human rights worldwide. There are several ways through which ICT is revolutionizing conflict resolution, promoting access to justice, and advancing human rights in diverse contexts.

11.3.1 ICT and Women's Health

About the attainment of Sustainable Development Goal-3 "*Ensure healthy lives and promote well-being for all at all ages*", providing access to quality healthcare and ensuring the well-being of its citizens is crucial for the development of any nation. Women are the pillars of a flourishing society, and healthy women may make decisions that propel the growth of their families and their nations. Globally, we have 50% women in the world.[7] However, in various nations across South and East Asia, particularly in countries like India and China, there exists a notable disparity in the proportion of females within the population, with numbers significantly lower compared to males. With the continuous and rigorous efforts of the government bodies, India has significantly improved its sex ratio to 1020 females per 1000 males from 991 females per 1000 males in 2015–2016 (National Health Survey 2022).[8] However, as a result of biological and gender-related differences, being male or female substantially impacts health. Several socio-economic factors contribute to the decline in the well-being of women, such as power imbalance between males and females, less educational and employment opportunities for women, less access to menstrual hygiene products and contraceptives, and reproductive and pregnancy issues.

Several health issues are exclusive to women and female organs. Apart from that, few health issues affect women differently than men. The major health issues where the intervention of technology can greatly assist are discussed below:

- *Critical diseases in women*: There are diseases unique to women due to their genital organs, such as menstruation-related diseases and general gynaecological conditions (such as uterine fibroid, ovarian cancer, breast cancer, and pelvic floor disorders). Apart from that, some of the diseases, such as diabetes, osteoporosis, arthritis, and thyroid disorder, affect women significantly and differently than men.
- *Maternal health*: Eliminating maternal mortality is an issue that must continue to be prioritized on a worldwide scale. The term "maternal health"

encompasses a woman's well-being before, during, and after giving birth. Blood loss, infections, hypertension, unsafe abortions, and obstructed labour are the leading causes of maternal injury and mortality, followed by anaemia, malaria, and cardiovascular disease as indirect causes [46].

- *Mental health*: Symptoms of depression, anxiety, unspecified psychiatric disorders, and psychological distress are more common in women, while symptoms of substance disorders are more common in men, according to the meta-analysis of empirical studies of mental disorders conducted in a wide range of social settings and cultural settings. World Bank's data on disability-adjusted life years reflects these variations [47]. Higher rates of psychiatric morbidity among women have been linked to factors, such as poverty, domestic isolation, powerlessness (due to factors such as low levels of education and economic dependency), and patriarchal oppression. Summing up, there is a lot of data suggesting that the mental health issues of women have social roots.
- *Impact of nutrition and healthy lifestyle*: For many reasons, including pregnancy and old age, women are at a higher risk of experiencing hunger than males. Evidence suggests that prenatal malnutrition increases the risk of developing chronic diseases later in life, such as diabetes and heart disease.

Therefore, it becomes crucial to identify the areas where intervention is needed. The healthcare sector is responsible for the production of an enormous quantity of data and is one of the potential domains where ICT can perform marvels. Yet, there is a persistent challenge in transforming this data into insights that might enhance patient outcomes and enhance operational efficiencies. Analytics forecasts the future and hidden patterns in the data of any domain. The application of ICT plays an important role in healthcare, including new research findings, emergencies, and disease outbreaks. With the help of sophisticated computational tools and technologies, we can aid the health sector in various tasks, such as early detection of diseases, designing preventive healthcare, prediction of health outcomes, analysis of contributing factors of mental health issues, and patient profiling. Thus, data analytics can be instrumental in providing necessary insights regarding an array of women's health issues, which can facilitate the identification of the areas that need intervention. The use of technologies seems to hold promise in gynaecology, offering opportunities to enhance accuracy and precision, stratify patients, and offer personalized treatment options instead of generic healthcare approaches. This could ultimately improve effectiveness across all stages of care.

Some of the key areas where ICT can assist are as follows:

- *Early disease diagnosis*: Early-stage detection of various critical diseases, such as breast cancer, ovarian cancer, uterine fibroids, and diabetes, could significantly affect death rates in the long term. Novel technological advancements, such as mammography, magnetic resonance imaging (MRI), ultrasound, computerized tomography (CT), and positron emission tomography (PET), produce large amounts of clinical data. With data analytics and AI, we can build prediction models from is big data to warn clinicians of high-risk conditions [48, 49]. Many studies have been conducted on breast cancer detection through imaging (ultrasound, CT, PET, MRI) or genomics (gene expressions and gene sequencing) [50–52]. Machine learning techniques, such as SVM, deep learning, decision tree, and CNN, have been widely applied [52].

- *Prognosis and recovery*: Thanks to significant technological breakthroughs, ICT is transforming healthcare through numerous means of improving medical practice. In addition to helping physicians diagnose patients more precisely, it also helps them recommend treatment options and forecast patients' chances of recovering well. Healthcare has long faced difficulties with patient engagement and adherence, but AI and big data are starting to solve these problems. AI may tailor therapy suggestions based on patient data and comparable effective treatment pathways by evaluating data from multiple sources, including conversational interfaces, cell phones, biosensors, and electronic health records (EHRs). In the end, these suggestions should improve outcomes and experiences in healthcare for nurses, doctors, patients, call centre representatives, and care delivery coordinators [53].
- *Pre- and post-natal care*: By increasing access to healthcare services, offering information and support, and enabling early diagnosis and management of possible difficulties, ICT initiatives in pre- and post-natal care help to improve the health outcomes for mothers and infants. To monitor the foetus and identify any high-risk issues, a woman requires continuous oversight and assistance from the healthcare professional. Pregnant women can use a variety of smartphone applications made just to cater to many of their needs regarding balanced dietary plans, maternal exercises, foetal development, and doctor's appointments and prescriptions. Pregnant ladies have the opportunity to interact with other women going through similar situations through online forums and social media groups. These platforms provide a forum for the exchange of knowledge, counsel, and emotional support. Pregnant women can consult with doctors remotely via telemedicine platforms, which lessens the need for frequent in-person visits—especially in places with poor access to medical facilities. It is possible to track the pregnancy's development and handle any issues through video consultations, chat, and remote monitoring [54]. During routine check-ups and labour, AI is utilized to monitor the foetal heart rate by analysing cardiotocographs and projecting potential outcomes. Maternal health metrics like heart rate, activity level, and sleep cycles can be monitored with wearable technology like fitness trackers and smartwatches. In addition, some wearable technology offers capabilities unique to pregnancy, such as recording foetal movements [55, 56].
- *Sexual and reproductive health (SRH) Awareness*: One crucial component of human health is SRH. It is particularly stated that "people are able to have a responsible, satisfying and safe sexual life, and that they have the capability to reproduce and the freedom to decide if, when and how often to do so" in the World Health Organization's (WHO's) conceptualization of SRH as a fundamental right. It is now crucial to empower people to take

charge of their reproductive health given the growth in STDs, infertility, and other problems related to sexual health. Regretfully, there are situations where talking about SRH is taboo. The benefits of computer- and technology-based interventions are as follows: reduced delivery costs, increased standardization, fidelity, and ease of replication, and increased flexibility in disseminating information through various channels (e.g., in-person, mail, internet, cell phone, or other) [57]. Digital campaigns may have as their main objectives the destigmatization of sexually transmitted infections, the promotion of healthy lifestyles, the support of access to healthcare, and the advancement of reproductive rights. Virtual support groups and online counselling services provide a secure, private setting where people may talk about issues related to their SRH, get advice, and connect with others going through similar struggles. These platforms could be especially helpful for stigmatized or marginalized groups who might have trouble getting access to standard healthcare services. Apart from this, technology also assists in promoting menstrual hygiene and supporting individuals during menstruation via various mobile apps for period tracking and pain management, online forums for discussions and dissemination of accurate information, and digital campaigns that aim to destigmatize menstruation.
- *Combating mental health issues*: As previously said, there are still many obstacles in the way of providing women with adequate mental healthcare. These include the stigma associated with mental illness, the fact that women sometimes do not realize when they need support, and the necessity for health professionals to be trained in mental illness and cultural sensitivity. With the advent of social networking sites, online groups, and forums, people are interacting virtually in a safe environment to discuss several issues that are impacting their mental health.

While technology has an impact on women's health in numerous ways, it is crucial to make sure that these developments are inclusive and cater to several inherent challenges in its adoption. Some of such inherent challenges are mentioned below:

- *Integration with existing infrastructure*: Integrating technology-based diagnosis and treatment suggestions into EHR systems and clinical workflows might present difficulties at times. Many ICT-based capabilities for diagnosis and treatment from tech firms are standalone or address only one aspect of care; these integration issues have likely posed a bigger obstacle to widespread adoption of technology than any incapacity to offer precise and effective recommendations [54, 55].
- *Unavailability of relevant data for medical research*: Before AI-based systems can be utilized in healthcare applications, they need to be "trained" utilizing data generated from clinical activities, such as diagnosis, treatment assignment, and screening. This is done to make it possible for the systems to recognize patterns among subject groups and connections between subject attributes and desired results. However, managing clinical data is a crucial task due to its volume, variety, veracity, and privacy concerns [57].

- *Accessibility to all*: Women's health behaviours, attitudes towards healthcare, and access to technology can all be significantly impacted by varying cultural ideas and practices. Furthermore, the development and provision of health information and services should take cultural sensitivity into account. This entails offering content in a variety of languages, presenting health information while taking cultural norms and taboos into account, and collaborating with community leaders and members on the creation and application of technological solutions [55].
- *Cyberharassment*: There is a rising risk of online crimes, such as cyberstalking and cyberharassment, as internet use rises. Cyberstalking and/or harassing victims suffer from a wide range of damaging effects on their mental health, such as panic attacks, depression, anxiety, and suicidal thoughts. The victims described how the criminal justice system failed to assist them and how, as a result, they came to distrust technology [58, 59].

11.3.2 ICT for Women's Empowerment

One valuable tool for lifting people out of poverty and giving them agency is education. It is widely recognized that efforts to enhance the well-being of individuals in developing nations must include advancements in empowering women. As society moves towards a greater emphasis on knowledge, the significance of ICTs, like email and the internet, in driving sustainable community and economic growth is growing more prominent. Some of the prominent ways in which ICT suffices for women empowerment [60, 61] are:

- *Economical empowerment*: ICTs play a crucial role in distributing a wide array of information and guidance, which can lead to the transformation of knowledge and attitudes among women. Accessing new and valuable knowledge, information, and awareness on various issues, subjects, and activities that are important to women is integral. This newfound information often provides cognitive stimulation and expands participants' perspectives. It also facilitates the development of new skills, abilities, confidence, competence required for engaging in different group communication and interaction processes within projects. Furthermore, ICT has redefined the concept of workspaces; emerging employment opportunities such as telecommuting are now feasible with advanced technology. In addition, ICT offers women flexibility in terms of time and location—an aspect particularly beneficial for those facing social isolation in developing countries. Women are frequently involved in unorganized economic activity in developing nations, such as sewing, rolling cigarettes, weaving baskets, and fabrics, and working as street sellers in cities without benefits or contracts. More than anybody else, these women need and deserve measures aimed at reducing poverty. These women will be exposed to media, broadcast, and communications services through information technology (IT), which will open marketplaces for their goods and services. This has facilitated many

women to showcase their skills from home at various online avenues like marketplaces, forums, and groups to gain popularity and improve their economic status.
- *Social empowerment*: ICTs have allowed women to connect with and seek support from other women in both rural and urban areas, who share similarities and differences. This has facilitated the building of a strong community where they can engage in discussions about various topics related to emotional, social, physical, and sexual health. Furthermore, ICTs play a crucial role in assisting networking with individuals involved in similar interests, such as rural community development, teleworking, and writing articles or books that extend their reach beyond geographical constraints.
- *Political empowerment*: The use of ICTs has empowered women to become more politically informed and vocal, allowing their viewpoints to be considered by researchers and decision-makers in government and industry. This technology facilitates equal engagement for women in shaping policies, influential decision-making processes related to state matters, as well as shedding light on various socio-economic and cultural challenges affecting the well-being of women for necessary interventions.

However, for better implementation of ICT for women empowerment, the following hurdles need to be overcome:

- *Lack of digital literacy*: To utilize the benefits of ICT tools for women empowerment, it is crucial that women have basic education and be equipped with digital literacy. In developing countries, having basic education is also a far-fetched dream for many. In those scenarios, technological advancements may be used merely as a tool of entertainment but not education.
- *Online frauds*: With the advancement of payment methodologies and e-marketplaces, it becomes critical for everyone to be cautious with malicious hackers. The privacy of the individual is breached very easily if one does not adopt digital security measures.
- *Societal conditioning*: For developing countries with gender disparity, use of technological tools is still not encouraged among females. However, access to technology is costly which further widens the gap between ICT usage and women empowerment.

11.3.3 ICT and Women's Safety

The safety of women has greatly benefited from the use of IT. To stop and address violence against women, a variety of technologies are being used, such as social networking, GPS tracking, and smartphone apps to assist in the following manners:

Location tracking: Women now have quick and simple access to emergency contacts and support in the event of danger thanks to the development of mobile apps, Internet of Things, wearable devices, etc. [62–64]. Aspects like GPS tracking, which lets friends and family know where the user is, and emergency alarms that may be set off if the user feels unsafe are common aspects of these apps. Studies indicate that these applications may be useful in helping women feel more secure and safe. Another suggestion for improving women's safety is GPS tracking. For instance, GPS-enabled cell phones can be used to locate and notify authorities of the presence of women who are in danger.

Social media for awareness: Social media has also been shown to increase women's safety. Social media platforms such as Facebook and Twitter have been used to raise awareness about violence against women and to support and assist survivors. Additionally, social media has been used to organize groups and push for legislative changes that will increase the protection of women [65]. Beyond the aforementioned, newer technologies like AI and machine learning can also be leveraged to improve women's safety. For example, surveillance cameras with AI capabilities can be employed, and machine learning algorithms can be trained to identify and stop online harassment of women.

Though there is hope that new technologies will improve women's safety, there are still issues that need to be resolved. As an illustration, privacy issues have been brought up in relation to GPS tracking, especially in light of the possibility of its abuse. Many of these technologies are also inaccessible to many women, especially those who live in remote places or have restricted access to technology. However, there are ethical, privacy, and bias concerns with the implementation and usage of these technologies. In addition, new forms of gender-based violence have been brought about by the technological revolution. These include hate speech, blackmail, cyberstalking, cyberbullying, and online discrimination [66, 67]. As they are altering women's responses to violence while also transforming the ways in which they encounter it, CTs can thus be a double-edged sword. Development organizations must aggressively address the current digital safety gap for women by supporting gender-sensitive legislation, enhancing data collection, encouraging safety training for advocates, and increasing awareness, all while spearheading campaigns to make the internet and technology more affordable and accessible.

11.4 ICT FOR CHILDREN

ICT has a profound impact on children in the modern world, shaping their learning, communication, and overall development. It can benefit children in developing critical thinking, creativity, and problem-solving abilities. Interactive whiteboards, iPads, online games, and instructional apps are examples of ICT tools. Additionally, ICT can assist educators in developing more dynamic and captivating learning environments for educating children. But, on the negative side, ICT can lead to cyberbullying and exposure to inappropriate content online, which can have serious negative effects on their mental health. Excessive screen time can lead to physical health problems like obesity and eye strain, while addiction to ICT, particularly social media and gaming, can impact self-control and social skills. Privacy concerns and the risk of identity theft are also significant. In the present environment, children can be affected by ICT in both positive and harmful ways. To make sure children take use of the benefits provided by ICT while lowering the risks associated with it, parents, schools, and governments must appropriately handle these effects. In general, it is essential to recognize these risks and take proactive steps to reduce them to guarantee that children use ICT in a safe and responsible manner. In the following subsections, we will discuss the positive and negative impact of ICT on children.

11.4.1 Positive Impact of ICT in Children

Children have benefited greatly from ICT because it gives them access to a plethora of knowledge and educational materials, enhances learning through interactive and engaging tools, fosters creativity and innovation, develops critical thinking and problem-solving abilities, gets them ready for the future of the digital age, offers equal opportunities for success, and promotes health and safety. ICT is essential in today's society because it bridges the technological gap, improves children's overall development, and offers resources to support health and safety in addition to preparing kids for future academic and professional prospects. But it is crucial to make sure children use ICT sensibly, securely, and under appropriate supervision. Following are some of the key points which can positively impact children in various fields:

- Access to educational resources: Children can access a wide range of educational resources through ICT, such as multimedia content, instructional apps, and online courses. Children can study subjects that interest them and learn at their own pace. In India, several government initiatives like—SAKSHAT, FOSSEE, UGC-INFONET, EDUSAT, e-YANTRA, and e-SIKSHAK [68]—have been implemented to provide educational resources to children as well as educators.
- *Interactive learning through games*: For children, learning becomes more dynamic and interesting when they use ICT tools like educational games and simulations. In [69], it has been identified that to increase the effectiveness of their teaching, educators must always look for new approaches, and these strategies should surely be intimately related to the integration of ICT into the classroom. It's still unclear how to effectively offer the games to the learners and integrate them into the instructional processes. These resources can enhance the ability to remember and comprehend difficult ideas.
- *Remote learning*: Especially relevant in times of pandemic, ICT enables remote learning, allowing children to continue their education from home. Better access options are made available to students with disabilities or immune disorders through remote learning. This also facilitates equal access to education for people who are visually impaired or deaf. This can help bridge gaps in access to education and ensure continuity of learning. The authors in [70] have suggested some general guidelines using ICT tools that maths teachers can use while teaching maths material remotely or in any other manner.

- *Creativity and innovation*: ICT tools like digital art programs and coding platforms foster creativity and innovation among children, encouraging them to explore new ideas and express themselves in new ways. Interactive educational settings encourage inquiry and discovery, while digital tools enable creators to express themselves through novel forms like animation and music [71]. By exposing students to cutting-edge technologies that encourage innovative thinking about the future and by giving them access to tools for prototyping and experimentation, ICT also contributes to the development of future innovators.
- *Communication and socialization*: Children can interact and converse with peers and family members via ICT, even when they live far apart. This can support children's social skills development and relationship maintenance. In [72], authors have discovered empirical support for the beneficial relationships between early adolescents in 20 ICILS participating nations' ICT-related behavioural and motivational traits and the frequency of ICT use for social contact.
- *Global awareness*: Children can learn about many cultures, languages, and viewpoints from around the world through ICT, which promotes cultural understanding and global consciousness. Educating our kids about globalization will help our nation get ready for the future. It is beneficial to comprehend and put the concept of globalization into practice by interacting with a group of teachers from a different nation.
- *Skill development*: Children who use ICT are able to acquire vital skills that are necessary in today's digital environment, like problem-solving, critical thinking, digital literacy, and teamwork. In [73], authors have reviewed the impact of children's informal computer use on their academic, cognitive, and social skills. They have also provided advice for parents, teachers, and other adults to set up informal computer encounters in order to maximize the potential benefits for children's development, based on the evidence that has been presented.
- *Accessibility*: Through the provision of tools and materials tailored to their individual requirements, ICT can increase the accessibility of learning for children with disabilities. Students with visual impairments can benefit from text-to-speech software [74, 75], while people with motor limitations can be empowered by speech recognition software. Children with learning challenges can find complex concepts entertaining when they play interactive learning games and simulations. ICT gives every kid the opportunity to participate in and succeed in school by customizing the learning process to meet their unique needs.

11.4.2 Negative Impact of ICT in Children

Children may experience negative consequences from ICT if it is not utilized responsibly or moderately. Digital gadget addiction and excessive screen time can cause physical health problems like obesity, bad posture, and eye strain. Unrestricted access to social media and the internet can also expose kids to predators, offensive information, and cyberbullying. Some of the key ways in which ICT can have negative effects on children are discussed below:

- *Cyberbullying*: ICT offers platforms for cyberbullying, where kids can be subjected to threats, abuse, or embarrassment on the internet. This may have detrimental implications on their well-being and mental health. The use of digital communication tools to harass, threaten, or intimidate others is known as cyberbullying, and it can have a detrimental impact on children's mental health and well-being. Cyberbullying, in contrast to traditional bullying, may happen around-the-clock and affect a large audience, making it challenging for victims to flee or get assistance. Cyberbullying can take many different forms, such as distributing rumours, sending harsh messages, or uploading embarrassing images or videos on the internet [76].
- *Exposure to inappropriate content:* ICT can expose children to improper content for a variety of reasons. Due to the abundance of information on the internet and the ease with which it can be accessed, children are more likely to stumble across unsuitable content whether using social media platforms, surfing, or conducting searches [77]. This problem is exacerbated by elements like user-generated content on social media, improper content on online gaming platforms, pop-up ads and misleading links, and a lack of parental monitoring. It is essential that parents and educators teach kids about safe internet behaviours, implement parental controls, use safe search settings, and keep an eye on their online activity to reduce exposure. Content blockers and filtering software can also aid in limiting access to objectionable content [78].
- *Health issues*: ICT-related sedentary behaviour and excessive screen time can cause physical health concerns like obesity, musculoskeletal disorders, and eye strain. Moreover, using ICT devices after midnight might mess with sleep cycles, which can result in weariness and sleep disorders. To address these health problems, it's critical to encourage a responsible use of ICT. Sports and outdoor play are two good ways to encourage kids to be physically active and prevent the negative impacts of being inactive. Enhancing the quality of sleep can also be accomplished by limiting screen time and creating a regular nighttime ritual. Musculoskeletal problems can also be avoided by teaching kids and parents the value of taking breaks from screens and maintaining proper posture when using ICT gadgets [79]. We can lessen the detrimental effects of ICT on children's health by encouraging good habits and appropriate ICT use.
- *Addiction*: For children, ICT—especially social media and gaming—can be addicting for a variety of reasons. Instant gratification from likes and comments is one of the characteristics that social media platforms use to feed users' need for social connection and ongoing reinforcement. It might be challenging to escape the rewarding, progressive, and socially interactive environment that gaming offers. These characteristics take advantage of children's brains' growing reward systems, which can result in obsessive

behaviour and possibly the neglect of other facets of life. Excessive use can lead to problems with self-control, time management, and social interactions [80].

- *Privacy concerns*: Children's limited experience and comprehension of privacy and security issues may prevent them from completely understanding the ramifications of sharing personal information online. They could be unaware that sharing details about themselves, like their entire name, residence, school, or images, puts them at risk of identity theft, cyberbullying, and other negative actions by unscrupulous people. Children may also be less cautious and more trusting when engaging online, which increases their risk of disclosing personal information carelessly [81]. To solve this problem, parents and educators must teach kids about internet privacy and safety, instil in them a sense of caution when disclosing personal information, and keep an eye on their online activities to make sure they are making safe decisions.
- *Impact on social skills*: Even though ICT provides amusement and connections, it can harm kids' social abilities in several ways. Overindulgence in screens deprives individuals of vital in-person relationships, impeding the growth of empathy and nonverbal cue interpretation abilities [82]. On social media, text-based communication can cause miscommunication and make it harder to identify the tone. Moreover, children's social comparison and anxiety might be exacerbated by the carefully controlled and frequently fictitious depictions on social media. In general, exposure to inaccurate online representations and a possible lack of in-person social interaction are the main causes of ICT's detrimental influence.
- *Educational impact*: Children who have easy access to information may be discouraged from exploring further, challenging sources, and honing their autonomous research abilities. In games and tutorials, pre-made answers and walkthroughs can reduce the requirement for original thought and innovative problem-solving. In addition, the constant barrage of stimuli and rapid reward provided by ICT might shorten attention spans and make it more difficult to concentrate on difficult activities or participate in imaginative play—all of which are essential for the development of creativity.
- *Digital divide*: Due to inadequate access to ICT, children from underprivileged families may already be more isolated in terms of educational and economic chances [83]. This phenomenon is known as the digital divide or digital gap. Their education is hampered by a lack of equipment and internet connection, since online learning tools and platforms are becoming more and more crucial. They lose out on important learning resources, virtual teamwork chances, and knowledge that could improve their academic experience. In addition, the social components of ICT are also inaccessible, which hinders their capacity to engage in online communities, establish online connections with peers, and acquire digital literacy abilities—all of which are essential in today's environment. Social inequality is maintained, and the achievement gap is widened by this digital exclusion.

11.5 CONCLUSION

Overall, ICT is essential to improving the legal system, advancing human rights, and empowering women and children. Through ICT, government agencies, a multitude of social organizations, and forums have been able to raise awareness regarding pressing problems, boost participation in outreach initiatives, promote the cause of marginalized groups' empowerment, and offer security and assistance. The development of support communities, the transparent dissemination of information, and the amplification of the voices of underrepresented groups in society have all been made easier by recent developments in communication technology. This results in a reduction of the gender disparity, readily accessible justice, the defence of children's rights, and an overall betterment of the society. Technology undoubtedly has the ability to improve society, but it's also necessary to take potential negative effects into account. The idea that ICT use contributes to marginalization and inequality is one argument against it. The divide between the rich and the marginalized is often widened because people who need support the most may not have access to the required technologies. Furthermore, vulnerable populations—such as women and children—may be seriously at danger from the dissemination of misleading information and damaging content on the internet. It is imperative to exercise caution when using ICT and to take potential unforeseen consequences into account. That being said, with cautious use of technology, we may work towards a future where the rights and welfare of women and children are respected, where justice and peace reign, by utilizing technology developments and creative solutions.

NOTES

1 https://ourworldindata.org/poverty
2 https://www.un.org/en/observances/world-population-day
3 https://data.worldbank.org/indicator/IT.CEL.SETS.P2
4 https://legalaffairs.gov.in/
5 https://www.scconline.com/, https://www.manupatrafast.com/ipAccess.aspx, https://www.aironline.in/,
6 indiankanoon.org, indiacode.nic.in
7 https://ourworldindata.org/gender-ratio
8 https://www.abs.gov.au/statistics/health/health-conditions-and-risks/national-health-survey/2022

REFERENCES

1. Vrasidas, C., Zembylas, M., & Glass, G. V. (Eds.). (2009). *ICT for Education, Development, and Social Justice*. IAP.
2. Benyekhlef, K., Amar, E., & Callipel, V. (2015). ICT-driven strategies for reforming access to justice mechanisms in developing countries. *World Bank Legal Review*, *6*, 325.
3. Ibekwe, C. S., & Onwuatuegwu, C. (2021). ICT in the administration of justice: Challenges and prospects for labour and productivity. *Journal of Commercial and Property Law*, *8*(1).

4. Abdulvaliev, A. (2017). Court, internet technologies and their role in ensuring the well-being of society. *European Proceedings of Social and Behavioural Sciences, 26*.
5. Yavuz, N., Karkin, N., & Yildiz, M. (2022). E-justice: A review and agenda for future research. In *Scientific Foundations of Digital Governance and Transformation*, 385–414. Springer.
6. Mehandru, N., & Koenig, A. (2018). ICTS, social media, & the future of human rights. *Duke Law & Technology Review, 17*, 129.
7. Jørgensen, R. F., Møller Pedersen, A., Benedek, W., & Nindler, R. (2015). *ICT and Human Rights*. FRAME.
8. Mackey, A., & Petrucka, P. (2021). Technology as the key to women's empowerment: A scoping review. *BMC Women's Health, 21*, 1–12.
9. Venkatesh, V., Sykes, T., & Zhang, X. (2020). ICT for development in rural India: A longitudinal study of women's health outcomes. *MIS Quarterly, 44*(2), 605–629.
10. Bakola, L., Chaidi, I., Drigas, A., Skianis, C., & Karagiannidis, C. (2022). Women with special educational needs. Policies & ICT for integration & equality. *Technium Social Sciences Journal, 28*, 67.
11. Sourdin, T., Li, B., & McNamara, D. M. (2020). Court innovations and access to justice in times of crisis. *Health Policy and Technology, 9*(4), 447–453.
12. Gladysheva, O. V., Kostenko, R. V., & Sementsov, V. A. (2019). Digitization: Problems of use and protection of information in criminal proceedings. In *Ubiquitous Computing and the Internet of Things: Prerequisites for the Development of ICT*, 395–401. Springer International Publishing.
13. Bailey, J. (2012). Digitization of court processes in Canada. In *Working Paper no 2*. Laboratory of Cyberjustice.
14. Liebman, B. L., Roberts, M. E., Stern, R. E., & Wang, A. Z. (2020). Mass digitization of Chinese court decisions: How to use text as data in the field of Chinese law. *Journal of Law and Courts, 8*(2), 177–201.
15. Sembiring, T. B., Maruf, I. R., Suryadi, S., Suyani, S., & Amin, M. (2022). Understanding the role of social media in shaping millenial generation legal awareness in the digital age. *Budapest International Research and Critics Institute-Journal (BIRCI-Journal), 5*(3), 18501–18511.
16. Vasiliy, L., & Vladimir, F. (2020). Legal awareness in a digital society. *Russian Law Journal, 8*(1), 138–157.
17. Barberá, P., Persily, N., & Tucker, J. A. (2020). Social media and democracy: The state of the field, prospects for reform.
18. Ahmed, R. K., Muhammed, K. H., Reitsakas, A., Pappel, I., & Draheim, D. (2020). Improving court efficiency through ICT integration: Identifying essential areas of improvement. In *ICT Analysis and Applications: Proceedings of ICT4SD 2019, Volume 2* (pp. 449–461). Springer Singapore.
19. Mohamad, A. M., & Sule, I. (2021). ICT-enabled applications for decision-making by the courts: Experiences from Malaysia and Nigeria. *International Journal of Law, Government and Communication, 6*(22), 189–196.
20. Aidonojie, P. A., Wakili, S. A., & Ayuba, D. (2023). Effectiveness of the administration of justice in Nigeria under the development of digital technologies. *Journal of Digital Technologies and Law, 1*(4), 1105–1131.
21. Walters, E. J. (Ed.). (2018). *Data-Driven Law: Data Analytics and the New Legal Services*. CRC Press.
22. Raghupathi, V., Zhou, Y., & Raghupathi, W. (2018). Legal decision support: Exploring big data analytics approach to modeling pharma patent validity cases. *IEEE Access, 6*, 41518–41528.

23. Flanagan, G. P., & Dewey, M. H. (2018). Where do we go from here: Transformation and acceleration of legal analytics in practice. *Georgia State University Law Review, 35*, 1245.
24. Bana, A., & Hertzberg, D. (2015). Data security and the legal profession: Risks, unique challenges and practical considerations. *Business Law International, 16*, 247.
25. Marune, A. E. M. S., & Hartanto, B. (2021). Strengthening personal data protection, cyber security, and improving public awareness in Indonesia: Progressive legal perspective. *International Journal of Business, Economics, and Social Development, 2*(4), 143–152.
26. Li, Y., & Liu, Q. (2021). A comprehensive review study of cyber-attacks and cyber security; Emerging trends and recent developments. *Energy Reports, 7*, 8176–8186.
27. St Eve, A. J., & Zuckerman, M. A. (2012). Ensuring an impartial jury in the age of social media. *Duke Law & Technology Review, 11*, 1.
28. Marder, N. S. (2014). Jurors and social media: Is a fair trial still possible. *SMU Law Review, 67*, 617.
29. Simpler, M. F., III (2012). The unjust web we weave: The evolution of social media and its psychological impact on juror impartiality and fair trials. *Law & Psychology Review, 36*, 275.
30. Kelly, L. (2019). Uses of digital technologies in managing and preventing conflict. *Brighton. Institute of Development Studies. K4D Helpdesk Report. Accessed April, 13*, 2023.
31. Cheshmehzangi, A. (2022). The role of ICT and smartness for peace-building processes and practices. In *ICT, Cities, and Reaching Positive Peace* (pp. 17–46). Springer Nature Singapore.
32. Alkhodair, S. A., Ding, S. H., Fung, B. C., & Liu, J. (2020). Detecting breaking news rumors of emerging topics in social media. *Information Processing & Management, 57*(2), 102018.
33. Mukoya, F., & Mukherjee, A. S. (2020). The Role of Social Capital in Mediating ICT-Enabled Peace Building Efforts: A Case Study from Kenya. In *The Future of Digital Work: The Challenge of Inequality: IFIP WG 8.2, 9.1, 9.4 Joint Working Conference, IFIPJWC 2020, Hyderabad, India, December 10–11, 2020, Proceedings* (pp. 326–340). Springer International Publishing.
34. Mukoya, F. (2023). Interplay of ICTs and social capital in building and scaling peace networks within contexts of violent ethnic conflicts: A study from Kenya.
35. Katz, Y. (2020). Interacting for peace: Rethinking peace through interactive digital platforms. *Social Media+ Society, 6*(2), 2056305120926620.
36. Yadav, U., & Soni, S. (2022). Communities strengthening peace and harmony: A technological perspective. *IITM Journal of Management and IT, 13*(2), 7–12.
37. Susanto, T., Sumardjo, S. S., & Rilus, A. K. (2022). The message of peace from the village: Development of religious harmony from Nglinggi Village. *Al-Balagh: Jurnal Dakwah Dan Komunikasi, 7*, 119–50.
38. Bungin, B., Wono, H. Y., & Shwari, E. J. A. (2021). Communication media technology and social harmony construction in the era of society 5.0 a critical view. *International Journal of Computer and Information System (IJCIS), 2*(4), 125–130.
39. Joseph, S. (2012). Social media, political change, and human rights. *Boston College International and Comparative Law Review, 35*, 145.
40. Miladi, N. (2016). Social media and social change. *Digest of Middle East Studies, 25*(1), 36–51.
41. Diamond, L., & Plattner, M. F. (Eds.). (2012). *Liberation Technology: Social Media and the Struggle for Democracy*. JHU Press.

42. Zubiaga, A., Liakata, M., Procter, R., Wong Sak Hoi, G., & Tolmie, P. (2016). Analysing how people orient to and spread rumours in social media by looking at conversational threads. *PLOS One*, *11*(3), e0150989.
43. Islam, M. S., Kamal, A. H. M., Kabir, A., Southern, D. L., Khan, S. H., Hasan, S. M., …, & Seale, H. (2021). COVID-19 vaccine rumors and conspiracy theories: The need for cognitive inoculation against misinformation to improve vaccine adherence. *PLOS One*, *16*(5), e0251605.
44. Bondielli, A., & Marcelloni, F. (2019). A survey on fake news and rumour detection techniques. *Information Sciences*, *497*, 38–55.
45. Mittelstadt, B. (2019). Principles alone cannot guarantee ethical AI. *Nature Machine Intelligence*, *1*(11), 501–507.
46. Hamal, M., Dieleman, M., De Brouwere, V., & de Cock Buning, T. (2020). Social determinants of maternal health: A scoping review of factors influencing maternal mortality and maternal health service use in India. *Public Health Reviews*, *41*, 1–24.
47. Silverio, S. A. (2021). Women's mental health as a public health priority: A call for action. *Journal of Public Mental Health*, *20*(1), 60–68.
48. Davenport, T., & Kalakota, R. (2019). The potential for artificial intelligence in healthcare. *Future Healthcare Journal*, *6*(2), 94–98.
49. Kumar, N., Narayan Das, N., Gupta, D., Gupta, K., & Bindra, J. (2021). Efficient automated disease diagnosis using machine learning models. *Journal of Healthcare Engineering*, *2021*(1), 9983652.
50. Nassif, A. B., Talib, M. A., Nasir, Q., Afadar, Y., & Elgendy, O. (2022). Breast cancer detection using artificial intelligence techniques: A systematic literature review. *Artificial Intelligence in Medicine*, *127*, 102276.
51. Dar, R. A., Rasool, M., & Assad, A. (2022). Breast cancer detection using deep learning: Datasets, methods, and challenges ahead. *Computers in Biology and Medicine*, *149*, 106073.
52. Mohammed, S. A., Darrab, S., Noaman, S. A., & Saake, G. (2020). Analysis of Breast Cancer Detection Using Different Machine Learning Techniques. In *Data Mining and Big Data: 5th International Conference, DMBD 2020, Belgrade, Serbia, July 14–20, 2020, Proceedings 5* (pp. 108–117). Springer Singapore.
53. Shankar, S. P., Supriya, M. S., Varadam, D., Kumar, M., Gupta, H., & Saha, R. (2023). A comprehensive study on algorithms and applications of artificial intelligence in diagnosis and prognosis: AI for healthcare. In *Digital Twins and Healthcare: Trends, Techniques, and Challenges* (pp. 35–54). IGI Global.
54. Khamisy-Farah, R., Furstenau, L. B., Kong, J. D., Wu, J., & Bragazzi, N. L. (2021). Gynecology meets big data in the disruptive innovation medical era: State-of-art and future prospects. *International Journal of Environmental Research and Public Health*, *18*(10), 5058.
55. Stoumpos, A. I., Kitsios, F., & Talias, M. A. (2023). Digital transformation in healthcare: Technology acceptance and its applications. *International Journal of Environmental Research and Public Health*, *20*(4), 3407.
56. Srivastava, D., Pandey, H., & Agarwal, A. K. (2023). Complex predictive analysis for health care: A comprehensive review. *Bulletin of Electrical Engineering and Informatics*, *12*(1), 521–531.
57. Adoun, M. A. S. D., Gagnon, M. P., Godin, G., Tremblay, N., Njoya, M. M., Ratté, S., …, & Ly, B. A. (2017). Information and communication technologies (ICT) for promoting sexual and reproductive health (SRH) and preventing HIV infection in adolescents and young adults. *The Cochrane Database of Systematic Reviews*, *2017*(2).

58. Stevens, F., Nurse, J. R., & Arief, B. (2021). Cyber stalking, cyber harassment, and adult mental health: A systematic review. *Cyberpsychology, Behavior, and Social Networking*, *24*(6), 367–376.
59. Brands, J., & Van Doorn, J. (2022). The measurement, intensity and determinants of fear of cybercrime: A systematic review. *Computers in Human Behavior*, *127*, 107082.
60. Anitha, L., & Sundharavadivel, D. (2012). Information and communication technology (ICT) and women empowerment. *International Journal of Advanced Research in Management and Social Sciences*, *1*(4), 143–152.
61. Abubakar, N., Dasuki, S. I., & Quaye, A. (2017). The contribution of ICTs to women empowerment: A capability perspective.
62. Monisha, D. G., Monisha, M., Pavithra, G., & Subhashini, R. (2016). Women safety device and application-FEMME. *Indian Journal of Science and Technology*, *9*(10), 1–6.
63. Hyndavi, V., Nikhita, N. S., & Rakesh, S. (2020, June). Smart Wearable Device for Women Safety Using IoT. In *2020 5th International Conference on Communication and Electronics Systems (ICCES)* (pp. 459–463). IEEE.
64. Gulati, G., Lohani, B. P., & Kushwaha, P. K. (2020, February). A Novel Application of IoT in Empowering Women Safety Using GPS Tracking Module. In *2020 Research, Innovation, Knowledge Management and Technology Application for Business Sustainability (INBUSH)* (pp. 131–137). IEEE.
65. Reddy, A. Y., Nikhitha, B., Manideep, B., Vivek, A., & Akshay, L. (2023). The role of social media in promoting the safety of women in Indian cities. *Turkish Journal of Computer and Mathematics Education (TURCOMAT)*, *14*(03), 1342–1351.
66. Abdel-Fattah, A. K. (2022). Women and cyberbullying. *International Journal of Childhood and Women's Studies*, *2*(1), 49–58.
67. Wang, M. J., Yogeeswaran, K., Andrews, N. P., Hawi, D. R., & Sibley, C. G. (2019). How common is cyberbullying among adults? Exploring gender, ethnic, and age differences in the prevalence of cyberbullying. *Cyberpsychology, Behavior, and Social Networking*, *22*(11), 736–741.
68. Das, K. (2019). The role and impact of ICT in improving the quality of education: An overview. *International Journal of Innovative Studies in Sociology and Humanities*, *4*(6), 97–103.
69. Chao-Fernandez, R., Román-García, S., & Chao-Fernandez, A. (2017). Analysis of the use of ICT through music interactive games as educational strategy. *Procedia-Social and Behavioral Sciences*, *237*, 576–580.
70. Dahal, N., Manandhar, N. K., Luitel, L., Luitel, B. C., Pant, B. P., & Shrestha, I. M. (2022). ICT tools for remote teaching and learning mathematics: A proposal for autonomy and engagements. *Online Submission*, *2*(1), 289–296.
71. Ala-Mutka, K., Punie, Y., & Redecker, C. (2008). ICT for learning, innovation and creativity. *Institute for Prospective Technological Studies (IPTS), European Commission, Joint Research Center. Technical Note: JRC, 48707.*
72. Areepattamannil, S., & Khine, M. S. (2017). Early adolescents' use of information and communication technologies (ICTs) for social communication in 20 countries: Examining the roles of ICT-related behavioral and motivational characteristics. *Computers in Human Behavior*, *73*, 263–272.
73. Wang, S. K., McPherson, S., Hsu, H. Y., & Tsuei, M. (2008). Information and communication technologies (ICTs) to develop teachers' global awareness. *International Journal of Education and Development Using ICT*, *4*(2), 89–104.
74. Isewon, I., Oyelade, J., & Oladipupo, O. (2014). Design and implementation of text to speech conversion for visually impaired people. *International Journal of Applied Information Systems*, *7*(2), 25–30.

75. Hagargund, A. G., Thota, S. V., Bera, M., & Shaik, E. F. (2017). Image to speech conversion for visually impaired. *International Journal of Latest Research in Engineering and Technology*, *3*(06), 09–15.
76. Nocentini, A., Zambuto, V., & Menesini, E. (2015). Anti-bullying programs and information and communication technologies (ICTs): A systematic review. *Aggression and Violent Behavior*, *23*, 52–60.
77. Bozzola, E., Spina, G., Agostiniani, R., Barni, S., Russo, R., Scarpato, E., …, & Staiano, A. (2022). The use of social media in children and adolescents: Scoping review on the potential risks. *International Journal of Environmental Research and Public Health*, *19*(16), 9960.
78. Ybarra, M. L., Finkelhor, D., Mitchell, K. J., & Wolak, J. (2009). Associations between blocking, monitoring, and filtering software on the home computer and youth-reported unwanted exposure to sexual material online. *Child Abuse & Neglect*, *33*(12), 857–869.
79. Lim, W., Lau, B., Chua, C., & Islam, F. (2021). Do information and communication technologies influence skills, competencies, health and well-being of teenagers? Current evidence. *EAI Endorsed Transactions on Pervasive Health and Technology*, *7*(27).
80. Li, S., Ren, P., Chiu, M. M., Wang, C., & Lei, H. (2021). The relationship between self-control and internet addiction among students: A meta-analysis. *Frontiers in Psychology*, *12*, 735755.
81. Acquisti, A., Brandimarte, L., & Loewenstein, G. (2020). Secrets and likes: The drive for privacy and the difficulty of achieving it in the digital age. *Journal of Consumer Psychology*, *30*(4), 736–758.
82. Graafland, J. H. (2018). New technologies and 21st century children: Recent trends and outcomes. OECD Education Working Papers, No. 179. OECD Publishing.
83. Ridge, T. (2002). *Childhood Poverty and Social Exclusion: From a Child's Perspective*. Policy Press.

12 Integration of Green Computing and E-Waste Management

Prerna Agarwal, Prateek Gupta, Pranav Shrivastava, Bharat Gupta, and Umang Mehrotra

12.1 INTRODUCTION

The past decade has seen an increase in electronic devices and the development of digital technologies, leading to various environmental issues especially energy usage and e-waste management [1]. Green computing, which identifies how people can reduce the impact of information technology (IT) activities through information and data, and e-waste management, which focusses on the safe disposal and recycling of electronic gadgets, are some of the most critical research areas in the technology industry that address the sustainability of the environment [2]. To avert the adverse impact of technology and guarantee environmental safety, it is vital to link green computing with e-waste management. The current chapter elaborates the relationship between the two in terms of the need to ensure that sustainable computing practices contribute to the proper management of electronic waste. The overall purpose is to determine how education and community involvement can foster sustainable practices by reinforcing sustainable computing while tackling the difficulties caused by electronic waste.

Green computing is alternatively known as sustainable computing or eco-friendly computing. It involves the implementation of principles and practices that could help reduce the environmental impact that IT operations have. These practices may include cutting down energy use, ensuring optimal use of resources, and reducing electronic waste at various stages of a computing device's life cycle [3]. The concept of green computing is drawn from the need to address the huge carbon footprint that defines the IT sector [4]. As the sector continues to grow and become an integral component of all aspects of human life, more emphasis is put on ensuring that it is environment friendly. E-waste management refers to the responsible handling, disposal, and recycling of electronic gadgets to control their environmental and health effects. Due to the high rate of electronic gadgets' growth and the short life of the products, e-waste is a significant problem all over the world. Poor disposal of the products leads to contamination of the toxins contained in the products leading to a health hazard. For proper disposal and resource recovery, the management approach must cut across the collection, recycling, and policy framework [5]. The purpose of this chapter includes the following:

1. To provide a comprehensive review of literature on green computing and e-waste management, including definitions, principles, key components, current practices, and technologies.

DOI: 10.1201/9781003471356-12

2. To examine the role of education in promoting e-waste awareness and sustainable practices.
3. To explore community engagement strategies for fostering sustainable e-waste management practices.
4. To analyse the synergies between green computing, education, and community engagement in addressing the challenges of electronic waste.
5. To identify challenges and future prospects for integrating green computing and e-waste management practices.

The chapter will provide a comprehensive analysis of the integration of green computing and e-waste management, highlighting the importance of this synergy in achieving a sustainable future.

12.2 GREEN COMPUTING

Green computing also referred to as green IT or green technology is the use of computing resources in a sustainable and environmentally sound manner. In broader terms, it can also be defined as the study and exploration of designing, manufacturing, using, and discarding or disposing of different computing devices like monitors, CPUs, and servers efficiently and in a way that minimizes their impact on the environment [6]. Green computing strives to reduce the environmental impact of computers and other devices. The main goals of green computing include the following:

- *Promote recycling*: One of the major goals of green computing is to promote recycling by promoting circular economy. It aims to reduce the impact on environment by reducing the amounts of non-renewable resources as well as non-biodegradable materials like plastics needed for production of electronic devices.
- *Minimizing cost*: Green computing also aims to cut down the energy consumed for computing resources. One example of this is the "sleep mode", now available in almost all devices which switch off the device when it is not in use which reduce the consumption of energy.
- *Sustainability*: Data centres consume a lot of energy and thus also produce a lot of carbon dioxide. By following green computing practices, these carbon emissions can be reduced.
- *Switching to renewable energy sources*: The switch from non-renewable to renewable sources of energy will be a big step towards reducing the global carbon emissions.

The ultimate goal of green computing is to make efficient computing devices which are further powered as efficient as possible to help reduce their impact on the environment. Green computing is majorly divided into four components which are necessary to be implemented to completely address environmental impacts of computing [7]:

1. *Green use*: It involves reducing the energy consumption of computers, data centres, and other computing devices and using them in a more environment-friendly manner. In case of data centres, this can be done with the

help of virtualization. The "sleep mode" in computing devices was invented as a way to save energy while they were not in use.

2. *Green disposal*: It involves reusing computing devices which can be reused and if not then refurbishing or recycling those computing devices and other electronic equipment.
3. *Green design*: It involves designing computing devices which can last longer without the need to be replaced. They have to be designed while keeping energy-efficiency and environment in mind.
4. *Green manufacturing*: Manufacturers should be able to produce computing devices and other equipment with minimal impact on the environment.

12.2.1 Energy-efficient Computing

Energy-efficient computing simply means designing and building computer systems in a way that they utilize energy efficiently and also try to minimize its consumption. Computer systems are very heavily reliant on energy and it is the only factor that limits their computing capabilities. Designing energy-efficient algorithms is also a crucial step in achieving energy-efficient computing [8].

As the use of different computing devices and networks is increasing all over the world, there is a need to make them more energy-efficient so that they have less impact on the environment. This energy-efficiency can also help in saving operational costs in big businesses all over the world. Many researches into energy-efficient computing are already going on in many universities all over the world. Researchers have also proposed some minor changes in hardware and software of computing devices that would help them consume less energy than they currently do. Many researchers have also suggested energy-efficient algorithms for everyday activities like sorting and web searches that consume less resources. These algorithms could also have a huge impact on processing of big data.

The carbon emissions from the IT sector amounted to about 1.8%–2.8% of the global emission in 2020. In retrospect this amount might seem negligible but it is equivalent to about 730 Mt CO_2. The IT sector also uses 3.6% or 800 TWh of the total electricity produced globally [9]. Most of the power consumption comes from user devices, data centres, etc. Thus, designing more efficient computing devices (mobile phones, computers, etc.) and algorithms could go a long way in reducing the amount of carbon produced globally.

12.2.2 Sustainable Design and Manufacturing

When any electronic product is designed and manufactured, the role of the company/manufacturer is very important. The first requirement should always be demand and usefulness of the product. A sustainable design for the product means the way it can be made more eco-friendly at all stages of its life [10]. Mainly, the components used while designing and manufacturing should be such that they should emit less radiations and built-in parts so that they can be removed or dismantled easily.

The transport and distribution can be done without much hassles, which means the packaging should be with green material or can be recycled. Also, when it is no longer in use, it can be easily recycled or disposed of safely. Manufacturers/industries can help directly to the consumers:

- They can provide options or facilitate the consumer to get the repair of the products at their place so that the product should not become an e-waste.
- Make the products which are long lasting.
- The electronic product should be such that the components used should be of good quality and can be recycled.
- The manufacturers should set up a utility to further collect the e-waste from their consumers so that it can be disposed safely.

12.2.3 Recycling and Circular Economy in IT

With the rapidly advancing technologies all around the world and the rapid consumption of resources, we have a responsibility to follow sustainable practices and reduce the amount of resources used as much as we can. One thing for allowing this to happen is by following the circular economy model/framework. To fully understand the need of circular economy, we have to first understand its counterpart, the traditional linear economy model [11].

Linear economy follows a simple take-make-dispose model. It is simple in its design and is followed with a short-term profit in mind. It simply involves collecting resources (take), transforming the collected resources into products for consumption (make), and finally discarding the unwanted materials (dispose). Linear economy consumes a lot of resources and does not make complete use of them in a sustainable manner. It also produces a lot of CO_2 emissions which are very harmful to our already delicate atmosphere [12].

Herein comes the concept of circular economy. Circular economy involves the use of limited resources in a more sustainable manner. It focusses on designing and manufacturing products that can be used for as long as possible and later can be recycled and reused again for production [13]. It believes in keeping the added value of a product and reduces the number of raw materials needed as much as possible. It is primarily based on the 3R (Reduce, Reuse, and Recycle) approach.

One prime example of this economy being followed for green computing is urban mining. As its name might suggest, it involves mining or extraction of precious metals from thrown-away electronic devices. Manufacturers use many precious materials like gold and copper in making different circuit boards and machinery for electronic devices. These metals can be extracted from these devices when they become old and are discarded and can be used again for production purposes. The total e-waste produced in 2019 was 53.6 million tonnes. The raw materials inside this waste were worth more than $57 billion but only some of this value could be recovered with sustainable practices [14].

To demonstrate how profitable as well as sustainable urban mining can be, we will take a look at a company from New Zealand called Mint Innovation [15].

Mint Innovation uses naturally sourced microbes as well as inexpensive chemicals to extract precious metals from the discarded electronic waste. It is estimated that they have the capabilities of generating about $30 million every year. They demonstrate how the e-waste industry is a literal treasure trove. But the problem encountered in this processing of e-waste is that there is still not a lot of infrastructure built for e-waste processing (Figure 12.4).

Many countries from around the world have also started adopting circular economy (Figure 12.1) as a way to curb the damage caused by the production of e-waste. One such country is Japan. It has one of the most advanced e-waste legislations in Asia [16]. Most of the e-waste produced in Japan is recycled under two acts: The act of promotion of recycling of small EEE (2011) and the act on recycling of specific kinds of home appliances. Japan also has a very strong system for collection of different kinds of e-waste. Under this system the consumers are liable to deliver end-of-life products to a collection point. From this collection point, collection services are provided by the manufacturer and retailers or some other organization like the AEHA. Manufacturers are encouraged to use recycled materials in their products and they are also responsible to finance the recycling of their own product. Japan also has a monitoring system in which special receipts are provided to end users from retailers which helps them keep track of how their collected products are treated.

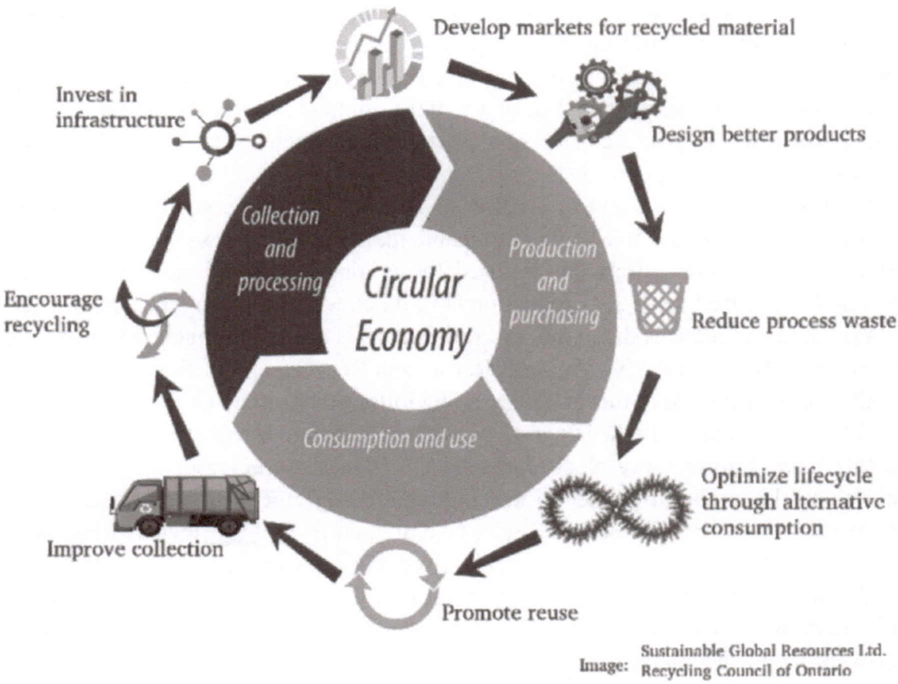

FIGURE 12.1 The circular economy model [17].

12.3 E-WASTE MANAGEMENT STRATEGIES

E-waste short for electronic and electrical waste consists of all items electrical in nature (containing some circuitry) and their components that have been discarded by their owners or have reached their end of life. It consists of many hazardous materials like lead, cadmium, and PCB that can be harmful to the environment as well as the human well-being. Figure 12.2 shows some of the major hazardous materials and emissions from e-waste [18].

According to the latest statistics, more than 50 million metric tons of e-waste are produced every year which is about 2.6% of the total waste (more than 2 billion metric tons) [20]. In hindsight this may look like a very small amount but it is almost equivalent to the weight of 3.3 lakh blue whales or 10 million elephants. Of the total e-waste produced that is actually recycled only amounts to about 17%. Figure 12.3 shows the global e-waste generation (year 2010–2019) and projected e-waste generation (year 2020–2030) [20].

E-waste can be briefly categorized into six categories [21]:

1. *Temperature exchange equipment*: It can also be referred to as cooling and heating equipment, including refrigerators, air conditioners, and heaters
2. *Large equipment*: Items like washing machines, dryers, printers, and dish-washers
3. *Small equipment*: Common household items like microwaves, vacuum cleaners, cameras, and calculators; also includes small medical devices
4. *Small IT and telecommunication equipment*: Mobile phones, routers, PCs, etc.
5. *Lamps*: Fluorescent lamps, LEDs
6. *Screens and monitors*: Televisions, monitors, laptops, etc.

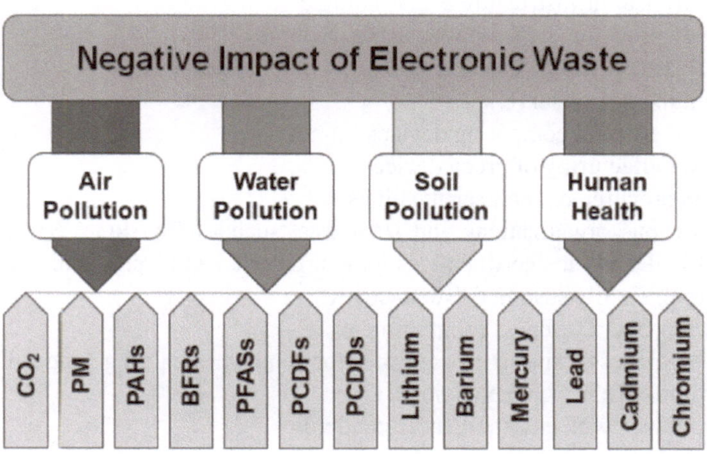

FIGURE 12.2 Major pollutants and hazardous materials that can be generated from e-waste when improperly dumped or managed [19].

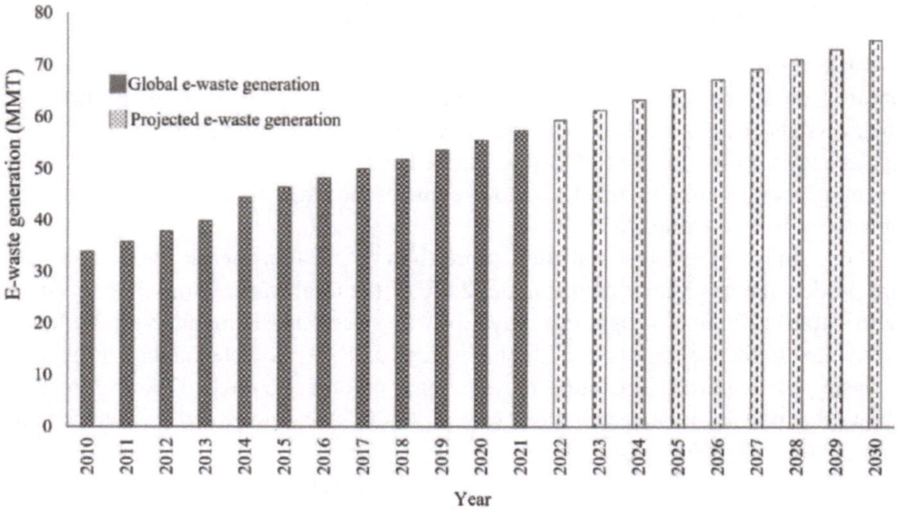

FIGURE 12.3 Global e-waste generation (year 2010–2019) and projected e-waste generation (year 2020–2030).

Government all over the world adopted some best practices to promote green computing and reduce the impact of e-waste:

1. Energy-efficient Data centre
   a. Advanced cooling technologies usage in data centres
   b. Efficient power distribution systems
   c. Optimized server configurations to minimize energy consumption.
2. Cloud computing
   a. Sharing of computer resources among different or multiple users
   b. Physical infrastructure is not required
3. Energy procurement from renewable resources
   a. Power should be used using solar, wind, or hydropower
4. Virtualization of servers
5. Energy-efficient computing devices
   a. Manufacturing of green devices
6. Green procurement and certifications
   a. Various organizations and standards, such as ENERGY STAR and LEED, provide certifications for energy-efficient IT products and environmentally sustainable data centres
7. Training and awareness programme
   a. Awareness training programmes for employees on usage and safe disposal of electronic equipment
8. Compliance with environmental standards
9. Smart grids
   a. Energy-efficient smart building technologies and smart grids allow organizations to optimize energy use based on real-time demand and availability

10. Recycling
    a. Safe disposal and recycling of e-waste

12.3.1 Legislative Frameworks and Policies

Every country has different frameworks and policies but globally the goal is same, i.e. recycling and safe disposal of e-waste to save the environment [16].

- **European Union:**
  - *Waste Electrical and Electronic Equipment (WEEE) Directive*: The EU has the WEEE Directive, which establishes guidelines for the collection, recycling, and treatment of e-waste. It places responsibility on manufacturers to manage the end-of-life planning and future treatment of their products and sets targets for collection and recycling.
  - Under EU directives and national implementing laws, consumers can return any e-waste, packaging, or batteries to a municipal collection point or to a retail outlet free of charge. Manufacturers are then responsible for financing collection, recycling, and recovery from collection points onwards. Mainly, manufacturers/producers are responsible for paying costs.
- The **United States:**
  - *Resource Conservation and Recovery Act (RCRA)*: The U.S. EPA administers the RCRA, which addresses hazardous waste management, including e-waste.
- **China:**
  - China has regulations for management methods for the restriction of the use of hazardous substances in electrical and electronic products.
  - The guidelines for safe treatment and disposal of electronic waste are already in place to save the environment.
  - Legislations include prevention and control of pollution from WEEE.
  - It controls use of hazardous substances in e-waste and management through "3R– reduce, reuse, recycle".
  - The focus on eco-design while manufacturing the products, storage, and safe recycling results in the prevention of pollution.
  - The Circular Economy Promotion Law, Administrative Rules on Prevention of Pollution by WEEE in 2008, put forward the EPR principle, which was formalized in 2012, requiring manufacturers to carry out environmentally safe management.
- **Japan:**
  - In Japan, two main legislations control the management of e-waste. Under these rules, a recycling-based economic system is established in which home appliances are regulated. The rules define the responsibilities of stakeholders and determine waste collection points. The rules ensure that waste parts collected are reused, standards and minimum targets for recycling rate are set, and new measures to reduce waste and extend product life are introduced.

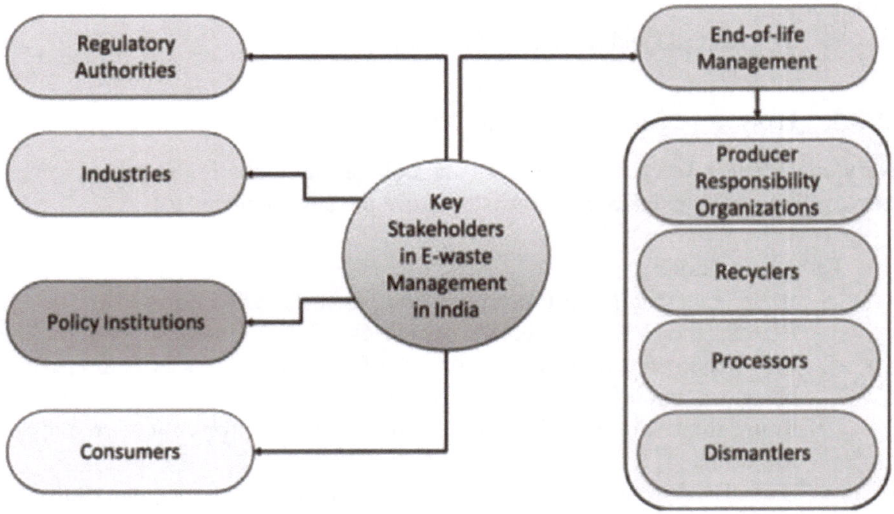

FIGURE 12.4 Key stakeholders in e-waste management in India [16].

- **India:**
  - *E-Waste (Management and Handling) Rules, 2011*: India has specific rules for the management and handling of e-waste.
  - These rules require manufacturers to implement extended producer responsibility (EPR), set up collection centres, and ensure environmentally sound recycling.
  - India has separate rules for management of spent batteries which are regulated by the Battery (Management and Handling) Rules, 2001. The objective of the battery rules is to channelize used lead-acid batteries for recycling in an environmentally sound manner. The 2020 amendments have further expanded the battery chemistries covered under the rules to new lithium-ion and other similar batteries. They have mandated tracking through online records, safe formal recycling, and data management, with clear outline of roles and responsibilities for the involved stakeholders (Figure 12.4).

12.3.2 Technological Innovations in E-Waste Recycling

Many innovations in technology have taken place in recent years which can bring revolution for managing e-waste [22]:

1. Robotics and AI can be used for segregation practice of e-waste components. Using proper AI algorithms, the model can be trained.
2. Waste to energy can be made by using incinerators which further produce energy that can be utilized as a fuel.
3. Advanced shredding and crushing techniques can be used to break down the bigger components into smaller parts.

4. Some electronic and electrical components use rare and costly metals also, and biometallurgical techniques can be used for the proper segregation and reuse.
5. Closed-loop recycling is done so that some e-waste components can be used again in manufacturing. This is the main concept of circular economy also.
6. Blockchain can be used to improve transparency. Blockchain can track the movement of electronic waste from collection to recycling, ensuring responsible and accountable disposal practices.
7. The manufacturers or NGOs or government organizations can introduce methods to collect e-waste directly from source, i.e. citizens/consumers.
8. The buyback policy should be introduced by manufacturers so that e-waste can be collected and incentives should be given to consumers.

12.3.3 Challenges in e-waste Management

E-waste represents a huge threat to our world. Many of the devices coming under e-waste are made from harmful chemicals and metals. There is a need for proper management and disposal of e-waste, but dealing with e-waste is not as easy as it may look. Some of the challenges faced in e-waste management and disposal are listed below [23, 24]:

1. *Material separation*: With the evolving technology, electronic devices have also become increasingly complex. For proper recycling of e-waste, different components and materials of a device must be separated. But due to the complexity of devices made today, this process is very resource intensive.
2. *Efficiency*: The consumption of electronics is rising day by day. As a result, the amount of e-waste produced is on a constant rise. The sorting centres (where different components like precious metals are extracted from e-waste) require more cost-efficient methods to deal with e-waste. These solutions have to be able to deal with a large influx of waste and to do it in as less time as possible.
3. *Lack of uniform regulations*: The regulations regarding the management of e-waste vary from region to region. In some places it is very strict, while in others it is quite lax. The absence of uniform international regulations makes it harder for different industries to adopt a standardized practice for recycling e-waste.
4. *Infrastructure*: A big obstacle that hampers the management of e-waste is the availability of proper infrastructure. Despite the growing concerns surrounding e-waste, the infrastructure need for its proper handling is still inadequate on a global scale. Without the proper facilities, the e-waste collected is either dumped in landfills or improperly disposed of.
5. *Lack of awareness*: Perhaps one of the most dangerous challenges faced by e-waste management is the lack of awareness of people about e-waste and its harmful impact on the environment. There are still many places in the world where people are not aware of the threat that e-waste represents and are thus ignorant to its proper disposal.

To win the war against e-waste and bring about a change in our world, it is important for us to tackle the above-mentioned challenges. Only by doing so can we develop solution and strategies which will work against e-waste.

12.3.4 E-Waste and Sustainable Development

The United Nations (UN) and its member states adopted the 2030 agenda in September 2017, which outlined 17 sustainable development goals for protecting the planet, ending poverty, etc. to be achieved by 2030 [25]. The increase of e-waste and its improper disposal in landfills or with the help of incineration are a detriment to achieving the SDGs. According to GEM (Global E-waste Monitor) 2020 report, the management of e-waste is directly linked with many SDGs like

SDG 3: Good health and well-being
SDG 6: Clean water and sanitation
SDG 8: Descent work and economic growth
SDG 14: Life below water

The indicator adopted by UN for e-waste is as follows:

$$\text{Sub}-\text{indicator one}-\text{waste} = \frac{Totale-waste\ recycled}{Totale-waste\ generated}$$

The proper handling of e-waste comes under the following SDGs as defined by the UN:

SDG 11: Make cities and human settlements inclusive, safe, resilient, and sustainable

Most of the e-waste is produced in urban areas like cities. With the increasing population and rapid urbanization, there is a need for development of solutions and new technologies for improving recycling and collection rates as well as for proper handling of e-waste.

SDG 12: Ensure sustainable consumption and production patterns

As the population of the world is increasing, they are consuming more and more products. Therefore, it is important to make the production and consumption of these products more sustainable. One way of achieving this is with the help of circular economy.

12.4 ROLE OF EDUCATION IN E-WASTE AWARENESS

Incorporating the study of e-waste and its management into the curricula of different schools is a crucial step in dealing with the threat that e-waste represents [26]. There is a need for future generations to understand the impact e-waste or waste in general has on our mother earth. They need to be taught the steps that have to be taken to reduce e-waste (Figure 12.5). The war against e-waste is not one that can be won in a small amount of time. It requires the work of many generations to have a significant impact. We must not pass a world already on course to doom to our future generations and have them curse us for the steps we did not take to make it better. It is important to teach children in schools about e-waste and its impact so that they can learn from previous generations and not repeat their mistakes. Teaching them about e-waste might also help them discover innovative and never before seen ideas that with successful implementation can help in reducing the dangers of e-waste and thus work to save our planet.

1. *Awareness and understanding*: To reduce the amount of e-waste produced or to be able to recycle more e-waste, spreading awareness about it is very important.
2. *Skill development*: Skills to professionals for manufacturing of green IT hardware and software and efficient ways to manage electronic waste.

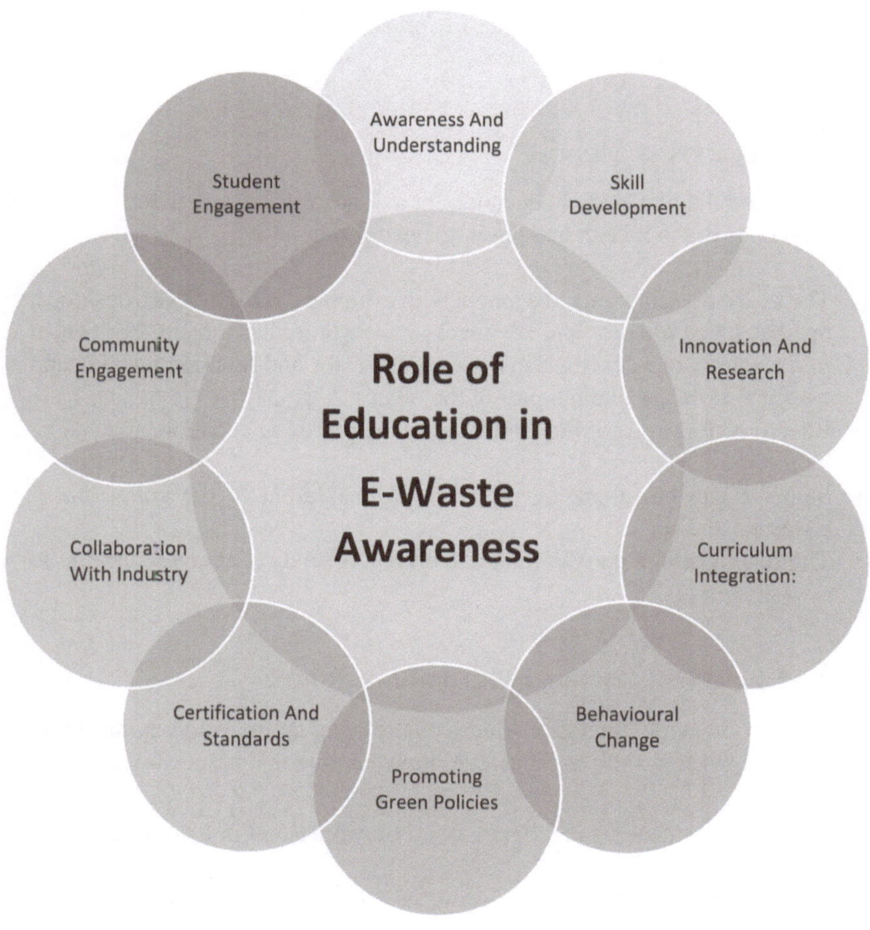

FIGURE 12.5 Role of education in e-waste awareness.

3. *Innovation and research*: development of environment friendly technologies and sustainable computing solutions.
4. *Curriculum integration*: This includes topics like energy-efficient programming, data centre management, and sustainable software design.
5. *Behavioural change*: This can include training employees and students to turn off devices when not in use, optimizing energy settings, and promoting the use of energy-efficient hardware.
6. *Promoting green policies*: Use of renewable energy sources, reducing electronic waste, and adopting sustainable IT procurement practices.
7. Certification and standards
8. Collaboration with Industry
9. *Community engagement*: Community engagement plays a pivotal role in waste recycling and reduction. To promote a culture of environmental responsibility, it is important to engage in community engagement.
10. *Student-led engagement*: It is a very good way to make students aware about the detriments of e-waste. Students can also participate in various drives, organize workshops, etc. to spread awareness as well as increase their own knowledge.

12.4.1 Education in Schools

The schools are the first step of education for a child. Whatever activities and learning a child does in school can be seen in the behaviour.

- The use of reusability can be taught with examples like out of two desktops, one has a bad monitor and keyboard and the other has a bad CPU. Out of this scenario, one desktop can be repaired easily, and functioning CPU and working keyboard and monitor of the other.
- Bins to collect e-waste like batteries can be placed in corridors and can be monitored.
- Students can be taught by practical demonstration of the collection of e-waste exercise.
- The school can tie up with manufacturers to give discount on return of old e-waste items.

12.4.2 Education in Higher Education Institutions

Higher education institutions give wide scope to open up the young minds that can grasp more knowledge and are capable of implementing that practically.

- Awareness campaigns can be arranged by youngsters in a community for the collection of e-waste.
- Talks from the experts can be arranged for the young minds to increase their circumference on e-waste management.
- Nukkad natak (street play) can be presented to raise awareness in the localities.

- Knowledge about circular economy and its benefits should be given.
- Certification programmes can be arranged by government organization to motivate the youngsters.

12.5 COMMUNITY ENGAGEMENT FOR SUSTAINABLE E-WASTE PRACTICES

Community engagement plays a crucial role in promoting sustainable practices for the integration of green computing and e-waste management. By involving local communities, organizations, and stakeholders, initiatives can be developed and implemented to raise awareness, facilitate behaviour change, and foster collective action towards reducing electronic waste and promoting environmentally friendly computing practices. This section surveys numerous approaches for community engagement in sustainable practices associated with green computing and e-waste management. For instance, the Department of the Environment, San Francisco has implemented a community engagement programme called "Zero Waste", which aims to encourage recycling, composting, and waste reduction. The programme has notably boosted public involvement in sustainable waste disposal and reduced landfill waste and greenhouse gas emissions in San Francisco by as much as 80% and 25%, respectively. As San Francisco shows, community engagement ensures environmental sustainability by allowing residents, businesses, and schools to work on it.

Other communities can likewise effect such an achievement by sharing information. Sustainable solutions can be developed and implemented to address the growing challenges of electronic waste and climate change through collaborative efforts between government agencies, NGOs, businesses, and community groups.

12.5.1 Community Awareness Programmes

Community awareness programmes are a useful way of sensitizing people on the importance of sustainable computing and proper e-waste disposal. The programmes take the form of workshops, seminars, and public campaigns which are designed to enlighten people on the environmental effects of electronic gadgets, the merits of energy-wise computing, and the necessity for e-waste recycling. Community awareness programmes will work by enlisting the backing of non-governmental organizations (NGOs), local governments, and learning institutions to educate and sensitize people on the need to take an active part in sustainable computing practices.

Ways in which community awareness programmes can help to raise concern about e-waste are the following:

- Providing information about the environmental and health hazards associated with improper e-waste disposal.
- Raising awareness about the value of e-waste recycling and the potential for resource recovery.
- Informing about the usefulness of buyback policies for the consumer as well as manufacturer.

- Offering proper methods and information on e-waste disposal and recycling.
- Conducting training sessions and workshops for demonstrating the correct procedures for segregating, collecting, and disposing of e-waste.
- Enhancing understanding and practical skills by hands-on sessions.
- Disseminating information by participation in local fairs, festivals, and community events.
- Launching awareness campaigns through posters, banners, and community announcements.
- Calling local celebrities to share awareness in the community.

12.5.2 Collaborative Initiatives with NGOs and Local Bodies

The NGOs and local governmental bodies can amplify the impact of community engagement efforts by collaborating with local communities. NGOs often have expertise in environmental advocacy and community outreach, while local governments can provide support through policy development, infrastructure investment, and public resources. The community groups can leverage their networks and resources to implement sustainable computing and e-waste management initiatives at the grassroots level by forming partnerships with these organizations [27].

12.5.3 The Role of Media and Social Platforms

Social media has become an important tool for providing a medium for the dissemination of information and participation of public and young generation in digital activities in the form of activities/quizzes etc. Media and social platforms play a vital role in disseminating information and mobilizing communities around environmental issues. Community engagement efforts can utilize traditional media channels such as television, radio, and newspapers, as well as social media platforms like Facebook, Twitter, and Instagram, to reach diverse audiences and promote sustainable practices. Creating engaging content, sharing success stories, and fostering online communities can help raise awareness and inspire individuals to take action towards greener computing and responsible e-waste disposal [28]. The awareness about green computing can be taken up as a challenge/short film/documentary/reels/contests etc. and winners can be announced. Examples of these platforms where these types of activities take place include the following:

- https://mygov.in,
- https://blog.mygov.in/closing-announcement-of-short-video-making-competition-on-green-clean-energy/,
- https://www.mygov.in/task/inviting-innovative-ideas-green-electronics-sustainable-future/.

Citizens can share information on social media platforms about the green clubs in their area and the innovative activities any community or society is doing for safe disposal and recycling of e-waste. Success stories can be shared on Facebook and

Instagram about the green initiatives taken by an individual/group. The collection and disposal of e-waste can be leveraged. Smart users can discuss and provide innovative ideas to reduce e-waste.

Media plays a crucial role to cover live events, news, and any social activity which can be of great help to general public. The society has many experts and people having this calibre but they are not known to the masses but media has the power to enlighten these pearls and show their social activity about their steps taken towards green computing. Also, media can raise awareness by organizing education programmes about the e-waste collection and safe disposal, reduction of usage, and harmful effects that can be generated if proper measures are not taken to handle the situation. The influence of media in the form of visuals and voices is such that its impact remains for a very long time in the mind of an individual, so any knowledge given through this will last longer.

12.6 SYNERGY BETWEEN GREEN COMPUTING, EDUCATION, AND COMMUNITY ENGAGEMENT

The green computing, education, and community engagement are linked with each other strongly as all these create environmental awareness, sustainable practices, and responsible use of technology within local communities. The awareness drives/campaigns are required to be organized for the community to be aware of the harmful effects of it. The informative material should be distributed through small booklets in schools, institutions, societies, etc. In this way only, society will be able to know that how e-waste can be recycled and properly disposed. The benefits should be known to the community that how carbon emissions can be reduced, reusability can be done, and depletion of renewable resources can be saved.

Education is the only tool through which young minds can participate in collection drives for e-waste, organize small workshops locally to aware the masses about the harmful impacts on the environment which can explode if action through education and involvement of communities is not taken at this time. Raising awareness through this can enhance the participation to a larger extent where with the help of government and NGOs, the practical action can be done. Also, collection centres can be built in an area where e-waste can be easily dropped by public from where proper transportation for safe disposal can be done.

12.6.1 The Role of Education in Creating Green Computing Professionals

The shared goal of green computing and e-waste management is to reduce impact of IT infrastructure on the environment. In the current scenario, the e-waste is treated as a normal waste for a consumer and mostly treated in a similar manner. For a sustainable e-waste management and green computing, joint efforts are required [26]. It is the time that every consumer, institution, and manufacturer should start implementing 3R, i.e. Reduce, Reuse, and Recycle. Reduce means that e-waste should be reduced as paperless systems can reduce the use of deployed printers. Reuse means using existing e-waste to produce some innovative things. Recycle the remaining e-waste, thus promoting circular economy.

For promoting green computing and e-waste management and for creating green computing professionals, the following steps are required:

- Educate people about the disposal of e-waste with proper segregation and classification.
- Green computing emphasizes on good and green design of any equipment and e-waste management focusses on long lifespan of electrical/electronic product so that it should not get obsolete.
- Green computing focusses on avoiding the use of harmful and hazardous electronic materials in products like lead and mercury. If used, then e-waste out of these devices needs safe handling and disposal to prevent pollution in the environment.
- Educate and train about the awareness and practices of management of e-waste with the help of communities, NGOs, and help groups.
- Extended producer responsibility (EPR) is the agenda for both; the manufacturer should be held responsible for improper disposal of their products.

12.6.2 Community-Led Sustainable Practices in E-Waste Reduction

The sector of e-waste management is informal so it is required that community/society be part of it to organize it up to some level. The community participation can improve the reduction of e-waste globally with aim to have less burden on landfills and hence better the environment.

- Collection drives for e-waste can be organized through communities. They can further arrange for segregation. Collection points can be set up in the societies/towns so that people donate or throw their e-waste at those collection points. The NGOs can facilitate further transportation to the recycling units.
- E-waste awareness campaigns should be organized to educate about the harmful impact of improper management. The youth can be an important part of the campaigns.
- The incentive programmes should be given to people by manufacturers/producers if they properly recycle the waste through them. This also initiates circular economy principles.

12.6.3 Benefits of Integrating Green Computing Education with Community Engagement

Integrating green computing education with community engagement offers numerous benefits for both individuals and society as a whole. Stakeholders can achieve greater awareness, participation, and impact in addressing environmental challenges associated with IT consumption and electronic waste (e-waste) by combining efforts to promote sustainable computing practices with community involvement. One significant benefit is the empowerment of individuals with knowledge and skills to adopt greener computing habits and make informed decisions about electronic device usage and disposal. Individuals can learn about energy-efficient computing practices, responsible e-waste management, and the environmental impacts of their digital footprint through educational initiatives and community engagement activities. This knowledge equips individuals with the tools to minimize their environmental impact, reduce energy consumption, and contribute to the circular economy by recycling and repurposing electronic devices [29].

Fostering a sense of collective responsibility and social cohesion around environmental sustainability could be achieved through integrating green computing education with community engagement. By leveraging diverse perspectives, resources, and networks to generate broader impact, initiatives would imply actively involving local communities, organizations, and stakeholders in shared activities to promote greener computing practices. For example, community-led projects such as electronic waste recycling drives, energy-saving competitions, and educational workshops facilitate opportunities for meaningful interaction and collaboration, promoting a sustainability mindset in neighbourhoods, workplaces, and schools.

Essentially, positive economic outcomes may derive from the integration of green computing education with community engagement. This activity could first and foremost spur innovation and job creation. As individuals and organizations adopt greener computing practices, there is a growing demand for sustainable technologies, products, and services, driving market growth and investment in green IT solutions. By fostering a skilled workforce and entrepreneurial ecosystem focussed on sustainability, communities can capitalize on emerging opportunities in the green economy while reducing environmental impacts and enhancing resilience to climate change [30]. Integrating green computing education with community engagement offers a wide range of benefits, including empowering individuals, fostering social cohesion, and stimulating economic growth. Stakeholders can achieve greater awareness, participation, and impact in promoting sustainable computing practices and addressing environmental challenges associated with electronic waste and energy consumption, by combining educational initiatives with collaborative community action.

12.7 CHALLENGES AND FUTURE PROSPECTS

12.7.1 Existing Challenges in Implementing Green Computing and E-Waste Management

Green computing and e-waste management are associated with many difficulties due to underdevelopment and its impact on the environment, albeit widely recognized. One of the fundamental problems is the lack of standardized electronic waste disposal and recycling policies and laws at the global level. In some countries, the lack of proper policymaking and enforcement mechanisms results in the illegal handling of electronic devices. It further causes environmental pollution and related health problems. The sector's complexity, characterized by multiple participants, technologies, and supply chains, makes it even more difficult to efficiently coordinate and be responsible for the process.

The second difficulty is the relatively low awareness of green computing and related laws and standards. Even though energy-efficient computing and sustainable design offer potential benefits, many individuals and organizations lack the knowledge and incentives to adopt greener technologies and practices. Additionally, the rapid pace of technological innovation and product obsolescence exacerbates the problem by generating large volumes of electronic waste with short lifespans [31].

12.7.2 Potential Solutions and Innovations

There are several possible solutions and innovative technologies that can address the above challenges and promote green computing while enhancing e-waste management practices. A potential solution involves creating EPR that would make producers financially and legally responsible for their products throughout the life cycle, including the post-consumer disposal. EPR can help to reduce e-waste generation and contribute to resource recovery by incentivizing producers to develop sustainable products and investing in recycling infrastructures.

Technological solutions include the use of blockchain, artificial intelligence, and Internet of Things to ensure traceability, transparency, and efficiency. Blockchain technology, for example, can enable secure and transparent tracking of electronic waste throughout the supply chain, while AI and IoT devices can optimize recycling operations and facilitate resource recovery [13].

12.7.3 Future Trends and Emerging Technologies

There are several future trends and emerging technologies that, if implemented, have the potential to revolutionize green computing and e-waste management in the IT industry. The first of these trends is the growing popularity of circular economy models that emphasize resource efficiency, product life extension, and closed-loop material cycling. These initiatives focus on waste reduction and resource maximization in the IT sector, ranging from product repair, refurbishment, and remanufacturing to recycling [32]. Moreover, progressive sustainable materials and design methodologies that allow for the creation of environmentally friendly electronics with a smaller ecological footprint have been developed. Biodegradable plastics as well as energy-efficient components and design strategies are all used to build greener technologies with minimal environmental impact and resource usage [33].

Even though there are some challenges in the implementation of green computing and adopting e-waste management policies, there are still some probable solutions and innovations that bring hope for addressing environmentalism and promoting sustainability in the IT sector. These include the enlightenment of emerging technologies, adopting the relevant regulatory frameworks, and embracing the circular economy systems among the IT stakeholders to achieve a more sustainable computing and e-waste management.

REFERENCES

1. Wendy, J., et al. (2017). Applied Sustainability. In Egenhoefer, R. B. (Ed.), *Routledge Handbook of Sustainable Design*. Taylor & Francis.
2. Kumar, R., Gupta, S. K., Wang, H. C., Kumari, C. S., & Korlam, S. S. V. P. (2023). From efficiency to sustainability: Exploring the potential of 6G for a greener future. *Sustainability*, *15*(23), 16387.
3. Bibri, S. E., Krogstie, J., Kaboli, A., & Alahi, A. (2024). Smarter eco-cities and their leading-edge artificial intelligence of things solutions for environmental sustainability: A comprehensive systematic review. *Environmental Science and Ecotechnology*, *19*, 100330.
4. Murugesan, S. (2008). Harnessing green IT: Principles and practices. *IT Professional*, *10*(1), 24–33.
5. Kumar, A., Holuszko, M., & Espinosa, D. C. R. (2017). E-waste: An overview on generation, collection, legislation and recycling practices. *Resources, Conservation and Recycling*, *122*, 32–42.
6. Garg, P., Pranav, S., & Prerna, A. (2021). Green internet of things (G-IoT): A solution for sustainable technological development. In *Green Internet of Things for Smart Cities* (pp. 23–46). CRC Press.
7. Le, M. H., Lu, W. M., & Chang, J. C. (2023). Recycling e-waste and the sustainable economy: A bibliometric exploration. *Sustainability*, *15*(22), 16108.
8. Mehrotra, U., Mehta, N., Agarwal, P., Gupta, S., & Shrivastava, P. (2022, December). Methodology to test Optimal Encryption Algorithms for IoT Applications. In *2022 5th International Conference on Contemporary Computing and Informatics (IC3I)* (pp. 1977–1980). IEEE.
9. Freitag, C., Berners-Lee, M., Widdicks, K., Knowles, B., Blair, G. S., & Friday, A. (2021). The real climate and transformative impact of ICT: A critique of estimates, trends, and regulations. *Patterns*, *2*(9).
10. Ahmad, S., Wong, K. Y., Tseng, M. L., & Wong, W. P. (2018). Sustainable product design and development: A review of tools, applications and research prospects. *Resources, Conservation and Recycling*, *132*, 49–61.
11. Agarwal, P., Shrivastava, P., & Singh, S. P. (2021). Green internet of things (G-IoT): An exposition for sustainable technological development. *Artificial Intelligence for a Sustainable Industry*, *4*(0), 31–53.
12. Sariatli, F. (2017). Linear economy versus circular economy: A comparative and analyzer study for optimization of economy for sustainability. *Visegrad Journal on Bioeconomy and Sustainable Development*, *6*(1), 31–34.
13. Sarkis, J., Cohen, M. J., Dewick, P., & Schröder, P. (2020). A brave new world: Lessons from the COVID-19 pandemic for transitioning to sustainable supply and production. *Resources, Conservation and Recycling*, *159*, 104894.
14. Baldé, C. P., Forti, V., Gray, V., Kuehr, R., & Stegmann, P. (2017). The global e-waste monitor. *United Nations University (UNU), International Telecommunication Union (ITU) & International Solid Waste Association (ISWA), Bonn/Geneva/Vienna*, 1–109.
15. Xia, J., & Ghahreman, A. (2024). Sustainable technologies for the recycling and upcycling of precious metals from e-waste. *Science of The Total Environment*, 170154.
16. Gautam, S. (2022). Executive Summary-White Paper on National EPR framework for E-waste Management in India.
17. Barbaritano, M., Bravi, L., & Savelli, E. (2019). Sustainability and quality management in the Italian luxury furniture sector: A circular economy perspective. *Sustainability*, *11*(11), 3089.

18. Ghulam, S. T., & Abushammala, H. (2023). Challenges and opportunities in the management of electronic waste and its impact on human health and environment. *Sustainability, 15*(3), 1837.
19. Zhao, R., Zhang, L., Liu, H., & Huang, S. (2020). Research on the Application of Community Engagement in Urban Renewal. In *2020 International Conference on Civil, Architecture and Urban Engineering (ICCAUE 2020).* Atlantis Press.
20. Forti, V., Balde, C. P., Kuehr, R., & Bel, G. (2020). *The Global E-waste Monitor 2020: Quantities, flows and the circular economy potential.*
21. Balde, C. P., Kuehr, R., Blumenthal, K., Fondeur Gill, S., Kern, M., Micheli, P., …, & Huisman, J. (2015). E-waste statistics-Guidelines on classification, reporting and indicators", United Nations University, IAS-SCYCLE, Bonn (Germany) 2015, 51 pages (ISBN Print: 978-92-808-4553-2)(with CP Balde, K. Blumenthal, S. Fondeur Gill, M. Kern, P. Micheli, E.
22. Shreyas Madhav, A. V., Rajaraman, R., Harini, S., & Kiliroor, C. C. (2022). Application of artificial intelligence to enhance collection of e-waste: A potential solution for household WEEE collection and segregation in India. *Waste Management & Research, 40*(7), 1047–1053.
23. Van Yken, J., Boxall, N. J., Cheng, K. Y., Nikoloski, A. N., Moheimani, N. R., & Kaksonen, A. H. (2021). E-waste recycling and resource recovery: A review on technologies, barriers and enablers with a focus on Oceania. *Metals, 11*(8), 1313.
24. Nwankwo, W., & Chinedu, P. U. (2021). Green computing: A machinery for sustainable development in the post-Covid era. In *Green Computing Technologies and Computing Industry in 2021.* IntechOpen.
25. Ghimire, H., & Ariya, P. A. (2020). E-wastes: Bridging the knowledge gaps in global production budgets, composition, recycling and sustainability implications. *Sustainable Chemistry, 1*(2), 154–182.
26. Adejumo, O. A., & Oluduro, O. F. (2021). Ticking time bomb: Implications of the COVID-19 lockdown on e-waste management in developing countries. *UCL Open Environment, 3.*
27. Leal Filho, W., Azul, A. M., Brandli, L. L., Özuyar, P. G., & Wall, T. (2021). Advancing community engagement in climate change research, policy, and action. *Environmental Science & Policy, 121*, 332–334.
28. Hadjri, K., Arif, M., Khalfan, M., Ullah, F., & Koskela, L. (2020). The potential of social media for community engagement with urban planning and design: A case study of Leicester, UK. *Journal of Urban Design, 25*(3), 310–334.
29. Zhou, L., Song, M., & Zhu, X. (2021). The effects of green IT education on green IT behavior: An extended theory of planned behavior model. *Sustainability, 13*(1), 143.
30. Chowdhury, R., Chowdhury, S. P., & Chowdhury, S. A. (2020). Green computing and sustainability: An analysis of research trends. *Journal of Cleaner Production, 277*, 123271.
31. Jin, Y., Geng, Y., Dong, H., Fujita, T., & Zhang, P. (2018). Quantifying the production, consumption, and exports of electrical and electronic equipment of nations. *Journal of Industrial Ecology, 22*(5), 1188–1198.
32. Geissdoerfer, M., Savaget, P., Bocken, N. M., & Hultink, E. J. (2017). The circular economy—A new sustainability paradigm? *Journal of Cleaner Production, 143*, 757–768.
33. Han, B. R. E. Z. E. T. (1997). *Ecodesign—A Promising Approach to Sustainable Production and Consumption.* United Nations Environmental Programme (UNEP).

13 Green IoT

Paving the Way for Eco-Friendly Smart Cities – Future Avenues and Opportunities for Sustainability

Abha Kiran Rajpoot, Gaurav Agrawal, Diksha Dani, and Hunar Sajjan Agrawal

13.1 INTRODUCTION

In an era of unmatched advancement in technology, the combination of innovation and ecological consciousness has resulted in a revolutionary concept known as green IoT (Internet of Things). This paradigm shift aims at balancing technological advancement with ecological sustainability along with creating a connected world. Highlighting this movement is the intention of creating eco-friendly smart cities, where IoT technologies are seamlessly integrated to improve urban living alongside reducing environmental effects.

The rise of green IoT indicates an essential phase in the pursuit of sustainable urban development. Eco-friendly smart cities offer a promising solution to issues like pollution, energy usage, and resource depletion that traditional cities experience. These cities seek to optimize resource use, minimize carbon footprints, and develop ecosystems that prioritize the health of our planet and its residents primarily through the intelligent deployment of IoT devices.

There is a wide range of potential applications for green IoT in the future that could transform the city's operations and citizen-environment interactions. The possibilities for sustainability-driven innovation are endless, ranging from trash management systems that optimize [1] collection routes to intelligent energy networks that adjust dynamically according to demand.

The potential for sustainability in the field of green IoT is not limited to technological advancements. They also involve promoting citizen engagement and a culture of environmental awareness [2]. Over time, residents in smart cities play an active role in developing their urban environments as they participate in decision-making processes and have access to real-time data.

Figure 13.1 explores the various aspects of developing eco-friendly smart cities in the context of green IoT. The journey toward greener, smarter cities is an exciting and dynamic endeavor, involving everything from the use of data-driven insights to

DOI: 10.1201/9781003471356-13

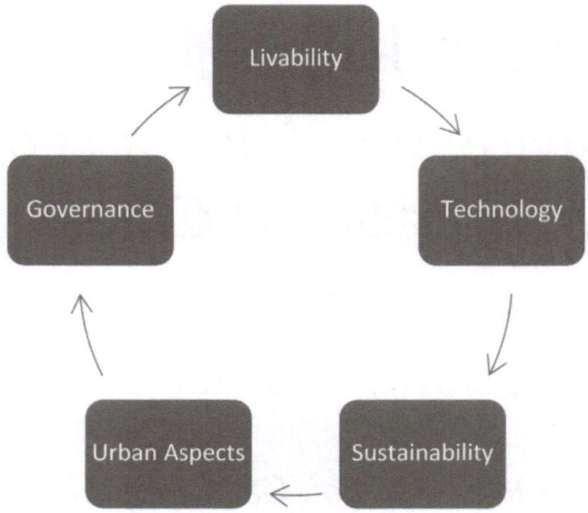

FIGURE 13.1 Characteristic of smart cities.

drive sustainable policies to the implementation of smart infrastructure that adjusts to the requirements of a growing population [3, 4]. As we navigate the landscape of green IoT, the vision of eco-friendly smart cities becomes not just a possibility but a beacon of hope for a sustainable and resilient future.

13.1.1 Related Work

The study focused on green IoT-based smart cities is fragmented [5, 6], resulting in insufficient awareness of the significance of green IoT. Current literature does not have the depth to explain in detail the technology of IoT systems that can reduce carbon dioxide emissions, reduce energy consumption, improve service quality [7], and support information and communication in smart cities. Current studies do not clarify smart city concepts and technologies to achieve green smart cities. As far as the author understands, there is no current research that specifically examines strategies and technologies for the development of smart cities [8] by promoting ICT, minimizing CO_2 emissions, and reducing energy efficiency.

In comparison, [9] discuss low-energy-consuming green IoT. This study focuses primarily on the development of energy-saving guidelines, energy-saving facilities, and data transfer from various IoT devices [10].

In [10] the author introduced the use of IoT in smart cities and green ICT concepts by discussing cities and technologies that will reduce the use of green IoT.

Sheikh et al. show the way to achieve green IoT using IoT technology. Figure 13.2 found IoT applications that can lower energy use and provide a healthier environment. Various technologies have been introduced to use green IoT [10] to improve the efficiency of energy.

The authors from [11] discuss the idea of smart city IoT and its benefits, various applications, and advantages. This study [12] does not discuss technologies to enhance IoT to improve the environmental friendliness and sustainability of the

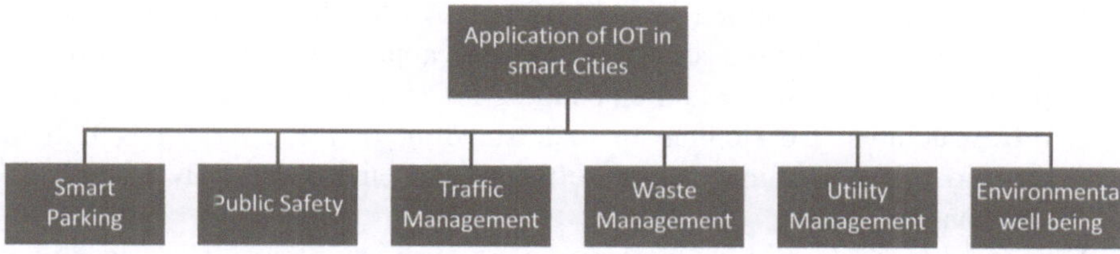

FIGURE 13.2 Smart city applications.

smart city. Table 13.1 shows the comparison between the existing study and the current study.

13.1.2 Contribution

Literature review for "Green IoT: Paving the Way for Future Opportunities and Pathways for Eco-Friendly Smart Cities for Sustainability" is essential for providing a comprehensive understanding of the current state of the field, identifying research gaps and challenges, evaluating existing practices and technologies, assessing environmental [20] impact, exploring policy frameworks, benchmarking against existing approaches, and informing future research directions.

Understanding the current landscape: A literature review helps researchers understand the state of the art at the moment in green IoT technologies and their applications [21] in building eco-friendly smart cities. It provides insights into existing research, technologies, methodologies, and findings related to sustainability in IoT and smart city development.

Identifying gaps and challenges: Through the process of synthesizing the existing literature, researchers are able to identify gaps, barriers, and opportunities for enhancement in the present green IoT implementations. By addressing these gaps with research questions and objectives, this identification enhances the study's relevance and impact.

TABLE 13.1
Comparison of the Present Work with Existing Surveys

[13]	Explore the concepts of green IoT for improving economic growth, environmental safety, and quality of life.
[14]	Smart City Green IoT
[15]	Use green IoT technology to improve the efficiency of energy consumption
[16]	IoT principles have implications for numerous uses in smart cities
[17]	We encourage green IoT technologies in smart cities
[18]	Fog computing and facilitating technologies for smart cities based on the Internet of Things environment.
[19]	Drone-supported smart city green IoT application based on B5G network

Reviewing sustainable practices: A literature review helps researchers study and analyze numerous sustainable practices, approaches, and frameworks presented in prior studies for embedding IoT technologies into smart city infrastructures. Developing an understanding of these strategies [22] can aid in the creation of more efficient and environmentally friendly solutions.

Examining technological innovations: To establish environmentally friendly smart cities, researchers may explore technical developments in IoT devices, sensors, communication protocols, and data analytics methods. This analysis supports the selection of suitable technologies for the suggested research and an understanding of their sustainability implications.

Assessing environmental impact: A literature study allows researchers to examine the environmental impact of IoT deployments in smart cities by [23] analyzing empirical studies, real-world environmental assessments, and case reports. Designing sustainable IoT solutions that reduce adverse environmental effects requires an understanding of the environmental implications.

Exploring policy and regulatory frameworks: A literature study enables researchers to look into existing policy frameworks, guidelines, standards, and suggestions relating to green IoT and sustainable smart city development. It is essential to understand the policy context [24], for the purpose of combining research goals with regulatory constraints and identifying possibilities for policy interventions to support environmentally friendly technology.

Informing future research directions: Finally, a literature analysis gives insight into future research approaches and emerging trends in green IoT and sustainable smart city development [25]. By synthesizing existing knowledge and identifying research gaps, researchers can suggest new research approaches and opportunities for developing the area of eco-friendly smart cities through IoT technology.

13.1.3 The Scope of Study and Structure

Green IoT technologies can be used in smart city development to enhance sustainability. It starts by emphasizing how crucial sustainability is to the development of smart city projects and presents the concept of green IoT to attain environmental friendliness. The study reviews current research on IoT applications in smart cities, sustainable urban practices, related challenges, and relevant policy frameworks through an in-depth review of the literature. The methodology section explains the research operation, including the strategies applied for data gathering [26] and analysis. The subsequent sections examine green IoT technology and solutions, such as devices, sensors, and communication protocols and case studies demonstrating successful deployments are also included. An examination of the environmental impact of IoT in smart cities follows, comparing the energy utilization, carbon footprint, and utilization of resources of traditional methods [13] to those of green IoT solutions. Along with identifying the potential and difficulties that come along with integrating green IoT, the study also makes recommendations for stakeholders and future research avenues. In conclusion, the study summarizes its findings, highlighting the importance of the future path of sustainable smart city development led by green IoT principles.

13.2 IoT TECHNOLOGIES FOR SMART CITIES

Green IoT technologies for smart cities offer a revolutionary way to promote sustainability and lessen the environmental effects of urban areas [14]. These innovative approaches optimize, maintain, and monitor a range of resources, such as waste, water, electricity, and transportation systems, through using the concepts of the IoT. The implementation of smart grids, which include IoT sensors and devices into electrical grids to facilitate real-time energy distribution monitoring and management, is one of the major uses.

Optimizing load distribution and promoting the installation of smart grids and renewable energy sources, such as solar and wind energy, can help in reducing energy consumption and encourage the use of clean, green energy in urban areas. Furthermore, smart lighting systems that are made possible by IoT technology automatically adjust lighting settings in response to factors like occupancy and daylight levels [15], which significantly reduces energy use in buildings and public areas.

Moreover, IoT-based smart building management systems (BMS) monitor factors, including energy consumption, temperature, humidity, and occupancy levels to help optimize how much energy is utilized in buildings. Furthermore, IoT-powered smart water management systems enhance irrigation in urban landscapes, monitor water usage, and find leaks. These systems provide accurate control of water distribution and conservation efforts by providing real-time data on water flow, quality, and soil moisture levels. Green IoT technology also contributes to waste management solutions. Smart garbage bins [16] with sensors that indicate when they need to be cleaned minimize the number of unnecessary collection trips and encourage recycling habits. Green IoT includes intelligent traffic control systems, intelligent transport systems, and infrastructure for electric vehicle (EV) charging.

These systems use IoT sensors and data analytics to reduce traffic congestion, enhance traffic flow, and promote the adoption of low-emission vehicles for sustainable urban transportation. Furthermore, IoT-powered environmental monitoring systems [17] monitor pollution, noise levels, and air quality in cities, giving authorities real-time information they need to act quickly to reduce pollutants and enhance resident quality of air.

Finally, in urban agriculture settings, green IoT technologies enable precision agriculture practices by monitoring soil moisture, temperature, and nutrient levels, thereby optimizing water and resource usage, improving crop yields, and promoting sustainable urban food [18] production. Overall, green IoT technologies hold immense potential to drive sustainability and foster eco-friendly practices within smart cities, contributing to a more resilient and livable urban environment. Figure 13.3 shows green IoT for sustainable and eco-friendly smart cities.

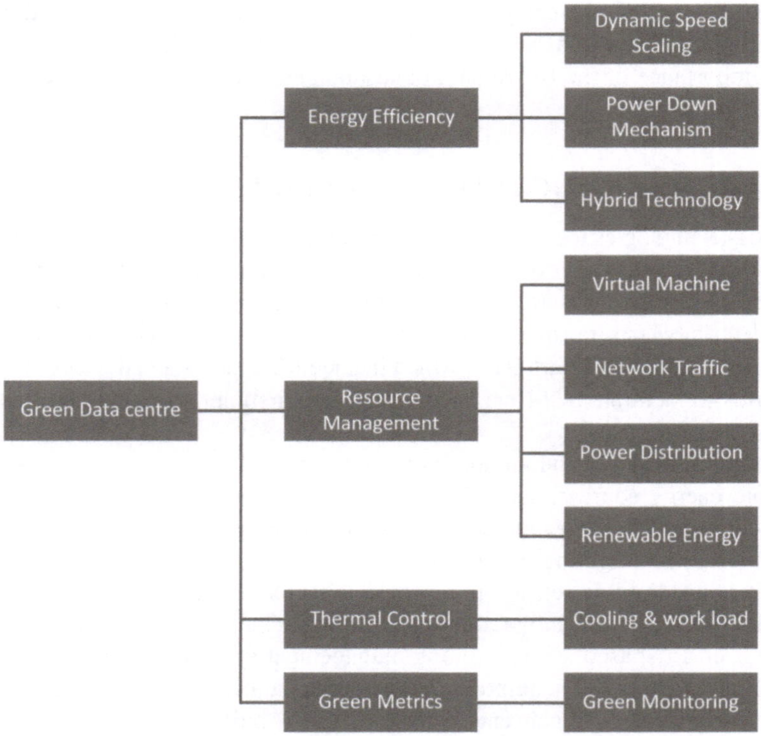

FIGURE 13.3 Green IoT for sustainable and eco-friendly smart cities.

13.2.1 Smart Data Center for Smart Cities

In the context of "Green IoT: Paving the Way for environmentally friendly Smart Cities - Future Avenues and Opportunities for Sustainability," a smart data center plays a pivotal role in helping the infrastructure necessary for managing and optimizing green IoT technologies [19] within smart cities. Here is how a smart data center contributes to the goals of sustainability and eco-friendliness in this context:

Efficient data management: A smart data center efficiently manages and processes the large amounts of data generated by green IoT devices and sensors deployed throughout the smart city. By consolidating and analyzing this data in real time, the data center enables [27] proactive decision-making to optimize resource utilization and enhance sustainability initiatives.

Energy efficiency: To align with the sustainability objectives of the study, a smart data center is designed with energy-efficient hardware and cooling systems. Advanced technologies such as energy-efficient servers, optimized cooling mechanisms, and intelligent power management strategies minimize energy consumption, reducing the carbon footprint of data center operations.

Renewable energy integration: To further enhance eco-friendliness, a smart data center can incorporate renewable source energy like wind and solar energy into its energy supply [28]. By utilizing renewable energy sources for powering data center operations, the overall environmental impact is reduced, contributing to a more sustainable energy ecosystem in the smart city.

Green building standards: The architecture and design of the smart data center can adhere to green building standards and certifications, incorporating sustainable materials, energy-efficient design principles, and eco-friendly practices. Features such as efficient lighting, natural ventilation, and optimized building layouts contribute to reducing energy consumption and environmental impact.

Interoperability and open data: A smart data center facilitates interoperability and open data standards to ensure seamless integration with green IoT devices and systems deployed across the smart city. Open data initiatives enable transparency and collaboration, empowering stakeholders to access and utilize environmental data for developing [29] innovative sustainability solutions and driving positive change.

Community engagement and education: The smart data center serves as a platform for community engagement and education on sustainability topics. Through initiatives such as open houses, educational workshops, and public forums, residents and stakeholders [30] are informed about the importance of eco-friendly practices and encouraged to participate in sustainability efforts within the smart city.

In order to manage and optimize green IoT technologies, a smart data center is essential for "Green IoT: Paving the Way for environmentally friendly Smart Cities - Future Avenues and Opportunities for Sustainability" [31]. It can be done by making community involvement a priority, integrating renewable energy sources, providing data analytics for sustainability, and emphasizing energy efficiency.

13.2.2 Communication Network for Smart Cities

In the dynamic landscape of urbanization, smart cities show a significant advancement toward sustainable development incorporating advanced technologies such as the IoT to optimize resources, enhance efficiency, and mitigate environmental impact. At the heart of this revolution is a complex web of communication networks that allow IoT devices to function, facilitating seamless connectivity and data exchange across multiple urban systems. However, the sustainability of smart cities relies heavily on the eco-friendliness and durability of these communication infrastructures. There are several challenges to overcome, from the technical difficulties of ensuring network security, scalability, and stability to the broader environmental problems of energy use and the generation of electronic trash [32]. However, amidst these challenges lie opportunities for innovation and optimization. Current solutions and best practices emphasize the adoption of energy-efficient communication technologies like 5G, LoRaWAN, and NB-IoT, supported by decentralized network designs and incorporating the utilization of renewable energy sources. Moreover, emerging trends such as artificial intelligence (AI)-driven network optimization and blockchain-based secure data exchange hold promise for further enhancing the sustainability of communication networks in smart cities [33, 34]. Real-world instances and case studies provide valuable insights, highlighting the real benefits of implementing environmentally friendly strategies for communication in urban environments. Collaboration among policymakers, technology providers, and urban planners is vital for developing legislative frameworks and carrying out guidelines that promote sustainability in communication network deployment. Smart cities can pave the way for a more resilient and environmentally friendly urban future where communication networks are essential for promoting sustainable development and enhancing the living standards of all citizens by addressing these issues and capturing innovation opportunities. With a focus on sustainability, let's take a closer look at some particular aspects of communication networks for smart cities:

Energy efficiency: Energy consumption is one of the main issues with smart city communication networks. Conventional networks have a tendency to consume a lot of power, which increases carbon emissions and affects the environment. On the other hand, energy efficiency is a key consideration in the design of modern communication technologies like 5G and LoRaWAN, which optimize power consumption and extend the battery life of IoT devices. Additional network management improvements that lower energy usage and improve the network's overall sustainability include dynamic energy allocation and activating sleep mode for inactive devices.

Renewable energy integration: To further enhance sustainability, smart cities can integrate renewable energy sources into their communication network infrastructure. This includes deploying solar panels, wind turbines, or other renewable energy generators [35] to power network equipment and IoT devices. By leveraging renewable energy, smart cities can reduce their reliance on non-renewable energy resources like fossil fuels, lower carbon emissions, and promote a more environmentally friendly approach to urban development.

Data privacy and security: As smart cities collect vast amounts of data via IoT devices, maintaining data privacy and security is critical. Smart cities can safeguard critical data from cyber risks and illegal access by setting up strong encryption methods, access control systems, and secure communication routes [36]. Additionally, implementing distributed ledger technologies like blockchain and decentralized architectures can improve data security and integrity, building confidence among stakeholders and residents in the smart city ecosystem.

Scalability and flexibility: Smart cities are dynamic environments that require scalable and flexible communication networks to adapt to changing needs and demands. Cloud-based network architectures: this flexibility ensures that communication networks are capable of handling the growing number of IoT devices and support emerging applications and services, ultimately contributing to the long-term sustainability of smart cities.

Community engagement and participation: Sustainability in smart city communication networks includes more than just technical solutions; it also involves engaging and strengthening the local population. Smart cities can address urban difficulties and encourage sustainable practices by promoting community participation through initiatives such as citizen co-creation and crowd-sourced data collection [37]. Furthermore, increasing awareness of the environmental benefits of eco-friendly communication networks can motivate behavioral changes and urge citizens to include sustainability in their daily lives.

By considering these aspects and implementing holistic strategies, smart cities can develop communication networks that not only enable efficient data exchange and connectivity but even contribute toward a better sustainable and resilient urban future. Table 13.2 summarizes the techniques and methodologies utilized for smart city communication networks.

13.2.2.1 Wireless Sensor Network for Smart Cities

The combination of various sensors and wireless communications has resulted in the emergence of wireless sensor networks. The wireless sensor networks have numerous applications like environmental monitoring, fire detection [32–34], response to changing military borders, object tracking, healthcare systems, and business processes. Observed, wireless sensor networks represent an important technology enabling the development of the IoT. The sensor integrates numerous small, weak, and cheap electrical equipment. Wireless sensor networks (WSN) components include base stations or receivers and many sensor nodes. It desires to use the nearest neighbor routing algorithm and find an idle mode, where the nearest node is active (sending and receiving information) while the remaining nodes are inactive. Therefore, every node that wants to share data with another node keeps all the nodes of its root node in its stand and sends data accordingly.

TABLE 13.2
Summary of the Communication Network Strategies and Techniques Used for Smart Cities

Ref	Techniques	Advantages
[15]	Energy-efficient	• Maximizing the energy • Efficient
[16]	Resource allocation	• Optimizing the energy efficiency • Improvising the integration of communication networks
[17]	Green cognitive radios	Minimum power transmissions of the information Signal
[19]	Smart grid	The enhanced power utilization of smart grid
[31]	Edge computing	Reduces the flow of traffic from edge computing by the utilization of a node-to-node-based communication protocol.

Many technologies, such as on-demand sensing, context-aware energy management, and sleep time, enable connected networks to enable green IoT, which can save energy and reduce the number of sensors in slow communication. Battery power appears to be the most important factor in wireless sensor connection that directly affects the life of the network. The concept of utility has been supported by Gupta et al. [35] who introduced regulatory measures to improve the efficiency of energy usage. Similarly, [38] discussed the benefit of IoT-flexible and hierarchical networks. However, the authors of [39] proposed green WSN to improve the path and life cycle of WSN. Although, the authors of [39] elaborate on a green WSN that focuses on reducing relay nodes, increasing energy efficiency, improving the network's lifetime, and developing resources to ensure security in the IoT environment. In addition, the authors from [31] work on an integrated approach to energy saving for green area WSN. This collaboration is based on technology where several hops act as network stations in order to ensure communication among sensors. Energy efficiency and link optimization are also discussed for increasing green wireless sensor networks in cloud computing platforms [31]. This work is carried out in four steps: creating a hierarchical system, finding sensor/actuator nodes, node clustering, creating a good model for green IoT applications, and finally performing calculations to find the minimum power. The outcomes demonstrate how adaptable, energy-efficient, and effective the plan is. It is also suitable for numerous IoT applications such as smart agriculture and smart cities. To improve the efficiency of green wireless sensor networks and lower CO_2 emissions, Hamood et al. [32] proposed line configuration, wireless energy harvesting, and error control coding. Moreover, combining wireless sensor networks and cloud computing can reduce high energy consumption and carbon dioxide emissions, which have a negative impact on the environment [33]. Balanced tree-based WSNs aim to extend the network lifetime and reduce the energy consumption of sensor nodes [34]. However, a green intelligence network has been proposed in wireless sensor networks [34]. Additionally Gupta et al. [35] proposed the realization of WSN for low power. Their work is presented and examined in three cases regarding the realization of WSN energy reduction and green systems development. For green WSN, the following technologies [36] can be used to save energy, such as sleep and motor sensor nodes, optimization of energy use, radio technology, data reduction techniques, and energy saving. A hybrid technology transport protocol provides reliability for a lifetime. Table 13.3 summarizes the strategies and techniques used in WSN for smart cities.

Recently, smart cities faced various issues such as waste management, pollution, traffic, and excessive energy consumption. Rapid growth and sustainable solutions require more water to improve the working environment. The authors in [37] introduced smart mobility and connectivity of autonomous vehicles and discussed the problems of smart cities, and the benefits of moving toward improving smart city security, including improving human safety, reducing noise, reducing pollution, increasing the pollution rate, reducing traffic, and reducing transfer costs [38]. Additionally, Al-Samhi and Rajput [39] discussed how IoT data sharing can help the value chain to be better connected.

TABLE 13.3
Summarizes the Strategies and Techniques Used in WSN for Smart Cities

Ref	Techniques	Advantages
[16]	Cloud computing and sensors	• Lower the adverse effects of computer resources and minimize energy consumption
[17]	Balanced tree node switching	• Counterbalancing energy use among sensor nodes
		• Improvising the lifetime network
[19]	Hybrid transmission protocol	• Conserve energy close to the sink regions
		• Enhance the network reliability and delay
[16]	WSN equipped with an energy harvest system	• Green world
		• Gives WSN nodes a long life
[18]	Duty-cycling	• Save energy
[19]	Scheduling Duty-cycling	• Energy saving
		• Minimize the latency in communication across sensor nodes
[27]	Clustering technique	• Saving the energy for greening WSNs
[28]	Cognitive WSN	• Minimize the use of excessive power
		• Green protocols
[27]	Shortest path	• Energy conservation
[28]	Application profile and event-driven self-healing	• Energy consumption
		• Provisioning for network resilience
[17]	Intelligent transportation	• Optimize and improve network capacity
		• Increase safety
		• Reduce pollution
		• Reduce congestion

13.3 EFFICIENT ENERGY FOR SMART CITIES

Efficient energy solutions are foundational to the development of smart cities, particularly in the context of green IoT, where sustainability is a central focus. These solutions encompass a range of strategies and technologies aimed at optimizing energy usage, reducing carbon emissions, and minimizing environmental impact. Diversifying energy sources and minimizing dependency on fossil fuels are made possible by the integration of renewable energy resources, such as wind, solar, and hydroelectric power. Demand-side management (DSM) techniques allow consumers to actively participate in energy conservation actions by utilizing smart meters, energy-efficient appliances, and real-time monitoring tools. Microgrids are energy storage systems that are examples of grid optimization technology that maximize energy efficiency while enhancing the electrical grid's resilience and reliability. Smart cities can develop environmentally friendly urban environments that support sustainability, resilience, and enhance resident quality of life by utilizing these economical energy solutions.

Efficient energy solutions for smart cities include a wide range of methods that not only optimize energy consumption but also encourage sustainability and environmental stewardship. Using renewable energy sources like hydroelectric, solar, and wind power in the urban energy mix is one of these alternatives. DSM programs encourage customers to participate in an active role in energy conservation by promoting the use of smart meters, energy-efficient equipment, and behavioral modifications. Furthermore, energy storage devices are essential for grid optimization because they reduce waste and improve grid stability by storing extra energy during times of low demand for later use. Integrating these efficient energy solutions into the fabric of smart cities not only minimizes greenhouse gas emissions and mitigates environmental impact but also creates more resilient and sustainable urban environments capable of satisfying both the current and future generations' energy needs.

Renewable energy integration: A major strategy for enhancing energy efficiency in smart cities is the use of renewable energy resources, including solar, wind, and hydroelectric power. The use of renewable energy can help smart cities reduce carbon emissions, lessen their reliance on fossil fuels, and minimize their negative environmental effects. Smart cities are becoming more environmentally friendly as a result of the smooth integration of renewable energy into urban infrastructure which was made possible by advances in technology in the industry, creative finance strategies, and supporting legal frameworks.

DSM: Strategies play a critical role in optimizing energy usage and reducing peak demand in smart cities. DSM offers customers with the capacity to monitor and manage their energy consumption in real time by deploying smart meters, energy-efficient appliances, and smart grid technology, allowing them to make informed decisions about their usage patterns. DSM contributes to a more sustainable energy ecology in smart cities by encouraging load shifting and energy saving. This reduces grid stress, enhances system stability, and eventually lowers consumer energy bills.

Grid optimization: It is another essential aspect of efficient energy solutions in smart cities, focusing on enhancing the resilience and reliability of the electrical grid while maximizing energy efficiency. Advanced grid technologies, such as microgrids, energy storage systems, and grid-edge intelligence, allow for decentralized energy generation, storage, and distribution, minimizing transmission losses and enhancing grid stability. Grid optimization strategies also make use of AI, predictive modeling, and data analytics to improve grid operations, predict demand variations, and enable dynamic energy management. All of these features support the integration of renewable energy resources and foster a more sustainable energy environment in smart cities.

13.4 REDUCING POLLUTION HAZARDOUS IN SMART CITIES

Reducing pollution dangers in smart cities requires a multidisciplinary approach that successfully addresses multiple sources of pollution by integrating different technologies, policies, and community involvement initiatives. Smart cities analyze pollution levels and locate pollution hotspots with precision thanks to sensor technologies, real-time monitoring, and data analytics. In order to give timely insights into pollution management, these systems—which are frequently installed as parts of IoT networks—continuously monitor air quality, noise levels, water quality and levels, and other environmental data.

In addition to monitoring, sustainable transportation options are given top priority in smart cities to reduce car emissions, which is a major driver of urban air pollution. In order to reduce traffic and enhance flow, this involves encouraging EVs, building infrastructure for EV charging, and implementing intelligent transportation systems (ITS). In order to reduce the need for private automobiles and lower pollution levels, intelligent urban planning also prioritizes mixed land-use development, pedestrian-friendly infrastructure, and effective public transportation networks.

Moreover, green infrastructure plays an important role in pollution reduction efforts. Smart cities invest in green spaces, urban forests, green rooftops, and permeable pavements to absorb air pollutants, reduce heat island effects, and enhance overall air quality [39]. These green infrastructure elements not only improve environmental quality but also contribute to the overall well-being and liveability of the urban areas.

Along with technical solutions, effective pollution reduction in smart cities requires strict environmental rules, legislative frameworks, and community involvement. Smart cities manage industrial emissions, enforce strict automobile emissions rules and regulations, and use financial incentives and legislative measures to encourage the use of clean energy technologies. Furthermore, through citizen science projects, environmental education programs, and community-led initiatives, community engagement initiatives enable residents to participate in pollution reduction efforts, encourage sustainable behaviors, and raise awareness about the hazards associated with pollution.

By integrating these approaches, smart cities can effectively reduce pollution hazards, protect public health, and create healthier, more sustainable urban environments for residents and future generations.

Smart cities leverage advanced technologies and data-driven solutions to address pollution challenges through various strategies:

Air quality monitoring and management: Smart cities deploy IoT-enabled air quality monitoring systems so that pollutants like nitrogen dioxide (NO_2), sulfur dioxide (SO_2), and particulate matter (PM) should be monitored continuously. Real-time data collected from these sensors helps city officials monitor and identify various pollution hotspots around the region, implement targeted mitigation measures, and provide timely alerts to residents, enabling them to take proactive steps to minimize exposure to harmful air pollutants.

Smart transportation solutions: Transportation contributes significantly to urban air pollution. ITS are used in smart cities to optimize traffic flow, limit emissions, and relieve congestion. These ITS are implemented through approaches like dynamic traffic routing, traffic signal synchronization, and encouraging the use of shared mobility and public transit. In addition, the use of electric cars (EVs) and the construction of EV charging infrastructure [40] also help to lessen air pollution caused by conventional combustion engine vehicles.

Green infrastructure and urban planning: Smart cities prioritize green infrastructure and sustainable urban growth approaches in order to reduce pollution risks. This includes putting in place green areas, urban forests, and green rooftops—all of which improve overall air quality by absorbing air pollutants and minimizing the heat island effects. In addition, compact city designs, pedestrian-friendly surroundings, and multi-use structures are the main goals of smart urban planning in order to reduce automobile emissions and encourage active transportation options like cycling and walking.

Waste management and recycling: Smart cities use smart waste management technologies to improve waste collection routes, lower collection frequency, and promote waste reduction and recycling diversion. IoT-enabled waste bins equipped with numerous sensors and radio frequency identification tags enable real-time monitoring of garbage levels, resulting in more efficient waste collection and minimizing the risk of pollution from overflowing bins and illegal dumping.

Environmental regulations and policy frameworks: Effective pollution control in smart cities requires robust environmental regulations and policy frameworks that incentivize sustainable practices and hold polluters accountable. Smart cities implement policies such as regulations on industrial emissions, emission standards for vehicles, and initiatives for clean energy adoption to promote pollution reduction and environmental sustainability.

By implementing these and other innovative solutions, smart cities can effectively reduce pollution hazards, protect public health, and develop sustainable urban environments for current and future generations.

13.5 WASTE MANAGEMENT IN SMART CITIES

Waste management in smart cities is an essential component of creating sustainable and eco-friendly urban environments, particularly when integrated with green IoT solutions. Through the utilization of data-driven approaches and advanced technologies, smart cities aim to optimize the process of waste management, reduce environmental impact, and promote resource efficiency. Here's how waste management in smart cities is related to green IoT:

IoT-enabled waste monitoring: Smart cities deploy IoT-enabled sensors in garbage bins to check on the fill levels in real time. These sensors transmit data to a centralized platform, allowing the waste management authorities to efficiently optimize the garbage collection routes, reducing unnecessary pickups, and minimizing fuel consumption and emissions from collection vehicles.

By efficiently managing waste collection, smart cities can reduce their carbon footprint and promote resource conservation.

Smart waste sorting and recycling: IoT technology can be used to improve the recycling process and waste sorting in smart cities. Smart waste bins are equipped with cameras and sensors that can automatically sort recyclable materials from general waste, streamlining the recycling process and increasing recycling rates. Additionally, IoT platforms can provide real-time information to residents about proper waste sorting practices, encouraging participation in recycling programs and reducing contamination in recyclable materials.

Optimized waste-to-energy conversion: Smart cities leverage IoT and data analytics to optimize waste-to-energy conversion processes. By monitoring waste composition, moisture levels, and other parameters in real-time, waste-to-energy facilities can adjust their operations to maximize energy recovery while minimizing emissions and environmental impact. Additionally, IoT-enabled predictive maintenance systems can ensure the efficient operation of waste-to-energy plants, reducing downtime and optimizing energy production.

Smart composting systems: Smart cities implement IoT-based composting systems to manage organic waste efficiently. IoT sensors monitor temperature, moisture levels, and oxygen levels in composting piles, ensuring optimal conditions for decomposition and reducing greenhouse gas emissions associated with anaerobic decomposition. Additionally, IoT platforms can provide valuable data insights to farmers and urban gardeners, enabling the production of high-quality compost for agricultural and landscaping purposes.

Data-driven waste reduction strategies: Green IoT solutions enable smart cities to implement data-driven waste reduction strategies. By analyzing waste generation patterns and identifying areas of high waste generation, cities can develop targeted waste reduction initiatives and educational campaigns to promote sustainable consumption practices and minimize waste generation at the source. Additionally, IoT platforms can facilitate the sharing and reuse of unwanted items through online marketplaces and community exchange programs, promoting a circular economy and reducing waste sent to landfills.

13.6 SUSTAINABILITY IN SMART CITIES

Adoption and integration of green IoT solutions in smart cities are linked to sustainability in a sophisticated way which holds advanced technologies to create an efficient, resource-conscious, and environmentally friendly urban environment. Green IoT plays a significant role through various interlinked mechanisms:

Efficient resource management: Green IoT enables urban areas to enhance resource usage and reduce waste from various domains, including water, transportation, and energy. Through the deployment of IoT sensors and smart meters, cities can survey and manage resource utilization instantaneously, Alsamhi [38] identify incompetency and implement useful inventions to improve efficiency and reduce waste. For example, smart meters help residents and organizations to track their energy utilization, which can benefit to make better decisions to reduce energy consumption and lower carbon emissions. Similarly, IoT-powered water management systems keep track of water quality, detect leaks, and enhance irrigation practices, leading to water conservation and reduced environmental impact.

Renewable energy integration: Green IoT makes it contented to integrate renewable energy resources, like wind and solar power, into urban infrastructure. IoT-powered smart grids and energy management systems help in the efficient distribution and utilization of renewable energy, maximizing its contribution to the overall energy mix, while minimizing dependency on fossil fuels. By controlling the usage of renewable energy resources, urban areas can enhance air quality, reduce greenhouse gas emissions, and improve energy resilience leading to long-term sustainability.

Eco-friendly mobility solutions: Green IoT plays a crucial role in promoting sustainable transportation alternatives in smart cities. IoT-enabled transportation systems, including EV charging infrastructure, intelligent traffic management systems, and smart public transportation networks, help reduce traffic congestion, lower emissions, and improve air quality. By providing real-time traffic data, optimizing traffic flow, and encouraging the use of EVs and public transit, green IoT solutions support the transition to cleaner and more sustainable mobility options, contributing to reduced carbon emissions and enhanced urban liveability.

Waste management and recycling: Green IoT solutions enhance waste management practices in smart cities, promoting recycling, waste reduction, and resource recovery. IoT-enabled waste management systems monitor the collection, sorting, and disposal processes in real time, optimizing collection routes, reducing landfill waste, and increasing recycling rates. By promoting circular economy principles and minimizing waste sent to landfills, green IoT solutions contribute toward the conservation of natural resources, reduction of environmental pollution, and overall sustainability of the urban environment.

Overall, green IoT solutions are instrumental in advancing sustainability in smart cities by promoting efficient resource management, renewable energy integration, eco-friendly mobility solutions, waste management and recycling, and data-driven [39] sustainability initiatives. By harnessing the power of IoT technology to address environmental challenges and promote sustainable practices, smart cities can create cleaner, healthier, more resilient, and environmentally friendly urban environments for current and future generations.

13.7 FUTURE DIRECTIONS

Future directions for green IoT in paving the way for eco-friendly smart cities involve innovative strategies and technologies aimed at further enhancing sustainability, resilience, and environmental stewardship. Here are some future avenues and opportunities for green IoT in smart cities:

Integration of AI and machine learning (ML): The green IoT solutions enable smarter and adaptive systems for resource management, energy optimization, and pollution control. AI models may analyze vast quantities of data collected by IoT sensors to identify patterns, optimize resource allocation, and forecast future environmental trends. ML algorithms can also enable independent decision-making in real time, leading to more responsive systems for managing energy, water, waste, and transportation in urban areas.

Blockchain for environmental accountability: Blockchain technology improves environmental accountability as well as liquidity in smart cities. By controlling blockchain-based segregated ledgers, green IoT systems can record environmental data, transactions, and actions, ensuring data security [40] and liability across various stakeholders. Blockchain technology can also facilitate automated records for carbon trading, renewable energy trading, and environmental credits, incentivizing sustainable operations and fostering a sustainable economy in urban areas.

Edge computing and fog computing: Edge and Fog are two computing technologies that play a vital role in increasing the scalability, responsiveness, and efficiency of green IoT systems in urban areas. By decentralizing data processing and analytics at the network's edge, edge and fog computing reduces energy consumption, bandwidth, and latency, enabling real-time decisions and optimized distributed IoT environments. Edge and Fog also enhance privacy by processing data and minimizing the need for data broadcasting over the network.

Internet of bio-nano things (IoBNT): The IoBNT offers up new possibilities for integrating biological and nanotechnology-based sensors into green IoT systems to monitor the environment and assure its sustainability. IoBNT sensors offer vital insights into ecosystem health and biodiversity in smart cities by detecting and analyzing biological and chemical environmental health indicators [41], such as microbial contamination, air quality, and soil fertility. Green IoT in smart cities is being developed by IoBNT, which also makes it possible for cutting-edge applications like bioinspired sensors, biodegradable sensors, and self-healing sensor networks.

Interoperability and standardization: Interoperability and standardization efforts will be essential for ensuring seamless integration and compatibility of green IoT solutions across different smart city applications and domains. Common data formats, communication protocols, and interoperability standards will enable seamless data exchange and integration between diverse IoT devices, platforms, and systems, facilitating holistic and integrated approaches to sustainability in smart cities. Interoperability and standardization also promote scalability, vendor neutrality, and futureproofing of green IoT deployments, ensuring long-term viability and sustainability in smart city ecosystems [41].

By embracing these future directions and opportunities for green IoT, smart cities can further advance their sustainability goals, enhance environmental resilience, and create healthier, more livable urban environments for residents and future generations.

13.8 CONCLUSION

Green IoT holds immense potential in paving the way for eco-friendly smart cities, offering innovative solutions and technologies that promote sustainability, resilience, and environmental stewardship. By leveraging advanced sensors, data analytics, and connectivity, green IoT enables smart cities to optimizing resource management, reducing pollution, and enhancing the quality of life for residents. Future avenues and opportunities for green IoT in smart cities include the integration of AI, blockchain, edge computing, and the IoBNT, which promise to further enhance the sustainability, efficiency, and effectiveness of IoT solutions. Moreover, citizen science, participatory sensing, and interoperability efforts will be essential for engaging communities, fostering collaboration, and ensuring seamless integration of green IoT solutions across diverse smart city applications and domains. As smart cities continue to evolve, green IoT will be playing an essential role in shaping the future of urban sustainability, creating healthier, more livable, cleaner, and environmentally friendly cities for generations to come.

REFERENCES

1. Atzori, L., Iera, A., & Morabito, G. (2010). The internet of things: A survey. *Computer Networks*, *54*(15), 2787–2805.
2. Minerva, R., Biru, A., & Rotondi, D. (2015). Towards a definition of the internet of things (IoT). *IEEE Internet Initiative*, *1*(1), 1–86.
3. Perera, C., Zaslavsky, A., Christen, P., & Georgakopoulos, D. (2013). Context aware computing for the internet of things: A survey. *IEEE Communications Surveys & Tutorials*, *16*(1), 414–454.
4. Gubbi, J., Buyya, R., Marusic, S., & Palaniswami, M. (2013). Internet of things (IoT): A vision, architectural elements, and future directions. *Future Generation Computer Systems*, *29*(7), 1645–1660.
5. Tellez, M., El-Tawab, S., & Heydari, H. M. (2016, April). Improving the security of wireless sensor networks in an IoT environmental monitoring system. In *2016 IEEE systems and information engineering design symposium (SIEDS)* (pp. 72–77). IEEE.
6. Shah, J., & Mishra, B. (2016, January). IoT enabled environmental monitoring system for smart cities. In *2016 international conference on internet of things and applications (IOTA)* (pp. 383–388). IEEE.

7. Chen, X., Ma, M., & Liu, A. (2018). Dynamic power management and adaptive packet size selection for IoT in e-Healthcare. *Computers & Electrical Engineering*, *65*, 357–375.
8. Popa, D., Popa, D. D., & Codescu, M. M. (2017). Reliability for a green internet of things. *Buletinul AGIR*, 1.
9. Kong, L., Khan, M. K., Wu, F., Chen, G., & Zeng, P. (2017). Millimeter-wave wireless communications for IoT-cloud supported autonomous vehicles: Overview, design, and challenges. *IEEE Communications Magazine*, *55*(1), 62–68.
10. Prasad, S. S., & Kumar, C. (2013). A green and reliable internet of things. *Communications and Network*, *5*(1), 44–48.
11. Pavithra, D., & Balakrishnan, R. (2015, April). IoT based monitoring and control system for home automation. In *2015 global conference on communication technologies (GCCT)* (pp. 169–173). IEEE.
12. Kodali, R. K., Jain, V., Bose, S., & Boppana, L. (2016, April). IoT based smart security and home automation system. In *2016 international conference on computing, communication and automation (ICCCA)* (pp. 1286–1289). IEEE.
13. Khan, R., Khan, S. U., Zaheer, R., & Khan, S. (2012, December). Future internet: the internet of things architecture, possible applications and key challenges. In *2012 10th international conference on frontiers of information technology* (pp. 257–260). IEEE.
14. Zhu, C., Leung, V. C., Shu, L., & Ngai, E. C. H. (2015). Green internet of things for smart world. *IEEE Access*, *3*, 2151–2162.
15. Shaikh, F. K., Zeadally, S., & Exposito, E. (2015). Enabling technologies for green internet of things. *IEEE Systems Journal*, *11*(2), 983–994.
16. Talari, S., Shafie-Khah, M., Siano, P., Loia, V., Tommasetti, A., & Catalão, J. P. (2017). A review of smart cities based on the internet of things concept. *Energies*, *10*(4), 421.
17. Alsamhi, S. H., Ma, O., Ansari, M. S., & Meng, Q. (2019). Greening internet of things for greener and smarter cities: A survey and future prospects. *Telecommunication Systems*, *72*, 609–632.
18. Zahmatkesh, H., & Al-Turjman, F. (2020). Fog computing for sustainable smart cities in the IoT era: Caching techniques and enabling technologies-an overview. *Sustainable Cities and Society*, *59*, 102139.
19. Alsamhi, S. H., & Rajput, N. S. (2016). Implementation of call admission control technique in HAP for enhanced QoS in wireless network deployment. *Telecommunication Systems*, *63*, 141–151.
20. Gu, M., Li, X., & Cao, Y. (2014). Optical storage arrays: A perspective for future big data storage. *Light: Science & Applications*, *3*(5), e177–e177.
21. Hashem, I. A. T., Yaqoob, I., Anuar, N. B., Mokhtar, S., Gani, A., & Khan, S. U. (2015). The rise of "big data" on cloud computing: Review and open research issues. *Information Systems*, *47*, 98–115.
22. Syed, F., Gupta, S. K., Hamood Alsamhi, S., Rashid, M., & Liu, X. (2021). A survey on recent optimal techniques for securing unmanned aerial vehicles applications. *Transactions on Emerging Telecommunications Technologies*, *32*(7), e4133.
23. Alsamhi, S. H., Ansari, M. S., Zhao, L., Van, S. N., Gupta, S. K., Alammari, A. A., …, & Srivastava, A. (2019, December). Tethered balloon technology for green communication in smart cities and healthy environment. In *2019 First International Conference of Intelligent Computing and Engineering (ICOICE)* (pp. 1–7). IEEE.
24. Shuja, J., Ahmad, R. W., Gani, A., Abdalla Ahmed, A. I., Siddiqa, A., Nisar, K., …, & Zomaya, A. Y. (2017). Greening emerging IT technologies: Techniques and practices. *Journal of Internet Services and Applications*, *8*, 1–11.
25. Vidyasekar, A. D. (2013). Strategic opportunity analysis of the global smart city market: Smart city market is likely to be worth a cumulative 1.565 trillion by 2020. *Frost & Sullivan*.

26. Arshad, R., Zahoor, S., Shah, M. A., Wahid, A., & Yu, H. (2017). Green IoT: An investigation on energy saving practices for 2020 and beyond. *IEEE Access*, *5*, 15667–15681.
27. Alsamhi, S. H. A., & Rajput, N. S. (2012). Methodology for coexistence of high altitude platform ground stations and radio relay stations with reduced interference. *International Journal of Scientific Engineering and Research*, *3*, 1–7.
28. Alsamhi, S. H., Ma, O., Ansari, M. S., & Gupta, S. K. (2019). Collaboration of drone and internet of public safety things in smart cities: An overview of QoS and network performance optimization. *Drones*, *3*(1), 13.
29. Alsamhi, S. H., & Rajput, N. S. (2014). Neural network in intelligent handoff for QoS in HAP and terrestrial systems. *International Journal of Materials Science and Engineering*, *2*(2), 141–146.
30. Alsamhi, S. H., & Rajput, N. S. (2015). An intelligent HAP for broadband wireless communications: Developments, QoS and applications. *International Journal of Electronics and Electrical Engineering*, *3*(2), 134–143.
31. Saif, A., Dimyati, K. B., Noordin, K. A. B., Shah, N. S. M., Alsamhi, S. H., Abdullah, Q., & Farah, N. (2021). Distributed clustering for user devices under unmanned aerial vehicle coverage area during disaster recovery. *arXiv preprint arXiv:2103.07931.*
32. Alsamhi, S. H., Almalki, F. A., Ma, O., Ansari, M. S., & Lee, B. (2021). Predictive estimation of optimal signal strength from drones over IoT frameworks in smart cities. *IEEE Transactions on Mobile Computing*, *22*(1), 402–416.
33. Alsamhi, S. H., & Rajput, N. S. (2014, March). Performance and analysis of propagation models for efficient handoff in high altitude platform system to sustain QoS. In *2014 IEEE Students' Conference on Electrical, Electronics and Computer Science* (pp. 1–6). IEEE.
34. Gupta, A., Sundhan, S., Alsamhi, S. H., & Gupta, S. K. (2020). Review for capacity and coverage improvement in aerially controlled heterogeneous network. *Optical and Wireless Technologies: Proceedings of OWT 2018*, 365–376.
35. Gupta, A., Sundhan, S., Gupta, S. K., Alsamhi, S. H., & Rashid, M. (2020). Collaboration of UAV and HetNet for better QoS: A comparative study. *International Journal of Vehicle Information and Communication Systems*, *5*(3), 309–333.
36. Almalki, F. A., & Angelides, M. C. (2020). Deployment of an aerial platform system for rapid restoration of communications links after a disaster: A machine learning approach. *Computing*, *102*(4), 829–864.
37. Alsamhi, S. H., Afghah, F., Sahal, R., Hawbani, A., Al-qaness, M. A., Lee, B., & Guizani, M. (2021). Green internet of things using UAVs in B5G networks: A review of applications and strategies. *Ad Hoc Networks*, *117*, 102505.
38. Alsamhi, S. H. A. M. (2015). Quality of Service QoS Enhancement Techniques in high Altitude platform HAP Based Communication Networks.
39. Al-Samhi, S., & Rajput, N. (2012). Interference environment between high altitude platform station and fixed wireless access stations. *System*, *4*(5).
40. Nandyala, C. S., & Kim, H. K. (2016). Green IoT agriculture and healthcare application (GAHA). *International Journal of Smart Home*, *10*(4), 289–300.
41. Nandyala, C. S., & Kim, H. K. (2023). Green IoT for eco-friendly and sustainable smart cities: future directions and opportunities. *Open Access*, *26*, 178–202.

Index

Note: **Bold** and *italic* page numbers refer to **tables** and *figures*

F

G

H

I

K

L

M

N

O

P

Q

R

S